British-German Defence Co-operation

British-German Defence Co-operation:

Partners within the Alliance

edited by
KARL KAISER and JOHN ROPER

JANE'S

for
THE ROYAL INSTITUTE OF INTERNATIONAL AFFAIRS
London
and
FORSCHUNGSINSTITUT DER DEUTSCHEN
GESELLSCHAFT FÜR AUSWÄRTIGE POLITIK
Bonn

345620

First published in 1988 by
Jane's Publishing Company Limited
238 City Road, London EC1V 2PU

Distributed in the Philippines and
the USA and its dependencies by
Jane's Publishing Inc.
115 5th Avenue, New York, NY10003

ISBN 0 7106 0498 X

Typeset in English Times by
Colset Pte Ltd., Singapore
Printed in United Kingdom by
Biddles Limited, Guildford and King's Lynn

c

Contents

Contributors

The late *Jonathan Alford*, former Deputy Director, International Institute for Strategic Studies

Clive Archer, Deputy Director, Centre for Defence Studies, University of Aberdeen

Sir Hugh Beach, GBE, Director, Council for Arms Control, London

Christoph Bertram, Editor, *Die Zeit*, Hamburg

Christoph Bluth, Research Student, King's College, London

Michael Clarke, Senior Lecturer, Department of Politics, University of Newcastle

Stuart Croft, Research Student, University of Southampton

Lawrence Freedman, Professor of War Studies, King's College, London

Keith Hartley, Reader in Economics, University of York

Karl Kaiser, Director, Forschungsinstitut der Deutschen Gesellschaft für Auswärtige Politik, Bonn

Frank Kupferschmidt, Assistant Naval Attaché, Embassy of West Germany, London

Timm R. Meyer, Head of the Public-Sector Markets/Defence Industry Department, Bundesverband der Deutschen Industrie, Cologne

John Roper, Head of the International Security Programme, Royal Institute of International Affairs

Harald Rüddenklau, Scientific Rapporteur, Study Group on International Security, Forschungsinstitut der Deutschen Gesellschaft für Auswärtige Politik, Bonn

Franz-Joseph Schultze, former Commander-in-Chief, German Forces in Central Europe

K. Peter Stratmann, Research Associate, Stiftung Wissenschaft und Politik, Ebenhausen

Trevor Taylor, Senior Lecturer, Department of International Relations, Polytechnic of North Staffordshire

Angelika Volle, Research Fellow, Forschungsinstitut der Deutschen Gesellschaft für Auswärtige Politik, Bonn

Phil Williams, Lecturer in International Relations, Department of Politics, University of Southampton

Preface

This volume, which is the result of co-operation between the Royal Institute of International Affairs and the Forschungsinstitut der Deutschen Gesellschaft für Auswärtige Politik, is the first attempt to look at British-German defence collaboration with authors from both countries.

As a result of a grant from the Ford Foundation, it was possible to organise a conference in London in November 1986, at which the chapters of this volume were discussed. The authors have subsequently amended their papers in the light of this discussion.

We are grateful to the Ford Foundation for the grant, without which this conference would not have been possible, and to Christoph Bluth and Angelika Volle for assistance in the editing and preparation of the volume.

June 1987   K.K.
                                                                    J.R.

List of Abbreviations

ACE	Allied Command Europe
AD	air defence
ADM	atomic demolition mines
ADP	automatic data processing
AFCENT	Allied Forces Central Europe
AFNORTH	Allied Forces Northern Europe
AGAEC	Anglo-German Army Equipment Commission
ANF	Atlantic Nuclear Force
ASW	anti-submarine warfare
ATM/ATBM	anti-tactical missile/anti-tactical ballistic missile
BAOR	British Army of the Rhine
C^3I	command, control, communications, intelligence
CDU	Christian Democratic Union
CENTAG	Central Army Group Europe
CNAD	Committee of National Armaments Directors
CSCE	Conference on Security and Co-operation in Europe
CSU	Christian Socialist Union
EDC	European Defence Community
EDIP	European Defence Improvement Programme
EFA	European fighter aircraft
EPC	European Political Co-operation
ERW	enhanced radiation warheads
ESA	European Space Agency
ESECS	European Security Study
EURONAD	European National Armaments Directors
FBS	forward-based systems
FACS	future armour-based combat systems
FOFA	follow-on-forces attack
HLG	high-level group
IEPG	International European Planning Group
IMF	International Monetary Fund
INF	intermediate-range nuclear forces
IPMO	International Project Management Offices

IRBM	intermediate-range ballistic missiles
JSTPS	Joint Strategic Target Planning Staff
KDAR	anti-radar drone
LRTNF	long-range theatre nuclear forces
LTDP	Long Term Defence Programme
MBFR	mutual balanced force reductions
MICV	mechanised infantry combat vehicle
MLRS	multiple-launch rocket system
MRBM	medium-range ballistic missile
NATO	North Atlantic Treaty Organisation
NORTHAG	Northern Army Group Central Europe
NPG	Nuclear Planning Group
NPT	Non-Proliferation Treaty
OMG	Operational Manouever Group
PTP	Partial Test-Ban Treaty
SACEUR	Supreme Allied Commander Europe
SALT	Strategic Arms Limitation Talks
SAM	surface-air missiles
SDI	Strategic Defense Initiative
SHAPE	Supreme Headquarters Allied Powers Europe
SIOP	Single Integrated Operational Plan
SLBM	submarined-launched ballistic missiles
SPAT	self-propelled anti-tank vehicles
SRBM	short-range ballistic missile
TA	Territorial Army
TNF	theatre nuclear forces
TNW	tactical nuclear weapon
VD	variable depth
VSTOL	vertical/short takeoff landing
WEU	Western European Union

Chapter 1
British-German Defence Relations, 1950–80: A Survey

CHRISTOPH BLUTH

I British-German relations and Western security, 1945–54

The most remarkable feature of Anglo-German relations since World War II has been the close and cordial relationship between two nations that were such great adversaries during World War II. West Germany has become Britain's most important partner in Europe, and all those involved testify to the very close collaboration in security and defence matters.

British foreign policy after World War II

Great Britain emerged from the war as a victor, as one of the Big Three powers, with its global role apparently still intact. The central factors of the balance of power in the post-war world – namely the strategic role of nuclear weapons and the resultant bipolarity of world power relations, and the new alignment of world economic relations – did not emerge for some time after the war.[1] For these reasons, there was a marked continuity in British foreign policy in the first years of the post-war era, during which Britain continued to pursue its great-power role in terms of global commitments as the major power in Western Europe.

Despite impressive elements of continuity, however, profound changes were already beginning to make themselves felt. The United States had without doubt emerged as the dominant partner of the Allies. Britain, while still clearly the third most powerful nation in the world, could not come near to matching American or Soviet power. While Britain was still at the centre of a large Empire, the period of decolonisation began with India and Pakistan gaining independence in 1947. Unlike France, Britain did not attempt to hold on to its colonies by force.

In attempting to understand Britain's post-war security policy, the central question is: Who was it directed against? Clearly, the containment of post-war Germany was still high on the agenda of all the Allies. But the conciliatory attitude to the war-time ally, the Soviet Union, did not last as long in London as it did in Washington, and thus, for Britain, the Soviet Union assumed much earlier the central position as the main threat to Western security.[2]

The fundamental dilemma for Western security, as perceived in Britain, was the weakness of Western Europe and its openness to Soviet subversion. The particular focus of British concern was France; it was economically weak, politically vulnerable (given the large support for the French Communist Party) and lacking in military strength. Thus Britain became the main supporter of France being accorded great power status and an occupation zone in Germany, participation in the Allied Control Council for Germany and a permanent seat in the United Nations Security Council. The Anglo-French Treaty of Dunkirk, signed on 4 March 1947, involved a British commitment of support against any future German aggression, a possibility which still preoccupied the French, although Germany was no longer seen as the most serious threat in London.

As relations with the Soviet Union deteriorated, the need for a Western alliance to take the place of four-power co-operation began to dominate the foreign policy agenda in Britain. An important step was the Brussels Treaty, signed on 17 March 1948, establishing the Western Union (involving Britain, France and the Benelux countries) and a defence organisation consisting of a committee of Defence Ministers and a committee of Finance Ministers.

One of the British Foreign Secretary, Ernest Bevin's hopes in creating the Western Union was to draw the United States into a security alliance. In the face of growing tension in East-West relations, and particularly the Communist coup in Czechoslovakia in February 1948 and the Berlin blockade which began on 20 June 1948, this found both Presidential and Congressional approval. In July 1948 B-29 bombers with nuclear capability were dispatched to British bases, and serious planning for the defence of Western Europe was initiated by the American Joint Chiefs of Staff. On 4 April 1949, the United States put its signature to the treaty establishing the North Atlantic Treaty Organisation (NATO). Thus the British efforts to include the United States and Canada in a Western defence pact had come to fruition.

In the late 1940s, the logic of European integration appeared to be irresistible. There were differences of approach: France was still concerned to preserve some degree of co-operation with the Soviet Union and was highly suspicious of Germany and the United States. Furthermore, France saw itself, despite its present weakness, as the leader of a future united Europe. Britain and Germany (which until September 1949, when the Federal Republic was established, was still under direct Allied rule) took a more pro-American stance. However, even in Britain there was a great deal of enthusiasm for European unity. The Brussels Treaty was one step towards this. Another was the creation of the Council of Europe in May 1949 as the outcome of a Ten-Power Conference in The Hague. Significantly, Britain was a participant. The British Government, favouring some sort of 'European unity', was not very enamoured with the supranationalism or federalism advocated by the supporters of European integration; it certainly did not want Britain to join a "European state." But Ernest Bevin supported the Council of Europe because the United States strongly favoured the movement towards European unity, as symbolised by the Council, and also as a means of involving West Germany in Europe (West German membership became possible only after the formation of the Federal Republic). The Council of Europe failed to become the focus of European unity because Britain always insisted on limiting the whole process, keeping it under tight government control and failing to give the Council any significant functions.

The next major initiative towards European unity was the so-called Schuman Plan, launched in April 1950, which eventually led to the establishment of the European Coal and Steel Community. Its purpose was quite clear: it was designed to bind Germany into a European framework and at the same time to serve as a basis for overcoming European weakness in the face of the Russian threat. An Atlantic framework was not sufficient for the French; the perception in Paris was that the need to constrain Germany was not shared by America or even Britain in the same way. The British, while anxious to co-operate with Europe, were not able to accept the principle of supranationality inherent in the Schuman Plan and so did not join.

The European Defence Community

The deterioration of East-West relations after the War soon caused the Allies, who as occupying powers were pursuing the demilitarisation of Germany, to think about a West German contribution to the defence of Europe against the perceived Soviet threat. Ernest Bevin referred to a future West German contribution to an Atlantic-European defence system in a paper for the US State Department in January 1948. Without Germany, he wrote, "no Western system can be complete".[3] Despite this statement, for the present, the official British position was to oppose German rearmament. The French very strongly opposed it and made their views known to the British. Nonetheless, by 1949, in the aftermath of the 1948 Berlin blockade and the first Soviet atomic bomb test in the autumn of 1949, there was a great deal of public discussion about the issue of German rearmament.

The entire situation was transformed by the Korean War. To the Americans, the invasion of South Korea on 25 June 1950 signified that the Soviets were willing to gamble on the risks of military aggression and that the Soviet threat to Western Europe was real. This led to an immediate rearmament programme resulting in a considerable increase in defence expenditure both in the United States and Britain. Given the existing military balance in Europe, the Americans accepted the need to keep a significant troop presence in Central Europe, and it was apparent that NATO needed to be given more substance in military terms. However, there was still no consensus on German rearmament. In 1950 the British government still supported the French in their opposition to any kind of German army (even though the Chiefs of Staff had come to the conclusion that a West German army was what was needed in military terms, and Churchill had proposed the creation of a Federal European Army along the lines of Adenauer's suggestion at the Council of Europe). In the United States the clear conviction was emerging that a credible force posture in Europe was not possible without a German contribution. President Truman accepted in September 1950 the proposal by the Joint Chiefs for the immediate rearmament of West Germany within the NATO structure; West Germany was to provide 12 divisions. The Americans were able to persuade the British to agree to their proposals in principle, but not the French to whom it was quite unacceptable.

The Pleven Plan

Although neither the French Cabinet (in particular French Defence Minister Jules Moch) nor French public opinion was ready to accept the rearmament of West Germany, Schuman realised that the French position was jeopardising NATO defence preparations and putting in doubt the continued presence of the United States in Europe. It was therefore necessary to respond to the Americans positively. Thus, on 24 October 1950, the French Prime Minister, René Pleven, proposed the so-called Pleven Plan, which foresaw the creation of a European army with a West German component. Political leadership should be provided by appropriate European political institutions, including a European Assembly; a European Defence Minister would be appointed and operate under the guidance of a European Defence Council of Ministers; there would also be a common European Defence Budget. The participating states were to provide contingents at the level of the smallest possible unit (ie the battalion). The plan assumed that not all the forces of the participating states (except for Germany which was to have no other forces of its own) would be integrated; France, for example, would retain control over its forces deployed overseas. The Pleven Plan was endorsed by the French National Assembly with 343 votes to 225 on 24 October 1950.[4]

The Spofford Plan

An American attempt to heal the divide among the Allies over German rearmament was the Spofford Plan. Its central idea was to allow both for a NATO and a European army. Thus it provided for the creation of an integrated NATO force in Europe with an American Supreme Commander. The creation of a European army was seen as desirable if it was militarily effective and would fit into a North Atlantic framework.

The acceptance of the Spofford Plan by France, Britain and the United States in December 1950 did not end the deep differences of view on the issue of German rearmament; it merely papered over them. As a result, early in 1951 two parallel conferences began. In February 1951, a conference to discuss the creation of a European Defence Community (EDC) began in Paris, with France, West Germany, Italy, Belgium, Luxembourg and (at a later stage) the Netherlands taking part as full members. The United States, Britain, Canada, Portugal and Norway sent observers. To implement the other part of the Spofford Plan, the Petersberg Conference opened on 9 January 1951 at which talks were held between the three Allied High Commissioners and the West German government about a German defence contribution, which the Americans considered an essential prerequisite for the ending of the occupation.

The Petersberg Conference soon ended in failure, principally because the French were clearly unwilling to accept German rearmament on the basis of German "equality" – the principal indicator of this being interminable arguments about the size of the "units" of the German defence contribution. Thus it seemed that active French cooperation could only be hoped for in an EDC framework.

The French were aware that if they did not now proceed with the European army concept, the Americans would once again bring up the issue of German rearmament in the NATO context. After long and difficult negotiations, a compromise solution was reached which essentially satisfied German concerns but could be considered an acceptable face-saving device by the French, and thus the EDC Treaty was signed by the six participating European nations on 27 May 1952.

The failure of the EDC

The United States was now strongly backing the EDC. One issue which acquired great importance was that of British participation. In October 1951, the Conservative Party under the leadership of Winston

Churchill had regained power. Its attitude to the EDC was that Britain could not accept the notion of giving up the degree of sovereignty that would be required and thus could not become part of the EDC, but it would take a positive attitude and seek some degree of association with it. The six EDC states were somewhat disappointed by Churchill's approach, and the Americans were suggesting that the British should after all reconsider joining. The question of British participation became part of the debate about the relationship between the EDC and NATO and in particular the status of the commitments to the response in case of armed attack. What would happen if the EDC treaty were to be violated by a member state (*eg* Germany)? The French sought American and British guarantees in case of the breakdown of the EDC. These were given in definite, if rather general, terms and played a significant part in the fact that agreement was reached.

Despite the impressive display of European unity at the establishment of the institutions of the ECSC in the autumn of 1952, French support for the EDC, even though it was originally a French idea, began to crumble after the signing of the treaty. Added to the existing apprehensions about German rearmament came General de Gaulle's vision of the *Union Française*, predicated on the notion that France was still a world power, and this clashed with the idea of subordinating the French Army into a supranational structure (even though some forces could have been retained for the defence of French overseas commitments). For a long time the French government, itself not certain about the EDC, failed to submit the treaty to the National Assembly as they considered that it was likely to fail. After unsuccessful attempts to renegotiate the EDC Treaty, it was finally put to the National Assembly in August 1954. The debate in the National Assembly ended in a procedural motion whereby the Assembly voted by 319 to 264 (with 43 abstentions) to move on to other business, thus effectively defeating the proposal for a European Defence Community.[5]

British proposal of a Western European Union

While France was agonising about the EDC, the United States and Britain had been discussing fallback positions in case, as had appeared increasingly likely, the EDC should fail. American and Britain were both still determined that Germany should rearm and become part of the Western Alliance. The Foreign Secretary, Anthony Eden's solution was to make use of the framework of the Brussels Treaty for this purpose.

The central element of the Eden plan was the expansion of the Western Union into a Western European Union (WEU) with the inclusion of Italy and West Germany. The Brussels Treaty should become a mutual guarantee pact; the occupying powers should restore sovereignty to Germany; Germany should be rearmed within the WEU framework and become a member of NATO. With this package, Eden went on a tour of European capitals on 11 September 1954 to obtain agreement for a conference where the WEU should come into being.

In Bonn and Rome Eden's proposal was warmly received. Despite strong reservations about West German membership of NATO, France agreed to participate in a conference involving all the EDC participants, Britain, the United States and Canada.

The London Conference of Nine Powers began on 28 September 1954 at Lancaster House under the chairmanship of Anthony Eden. The French were subject to severe pressure because they provided the main obstacle to success and were severely criticised for causing the failure of the EDC. The Anglo-American strategy was to make their security guarantees the primary means of convincing the French; Eden was quite blunt in indicating that if the Conference failed the British commitments to the defence of Europe would no longer be considered binding. Mendès-France unwittingly co-operated with the Anglo-American strategy by making the weakness of American and British security guarantees the focus of his attack. At a strategic moment in the discussions Eden suddenly produced his astonishing offer to station four divisions and a tactical air force permanently in Germany. This was the turning point: Mendès-France recognised that the situation had been transformed; there was no going back.

The central concessions on the American and British side then consisted in the guarantee of committing forces permanently to the defence of Europe, something which both the United States and Britain had up to this point staunchly resisted. The Germans were to gain by the ending of the occupation status. They would regain full sovereignty and be accepted as full members of the Western Alliance, but would have to accept a whole series of restrictions on the production of armaments (including certain classes of ships and missiles and, most importantly, a ban on the production of nuclear, biological and chemical weapons). The French had to concede German rearmament and membership of NATO.

After basic agreement had been reached at Lancaster House, the detailed work was completed at the Paris Conference from 20–22 October 1954. The Paris Agreements were accepted by all signatories. In December 1954, the French Assembly finally approved the last of them, removing the final obstacle to the birth of the Western European Union.

Conflicting nuclear weapons interests, 1954–64

As a result of West German rearmament in the context of the WEU the path was clear for West German accession to NATO membership on 5 May 1955. Thus West Germany was now engaged in developing appropriate military capabilities and strategies to defend itself against military aggression as part of the Western Alliance. Since West Germany had renounced the production and possession of nuclear weapons as a condition of membership in WEU and NATO, the issue of consultation about nuclear policy became central to West Germany's relationship with the Alliance as a whole and in particular with Britain, as one of the nuclear powers. Although the defence of Western Europe since the end of World War II has rested on the American nuclear guarantee, it was only in 1954 that the question of nuclear consultation and sharing emerged as a vital military and political issue for NATO. West Germany and Britain naturally approached it from very different standpoints and with diverging military and political interests, even though at times there were important and fruitful ventures into co-operation.

The issue arose as a result of the adoption by the NATO Council meeting of December 1954 of a report by the NATO military committee designated MC 48 which, by way of implementation of Eisenhower's "New Look" strategy, provided for the introduction of tactical and battlefield nuclear weapons in Europe. This was designed to deal with both the strategic military and the political problems; in the words of Secretary of State John Foster Dulles, it made collective security both "more effective" and "less costly". Pointing to the failure of the Allies to meet the force goals agreed at the NATO Council meeting in February 1952, the American Administration reduced total military manpower and at the same time exhorted its NATO Allies to increase its contributions and build up local military strength. The basic planning document of the new look strategy, NSC 162/2, appeared contradictory on this point. If nuclear strikepower was now to represent the principal means of deterring a Soviet attack, there was little incentive to invest scarce resources in building up conventional forces.

West Germany: security policy and political objectives

Whereas Britain in the 1950s was itself an emerging nuclear power, West Germany was in a position of particular dependence on its Allies for its security needs, as a result of its defeat in World War II and the development of the post-war settlement.

Originally the German emphasis was on conventional defence. Federal Chancellor Adenauer did not want Germany to be a nuclear battlefield. In the age of American strategic superiority, the American nuclear guarantee was accepted as a credible deterrent against a Soviet conventional attack; the response would be an American strategic attack against targets in the Soviet Union. A strong West German conventional contribution might serve to localise a smaller conflict while reducing Soviet conventional superiority in the European theatre and strengthening West Germany's political position in the alliance.

The strategic review in the United States had stressed the extreme difficulties facing a conventional defence strategy in West Germany, The strategy of "forward defence", according to which every inch of West German territory was to be defended, would be extremely hard to implement because the nature of the terrain of the north German plains leaves them wide open to penetration by large tank armies. A mobile defence strategy required space – but the territory to be defended had very little depth. The requirement for a credible conventional force posture thus demanded a large number of very heavily armed troops. But the Allies were unwilling to make the necessary financial and manpower resources available; hence the necessity of tactical nuclear weapons. The strategic concept involving tactical nuclear weapons was that conventional forces were now considered to be a "defensive shield", giving the Allies the time to gather their resources and prepare to wield the "sword" of nuclear weapons to defeat the enemy. Conventional forces thus acquired something of the character of a tripwire, which would cause nuclear weapons to be unleashed. However, the entire strategy was conceived with the purpose of preventing conflicts from starting in the first place by adequate nuclear deterrence.

Adenauer was not in favour of the "nuclearisation" of NATO. Moreover, when MC 48 was approved by the NATO Council. West Germany was not a member of NATO and was thus not informed about these decisions.[6] Consequently he and his Defence Minister, Theodor Blank, went ahead with a build-up of the Bundeswehr (including forcing a draft law through in the Bundestag) as if nuclear weapons had not been invented. The first clear indication about the possible effects of nuclear weapons came as a result of the *Carte Blanche* exercises in 1955, in which the simulated use of 355 nuclear weapons "resulted" in 1.7 million German deaths and 3.5 million wounded. Despite the major public controversy which ensued, during which the opposition pointed out the futility of building up conventional forces in Germany, Adenauer and Blank did not appear to have absorbed the significance of the New Look.[7]

Another major public controversy came about as a result of a proposal in July 1956 by the Chairman of the Joint Chiefs of Staff, Admiral Radford, for an 800,000 manpower cut, involving also the withdrawal of troops from Europe. Adenauer organised a determined rearguard action against the perceived shifts in strategy in Washington and London, to prevent the implementation of the Radford proposal and any American or British troop withdrawals. However, his defence policy and his Defence Minister were coming under increasing attack, not only from the opposition, which rejected the draft laws and called for a professional standing army half the size of the projected Bundeswehr, but also from the energetic defence expert of the CSU, Franz-Josef Strauss, who had already recognised the significance of nuclear weapons and placed less emphasis on conventional strength. In October 1956 Strauss replaced Blank as Defence Minister, a move that marked the acceptance of the new look strategy which Adenauer accepted as necessary even though he personally opposed it. The period of military service was reduced from 18 to 12 months, thus accepting somewhat more modest manpower goals for the Bundeswehr. From then on, Adenauer and Strauss urged the equipment of the Bundeswehr with short range nuclear battlefield weapons according to NATO plans, with the nuclear warheads remaining under American custody.

The inadequacy of a purely conventional force posture had now been accepted. As a result, West German defence planners saw themselves confronted with the extraordinary dilemma which remains to this day at the centre of the German debate about security policies: the defence of West Germany is not possible without nuclear weapons, but if nuclear weapons were detonated in large numbers on German soil (West or East), the resulting damage and the number of deaths would be catastrophic. Given that nuclear weapons would be fired from West German territory which could well lead to nuclear weapons being used against Germany, the need for German ministers to have a say about when and how they would be used became a burning issue as the years went by.

The issue of nuclear decision-making became top of NATO's agenda not merely for military but also for political reasons. A central goal of West German foreign policy was rehabilitation as a member of international society in general, and the acceptance of the Federal Republic as an equal member of the Alliance in particular. The nuclear non-production pledge excluded the possibility of the FRG itself becoming a nuclear power. Given the conviction in France and Britain that possession of nuclear weapons was a prerequisite of great power status and also conferred greater weight within the Alliance, it became a central object of West German policy to escape any possible discriminatory effects that might (and did) result from the non-production pledge. This goal was pursued through a variety of diplomatic means, including subtle hints that unless satisfactory arrangements for nuclear sharing were achieved, the FRG might have to think again about the possibility of itself acquiring nuclear weapons.[8]

One fundamental objective of West German foreign policy, given its vulnerability to Soviet aggression, was to enhance its security; another was the reunification of Germany. In 1952, the Soviet Union had indicated that it might accept the reunification on the basis of free elections, provided Germany would become neutral. The hostile reaction of the Adenauer administration demonstrated very clearly the possibility of a fundamental conflict between security and reunification as policy objectives. From then on, Adenauer emphasised that he was seeking reunification from a position of strength – which meant, in practice, that the goal of reunification had been subordinated to the requirements of security policy. West German membership of the WEU and NATO elicited from the Allies pledges of support of German reunification. Germany was not able to pursue a policy of "reunification through strength" on her own, and therefore sought to harness the forces of the Western Allies towards this end. Instead of acquiring its own nuclear weapons, which would have been totally unacceptable to the Soviet Union and the Western Allies alike, German policy was to achieve the same degree of political power by means of "nuclear participation" in the Alliance, as a way of pursuing its policy over the German question.

British security policy

The British decision after the war to become a self-sufficient nuclear power was based on the assumption that it was necessary for a major power to be in possession of the most modern weapons, recognised to be of possibly decisive military significance in the future.

With the decline of the British Empire and status as a world power at the end of World War II, Britain was faced with the vital issue of its role in the post-war world. Economically weak, unable to maintain its overseas presence, the possession of nuclear weapons appeared to be one way for Britain to preserve its status as a major power.

The political implications of the pursuit of this objective were highly paradoxical. On the one hand the)whole purpose of the independent nuclear deterrent, as it came to be called, was to preserve a degree of independence from the United States, even though it was clearly recognised that the defence of Europe depended on American strategic nuclear forces. In time, however, it became clear that Britain could not develop even a small strategic capability itself and increasingly relied on technological assistance from the United States, thus significantly diminishing the independence of its nuclear deterrent. Britain therefore continually emphasised its "special relationship" with the United States, arising out of the partnership during the war and for ethnic and cultural reasons. Its preservation became another principal objective in British foreign policy.

The election of a Conservative Government under Winston Churchill in 1951 marked the conversion of British strategy from an emphasis on conventional rearmament to an increased emphasis on nuclear weapons. Britain exploded its first fission device in the same year. The Chiefs-of-Staff produced a "Global Strategy" paper which argued that nuclear strike power was a more cost-effective way of dealing with the Soviet threat than building up conventional forces. In this way the British Chiefs-of-Staff anticipated by more than a year some of the ideas expressed in NSC 162/2 and Britain was converted to the new look before it became American and NATO policy. Some of the implications met with resistance in the British defence establishment, particularly when it came to cutting the army and navy budgets. However, by 1957, in the wake of the Suez crisis and the further reduction in British overseas commitments, the defence policy set out in a White Paper by Duncan Sandys as Minister of Defence involved substantial reductions in the army and navy budgets and a major shift towards nuclear deterrence.

Nuclear sharing: the MLF controversy

In the discussions about nuclear sharing within NATO, Britain and Germany had very different interests. Britain's primary objective was to maintain and enhance its independent nuclear deterrent. The United States was hoping to use nuclear sharing arrangements, which were seen to be necessary to satisfy West Germany, to channel the British nuclear forces into such arrangements, thus considerably reducing, if not altogether eliminating their significance as national forces. The West Germans were obviously interested in seeing the United States succeed in its endeavours. On the political front, West Germany and Britain were competing to some extent to enhance their respective "special relationship" with the United States.

The central issue occupying the United States in the late 1950s was the growing strategic power of the Soviet Union, dramatically demonstrated in the launch of Sputnik in 1957 and the resulting Soviet claims with regard to their ICBM capabilities. Although the United States had a substantial long-range nuclear bomber force to cover targets in the Soviet Union, there was a growing perception of a gap in the development and deployment of missiles capable of reaching the Soviet Union. The accelerated Soviet deployment of medium-range nuclear missiles in Europe and concerns about the strategic balance combined to increase European doubts about reliance on American strategic capabilities for deterrence and the concern for European involvement in the control of nuclear weapons.

To meet these twin concerns, the United States proposed the deployment of intermediate-range ballistic missiles (IRBMs) in Europe. As a result, Thor missiles were deployed in Britain in 1958 under a "dual-key" system and Jupiter missiles in Turkey and Italy. Another important element of the American response was the decision, endorsed by NATO, to create a stockpile of nuclear warheads.

Adenauer was opposed to stationing IRBMs on German soil, because of their vulnerability, and because of the political effects both domestically and in relations with the Soviet Union. Nonetheless, Defence Minister Strauss was keen to equip the Bundeswehr with modern tactical nuclear weapons; the announcement in March 1958 that the Bundeswehr should receive Matador C nuclear-capable cruise missiles and Nike-Ajax air defence missiles (under a dual-key arrangement) touched off a storm of controversy and the formation of a broad anti-nuclear coalition called *Kampf dem Atomtod* (Struggle against atomic death).

Discussions continued about extending nuclear sharing even further. In 1959 General Norstad proposed the deployment of medium-range ballistic missiles in Europe in addition to the IRBMs already deployed; his proposal also involved the American surrender of exclusive control of nuclear warheads in favour of joint allied control such as to make NATO in effect a fourth nuclear power. Norstad's proposal was not accepted, and instead US Secretary of State Christian Herter proposed in 1960 a different concept to deal with the problem of nuclear sharing: the multilateral force (MLF). This involved the commitment to NATO by the United States of five submarines armed with 80 Polaris missiles. Furthermore:

> If our allies provided [100] additional missiles on a multilaterally manned, owned, and controlled basis, deployed either in submarines, in surface vessels, or on land, the United States would then combine its five submarines with the contribution made by our allies into a NATO deterrent force under NATO command. How the NATO command should be constituted was left for subsequent consideration.[9]

The evolution of flexible response

When John F. Kennedy became President in 1961, his administration undertook a comprehensive review of United States security policy. As the United States itself had become vulnerable to Soviet nuclear attack and some degree of nuclear stalemate had developed between the super-powers, the almost automatic recourse to massive nuclear retaliation against any level of Warsaw Pact aggression had lost credibility. The new strategy eventually proposed by Defence Secretary Robert McNamara at the North Atlantic Council ministerial meeting in Athens in May 1962 became known as the strategy of "flexible response". It proposed that the Alliance should be able to respond initially to a limited attack by conventional means, thereby raising the threshold at which the use of nuclear weapons would become necessary. Even after the crossing of the nuclear threshold, however, the emphasis was on *escalation control*. Instead of immediately escalating to the level of all-out nuclear war, flexible response was designed to give NATO a range of options, beginning with very limited counterforce strikes.[10]

In France and West Germany, McNamara's proposal received a less than enthusiastic response; it was generally interpreted as signifying a diminution in United States' willingness to use its strategic nuclear arsenal for the defence of Western Europe. In 1957–8 the Adenauer administration had, with deep-seated reservations, agreed to the "nuclearisation" of NATO. Having been convinced that a conventional defence of Western Europe was not possible and that the early use of tactical nuclear weapons would be necessary, it had in essence accepted the practical impossibility of any kind of realistic defence strategy. The purpose of NATO must therefore be to deter war from breaking out in the first place. It was precisely the realism of the proposals for nuclear war-fighting inherent in McNamara's strategic thinking (involving an attempt to develop realistic responses in the event that deterrence should fail) that was unacceptable to the West German leadership.

The new strategy also had direct implications for the issue of nuclear participation, since escalation control implied very tight, centralised control over the use of nuclear weapons. Indeed, the United States was now demanding central and exclusive control over all nuclear weapons as well as complete freedom of action in case of war – demands wholly unacceptable to the Germans and the French. Proposals about separate conventional and nuclear command structure created the impression for the West Germans that they would become the conventional infantry (*konventionelles Fussvolk*) with the Americans being the "nuclear knights" (*nukleare Ritter*). The result seemed to be that the Germans would have even less control over the use of nuclear weapons than under the dual-key system. Furthermore, deterrence on the whole would be diminished, given that the consequences of an attack would become less incalculable if, as the result of raising the nuclear threshold, no immediate nuclear response was threatened.

During 1961, East-West relations and the Berlin crisis were at the centre of world attention. Doubts about the extent to which the United States would be prepared to act in the interests of their West European Allies were strengthened. The issue of nuclear sharing received renewed attention as a result of a French request for help with technological components for its developing independent nuclear force. The administration consensus in favour of non-proliferation and thus rejection of the French request gave the State Department the opportunity to advance the MLF as a solution to the political problems of Alliance management; the hope was that French (and eventually potential German) nuclear aspirations could be contained by participation in the MLF. In this way, the creation of the MLF moved to the top of the agenda of American alliance policy.[11]

In the State Department, the concept of the MLF had meanwhile evolved considerably. The proposal presented by American spokesmen in the European capitals in the summer of 1962 involved a surface fleet of 25 vessels, each to be armed with eight Polaris MRBMs. It was to be owned, controlled and operated on a multilateral basis, with each vessel being manned by a mixed crew from at least three different nations. The United States would retain a veto over the launch of the nuclear missiles, but the briefings mentioned the possibility that at some future date the United States might consider relinquishing its veto.

In Britain, the American proposal was greeted with scepticism. This is hardly surprising since the MLF was militarily unnecessary (as the Americans themselves often emphasised); in particular, the proposal as it stood appeared very dubious owing to the potential vulnerability of surface vessels, and the British were also not happy about the mixed-manning proposal. More fundamentally, the political objectives of the MLF ran directly counter to British security policy objectives. Although the Foreign Office recommended giving the MLF "a fair wind" in order not to upset the Americans and the "special relationship", there was no enthusiastic support in Britain and Macmillan did not want to commit himself to participate.

At this point, however, another issue intruded on British deliberations. After scrapping the development of its own silo-based missile programme Blue Streak, Britain had hoped to maintain an independent deterrent by purchasing the American air-launched missile Skybolt. Skybolt, however, ran into similar difficulties in the US and was eventually cancelled in November 1962, leading to a crisis in Anglo-American relations.[12] After a convoluted saga of misunderstandings, Macmillan eventually obtained at Nassau on 21 December 1962 an American offer to sell them Polaris missiles. The agreement specified that the British Polaris force "would be made available for inclusion in a NATO multilateral nuclear force".[13]

While, despite the Nassau agreement, the British still banked on the failure of the MLF project, the West German government supported it from the start. Their support was strengthened by the Nassau agreement, with the offer of Polaris missiles to Britain and France. This to the Germans, looked like a disturbing step in the direction of the nuclear triumvirate between America, Britain and France proposed by de Gaulle in 1958. Another significant event was the conclusion of the Treaty of Franco-German Co-operation which was signed on the 23 January 1963. As a result of de Gaulle's dramatic rejection of Britain's application for membership of the EEC, it acquired a potential symbolic significance not intended by Adenauer. Coupled with de Gaulle's rejection of Kennedy's offer to France of the same deal on Polaris that Britain had accepted at Nassau, this raised for the Americans and the British the ominous spectre of a Franco-German nuclear co-operation and a reorientation away from an Atlanticist position. Adenauer's commitment to Under-Secretary of State George Ball, on the very same day in January 1963 that de Gaulle rejected the Polaris offer that West Germany would participate in the MLF was a deliberate signal that Adenauer was not prepared to choose between a close relationship with France and the United States.

The first and paramount reason why the MLF proposal was so attractive to the West German leadership was security. The MLF was intended to serve as a strategic force to counter the Soviet MRBM threat. Although West Germany had been repeatedly assured that American strategic forces were more than adequate to deal with that threat, the American nuclear guarantee had lost credibility owing to the vulnerability of the United States itself to Soviet strategic forces and the debates surrounding the strategy of flexible response, in which, in German eyes, the importance of nuclear weapons was being down-graded in a way that made it look like a form of American nuclear disengagement (a concern very much shared by the French). Although from a strictly military point of view there might be no need for the MLF, the existence of a European-based nuclear strike force would significantly enhance the credibility of deterrence against a Soviet attack on Western Europe, particularly if the country immediately affected (*ie* West Germany) would have a say in the use of this force.[14]

The most important benefit promised by the MLF from the German perspective was thus the strengthening of American commitments and closer co-operation within the Alliance, thereby counteracting the effects of French policies which threatened to disintegrate the Alliance. A close integration of European and North American security policies and defence would serve to dispel the spectre of an American departure from Europe for the foreseeable future. It would enhance German influence on American (and NATO) military strategy, lead to a close co-ordination of European nuclear defence, degrade the value of independent nuclear deterrent forces (if not absorb them entirely) and remove the discrimination arising out of the non-production pledge.

While the MLF was enjoying considerable support in the United States and West Germany, it was in trouble virtually everywhere else in the Alliance. At the beginning of 1963, France, Canada, Norway, Denmark and Portugal had declared that they were not interested in taking part. Forthcoming elections in Italy and Holland precluded a response for the present.

The British Labour Party had argued against the MLF in its 1964 election campaign. When the new Labour Government assumed office in October 1964 under the leadership of Harold Wilson, it did not want to do anything which would damage the "special relationship" with the United States. Thus instead of rejecting the MLF outright, Wilson suggested an alternative proposal, the Atlantic Nuclear Force (ANF), in which Britain's contribution would involve mainly existing (or projected) British forces which were to be nationally manned. The purpose of this proposal was not that the MLF should assume a more acceptable form, but rather that it should be defeated altogether.[15] The ANF proposal elicited a strong French reaction because it appeared to the French that while the MLF proposal would have ultimately been clearly unacceptable to the British, and thus stood no chance of being realised, the ANF proposal might be different. Contrary to French expectations, Labour's election victory did not spell the end of the MLF; indeed, its realisation appeared to be closer than ever and threatened two areas of French interests. It could indirectly lead to a form of British involvement in Europe which France had believed it had foreclosed by rejecting the British application for EEC membership; and it could also lead to a close relationship between Britain and the FRG. Thus France became diplomatically very active in opposition to the

MLF/ANF, accompanied by an intensive campaign by the French media and politicians. In the course of their efforts, every conceivable means was employed, from diplomatic overtures to the Soviet Union to threats of leaving NATO. It was even hinted that if Germany participated in the MLF, France would have to join Eastern European states in opposing German reunification (raising the spectre of a nuclear-armed Germany).

The French campaign (and in particular the threat to leave NATO) had a significant effect in the United States and by the end of 1964 President Johnson was faced with growing domestic opposition to the MLF. The French campaign also sharpened the divisions in the FRG, where support for the MLF was diminishing.

There was no explicit rejection of the MLF either in Germany or the United States. But after Adenauer's successor, Erhard, was forced to announce a "delay" in West German participation in the MLF in the Bundestag in November 1964, support for the MLF had all but evaporated. The project was never cancelled – it was simply forgotten.

Anglo-German nuclear consultation, 1964–79

British defence policy: the shift towards Europe

Harold Wilson became Prime Minister in 1964 with a commitment to "renegotiate" the Nassau Agreement. In the end his government went ahead with building four of the five projected Polaris vessels, after he and Denis Healey had come to the conclusion that the Polaris deal was a very cost-effective way for Britain to remain in the nuclear business and maintain its influence as a world power.[16] However, it soon became apparent that Britain would no longer be able to continue in its global role in view of the severe problems of the British economy. The progressive withdrawal from East of Suez, which had become inevitable, had resulted in a fundamental reorientation of British defence policy; the Defence Review of February 1966 had supported a reduced military presence in the Far East; also indicative of the trend was the decision to phase out the British aircraft-carrier programme which would have been crucial to global power projection. A supplementary White Paper on Defence in July 1967 went considerably further, calling for the complete withdrawal from East of Suez of British forces by the mid-1970s.[17] In May 1967 Britain made its second application for membership of the EEC.

The moment for the shift to Europe occurred at a difficult time for the Western Alliance. The French withdrawal from the military structure of NATO in 1966 suddenly reduced considerably the depth of the territory to be defended (given the small width of the Federal Republic and that French territory was now no longer available). It created a host of other problems, such as the lines of supply and communications. The United States was preoccupied with Vietnam and therefore Alliance problems received a much lower priority. A perception of some relaxation in tensions between East and West, and thus a reduced Soviet threat, made the rationale for the existence of NATO appear less convincing. Paradoxically, the "shift to Europe" in 1968 coincided not only with the withdrawal of British forces from East of Suez, but also of a full brigade from British Army of the Rhine (BAOR). Britain's second attempt to join the EEC was rejected by the French in 1968.

However, defence, and thus Alliance concerns, returned to the top of the agenda with the Soviet invasion of Czechoslovakia in August 1968. While the trend to reduce NATO forces was halted, the British interpretation of events was that, although they were tragic and to be condemned, the Soviet action was designed to preserve a stable *status quo* in Europe and did not imply an increased likelihood of Soviet attack against Western Europe. Consequently, no increase of British forces in Germany occurred.[18]

As far as the fundamental question of NATO strategy for the defence of Europe was concerned, Defence Secretary Denis Healey was a firm supporter of the strategy of flexible response. However, he was extremely critical of wishful thinking about the role of conventional forces. Here, Healey shared many of the concerns of the German opponents of flexible response. In his view, the emphasis should not be on war-fighting, but on nuclear deterrence. He considered the threat of an early use of tactical nuclear weapons to be a likely requirement of a successful deterrence strategy. Healey feared that if doubt was cast on the American commitment to the strategy of nuclear deterrence in Europe, this would feed the pressures on European nations to acquire independent nuclear deterrents (rather than inducing them to build up their conventional forces).[19]

Although Healey argued quite strongly that there was no realistic hope of NATO increasing conventional forces to levels which would enable it to counter a Soviet attack on a purely conventional level, thus by implication rejecting the notion of significantly raising the nuclear threshold, his views were in accordance with the idea of flexible response (which became official NATO doctrine with the adoption of MC 14/3 by the Military Committee and the North Atlantic Council in 1967) insofar as he saw tactical nuclear weapons as a counter to the "middle-range" of aggression and, in the event of deterrence failing, opening up the possibility of holding out against the aggressor's forces long enough to allow for diplomatic attempts to end the conflict before escalation to the strategic level. This contradicted McNamara's original concept of flexible response, which was designed to force the *enemy* to make the decision to use nuclear weapons first, with all the associated risks. Healey's views, however, were much closer to, for example, German views (at the time) and to those that were actually adopted by NATO.[20]

The evolution of German security policy after Adenauer

The departure of Franz-Josef Strauss from the Ministry of Defence and Adenauer's retirement in October 1963 marked a reaffirmation of the Atlanticist orientation of German foreign policy. Foreign Minister Gerhard Schröder favoured a greater integration of the Bundeswehr with NATO and also the expansion of the EEC to include British membership. Defence Minister Kai-Uwe von Hassel, who on Washington's initiative became involved in regular bilateral consultations with McNamara (similar consultations also took place between the Chairman of the Joint Chiefs of Staff and the Inspector General of the Bundeswehr), accepted the principles of flexible response but insisted on an interpretation which, as in the British case, differed from the American concept. From a West German perspective, it was essential that the foundation of Western security policy must be deterrence, with the corollary of willingness to engage in the early use of tactical nuclear weapons. Instead of a rigid pause or firebreak, the German concept involved a ladder of escalation. Linked to that must be the preparedness to escalate to the strategic level.[21]

The mid-1960s saw a fundamental shift in West German security policy when the Grand Coalition between the CDU/CSU and the SPD was formed after the fall of the Erhard Government in November 1966. Until then, the German view of East-West relations had differed from that of the United States and Britain. Particular suspicion was directed at the détente and the arms control processes. The root cause of this lay in a strong ideological commitment to German reunification, as particularly indicated by the adamant refusal to recognise the German Democratic Republic and accept the Oder-Neisse borderline between Poland and East Germany. The recognition of the *status quo* in Europe, however, was the assumption underlying most proposals to improve East-West relations (including arms control proposals which were intended to further détente in general).

The German problem was, of course, central to East-West relations and therefore also to arms control. The objectives pursued by the Soviet Union in arms control negotiations were designed to limit German rearmament, to prevent German access to nuclear weapons in any form and to keep the FRG voice in the Western alliance at the lowest level possible.

One of the major arms control negotiations in the 1960s resulted in the Partial Test Ban (PTB) Treaty. While Britain was actively involved in the negotiations as a nuclear power, the Federal Government had deep reservations about its possible implications for *Deutschlandpolitik*; in particular it was concerned about the Treaty clause which allowed "all states" to become signatories, which implied that East Germany might acquire some sort of diplomatic recognition simply by virtue of signing the PTB Treaty. Eventually the United States and Britain managed to reassure the Federal Government on this point and in August 1963 the West German cabinet decided unanimously that the FRG should become a signatory to the Treaty.

But the coalition government under the leadership of Federal Chancellor Kurt Georg Kiesinger, brought about a fundamental change of attitude. Willy Brandt and Egon Bahr, in particular, had realised (as a result of the traumatic building of the Berlin Wall in 1961 when Brandt was Mayor of Berlin) that a foreign policy based on the Hallstein Doctrine, according to which the Federal Republic assumed the right of sole representation of all Germans and which led to a policy designed to isolate the German Democratic Republic diplomatically, was no longer realistic, since the Soviet Union was determined not to release the GDR from its sphere of influence. Bahr explained in a speech in July 1963 that the division of Germany, as symbolised by the Berlin Wall, could not be overcome by a policy of confrontation, but only by a relaxation of tension between the two Germanies, a long "process of many steps and stations".[22] Willy Brandt explicitly called for a new policy towards the Soviet Union:

> There is a solution to the German question only with the Soviet Union, not in opposition to it. We cannot give up our rights, but we must recognise that a new relationship between East and West is imperative, and with it a new relationship between Germany and the Soviet Union.[23]

Recognition of the need for a new approach had also been developing in the CDU, although it did not nearly go as far as the radical ideas espoused by Brandt and Bahr. There were some significant initiatives during the Grand Coalition, but the new *Ostpolitik* did not really get under way until Brandt became Chancellor in the SPD/FDP coalition which came to power as a result of the elections in 1969. Then, however, it moved at a dizzy speed, resulting in a number of treaties regularising West Germany's relationship with the Soviet Union and establishing the basic rules of diplomatic relations between the two German states.

Although West Germany did not entirely renounce reunification as a future goal, there was an explicit renunciation of force and an acceptance of the inviolability of the post-war borders in Europe. As Wolfram F. Hanrieder has pointed out, *Ostpolitik* had important implications for West German security policies 'because Bonn's readiness to accept the territorial *status quo* tackled German security problems at their political roots.'[24] When Willy Brandt became Chancellor in 1969, Helmut Schmidt took over from Gerhard Schröder as Defence Minister. Schmidt had always taken issue with the emphasis on nuclear weapons and in 1962 had declared himself in favour of the strategy of flexible response. His appointment as Defence Minister resulted in a substantial shift towards the American concept of flexible response; while under von Hassel German policy was designed to keep the nuclear threshold low, Schmidt was in favour of raising the nuclear threshold as high as possible.

This shift also became discernible in the attitude of the FRG to arms control. In respect of the Non-Proliferation Treaty (NPT) negotiations (begun in 1965), where Britain again saw itself in an important role, the initial German position was either to prevent a general NPT entirely or to radically revise the proposals. While the Federal Republic had no interest in acquiring nuclear weapons itself, it was feared that the NPT could reduce or even exclude a German role in nuclear consultation within the NATO framework. Furthermore, the NPT had potentially negative implications for *Deutschlandpolitik*; the Federal Republic was concerned that procedures which would result in recognition of the GDR should be avoided. Another concern was that the NPT would restrain the FRG from developing its peaceful use of atomic energy, as it had hitherto been able to do in the framework of EURATOM.

In time, the United States and Britain managed to allay some of these fears. The demise of the MLF proposals clearly removed a central obstacle to the NPT. But it was not until the end of the Grand Coalition and the beginning of Willy Brandt's Chancellorship that the internal debate in West Germany was resolved in favour of the NPT.

By the end of the 1960s, West Germany had moved very close to Britain on arms control issues. The new *Ostpolitik* was entirely in sympathy with the political aims of arms control as it was being practised by the United States and the United Kingdom.

The genesis of the Nuclear Planning Group

In 1965 the American Defence Secretary McNamara put forward a proposal for a forum for consultations about nuclear policy. This was principally the result of German pressure. Former German Defence Minister Kai-Uwe von Hassel told the author that he "demanded the Nuclear Planning Group" (NPG) from McNamara. The British favoured the NPG because it provided a way of satisfying the demands for nuclear sharing without involving hardware proposals like the MLF which were considered impractical and would have reduced the independence of British nuclear forces. The French, on the other hand, were quite hostile to the idea of the NPG.

On 10 November 1965, Defence Ministers met as a "Special Committee on Nuclear Consultation" and set up three working groups covering the areas of communications, data exchange and nuclear planning. It was agreed that the United States, Britain, West Germany and Italy should be members of the group on nuclear planning. One seat was provided to represent the smaller members of the alliance (occupied initially by Turkey). The first meeting of the Nuclear

Planning Working Group was held in Washington in February 1966. There the participants received the most comprehensive US briefing on nuclear targeting and the nuclear force posture ever given to the alliance partners. Although broader aspects of nuclear strategy were also discussed, the subsequent work of the NPG concerned itself mostly with questions affecting Europe more directly, such as the strategic doctrines governing battlefield nuclear weapons. In 1968 the NPG commissioned a number of studies: the British were to present a report on the use of nuclear weapons at sea, Italy on the use of atomic demolition mines (ADMs) and nuclear anti-aircraft weapons, Germany on the tactical use of nuclear weapons on the battlefield, and the United States on the bargaining use of nuclear weapons and demonstration shots.[25]

These reports were presented at the NPG meeting in Bonn in October 1968 and duly accepted. However, in the course of the discussions it became clear that the issue of tactical nuclear weapons required further study. On the initiative of Denis Healey, Germany and Britain were given the task of jointly working out draft guidelines for the possible employment of TNFs within the strategy of flexible response. There are indications that this represented a deliberate initiative by Healey to achieve closer Anglo-German co-operation, as part of his general strategy towards closer European co-operation on defence issues, despite the continuing French veto of British membership of the EEC.[26] The Anglo-German study was the central issue at the NPG meeting in London in May 1969 as well as in Warrington, Virginia, in November 1969, after the general election in Germany which had resulted in a coalition government of the SPD and FDP. Helmut Schmidt, the new Minister of Defence, approved the joint Anglo-German proposals, even though he was to interpret them somewhat differently from his predecessor. Two separate papers resulting from this study were approved at the Warrington meeting: one established guidelines for the initial use of TNFs and the other outlined procedures of consultation between the allies if the use of TNFs was being considered. A significant element in the guidelines was the emphasis on the consent of the "host country" in the event of the use of TNFs being considered. This had been a central concern of German policymakers for many years. Although there was no "host country veto" (which the Germans had sought since 1966), and the final authority of the US President for the release of nuclear weapons was not questioned, there was some attempt to meet West German concerns in this area.

Anglo-German co-operation and the NPG

At the end of the 1960s the Anglo-German relationship was very close on a whole range of significant areas. As William Wallace has pointed out, "in almost every dimension of that relationship West Germany ranks as one of Britain's two or three most important partners."[27] The important issues of security policy, such as *Ostpolitik*, in which Britain had a particular role to play because of the four-power status of Berlin, and the more general emergence of détente and the CSCE process necessitated close consultations between Britain and West Germany which, unlike the climate of the 1950s, took place in an atmosphere of mutual trust. Other important issues were the prospective British membership of the EEC and West German membership of the United Nations.

As a result, different government agencies in both countries developed very close relations in what William Wallace has termed an "interpenetration between the two administrations".[28] Particularly close relationships existed between the two ministries of defence, and Helmut Schmidt would consult Denis Healey almost every day by telephone.

Apart from direct bilateral links between German and British defence officials, the NPG also served as a link between the two administrations. The NPG framework provides for consultation on three different levels. The highest is obviously the Ministerial level at NPG general meetings. As a consequence of the need for administrative back-up there is considerable bilateral and multilateral consultation at national staff level. Thirdly, there is also a permanent staff. Another context for close Anglo-German co-operation was provided by participation in the Joint Strategic Target Planning Staff (JSTPS). This was established by the United States in 1960 at Offutt Air Force Base near Omaha to construct the Single Integrated Operational Plan (SIOP) in the event of a major conflict. In 1963 the NATO Council agreed that there should be European participation in operational planning. From 1963 officers from France, Italy, Germany and Britain were assigned to the JSTPS. The general principle agreed was that the four positions for Europeans on the JSTPS would be rotated among the NATO members which contributed forces to NATO's nuclear missions on a three-yearly basis. In 1968 Britain, Germany and Italy were given permanent positions at JSTPS (France having withdrawn from NATO's integrated military command).

Although the European representatives on the JSTPS are concerned only with planning related to SACEUR's command responsibilities, and thus do not have access to all American strategic plans, their presence provides for close co-operation on the highly secret operational level of nuclear targeting, which is of particular significance for Britain and Germany given their special position as two of the three permanent representatives and their role in forward defence.[29]

An important focus of Anglo-German co-operation was also provided by the Eurogroup formed on the initiative of Denis Healey in the autumn of 1968 at an informal meeting of Defence Ministers in NATO. (There is now a Eurogroup Secretariat at the UK Delegation to NATO in Brussels.) The political context of the initiative was, on the one hand, the British endeavour to join the EEC and, on the other, the controversies about "burden sharing" within the Alliance. American misgivings about the substantial costs of their defence effort in Europe (aggravated by the costs of the Vietnam War and a rising balance-of-payments deficit) led to feelings in the United States that Europeans did not sufficiently share in the financial burden of their own security. This resulted in pressure on West Germany for more generous offset arrangements and the Mansfield Resolutions in the US Senate for substantial troop reductions in Europe which attracted considerable support.

Central to the early work of Eurogroup was the awareness of the possibility of a major shift in the security relationship between the United States and Europe. It was the purpose of Eurogroup to create the foundation for a European defence structure which could be developed should such a shift materialise, while at the same time striving to prevent its occurring. There was some encouragement from a statement by US Secretary of State Dean Rusk to the effect that the United States would favour a European caucus within the NATO framework, and it appeared that this might be used to prove that the Europeans were taking their own defence seriously. Initially, apart from issuing warnings about the possible consequences of American troop reductions, there was an attempt to create a European fund to contribute towards the costs of the American presence in Europe. The Americans, however, made it clear that they "would prefer to see them spend that money on force improvements and defence improvements in Europe".[30]

On 1 October 1970 the Eurogroup met for the first time independently from the NATO Defence Planning Committee. The work of this meeting culminated in the decision in December 1970 to create the European Defence Improvement Programme (EDIP), on the basis of the fund which had originally been designed as a direct financial contribution to the United States. The EDIP involved an explicit linkage between an increased European effort to contribute to the improvement of their own defence capabilities and American commitments not to reduce their force levels in Europe. The actual size of the effort, however, was not very substantial; it represented a total of $1 billion over five years, ie a mere ¾% of the combined defence budgets of all European NATO allies (even though alongside the financial commitment it represented an effort which became central to Eurogroup's activities to organise and use more efficiently existing defence resources).[31] As a result, although the initiative was welcomed in the United States, and in 1971 the Mansfield Resolution was defeated, there was some scepticism in Congress about the small size of the fund.

In December 1971 Eurogroup approved the so-called Europackage, ie a collection of measures which in 1972 amounted to $1.3 billion extra defence expenditure (with a second Europackage in 1973 resulting in a

$2.9 billion dollar increase in the defence budgets of Eurogroup). The name of this programme was rather appropriate, since there was more packaging than reality, given that much of this expenditure would have occurred in any event through normal equipment modernisation procurement and inflationary pressures. Nonetheless, Eurogroup was successful in upgrading the visibility and thus the political significance of measures that were mostly routine.[32]

It is important to point out that France declined the invitation to join Eurogroup which consequently became a special focus for Anglo-German co-operation. Britain and West Germany displayed the most consistent enthusiasm and support for Eurogroup and provided much of its leadership, whereas a number of other members displayed at best marginal interest.[33] The United Kingdom contributed much to sustain the Eurogroup initiative through its leadership role and efficient administrative service. For the FRG, Helmut Schmidt was very aware of the limits in the freedom of action imposed on the superpowers by nuclear parity and mutual deterrence and was thus keen to emphasise the responsibility of Europe for its own security, while at the same time stressing the need for the United States to maintain its military presence in Europe, helped by the efforts of Eurogroup. It appears that the Federal Republic was prepared to move further in the direction of consultation and the creation of a European defence identity (in support of NATO) than many other participants. Indeed, it envisaged the possibility of Eurogroup becoming *the* central focus of European defence co-operation which could ultimately converge with the EEC (even though Britain was not a member at that stage). The German commitment can be measured by the fact that the FRG provided more than 47% of the EDIP approved in December 1970 (while at the same time raising the possibility of constructing a framework in which Eurogroup could provide a multilateral system for offset payments to the US).

To implement its goal of achieving a more efficient use of resources by way of European co-operation, Eurogroup set up a number of subgroups dealing with training, tactical concepts, logistics and collaboration in weapons procurement. The latter sub-group was called EURONAD and consisted of the national armaments directors of the Eurogroup states; but the absence of France was a severe disadvantage and when the Independent European Programme Group (IEPG) was established in 1976 with full French participation it more or less took over the functions of EURONAD.

Despite all the initial enthusiasm, Eurogroup has in the end failed to become the kind of centre for the organisation of European defence co-operation that was envisaged by West Germany and to some extent by Britain. The fundamental reason lies in the non-participation of France. Since France is a member of the WEU and has actively sought increased European defence co-operation within its context, it is now the Western European Union rather than Eurogroup which holds the most promise as a political vehicle for European defence collaboration.[34]

Arms control and nuclear co-operation

The Healey-Schröder paper on the use of theatre nuclear weapons (TNWs) became the basis of the Provisional Political Guidelines for the Initial Defensive Tactical Use of Nuclear Weapons (or PPGs). The most significant emphasis in the PPGs was that the use of tactical weapons should have an essentially political purpose in convincing the adversary of the risk of continued military action, *ie* their use should be designed to restore a state of deterrence. Although the inherent risk of escalation becoming out of control very quickly was clearly recognised, the Healey-Schröder paper still emphasised the idea of a gradualist response (similar to von Hassel's ladder concept). The notion that TNWs should also have a real military significance on the battlefield situation was not denied, but it was not given anything near the degree of importance attached to it by (mostly American) adherents to the "warfighting" school of thought. The German point of view was that the use of battlefield weapons on NATO territory should only be an adjunct to strikes on Warsaw Pact territory.

Between May 1971 and May 1973 a number of studies were undertaken on the follow-on use of TNWs. Again, the NPG provided the focus of very close co-operation between Britain and Germany on vital issues of defence policy, since the work was done by a trilateral group involving the United States, Britain and West Germany. The results pointed inescapably to the conclusion that even a large-scale use of TNWs would not necessarily result in regaining the military advantage. Again therefore the primary utility of TNWs was their function as a political signal to show the resolve of the Alliance to escalate even further if necessary.[35]

Those who rejected these conclusions were unable to dispute the validity of the findings of these studies. This prompted them to look in a new direction. If existing forces did not make for a coherent warfighting strategy, perhaps the solution lay in improving the effectiveness of NATO forces quite substantially by the application of more advanced technology.

In November 1973 the NATO Defence Ministers decided to undertake two studies about the effect of new technologies for TNWs: the Germans would analyse the political implications of technology (PIT) while the British were given the task of studying the military implications (MIT). To provide a framework, US Secretary of Defence Schlesinger gave a briefing at the NPG meeting in Bergen in June 1974 on the development of new weapon technologies in the United States. The possible directions of study involved low yield nuclear weapons (which led to public controversy) or enhanced radiation warheads, precision-guided munitions and new methods of target acquisition, advanced cruise missiles and finally improvements in C³I (command, control, communications, intelligence). It is important to note that the new technologies were considered not merely as a way of improving the TNW arsenal, but also as opening up the option of substituting to some extent the military role of some TNWs with new, more powerful and sophisticated conventional weapons. The British were interested in upgrading the V-bombers and F-111s[36], thus leading to great interest in air-launched cruise missiles, while the German Defence Ministry had developed some scepticism about the role of the Poseidon submarines assigned to SACEUR and was therefore also very interested in the cruise missile option.

In his report to Congress in March 1974, James R. Schlesinger announced what in effect amounted to a change in strategic doctrine, proposing an even greater flexibility in the planning and targeting of nuclear weapons, both on the strategic and theatre level, a modernisation of existing weapons systems and C³I as well as political measures (mostly arms control) to establish the equivalence of strategic nuclear capabilities on the lowest possible level.[37] A very clear implication was that Schlesinger intended to reduce the significance of TNWs in Europe. Aided by the results of the studies of the NPG he was now dragging the allies towards an even stronger version of McNamara's original concept. It is interesting to note that while Schlesinger's report stated clearly that the nuclear threshold should be as high as possible, the 1975–6 FRG White Paper stated merely that it was "in the common interest of the Americans and Europeans not to lower the nuclear threshold".[38] The Germans now emphasised the political function of TNWs both in warning the aggressor and in coupling the strategic American deterrent to the defence of Europe.

Schlesinger was pushed in the direction in which he was already moving by Congress. Senator Nunn, whose preferences also lay in reducing the stockpile of TNWs and increasing the significance of conventional forces in Europe, sponsored an amendment which demanded that the Secretary of Defence should give a detailed report to Congress about an overall concept for the use of tactical nuclear weapons in Europe which would be compatible with an increased emphasis on conventional forces, a demand which resulted in a further refinement of the Schlesinger doctrine.

A further constraint was introduced by the arms control dimension. Although American forward-based systems (FBS) had been excluded from SALT I, the Americans made it clear to the Europeans that arms control could be expected to affect theatre deployment options in the future. In the event, not much came of it due to domestic opposition in the US to the inclusion of cruise missiles in SALT II (SALT II involved a merely temporary ban on the deployment of land-based cruise missiles in Europe).

The origins of the dual-track decision

The studies on the implications of new technologies were presented to the NPG in November 1976 and June 1977. Their result was another rebuff to the war-fighters. The conclusion regarding the use of TNWs was virtually the same as in the previous studies, but it did represent a shift towards the American perspective insofar as a survey of existing weapons showed that many of them were obsolete and could either be replaced by modernisation or phased out completely. Although not confirming the Schlesinger doctrine, the report represented another significant push in the direction of modernisation. In May 1977, NATO's Defence Planning Committee decided to institute a Long Term Defence Programme (LTDP) involving 10 committees to work out proposals for the various areas of defence planning. One of these committees, which was to deal with TNWs, was to report to the NPG. The meeting also announced the target of an annual real increase of 3% in defence expenditure by NATO states.

An important stimulus to the gathering momentum for theatre force modernisation was of course the considerable Soviet modernisation programme. One particular aspect, which came to play a pivotal role, was the replacement of SS-4/SS-5 missiles by the SS-20. On October 1977, Helmut Schmidt gave the Alastair Buchan Memorial Lecture at the International Institute for Strategic Studies in which he voiced some of his concerns.[39] While he welcomed the SALT process, he thought the neutralisation of the strategic nuclear capabilities of the superpowers could be dangerous for Europe unless the disparities of military power in Europe were also removed.

The Europeans had already been concerned about the emphasis on conventional forces in the LTDP which they perceived as a form of burden sharing which was to be foisted upon them. At the NPG meeting in October 1977, some days before Schmidt's speech, US Defence Secretary Harold Brown suggested that the Taskforce 10 of the LTDP (which was concerned with TNWs) should be elevated to a High Level Group (HLG) chaired by the US Assistant Secretary for International Security Affairs (then David McGiffert).

As a result, the HLG soon developed its own momentum independent of the LTDP. The British member, Michael Quinlan, from the Ministry of Defence, displayed particular initiative in directing the focus of attention of the HLG towards the issue of Long Range Theatre Nuclear Forces (LRTNFs).[40] In its deliberations, the HLG considered a range of options from no modernisation at all to building up a serious limited war-fighting capability. It came to the clear decision that the only option that would achieve consensus in the Alliance would be a limited modernisation of LRTNFs. This formed the basis of the report of the HLG to the NPG at Homestead, Florida in April 1979. The result was a commitment to reach a decision on LRTNF modernisation by the end of the year. The British and Germans, at this point, were also very concerned to preserve the momentum towards a decision.

The work of the HLG was of course closely followed by the governments. In Germany, the Foreign Ministry was particularly supportive of LRTNF modernisation, while Defence Minister Apel and Chancellor Schmidt were still hesitant and wanted to look at other options. One important factor in all this was the public controversy in 1977 about the proposal to deploy enhanced radiation warheads (ERW) in Europe. At great political cost Schmidt had given qualified support to deployment, only for President Carter to defer deployment. To forestall another political disaster, Schmidt suggested that the issue should be discussed at the level of Heads of Government. Thus the French President, Valéry Giscard d'Estaing, British Prime Minister, James Callaghan, Chancellor Helmut Schmidt and American President Jimmy Carter met in January 1979 in Guadeloupe. Carter spoke in favour of the deployment of new LRTNF; Callaghan suggested prior negotiation with the Soviet Union. Giscard d'Estaing took the view that an offer to negotiate should be linked to a decision to deploy should the negotiations proved unsuccessful within a specific time. Helmut Schmidt eventually agreed to this dual-track approach.

As a result of the Guadeloupe meeting, a "Special Group" was set up to study the arms control implications of LRTNF modernisation. The work of the HLG and the Special Group resulted in the "Integrated Decision Document" which formed the basis of the NATO dual-track decision in December 1979 to deploy 572 LRTNF warheads (on 108 Pershing II and 464 land-based cruise missiles) subject to the outcome of arms control negotiations with the Soviet Union.[41]

Anglo-German co-operation and contributions formed an essential strand of the whole debate about flexible response and TNWs which resulted in the INF decision. The Anglo-German contribution constituted a solid and direct participation in the strategic planning process. The divergences with regard to flexible response have largely been resolved and the Governments of Britain, West Germany and the United States are now all clearly agreed on the principle of maintaining the nuclear threshold as high as possible.[42] One reason for this consists in the modernisation programmes (in the framework of which the NPG decided at Montebello, Canada, in 1983 to withdraw 1,400 of the older tactical nuclear warheads from Europe), both in the nuclear and the conventional field; the latter at least raise the hope of a more credible conventional force posture. Another reason lies in the fact that as a result of the INF controversy the public consensus for a defence based on nuclear deterrence and a strategy of flexible response has been substantially undermined. Adherence to such a defence policy must now take place in the presence of strong public pressures for nuclear disarmament. A policy advocating the threat of the early use of nuclear weapons is therefore politically no longer acceptable.

Conventional forces and forward defence

The politics of BAOR

The most fundamental and significant fact underlying British-German defence co-operation is the presence of British forces in West Germany and their role in Germany's and NATO's forward defence strategy. Like Britain's other extra-territorial commitments, the British Army of the Rhine (BAOR) represents a continuous problem in terms of the national balance of payments, and this has created permanent pressure for a reduction of the commitment, despite FRG support payments which, for a period, were quite considerable. A very substantial reduction in the number of troops was announced in the Defence White Paper in 1957. Between 1957 and 1960 the troop strength of BAOR was reduced from 77,000 to 55,000. It eventually settled at a level of around 50,000 (now, again, at about 56,000).[43] These reductions came at a time when, as a result of the failure of NATO members to reach the Lisbon force goals, the new look strategy abandoned the notion of a purely conventional defence strategy in Europe and put much greater reliance on the use of TNWs, thus providing a rationale for some troop reductions. No doubt they were also strongly related to the decrease of German support contributions to BAOR from £40 million to £12 million, and the severe economic pressures which led to the gradual withdrawal East of Suez.[43]

The agreement for the period 1964–7 covered 70% of the cost; German payments declined under the 1971–6 agreement to a commitment to 20%, which by the end of this period had been reduced to 10%, because part of the 1971–6 package was a commitment to the purchase of military equipment from Britain. This general commitment, however, became difficult for the Germans to maintain owing to their close collaboration with France and purchases from the United States. (West Germany was also involved in considerable offset payments to the United States.) As a result there was another offset agreement covering the period until 1980. At this point, however, there was both German resentment against the principle of offset agreements (on the grounds that the British commitment to BAOR serves the defence of the Alliance as a whole and not just West Germany), and a certain inter-action between financial arrangements in the EEC (in particular a £200 million subsidy to Britain in 1976) and the IMF loan (to which the FRG had contributed). The lesson learnt from the previous agreement was not to make it dependent on procurement decisions; it consisted of a single payment of DM 475 million phased over three years. It was made clear then that there would be no bilateral offset arrangements after that.[44]

Apart from the initial concerns about German rearmament, which are now no longer important, there are some important political reasons for Britain to maintain the commitment. Since over a number of decades Britain has had difficulty in convincing her European partners of the seriousness of her interest in European co-operation, the large commitment to the defence of Europe assumed particular significance. It also gave Britain an influence in NATO and European defence which it otherwise would not have had, and served to balance the growing weight of West Germany. To maintain the commitment was also vital in the face of recurring American doubts about the seriousness of Europe about her own defence. Finally, it must be said that BAOR represented a militarily important contribution to the defence of the Western Alliance. For all the reasons adduced above, no Government ever attempted to significantly reduce its size[45], except that the Labour Party in Opposition, under the leadership of Michael Foot, developed a commitment to a reduction of BAOR to a level of 30,000 (which is no longer supported by the Labour Party leadership).

Criticism from another quarter came as a result of the defence programme announced by Secretary of Defence John Nott, which made a clear choice in favour of Britain's contribution to NATO and of building up Britain's nuclear deterrent as opposed to maintaining out-of-area naval capabilities.[46] BAOR did not escape entirely; one divisional headquarters was to be scrapped. The Navy, however, had to endure 57% of the cuts, while Polaris was to be replaced by Trident. This policy resulted in an intense controversy which led to debate during which the priorities of British defence policy were questioned, particularly with regard to the continental commitment. It now looks, however, as though BAOR will not represent a problem for Anglo-German relations in the near future.[47]

Co-operation between forces in West Germany

At the centre of British-German security co-operation is the presence of British forces in Germany and their participation in the forward defence of Western Europe. The crucial difference between Anglo-German co-operation on the central front and the participation of other European nations lies in the fact that both nations have a substantial part of their total manpower contribution to NATO's defence stationed at the front line in peacetime, whereas the Belgians have only two brigades and the Dutch one brigade on German soil, with the remainder having to be moved in from their home base in the event of war. (The French have three tank divisions in the CENTAG region in South West Germany close to the French border.)

(i) Strategy: flexible response and forward defence

The military concept of NATO just after its foundation in 1949 consisted primarily in deterring a Soviet attack. In the event of war,

West Germany was considered to be a *Verzögerungszone* in which the Soviet offensive was to be slowed down. A substantial defence effort with the aim of halting and if possible reversing the attack would only begin at the Rhine. Logistic preparations for this effort were established deep within French territory.[48]

The notion that, faced with a massive Soviet attack, NATO forces would, for tactical reasons, immediately surrender large parts of West German territory was for obvious reasons quite unacceptable to the Federal Republic, and in the course of the negotiations about German rearmament and her accession to NATO the FRG demanded as a precondition for Alliance membership the adoption of the principle that defence should begin at the East German border and that no West German territory should be given up without a fight.[49]

The principle of forward defence therefore became integral to the declared strategy of NATO. However, in the Alliance it was not regarded as militarily realistic that the enemy could be stopped right at the frontier. The formulation in official statements therefore referred to a defence "as far to the east as possible". It was generally understood that German rearmament and integration in NATO made it possible to shift the line of defence eastwards to the Weser-Fulda-Lech line. This is an interesting indication of the differences between British and German strategic thinking. British military commanders tend to think of natural barriers, such as rivers, as suitable lines of defence, whereas German strategy emphasises mobility rather than static defence and the need to maintain lines of supply across these natural barriers. In the context of the "shield and sword" strategy, conventional forces should hold the enemy until, through massive use of theatre nuclear weapons, the attack could be halted and driven back across the border.

With the advent in the 1960s of the vulnerability of the American continent to Soviet long-range missiles and the subsequent retreat from the doctrine of massive retaliation, the strategy of forward defence, as understood by the West Germans, appeared to suffer a further decline in credibility. Nonetheless the government of the FRG staunchly stuck to this principle and presented it to its own public as firmly established NATO strategy.

The reasons that impelled the Federal Government in this direction are quite clear: 30% of West Germany's population and 25% of its industrial capacity lie within 100 km of the border. A strategy predicated on giving up so much territory in the initial phase of hostilities, followed by protracted combat action possibly involving the use of theatre nuclear weapons, simply cannot be contemplated by any FRG government.[50]

The West German argument, that NATO's capabilities to stop an attack were increasing and that therefore the defence line could be moved further east, began to find some degree of acceptance in NATO by 1963, when the principle that a determined defence should take place "as far to the east as possible" was replaced by the notion that it should take place "on the eastern boundary of NATO territory".[51] Furthermore, it was now expected that conventional operations to force a "pause" in hostilities would last a relatively short time, a few hours or days at most.

Since then, forward defence has been the declared strategy of NATO, but it must be understood that all the political declarations do not necessarily coincide with the perceptions of the likely course of a conflict in the military thinking of the Allies; the firm political commitment to forward defence has not necessarily removed all the doubts; nor has it created the force posture and deployment that makes it the actual and not merely the declared strategy. British military commanders have never really accepted the strategy of forward defence as it is understood by the West Germans. Despite the official position, they still think and plan in terms of tactical retreat to regain some depth of territory for defence, and a substantial defence effort, according to (private) British thinking, still begins at the Weser.[52] During the Lionheart exercises in 1984, for example, the British forces gave up 140 km before mounting their defence. It must also be added that the peacetime deployment of troops is not forward enough for a forward defence strategy in the case of a surprise attack.[53]

Given the divergence between political commitment and military reality, the issue of forward defence has become somewhat of a taboo subject within NATO.[54] There are the ritual affirmations of adherence to the strategy. The Germans for their part continue to say that adherence by NATO to forward defence remains a basic condition of West German membership of the Alliance, although even the Germans realise that in the event of war it is unlikely that the strategy will be implemented in the way in which it is officially described. As a result, the discussions within NATO have, since 1963, been based on the assumed commitment to forward defence and thus have concentrated not on the nature of the objective but rather on the means of achieving it. British operational strategy has traditionally been based on area defence, combined with some notion of using natural defence lines such as rivers as barriers against the enemy, reminiscent of the notions involved in linear defence. Thus, the operational concept on which BAOR was basing itself was always, to some extent, in contradiction to the German understanding of forward defence and the German strategy of mobile defence, even though the British Army has never been subject to strict doctrinal guidelines, thus allowing for considerable adaptation and changes. There have been some very interesting developments in British thinking recently which may have brought British and German operational concepts much closer. Gen. Sir Nigel Bagnall, when Commander of BAOR and NORTHAG, stressed the advantages of mobile defence and developed an agreed operational concept for NORTHAG. His concept involves a combination of area and mobile defence, with stress on flexibility (by giving mission-related orders and thus much greater flexibility to the individual commanders) and mobile reserves in particular. The acceptance of a unified operational concept for NORTHAG is a unique achievement, due mostly to British-German co-operation. There are, however, still considerable difficulties over implementation, because Britain lacks the quantity and quality of armoured infantry which form the equipment basis of the German strategy, and the creation of mobile reserves is more in the realm of a future objective than present reality.[55]

There is also close co-operation between the British and German air forces which are assigned to the 2nd Allied Tactical Air Force (2 ATAF). The RAF has three main missions: (a) to gain and maintain air superiority; (b) close support of land forces; (c) long-range interdiction of enemy second echelon forces. Phantoms, which are operated both by the RAF and the Luftwaffe, are the main means of carrying out the first mission. The second is effected (in the RAF) by Harriers and helicopters (Pumas and Chinooks). The third is the principal role of the Tornado (although at present Jaguars are still deployed for this task). The Tornado is again a major achievement of British-German co-operation (with Italian participation), and the adoption of the same aircraft solves major logistic problems of inter-operability of equipment and makes co-operation on the battlefield much easier. There is some difference between the American and British approach to long-range interdiction. While the British emphasise low-level approaches in small groups to evade radar detection, the American approach tends to be to go in with a much larger number of aircraft equipped with a great deal of electronic countermeasures. The Luftwaffe which is greatly involved in training both with the RAF and the USAF, operates on a basis compatible with the British approach, but has also adopted some aspects of the American approach. Thus (unlike the RAF) it has ordered 36 Tornados especially equipped for electronic warfare. Even so, there is not much disagreement on long-range interdiction tactics between the RAF and the Luftwaffe.

Discussions on conventional strategy have concentrated on "deep strike" concepts which focus on attacking the second echelon of Warsaw Pact forces and key C^3I installations in enemy territory such as Air Land Battle which is the US Army doctrine and Follow-on-Forces-Attack (FOFA), an operationally different concept evolved by SHAPE. Both concepts have focussed attention on "emerging technologies" which, it is hoped, will make second echelon interdiction a viable military option. The differences in the operational concepts, as well as the maldeployment of NATO forces on the central front (with the strongest forces being deployed by CENTAG, even though the most likely route for a conventional attack by Warsaw Pact forces is through the territory of NORTHAG) constitute a difficult problem for NATO's conventional posture. Whether the example of Britain and West Germany in the co-operative development of operational concepts will be emulated in future attempts by NATO planners to grapple with these issues remains to be seen, particularly in view of the gap in operational strategy between NORTHAG and CENTAG.[56]

(ii) Co-operation in leadership

In contrast to the proposals of a European Defence Community in the 1950s, NATO forces remain part of their national forces and command structure, with an integrated leadership above Corps level. Participating in the defence of Central Europe are: 1 British Corps, 1 Dutch Corps, 1 Belgian Corps, 2 American Corps, 1 Canadian Brigade and 3 West German Corps. The FRG contributes 50% of the peacetime land forces in Central Europe. In peacetime the Bundeswehr Corps are under the command of the Army Inspector; in a crisis situation there is a system whereby they are assigned in various phases (depending on the seriousness of the situation) to NATO command. Co-operation between British and German forces at and below the Corps level is said to be very close. There are regular contacts at the level of Corps Commander involving discussions about the co-ordination of operational war plans, tactical doctrine and training objectives.[57]

NATO leadership is, of course, under political control, and on top of the hierarchy in the decision-making process is a political body, known as the North Atlantic Council. All member countries are represented in the Council and have an equal vote.

There has been some discussion in West Germany as to whether the FRG is adequately represented in the NATO integrated military structure.[58] Although the German contribution to NATO is clearly comparable to the British, the latter have a much greater representation in the NATO leadership. Thus Britain is strongly involved with all three major NATO Commands (and the Commander of Allied Command Channel is British), while Germany occupies top positions only in the Allied Command Europe (ACE). There are some perceived imbalances even in ACE; although in SHAPE Germany is represented in six of 32 positions at the level of General, thus occupying the same number of positions as the British, and is also well represented in the command structure of AFCENT, there are some problems in AFNORTH where Germany now provides more than 50% of the forces but, as a result of the 1961 Oslo agreement, is not well represented in the top commanding positions.

Despite these discussions, it must be said that no great problems arise from the nature of the NATO command structure where British-German co-operation particularly is extremely close. The deep-seated problems in NATO are located not in the integrated structure, but rather in the existence of the widely diverging operational principles described above, arising from the way in which NATO forces are deployed, and in logistics and inter-operability of equipment, the resolution of which will demand a great deal of political will.

Conclusion

The close and cordial relations between West Germany and the United Kingdom have been of central importance to the political development of Europe since World War II and West Germany has become Britain's most important partner in Europe. The emergence of the superpowers and the advent of nuclear weapons leading to the "transatlantic bargain" with the United States, has compelled different European nations to look for different, and often conflicting, solutions to their security dilemmas. What should be clear from the tangled history of what are now sometimes called the "variable geometries" of relationships in Europe is that the paradoxes inherent in the issues of nuclear strategy and nuclear sharing are incapable of logical resolution; this is particularly true for West Germany which finds itself in such an exposed position. The primary challenge ahead lies not so much in resolving the incongruities and deficiences in NATO military strategy and the defence procurement systems, but rather in developing a coherent approach towards a political resolution of the security dilemmas. This is an immensely difficult task, which in the past has seen successes and failures. Its success, on which all our futures depend, demands close European co-operation in which the Anglo-German relationship will play a critical part.

Notes

1. Grame P. Auton and Wolfram Hanrieder, *The Foreign Policies of West Germany, France & Britain*, (Englewood Cliffs: Prentice Hall 1980, Chapter 9).
2. Auton and Hanrieder, *op. cit.*, p. 185f.
3. See Norbert Wiggershaus, "The Decision for a West German Defence Contribution", in Olav Riste (ed.) *Western Security: The Formative Years (European and Atlantic Defence 1947-1953)*, (Oslo: Universtetsforlaget AS 1985, 198–214, p. 198).
4. See Fred Mulley, *The Politics of Western Defence*, (London: Thames and Hudson 1962, p. 23.)
5. Royal Institute of International Affairs, *Britain in Western Europe*, (London: Oxford University Press 1956, Ch. VI); Edward Fursdon, *The European Defence Community: A History* (London: Macmillan Press 1980, Part III).
6. For a more detailed analysis of these controversies see Dieter Mahncke, *Nukleare Mitwirkung* (Berlin: Walter de Gruyter 1972, p. 12); Catherine McArdle Kelleher, *Germany and the Politics of Nuclear Weapons* (New York: Columbia University Press 1975, Ch. 2).
7. See David N. Schwartz, *NATO's Nuclear Dilemmas*, (Washington: Brookings Institute 1983, pp. 42–46.)
8. See Konrad Adenauer, *Erinnerungen 1953-1955*, (Stuttgart: Deutsche Verlags-Anstalt 1966, p. 347). While with regard to other Western nations, West Germany

emphasised the possibility of a joint nuclear force, it emphasised another aspect with regard to the Soviet Union, namely the possibility of a final and complete renunciation of nuclear weapons (an issue which had not been entirely clarified in 1954, initially partly due to hasty drafting of the agreements – see Note 1). The intention was to obtain concessions from the Soviet Union with regard to the German question in exchange. This policy was not very successful. As Dieter Mahncke has pointed out: "The value of a promise to renounce something that one does not possess and probably will not acquire does not appear to be very great". (Mahncke, *op. cit.*, p. 27).

9. Christian A. Herter, *Toward an Atlantic Community*, (New York: Harper & Row, 1963, pp. 41–42).

10. For more details about the internal American debate about flexible response, see Schwartz, *op. cit.*, Ch. 6.

11. See Schwartz, *op. cit.*, Ch. 5; T.C. Wiegele, "The Origins of the MLF Concept 1957–60," *Orbis*, **XII**:2, Summer 1968, pp. 465–489.

12. John Baylis has suggested that the crisis was overdramatised by the British to put pressure on the Americans with regard to Polaris. See John Baylis, *Anglo-American Defence Relations 1939–1980* (London: Macmillan Press 1981).

13. Baylis *op. cit.*, pp. 77–80; Lawrence Freedman, *Britain and Nuclear Weapons* (London: Macmillan, 1980, pp. 21–23).

14. For an exposition of official BMVg views on the MLF, see Kai-Uwe von Hassel, "Organising Western Defense: The Search for Consensus". *Foreign Affairs*, **43**:2, January 1965, 209–216. See also Mahncke, *op. cit.*, pp. 157–169; Kelleher, *op. cit.*, Ch. 9. It was even mooted that at some distant point in the future the United States might sell its share in the MLF to the Europeans. Statements suggesting a possible relinquishing of US control were made in 1963 by George Ball, Vice-President Johnson and even President Kennedy himself. See Mahncke, *op. cit.*, p. 142. However, American statements on this point were generally ambiguous, and the general preoccupation with non-proliferation and American attitudes to control sharing make it appear rather doubtful that there could be a realistic expectation of the American veto being ultimately relinquished.

15. See Mahncke, *ibid.* This interpretation was confirmed to the author in a personal conversation with Lord Chalfont, then Minister of State at the Foreign & Commonwealth Office.

16. See Maria Meyer zu Natrup, *Der strittige Weg zum Frieden – Die Sicherheitspolitik der britischen Labour Party 1970 bis 1979*, Ph.D. Dissertation, Köln University 1984, pp. 92–98; Schwartz *op. cit.*, pp. 96–105; Baylis, *op. cit.*, Chapter 3 and Lawrence Freedman, *op. cit.*, Chapter 4.

17. Neville Brown, "British Arms and the Switch towards Europe", *International Affairs*, **43**:3, July 1967, 468–482; Grame P. Auton and Wolfram Hanrieder, *The Foreign Policies of West Germany, France & Britain* (Englewood Cliffs: Prentice Hall 1980, Chapters 9 & 10); Richard Löwenthal (ed.), *Aussenpolitische Perspektiven des westdeutschen Staates, Bd. 3, Der Zwang zur Partnerschaft* (München: R. Oldenbourg 1972, pp. 34–43); Edward Heath, "Realism in British Foreign Policy", *Foreign Affairs*, **48**:1, 1969, p. 49; Andrew J. Pierre, "Britain and European Security: Issues and Choices for the 1970s", in William T.R. Fox and Warner R. Schilling (eds.), *European Security and the Atlantic System* (New York: Columbia University Press 1973, pp. 73–118).

18. See Auton and Hanrieder, *op. cit.*, p. 206.

19. Denis Healey, "NATO, Britain and Soviet Military Policy", *Orbis*. **XIII**:1, Spring 1969, 48–58, p. 51; see particularly p. 52. He believed that "this would do more to destabilise the existing relationships between Eastern and Western Europe than any other foreseeable development". This statement appears somewhat incongruous in the light of Britain's policy with regard to her own nuclear deterrent. See also: Roger Carey, "British Thinking on Tactical Nuclear Deterrence in Europe", *World Today*, **25**:4. April 1969, 172–177. For a slightly earlier German view, see Peter Wittig,

"Einige Fragen der Abschreckungstrategie aus deutscher Sicht", *Wehrkunde*, **XV**: 6, June 1966, 277–283.

20. Bruce Reed and Geoffrey Williams, *Denis Healey and the Politics of Power* (London: Sidgwick & Jackson 1971, pp. 251–262); Schwartz, *op. cit.*, Ch. 6.

21. See the various discussions in this theme in Kelleher, *op. cit.*, particularly Chs. 6 & 8; Paul Buteux, *The Politics of Nuclear Consultation in NATO 1965–1980* (Cambridge: Cambridge University Press 1983, Chapter 1); Schwartz, *ibid*; Kai-Uwe von Hassel, "Organizing Western Defence", *Foreign Affairs*, **43**:2, October 1964, 209–218; a fascinating insight into Soviet understanding of NATO debates about nuclear strategy is given in the article by Capt. Yu. Nepodayev, "On Nuclear Threshold in NATO Strategy", *Voennaya Mysl*, No. 6, June 1966 (pp. 77–79 translated version).

22. Walter F. Hahn, *Between Westpolitik and Ostpolitik* (Beverly Hills: Sage Publications 1975, p. 26).

23. Hahn, *op. cit.*, p. 26.

24. Wolfram F. Hanrieder, "Arms Control and the European Political Order", *Bulletin of Peace Proposals*, **16**:3 (1985), pp. 291–301, p. 2925. For an authoritative account of this history of *Ostpolitik*, see Arnulf Baring, *Machtwechsel* (Stuttgart: DVA 1982).

25. Buteux, *op. cit.*, Ch. 2.

26. Reed and Williams, *op. cit.*, pp. 251–263.

27. William Wallace, *The Foreign Policy Process In Britain* (London: George Allen & Unwin 1977, p. 226).

28. Wallace, *op. cit.*, p. 228.

29. Buteux, *op. cit.*, p. 87; Thomas C. Wiegele, "Nuclear Consultation Processes in NATO", *Orbis*, **XVI**:2, Summer 1972, 462–487, pp. 484–486.

30. Hearings before the Special Subcommittee on North Atlantic Treaty Organisation Commitments of the Committee on Armed Services, US House of Representatives, 92nd Congress, 1st and 2nd Sessions, October 26, 1971, p. 13093.

31. See Thomas Jansen, "Die Institutionen" in Karl Carstens and Dieter Mahncke (eds.), *Westeuropäische Verteidigungskooperation*, (München: R. Oldenbourg 1972, pp. 217–219); Phil Williams, "NATO and the European", in Kenneth J, Twichett (ed.), *European Co-operation Today*, (London: Europa Publications 1980, pp. 26–44); William C. Cromwell, *The Eurogroup and NATO* (Philadelphia: Foreign Policy Research Institute 1974, p. 16 f).

32. Cromwell, *op. cit.*, p. 16 f.

33. Cromwell, *op. cit.*, p. 6, has pointed out another reason why German and British contributions were of particular significance in Eurogroup:

    "It should also be pointed out that in some West European countries the position of the defence minister may be restricted by that of the foreign minister. In such cases a defence minister may be reluctant to commit his country to a position within Eurogroup which might be construed as an encroachment on the preserve of his foreign minister and thus risk jurisdictional and political quarrels within the government. Such a problem could be particularly sensitive in the case of a coalition government whose foreign and defence ministers may be from different political parties. In most cases, the range of the foreign minister's authority is greater than that of the defence minister, reaching into the broad arena of general security policy, and this may partially account for the reluctance of some defence ministers to undertake Eurogroup consultations on other than narrowly defined military defence topics. Though this situation creates no problems in the case of the Federal Republic and the United Kingdom, it does represent a factor, in varying degrees, for most other West European countries."

34. For more details, see the contributions by Werner Weidenfeld and Trevor Taylor in this volume.

35. Helga Haftendorn, "Das doppelte Missverständnis – zur Vorgeschichte des NATO-Doppelbeschlusses von 1979", *Vierteljahreshefte für Zeitgeschichte*, **33**:2, April

1965, 244–287, p. 249; J. Michael Legge, *Theatre Nuclear Weapons and the NATO Strategy of Flexible Response* (Santa Monica: Rand Corporation 1983, p. 26–28).

36. According to a personal conversation with former British Defence Secretary Lord Mulley.

37. James R. Schlesinger, "The Theater Nuclear Force Posture in Europe". A Report to the United States Congress, Washington DC, April 1975.

38. Ministry of Defence (Bonn), White Paper 1975/76, p. 50.

39. Schmidt later claimed to have some of the concerns expressed in his speech known at the NATO summit meeting in May 1977. This quotation is from Schwartz, *op. cit.*, p. 214.

40. This was confirmed by former British Foreign Secretary, Dr David Owen and officials in the German Ministry of Defence.

41. For more details, see John Cartwright and Julian Critchley, *Cruise, Pershing and SS-20*: A North Atlantic Assembly Report (London: Brassey's Defence Publishers 1985).

42. As a result, military planners proceed on the assumption that authorisation for the release of TNW will not be given at an early stage or at all, as the author was told during conversations at the Ministry of Defence in London.

43. Ministry of Defence, White Paper 1957, London: HMSO, Cmnd. 124; see also John Garnett, "BAOR and NATO", *International Affairs*, 46:4, October 1970, 670–681; J. Enoch Powell, "The Defence of Europe", No. 649, February 1968, 51–56.

44. These details are to be found in Lawrence Freedman, "British Foreign Policy to 1985 – II: Britain's Contribution to NATO", *International Affairs*, 54:1, January 1978, 30–47; see also Fred Mulley, *The Politics of Western Defence* (London: Thames and Hudson 1962, pp. 132–137).

45. One has also take into account, as Lawrence Freedman has pointed out, that the financial benefits of cuts in BAOR would only accrue gradually and in the short term a relocation of British troops would actually cause further outlays.

46. For more detailed discussion, see the contribution to this volume by the late Jonathan Alford.

47. See Meyer zu Natrup, *op. cit.*, pp. 138–143; 292–300 on the attitude of the Labour Party. See also Lawrence Freedman, "British Defence Policy after the Falklands", *The World Today*, September 1982, 331–339; and Michael Chichester, "Britain and NATO: the Case for Revision", *The World Today*, November 1982, 415–421. See also Alan Clark, *The Times*, 10 July 1982; Michael Chichester and John Wilkinson, *The Uncertain Ally* (Aldershot: Gower 1982).

48. Johannes Gerber, *Die Bundeswehr im nordatlantischen Bündnis* (Regensburg: Walhalla u. Praetoria Verlag 1985, p. 16 f).

49. Julian Lider, *Problems of Military Policy in the Konrad Adenauer Era (1949–1966)*, (Stockholm: Swedish Institute of International Affairs 1984, pp. 64–67).

50. Bundesminister für Verteidigung, *Weissbuch 1983*, Bonn 1983, p. 146.

51. Cf. Lider, *op. cit.*, p. 65.

52. According to interview evidence with defence experts, including a former British defence minister.

53. Roger L. Facer, *Conventional Forces and the NATO Strategy of Flexible Response* (Santa Monica: Rand Corporation Rand/R-3209-FF, p. 16); see also Chichester and Wilkinson, *op. cit.*, p. 228.

54. Philip R. Lindner has described this situation succinctly: "Some adherents to a defence option recognize the political need for forward defence and work around it in their strategy . . . On the whole . . . most analysts agree that enlightened criticism of forward defence must centre on the manner in which forward defence is conducted, *not on alternatives to replace it.*" [Emphasis added.] See also Philip R. Lindner, "Considerations of a Conventional Defense of Central Europe", in James R. Golden, Asa A. Clark and Bruce G. Arlinghaus (eds.), *Conventional Deterrence* (Lexington: D.C. Heath and Co., 1984, 109–120, p. 112).

55. This section is based on interview evidence with the Ministry of Defence in London

and British Forces in Germany. See also Sir Nigel Bagnall, "Möglichkeiten und Grenzen der europäischen Kooperation", in *Schutzschild für die Alte Welt*, Deutsches Strategie-Forum Bonn (Papers from a Seminar held in Bonn-Bad Godesberg on 13–15 March 1985 (Bonn: Mittler & Sohn 1985, 24–27).
56. This section is partly based on interview evidence. See also: Blackwell, *op. cit.*; Facer, *op. cit.*; Boyd D Sutton, John R. Landry, Malcolm B. Armstrong, Howell M. Estes and Wesley K. Clark, "Deep Attack Concepts and the Defence of Central Europe", *Survival*, **XXVI**:2, March April 1984, 50–69; Phil Williams and William Wallace, "Emerging Technologies and European Security", *Survival, ibid*, 70–78.
57. Bagnall, *op. cit.*, p. 25.
58. Günter Kiessling, "Die deutsche Repräsentation in der NATO", *Europäische Wehrkunde*, **31**:11, 1982, 481–486.

Chapter 2
The Political Debate on Security Policy in the Federal Republic

ANGELIKA VOLLE

The failure of détente – a German perspective

For the majority of the German population the *Ostpolitik* of the social-democratic/liberal coalition under Chancellor Willy Brandt was synonymous with the policy of détente between East and West. The "humanitarian improvements", which were achieved in the wake of *Ostpolitik* particularly for the people in East and West Germany as a result of tough negotiations, were tangible results of détente which the Germans felt and experienced themselves: "The new German *Ostpolitik* . . . filled the policy of détente with German substance in a pan-European perspective."[1] The establishment of cultural, economic and political relations between Europeans on both sides of the Iron Curtain promised hopes of an equilibrium of power between East and West.

The view of life of a whole generation which grew up during this period in the Federal Republic was moulded by the policy of détente. The media, which increasingly and lastingly influenced political consciousness, conveyed for the first time since the long period of Cold War an image of the East which no longer portrayed the political opponent as an enemy, but rather as a partner in negotiations. The "Soviet threat" on which NATO builds its strategy of deterrence, was no longer perceived as such. The abstract image of Communism, of the "enemy from the East", was replaced on television by real people in Eastern Europe, whose ordinary daily life and love of peace were apparently no different from that of the citizen of the Federal Republic.

The Federal government perceived in the policy of détente the opportunity to reconcile the relationship between the Federal Republic and the United States, its membership of the Western Alliance and integration into Western Europe with improved relations with the Soviet Union and Eastern Europe in general and the German Democratic Republic in particular, according to the principle of "change through rapprochement". The pursuit of this policy led at first to very harsh party political conflicts which very nearly resulted in the fall of Brandt's government, but by the time Helmut Schmidt became Chancellor in 1974 it gradually achieved the consent of all the parties represented in the Bundestag, especially when the results of détente became slowly discernible in inter-German relations.

With the signing of the CSCE Helsinki Final Act, East-West détente in Europe reached its climax in 1975. That at this time global détente was already on the decline was not a fact that political leaders in Europe – in contrast to the growing number of critics of détente in the United States – yet wanted to acknowledge. Chancellor Schmidt was the first European statesman publicly to condemn the production and deployment of accurate Soviet SS-20 medium-range missiles and the Backfire bomber, which threatened Western Europe ("blackmail of European states") and to criticise the American decision not to massproduce the neutron bomb and to cancel production of the B-1 bomber. The ensuing political discussion among Western Allies about the need for counter-deployments, triggered by Schmidt's speech at the International Institute for Strategic Studies in October 1977, coupled with an offer to the Soviet Union to negotiate to strengthen the security of Western Europe did not – in the German view – imply that the end of détente in Europe had arrived. On the contrary, inter-German relations received an important boost with the conclusion of negotiations about East-West transport and the signing of a border agreement at the end of 1978. But the announcement of the NATO dual-track decision on 12 December 1979 already foreshadowed the possibility of the failure of the "decade of détente". This finally occurred with the invasion of Afghanistan by the Soviet Army 15 days later.

The Germans in particular did not want to accept that Afghanistan should mark the end of the global policy of détente as well as the process of détente in Europe. The Federal Republic had the most to lose from the abandonment of *Entspannungspolitik*: namely the fragile, but nonetheless existing *modus vivendi* in *Ostpolitik* and *Deutschlandpolitik*. The government therefore attempted to keep détente in Europe alive under the slogan of the "divisibility of détente".[2] Some politicians attempted in vain to portray Afghanistan as an East-South type conflict, in order to save at least European détente. Chancellor Schmidt tried, to the chagrin of members of the American administration, to act as "interpreter" between East and West. He regretted the interruption in the United States of the process of ratification of the SALT II Treaty. The Federal government, with support from the

CDU/CSU opposition, successfully resisted the American demand for sanctions against the Soviet Union, particularly in the high-technology area, and consequently German companies participated in the Soviet gas pipeline project. It did, however, decide to boycott the Moscow Olympics (while Britain and France took part). It resisted (without success) the wholesale condemnation of the past policy of détente as misguided by the American presidential candidate Ronald Reagan. During his visit to Moscow in July 1980 Schmidt succeeded in persuading the Soviet Union to abandon one of its preconditions for the removal of medium-range weapons in Europe; the negotiations began on 30 November 1980 but were then postponed at the request of the United States until the autumn of 1981 because of the change of administration.

Nevertheless, the Federal Republic was unable to stop the gradual freezing of East-West relations. The raising of the minimum amount of currency that had to be exchanged by tourists to East Germany was a significant set-back, which was further underlined by the Gera demands of the Chairman of the SED, Erich Honecker, in October 1980. These were: recognition of a separate GDR citizenship; dissolution of the Central Registry Office of Criminal Offences against Human Rights by GDR authorities in Salzgitter; transformation of the permanent representatives of the two countries into embassies; and regulation of the Elbe demarcation line in the middle of the river. The election of President Reagan, who pursued a policy of military strength and superiority over the Soviet Union, set back the efforts of the Federal Republic for a resumption of the East-West dialogue. Particularly humiliating for Schmidt were the circumstances under which he was confronted with the collapse of détente in Europe: during his meeting with Honecker in the GDR on 13 December 1981 he received news of the imposition of martial law in Poland. The efforts of the Federal Government to continue to uphold *Entspannung* had failed.[3]

The public debate on security

Until the autumn of 1981 the discussion about the security policy and military strategy of NATO in the Federal Republic had been limited to a small circle of experts. Since the Easter marches and the *Kampf dem Atomtod* ('Struggle against atomic death') movement of the 1950s there had been no public controversies about the fact that the security of Western Europe relied essentially on the threat to use nuclear weapons. Because of the complexity of the issues involved with regard to nuclear deterrence, which were difficult to convey to the general public in a comprehensible manner, the media had shown little interest in the problem. A significant public interest in defence issues did not emerge until 1977/8, catalysed by the emotional domestic controversy with regard to the neutron weapon.

The neutron weapon controversy

On 6 June 1977, the *Washington Post* published an article with the sensational headline, "Neutron Killer Warhead Buried in ERDA Budget", in which it was claimed that American forces in Europe were to be equipped with a highly effective radiation weapon, the neutron weapon (ERW).[4]

The German Press described this weapon (which consists of warheads with enhanced radioactive radiation that, when detonated, would only cause minor collateral damage) as "the neut", or the "clean" and "humane" bomb, thus indirectly sparking off the subsequent discussion about moral values. After the Young Socialists, the SPD youth organisation, had protested in a public statement at the beginning of July 1977 against these characterisations which made the ERW appear more harmless, arguing that "thus a psychological climate is to be prepared, in which the use of such weapons no longer meets any resistance",[5] Egon Bahr, the General Secretary of the SPD, steered the discussion entirely into the emotional realm. Concerned that new steps of rearmament might endanger the policy of détente with the Soviet Union,[6] (and also for tactical political reasons) he protested in the party journal *Vorwärts* and in a number of other public statements that "humanity is going insane" if it entertained any idea of stationing in the Federal Republic this "symbol of the perversion of human thought", which was "inhumane in conception" and a "reversal of value concepts".

Compared with this form of argument, which was avidly taken up by the media, the rational expositions by Foreign Minister Genscher and CDU defence expert Wörner, which appeared to favour the introduction of the neutron weapon, looked rather pale (although, like some prominent German generals, they also warned that the weapon should not be treated as harmless). The same is true for the objective debate in the Bundestag in September 1977, in which the Federal Defence Minister Georg Leber (SPD) emphasised the deterrent character of the neutron weapon. However, conservative analysts pointed out at an early stage that the developing neutron discussion showed "that the West is acting irresponsibly from a psycho-strategic point of view. One can only be astonished at the light-heartedness with which this new weapon was introduced to the political scene."[7] The same light-heartedness, with which it was also removed from the political discussion, left the Federal Republic with grave doubts about the leadership qualities of the American President. By March 1978 Chancellor Schmidt had overcome the domestic political opposition (within and outside his own party) and the government had finally struggled to a position of agreeing to the deployment of neutron weapons – under certain conditions[8] – when President Carter suddenly announced on 7 April 1978 his decision to postpone production of the weapon.

The public debate continued to be fuelled by contradictory statements from the American administration, the domestic opposition in the United States and the President who was shying away from a decision.[9] Apart from the politicians, German peace researchers were particularly active in contributing to this debate among intellectuals. But even those arguments which sought to address the moral nature of the neutron weapon did not manage to capture the attention of the broad mass of the population in the issue. Apart from a number of demonstrations organized by the German Communist Party (DKP) and church organisations in the Federal Republic, and a mass demonstration in Amsterdam in March 1978 there were no large-scale public manifestations against the ERW.

The excited reaction in the Federal Republic to the neutron weapon, which was noted with surprise in NATO circles and in the United States since hitherto the stationing of American missiles in the Federal Republic had not been an issue, had been confined to a small (but audible) circle of experts. But the different views within the SPD leadership had been clearly exposed and the popular pressure for a public debate about securing peace by nuclear disarmament had increased. A political observer therefore warned:

> Given the discussion about a nuclear deterrent potential (and this is what the neutron weapon is, after all), one hardly dares to contemplate the controversy that might arise in the Federal Republic of Germany about weapons, whereby the territory of the Soviet Union can be threatened directly with nuclear weapons from German soil.[10]

This sceptical remark appears particularly prescient in view of the subsequent bitter controversy about the NATO dual-track decision.

NATO dual-track: the Schmidt government and the opposition

While the discussion in the Federal Republic about the neutron weapon was in full swing the Western Alliance was preparing its response to the Soviet medium-range missile deployments destabilising Western Europe.[11] From the American point of view the objective was a long-term improvement, especially in the conventional capabilities of the Alliance. The concept of the US government therefore favoured the modernisation of tactical nuclear weapons, *ie* rearmament; arms control was given little emphasis. In the Federal Republic there was little controversy about security political problems at the parliamentary level. The early briefing of the CDU/CSU party caucus by the government contributed to the moderate opposition stance, which mostly eschewed polemical statements; this helped considerably to keep the debate on a rational level. But inside the SPD/FDP government there were different views about the modernisation of NATO medium-range weapons. Foreign Minister Genscher was one of the main proponents of rearmament as presented in the American proposals, while Defence Minister Apel – in close collaboration with Chancellor Schmidt – stressed forcibly the negotiating option. Schmidt, who had expressed himself in favour of coupling modernisation with new offers for arms limitation negotiations to the Soviet Union such as were later manifested in the NATO dual-track decision, received full support for his policy from the CDU/CSU opposition.

Within his own party, however, Schmidt had great difficulty in gaining approval for the security political decisions of his government. He was therefore forced to emphasise the arms control aspects of the dual-track decision. Sections of the SPD, led by Egon Bahr and parliamentary party Chairman, Herbert Wehner, insisted that arms control negotiations should be given precedence. The foreign affairs and defence spokesmen of the SPD, Horst Ehmke and Alfons Pawelczyk, insisted on negotiations spread over several years before the Federal government should agree to the deployment of new weapons systems. Willy Brandt pronounced himself a "non-expert".[12] Schmidt was faced with the real problem of obtaining a majority for the NATO dual-track decision at the SPD Conference in Berlin from 3–7 December 1979, just a few days before the decisive NATO meeting. With great tactical skill he succeeded in obtaining conditional approval for his security policy, even though some positions taken by the party deviated from the dual-track decision: the goal of the negotiations should be the "zero option" and there should be nothing "automatic" about deployment (Karsten Voigt); the conference would not endorse the view that only the Soviet Union was responsible for the loss of military parity; and disparities in the military balance should only be "met" but not "countered". Soon it became evident that the security policy of the Federal government and the ambiguous formulations of the Berlin Party Conference, which were capable of varied interpretations, had become increasingly divergent.[13]

The peace movement's resistance to cruise and Pershing II

The general public in the Federal Republic knew little about the foreign policy and military context of the NATO dual-track decision. The maintenance of peace by nuclear weapons, the nuclear threat against Western Europe by Soviet SS-20 missiles, the loss of US nuclear superiority – all these were subjects reserved for experts. The media had not yet taken them up. Only when the peace movement initiated a campaign against the planned stationing of 108 Pershing II and 96 cruise missiles in the Federal Republic, and propagated the view that these constituted more of a threat than a protection for the population, did politicians, experts and the media take up the challenge and embark upon a public discussion of NATO strategy.

The *ex post facto* explanations of the NATO dual-track decision were not able to satisfy the public's growing demand for simple explanations; they were generally formulated in the abstract and full of technical jargon and thus incomprehensible to the layman. It appeared paradoxical that "the theory of deterrence must demonstrate that a nuclear war can be fought, in order to prevent it"[14] and as a result a large and vocal part of the population was more afraid of the nuclear weapons that were to be stationed in the Federal Republic from 1983 onwards than of the Soviet SS-20s which were actually targeted on Western Europe. The confidence of the population in the Chancellor's decisions on security policy were undermined by several statements from American politicians which were introduced into the discussion by the German media (partly taken out of context), such as on "prevailing in a limited nuclear war" (Defence Secretary Weinberger), that there were "more important things than living in peace" (Secretary of State Haig), or that "the United States will be once again No. 1 in the world" (presidential candidate Reagan). The average citizen, who had experienced his socialisation in the era of détente, was confused; this was more than he could cope with. The deterrent effect of nuclear weapons lost its credibility, since the immediate Soviet threat was no longer perceived. The peace movement detected this gap in information policy and appealed mainly to people's emotions, inciting fear of a nuclear war (which in their eyes seemed possible).

The origin, composition and value system of the peace movement is not the subject of this essay.[15] Here we merely wish to note that at the beginning of the 1980s the peace movement in the Federal Republic had become the reservoir of a large variety of groupings, brought together for the first time by agreeing on one minimal objective: opposition to the NATO dual-track decision. The leaders of the peace movement increasingly succeeded in the years 1980–1 in conveying a detailed scenario of the terrible consequences of a nuclear war in a manner comprehensible to everyone and thus stoked the fear among the population of an "atomic apocalypse". Newspapers, radio and particularly television at home and abroad took up these theses and gave them a completely disproportionate prominence, thus ensuring that they would spread among the public. With simple but effective slogans like "Create Peace Without Weapons" or the (significantly abbreviated) Brecht quotation "Imagine there is a war and no–one turns up,"[16] they gathered supporters. Apart from the reversal of the dual-track decision they demanded a "nuclear-free zone from Poland to Portugal" and the defence of the Federal Republic by defensive weapons. Furthermore, they propagated non-violent resistance and unilateral disarmament as concepts which could be realised politically.

Critics therefore accused them of being "parasitic security political drop-outs in their purest form".[17] The main strategy of the peace movement consisted initially in peace forums, peace workshops or "appeals" to the Federal government to withdraw approval for the stationing of American missiles; there were, for example, the Krefeld appeal of November 1980 (initiated by Communist groupings and signed by two million West German citizens within a year), and the Bielefeld appeal of 1981 (addressed by Social Democrats to the higher echelons of the SPD). From the autumn of 1981 the peace movement's emphasis shifted to peace demonstrations, which attracted an unexpectedly high number of people from all over the Federal Republic reaching a climax with a demonstration of 250,000 people in Bonn on 10 October 1981.

Within the SPD politicians with expertise and rhetorical skills like Erhard Eppler, Oskar Lafontaine and Egon Bahr, but also Willy Brandt, took up the theses of the peace movement and introduced them into the discussion on security policy within the party. The result was that an increasing number of SPD local committees, regional party conference delegates and in particular *die Basis* (the rank-and-file) began to reject the Chancellor's security policy. An American critic describing this process said: "Brandt's party brought down Schmidt's government".[18] The consensus on security policy, which for decades had been taken for granted by all parties represented in parliament, had broken down. It was not just a fringe group, the Greens, which rejected the consensus and advocated the rejection of all obligations to the Atlantic Alliance. A great national party, which was bearing the responsibility of government and hoped to do so again in future, denied its support for the implementation of a decision taken within the Alliance. At the SPD Conference in Munich in April 1982 an automatic linkage between the deployment of missiles and the failure of negotiations was rejected, and deployment was instead made dependent on a (subjectively evaluated) "seriousness of the negotiations". Schmidt could not and would not go along with such a policy. Although the coalition partner FDP and the CDU/CSU opposition expressed their confidence in Schmidt's security policy, the consensus in the coalition on questions of economic policy no longer existed. When the FDP left the coalition and Helmut Kohl was elected Chancellor on 1 October 1982, Schmidt's downfall was final.

The new Federal Government continued the security policy of the previous Chancellor, which had been formulated in agreement with the Atlantic Alliance. On this they had the support of the majority of the West German population: In July 1981 52% supported deployment in the event of negotiations failing; in March 1982 the figure had risen to over 60%. Only 39% had some sympathy with the peace movement.[19] The public mood was completely misread by the SPD. The election results of March 1983, which proved to be devastating for the

SPD, showed that it had been a mistake to fight the election – as the Greens had – entirely on the issue of the planned missile deployments. For the voters supporting the CDU/CSU/FDP coalition the hope of an economic upturn had been more important than the issue of cruise and Pershing II. Nevertheless, the newly-elected government had indirectly obtained a mandate to implement the NATO dual-track decision.

After the election the SPD finally turned full circle against the implementation of the 1979 decision; at the party conference at Cologne in April 1983 only Schmidt and a few of his loyal supporters voted in favour of implementing the dual-track policy. Together with the Greens (who had entered Parliament by obtaining 5.6% of the popular vote), the peace movement and a large number of non-organised, well-meaning SPD supporters, agitated against deployment. But despite 1.5 million participants in demonstrations in the Federal Republic on 22 October 1983, it was by no means a "long, hot autumn". The demonstrators were unable to prevent deployment in any event; the political decisions had already been taken. On 23 November the Bundestag voted in favour of deployment (against the opposition of the SPD and the Greens), after the state of negotiations in Geneva left no other option open. In mid-December 1983 the first Pershing II missiles were deployed in the Federal Republic.

The peace movement, which had single-mindedly concentrated on the issue of cruise and Pershing II, "faced the real danger that it might fall apart after failure to prevent deployment, just like the extra-parliamentary opposition at the end of the 1960s or the anti-nuclear movement of the 1950s".[20] However, it had gained representation in Parliament for the achievement of its political objectives via the Greens, and, more importantly, parts of the SPD. Its most significant success was that leading politicians in the Federal Republic now felt they had increasingly to justify their positions on security policy to an attentive public. In the long term the result was a controversial public concern about reliability of the Federal Republic in security matters, which frequently created confusion abroad.

Controversial reactions to SDI[21]

While the domestic political controversy about the deployment of long-range theatre nuclear forces was at its peak President Reagan on 23 March 1983 announced his decision to develop a protective shield in outer space to destroy hostile missiles. With his proposition to make nuclear weapons "ineffective and obsolete" and to develop "defensive technologies" by means of a gigantic research programme, Reagan undermined the efforts of all those arguing in favour of the deployment of LRTNF at a most inappropriate moment.[22] The first German response was, therefore, one of embarrassment, since there obviously had been no consultation about Reagan's plans. In 1983 the American

Strategic Defense Initiative (SDI) was not an issue of public controversy in the Federal Republic: the peace movement was occupied with cruise and Pershing II and the development of space weapons was still far in the future.

The first public reactions of the Government, which were "cautiously negative" (Foreign Minister Genscher and Defence Minister Wörner) did not occur until early 1984, after the executive committee of the Greens had taken a vehement posture against SDI, while the Bavarian Prime Minister Franz Josef Strauss had welcomed it whole-heartedly and SPD spokesmen like Bahr or Voigt had given a "cautiously positive" response.[23] Both Genscher and Wörner feared an extension of the arms race into space, a decoupling of the defence of Europe from the strategic arsenal of the United States and thus a change in NATO's military strategy, the growing risk of a conventional war in Europe and negative consequences for East-West relations. Furthermore, they believed that SDI could not be completely success-ful. But as by mid-1984 it had become apparent that the Americans would continue to pursue the SDI programme and Chancellor Kohl was adamantly opposed to disrupting US-German relations, the German position shifted. The Federal Government was increasingly concerned to emphasise the possibility of German participation in civil space research with all the economic advantages for German industry (ie a "technological innovatory push") and to play down the military aspects of SDI.

In April 1985, when the United States urged stronger European support for SDI, Chancellor Kohl gave qualified support for the project, subject to a large number of conditions[24] and stressed that Reagan's proposal had been paramount for the resumption of the arms control negotiations between the United States and the Soviet Union in Geneva, which were essentially in the German interest. At this time, however, the differences of view between various government Ministers about West German participation in SDI had not yet been reconciled: Defence Minister Wörner (CDU) now favoured a German role in SDI research, because he hoped that Germany would thus be able to exercise influence on the programme; Foreign Minister Genscher (FDP) hesitated for reasons of foreign and security policy;[25] Research Minister Riesenhuber (CDU) had doubts about the allegedly significant tech-nological spin-off of the programme; and Economics Minister Bange-mann (FDP) admitted that the expectations of German industry with regard to guarantees for an assured participation by German companies and lucrative SDI contracts had considerably sobered.

The SPD opposition, which initially had seen some hope of over-coming nuclear deterrence and abolishing nuclear weapons as a result of SDI, – its final goal as announced by President Reagan – had mean-while changed its view and now insisted on a total rejection of SDI in general and German participation in particular. It demanded an unrestricted prohibition of space-based weapons, since it feared that both nuclear powers could be led to believe they could initiate a nuclear war and "keep it under control, so that it would remain limited to Europe."[26] Leading SPD politicians like Ehmke, Bahr and Voigt urged the United States immediately to cease the development and testing of "killer satellites", because the strategic balance would be destabilised by space weapons and the arms spiral would increase indefinitely.

Chancellor Kohl did not allow himself to be diverted from his basic support for German participation in SDI either by the complete rejection of the SPD and the Greens, or by doubts within his government coalition. The optimistic impressions of a high level delegation to the United States, guided by a foreign policy adviser to the Chancellor, were greeted with scepticism particularly by Foreign Minister Genscher, who seemed to be fundamentally opposed to the general policy being pursued. Nevertheless, Economics Minister Bangemann signed two "secret" agreements in Washington in April 1986 about German SDI participation with the unanimous support of the Federal Government.[27] When, after wide-ranging financial cuts in the SDI programme by Congress in the autumn of 1986, voices were being raised in the United States demanding that SDI contracts for foreign companies and research institutes should be restricted, with the result that significant scientific-technical co-operation could not take place, some even in the government parties demanded, like the SPD and the Greens, that German support for SDI should be withdrawn.[28]

The crumbling consensus about security policy

Although the organised activities of the peace movement have decreased considerably since the decisive defeat on LRTNF deployment, the debate about security policy has been rekindled repeatedly in the Federal Republic. Various slogans like "creation of a nuclear-weapons-free-zone in central Europe", "neutralism", "drop out of the East-West conflict", "no first use of nuclear weapons", "security partnership", "withdrawal from NATO" gained credence. They were thrown into the public debate especially by the Greens and the Left wing of the SPD, with strong criticism of American policy and NATO. In the process a great gulf was revealed between, on the one hand, the "established parties", the CDU, CSU and FDP (as well as the Right wing of the SPD) who supported a continuation of Alliance policy on the basis of the hitherto valid concepts of deterrence and flexible response; and, on the other hand, the Left, glad to experiment and searching for new and unconventional ways of securing peace, which vehemently rejected deterrence with nuclear weapons and made arms control and disarmament the central theme of its security policy.

It was not only abroad that it was noticed with great disquiet that the SPD (often jointly with the Greens) assumed the role of spokesman for those searching for alternative security concepts. Since the SPD had abandoned the dual-track decision under pressure from the peace movement, was no longer bearing the responsibility for Government and no longer needed to seek legitimacy for its security policy from the public, it reflected more and more the opinion of its organised, usually younger rank-and-file members, to whom it felt a particular obligation as a "people's party". The hopes and fears of a generation, which as a result of the INF controversy had for the first time become aware of the precarious situation of their country in the East-West conflict and which no longer wanted to tolerate in the FRG the storage of an enormous arsenal of nuclear weapons under foreign control, were increasingly taken up by younger SPD politicians (for example, Lafontaine, von Bülow, Voigt). They hoped that these alternative concepts might lead to a new phase in the policy of détente and enable deterrence to be superseded by a "European peace order",[29] a decrease in West German dependence on the United States and a reduction of the nuclear threat. Their security policy proposals accord the utmost importance to arms control, the military requirements of security by contrast seeming to recede into the background.

Of the many alternative defence proposals which have been introduced into the specialist debate by the Greens and the Social Democrats, only a few can be mentioned here. The Greens, for example, support the concept of "social defence" (Theodor Ebert) and passive resistance by the entire population in case of an attack.[30] They also support (in contrast to the SPD) "unilateral disarmament" as a means of reducing mistrust on the other side and demonstrating peaceful intentions. Another proposal was "defensive defence" which involves equipping the army exclusively with defensive weapons, or "defence from depth" with light and mobile weapons (Horst Afheldt). The concept has been criticised on the grounds that this purely conventional defence no longer confronts the adversary (who most certainly enjoys conventional superiority) with the "risk of unacceptable damage to himself, such as he would incur as the result of the use of nuclear weapons", and thus "results in a considerable increase in the probability of a conflict".[31] The (old) concept of a nuclear-weapon-free-zone in Central Europe was taken up again by the SPD and the Greens: on 21 October 1986 a working party of the SPD and the East German SED presented their "*Principles for a nuclear-free corridor in Central Europe along the inner-German border*" at a Press conference in Bonn. Proposals for a further development of this concept towards a "completely de-militarised, neutralised zone" opened up the (vague) possibility of a reunification of both German states. The first step in the direction of a 'weapon-free' zone was taken by the SPD in June 1985 when it negotiated with the SED about a proposal for an agreement to establish a chemical-weapons-free zone in Europe.

The public took no notice of these alternative concepts because of their generally abstract and technical nature. Moreover, foreign policy agreements by opposition parties are in no way binding for governments; they merely constitute declarations of intent. However, when the SPD chose a candidate for the Chancellorship from the political centre (Johannes Rau), the security policy concepts of the SPD attracted more attention from government ranks as well as abroad. It was noted with concern that the SPD had committed itself to the political goal of a no-first-use of nuclear weapons[32] at its party conference in Essen in May 1984. Thereby nuclear weapons should be gradually detached from the defence strategy of the Alliance. The demand by the Prime Minister of the Saar, Lafontaine, that the Federal Republic should leave the military integration of NATO initiated a lively internal debate (the proposal being, of course, approved by the Greens). The explicit reassurance by Rau that the Federal Republic would remain a member of the Western Alliance if he became Chancellor, and his rejection of a coalition with the Greens, failed to remove all doubts about the SPD's loyalty to the Alliance and the orientation of its security policy.

Thus all government parties, the media and foreign observers (but not the general public) paid a great deal of attention to the (unanimously agreed) security policy decisions at the SPD conference in Nuremberg at the end of August 1986. These were: removal of American medium-range missiles from the Federal Republic; cancellation of the SDI agreements with the United States; reduction of the defence budget; a nuclear "build-down"; reductions in conventional forces; the creation of a nuclear-weapons-free corridor in Central Europe; a "security partnership" in the East-West conflict; creation of the "structural inability to engage in aggression" for the Bundeswehr; and the shortening of the draft period. These (partly contradictory or ambiguous) demands in the area of security policy indicate that in Nuremberg the left wing of the party prevailed and that the continuing deep differences between the right and left wings could not be bridged. Doubts about the credibility of the defence strategy of the party came even from its own ranks: "This cannot be called a credible security policy for a Party that wants to be taken seriously."[33] It is true that these SPD conference decisions are merely guidelines for an SPD government and do not represent a concrete government programme as such. Nevertheless, it became evident that by passing these decisions the party had turned away from a well-proven Alliance-oriented security policy, for which there is still an overwhelming public majority. In the autumn of 1984 57% of the West German population were of the opinion that peace could only be secured through the Western Alliance, whereas by Spring 1986 this number had risen to 62%. Except for the supporters of the Greens, this trend could be observed in all parties, including the SPD.[34]

Implications for the Alliance

The influence of the peace movement on the security policy of the Federal Republic which has been observed abroad with particular interest and concern has, according to the most recent evidence, remained extremely small. Indeed, it cannot be stated categorically that the public protest movement has had any influence on the political decision-makers.[35] The alternative security policies which have been developed since the beginning of the 1980s have remained the views of intellectual and politically-committed minority elites:

> What we are witnessing is not mass protest against established national security policy but a combination of minority protest and the dynamics of political mass communication.[36]

The peace movement fell apart after the deployment of cruise and Pershing II began (even though a central core remained). Their political representatives in the Bundestag, the Greens, will probably never achieve the degree of support and influence of the two great national parties. In the Federal Republic there will continue to be a clear majority for a continuation of close relations with the United States, membership of NATO and integration in the European Community (and also in a European Security Community which still has to be created).

Nevertheless, the controversial debate about security policy in the Federal Republic has domestic and foreign policy consequences. The rejection of NATO doctrines which were hitherto valid and undisputed, and the search for alternative defence strategies will result in endless internal party political disputes about this sensitive topic. The position of the Federal Government in the formulation of security policy has been weakened, since it continually has to justify its policy domestically; furthermore it cannot represent those abroad, who have broken with the consensus about defence. The differences of view between the two big national parties are publicly displayed and contribute to confusion among the Allies about the real position of the Federal Republic on security issues.[37]

The alternative defence positions of the SPD were clearly developed with a view to winning over voters in the 1987 elections among the Greens and the peace movement where the Party suspects there is a reservoir of votes outside its traditional areas of support. The Party also attempts to satisfy the growing proportion of its increasingly younger, academically educated and more radical members (Young Socialists, women, trades unionists) whose interest in security issues has increased, while their general level of information has not.[38] The danger of this strategy is, however, that this radicalisation will lead to a loss of votes in the centre which cannot possibly be compensated for by increased votes from sympathisers of the protest movements.[39]

This reservoir of protesters in the Federal Republic (with at times rather unconventional forms of protest) has to some extent alienated the Alliance partners who find it difficult to understand. This is a younger, self-confident generation which has been accused – sometimes rightly – of a lack of historical consciousness with regard to the recent past. This generation, from which the future leadership of the nation will be recruited, has little understanding of the fact that, because of its geographical position and Germany's historical past, the security policy of the Federal Republic is scrutinised more closely abroad. It does not understand, why a "good" German always has to affirm "150%" his or her loyalty to NATO or his friendship with the United States, whereas in other areas (love of order, punctuality) such an attitude is decried. It also does not understand or accept the excitement abroad about the Greens or the peace movement, when in France a similarly sizeable support for politicians of the extreme Right or for the Communist Party is accepted without much comment. It does not understand the disquiet among the Alliance partners about the demand of a vocal but insignificant minority that the Federal Republic should leave the military integration of NATO, when precisely this position, when maintained by Spain, is described as a success – to say nothing of France's half-hearted attitude to NATO. This generation does also not understand the concern abroad about alleged *incertitudes allemandes* with regard to a "reawakened nationalism" (alleged by some foreign observers) or a "newly-discovered inclination towards neutralism or pacifism", or a "growing anti-Americanism", when for example the British could indulge in excessive national sentiment during the Falklands war without having to justify themselves.

Such criticisms by the Alliance partners are for the most part unfounded and are refuted by statistics as well as scholarly research.[40] In the Federal Republic a loss of national consciousness is more likely to be found than a reawakened nationalism. The peace movement has reopened the subject of the German question as one among many, not in the fervent pursuit of reunification, but rather because this question must naturally arise in considering "dropping out" of the East-West confrontation. Its only nationalistic aspect is its aversion to the dominance of the Alliance, but this is more "an egocentricity of survival than nationalism in the traditional sense".[41] Neutralism has always had more supporters in the Federal Republic than elsewhere owing to its particular situation. The percentage of West Germans who believe that peace would be more secure in a neutralised Western Europe without NATO has averaged about 20% between 1984 and 1986.[42] Most of the supporters of neutrality, in particular the younger ones, see in this concept the image of an ideal world without great power rivalries; they dream of an equidistance between the superpowers, but have no clear concepts. There is no question either of a growing anti-Americanism. It is certainly true that the present generation is less prepared than their parents to adopt the "American model" uncritically. Nevertheless, continued co-operation with the United States is supported by the large majority of the German population: over more than three decades West German support for a close relationship with the United States has remained very stable at 80%![43] However, in the Federal Republic concern is increasing among all age groups and party political groupings that the United States is treating its adversaries and also its Alliance partners, with political carelessness. There is a lack of confidence in US political judgement as much as in the credibility of American information – Irangate demonstrated this persuasively. This means that the future orientation of West German security policy will also depend in no small measure on a rational American policy which takes account of the needs of the Europeans.[44]

The FRG's Alliance partners will continue to follow the developments in West German domestic politics, especially the implications for security policy, with close attention. However, those with doubts about the reliability of the Federal Republic's security policy should not to forget that NATO has up to now always demonstrated its ability

> to live with inner political tensions and considerable contradictions between declared military requirements and actual deployments. In this context one should remember that there were already powerful anti-nuclear protest movements in the 1950s and 1960s and that the currently valid NATO strategy resulted from a long and bitter controversy, which was triggered by the American attempt to distance itself from the concept of nuclear escalation. Doubts about the credibility of an extended strategic deterrence are therefore older than the strategy of flexible response.[45]

Notes

1. Werner Link, "Aussen- und Deutschlandpolitik in der Ära Brandt 1969–1974", in: Karl Dietrich Bracher, Wolfgang Jäger, Werner Link, *Republik im Wandel 1969–1974: Die Ära Brandt*, (Stuttgart: dva, Mannheim: Brockhaus 1986, p. 278). On West Germany and détente see Helga Haftendorn, *Sicherheit und Stabilität. Aussenbeziehungen der Bundesrepublik zwischen Ölkrise und NATO-Doppelbeschluss*, (München: dtv, 1986); Harald Rüddenklau, "Aspekte der innenpolitischen Kontroverse um die Sicherheitspolitik", in Erhard Frondran, Gert Krell (eds.), *Kernwaffen im Ost-West Vergleich*, (Baden-Baden: Nomos 1984, pp. 415–420); also Jeffrey Boutwell. "The German Search for Security", in Stephen Flanagan, Fen Osler Hampson, *Securing Europe's Future*, (London, Sydney, Croom Helm 1986, pp. 113–136).

2. In January 1980 74% of the population were in favour of a continuation of the policy of détente; in May 1981 the figure was still 68% and by Autumn 1983 had risen again to 87%. See Gebhard Schweigler, *Grundlagen der aussenpolitischen Orientierung der Bundesrepublik Deutschland*, (Baden-Baden: Nomos 1985, p. 143).

3. In the aftermath of the chill in East-West relations, however, Erich Honecker as well as the new Federal Government under Chancellor Helmut Kohl were concerned to maintain the "diplomacy of talking to each other" between the two German states and practise "damage limitation". The best examples of this policy were the billion

mark credits provided to the GDR by West German banks in 1983 and 1984, which had been made available with the active involvement of the Bavarian Prime Minister Franz-Josef Strauss. See Peter Danylow, "Die innerdeutschen Beziehungen – Kontinuitat und Wandel", in *Die Internationale Politik 1983/84*, Jahrbuch der DGAP, (Munich, R. Oldenbourg, 1986, pp. 176–188.)

4. See especially: Lothar Ruehl, "Das Ringen um die Neutronenwaffe", in *Die Internationale Politik 1977/78*, Jahrbücher der DGAP, (München, Wien: R. Oldenbourg, 1982, pp. 142–150); Ruehl, "Die Nichtentscheidung über die 'Neutronenwaffe' ", *Europa Archiv*, 5/1979, 137–150; also Sherri L. Wasserman, *The Neutron Bomb Controversy. A Study in Alliance Politics*, (New York: Praeger 1983.)

5. *Frankfurter Allgemeine Zeitung*, 20 July 1977.

6. Haftendorn, *op. cit.* p. 105.

7. Adelbert Weinstein, *Frankfurter Allgemeine Zeitung*, 6 August 1977.

8. The Federal Republic should not be the only country in which the weapon would be deployed; the decision for deployment would have to made jointly with all the NATO partners; at the same time arms control negotiations with the Soviet Union should be initiated.

9. Carter did not want to enter the annals of history as the "father of the neutron bomb".

10. Hans Rühle, "Das Kind liegt im Brunnen". Jimmy Carter's "Folgenschwerer Entscheid gegen die Neutronenwaffe", *Deutsche Zeitung – Christ und Welt*, 14 April 1978.

11. With regard to the domestic political debate about the NATO dual-track decision see especially: Haftendorn, *op. cit.* pp. 124–133; Rüddenklau, *op. cit.*,; Lothar Ruehl, "Belastungen des amerikanisch-europäischen Verhältnisses", in *Die Internationale Politik 1979/80*, Jahrbücher der DGAP, (*Munich, Vienna*: R. Oldenbourg, 1983, pp. 42–69); also Jeffrey Boutwell, Paul Doty, Gregory F. Treverton (eds)., *The Nuclear Confrontation in Europe*, (London, Sydney: Croom Helm 1985.)

12. Haftendorn, *op. cit.*, p. 129.

13. Rüddenklau, *op. cit.*, especially p. 429.

14. Karl Kaiser, in *Sicherheitspolitik contra Frieden? Ein Forum zur Friedensbewegung*, (Berlin, Bonn: Dietz 1981, p. 40.)

15. Angelika Volle, "Innere Wandlungen in Westeuropa", in *Die Internationale Politik 1981/82*, Jahrbücher der DGAP, (Munich: R. Oldenbourg 1984, pp. 76–91); Stephen Szabo (ed.), *The Successor Generation: International Perspectives of Postwar Europeans*, (London, Butterworth 1983); Lother Ruehl, "Fragen der Sicherheit zwischen Ost und West", in *Die Internationale Politik 1983/84*, *op. cit.*, 1986, pp. 92–110. For opposition to the dual-track decision see also Jeffrey Herff, "War, Peace and the Intellectuals; The West German Peace Movement", *International Security*, Spring 1986, 10:4, 172–199; Gregory Flynn, Hans Rattinger, *The Public and Atlantic Defence*, (London, Boston: Butterworth 1983); Schweigler, *op. cit.* pp. 153 ff.

16. The next line of the Brecht poem reads: "then war will come to you", (Bertolt Brecht, *Gedichte*, Frankfurt: Suhrkamp, 1981, p. 503).

17. Hans Peter Schwarz, "Die Rückkehr der Schwärmer. Fragen an die Christen in der sogenannten Friedensbewegung", *Die politische Meinung*, No. 205, Nov./Dec. 1982, p. 20.

18. Herff, *op. cit.*, p. 176.

19. Volle, *op. cit.*, p. 89.

20. Peter Glotz, "Am Widerstand scheiden sich die Geister", *Die Zeit*, 24 June 1983.

21. For the response of the Federal Republic of Germany to SDI see Karl Kaiser, "SDI und deutsche Politik", *Europa Archiv*, 19/1986, pp. 569–578 and Christoph Bluth, "SDI: The Challenge to West Germany", *International Affairs*, 2/1986, pp. 247–264.

22. SDI is almost a model of how not to introduce a new idea", Ralf Dahrendorf in *A Widening Atlantic? Domestic Change & Foreign Policy*, (New York: Council on Foreign Relations, 1986, p. 53.)

23. Kaiser, *op. cit.* pp. 570 and 573.

24. *SDI Fakten und Bewertungen, Fragen und Antworten*, (Bonn: Ministry of Defence, June 1986.)

25. Genscher was actively involved in creating a European technological community (EUREKA), designed as a non-military alternative to SDI.

26. Kaiser, *op. cit.*, p. 573.

27. The text of the agreements was published in the German Press on 18 April 1986 and confirmed the fears of the SDI critics that American concessions on the transfer of technology proved unobtainable; the final result of the negotiations was rather meagre from the German point of view.

28. *Frankfurter Allgemeine Zeitung*, 16 August 1986.

29. See especially: Andreas von Bülow, *Strategie vertrauenschaffender Sicherheitsstrukturen in Europa, Wege zur Sicherheitspartnerschaft*, (Bonn: SPD, September 1985.)

30. See, Ulrich de Maizière, "The Arguments of the German Peace Movement", in Walter Laqueur, Robert Hunter (eds.), *European Peace Movements and the Future of the Western Alliance*, (New Brunswick, Oxford: Transaction Books, 1985, pp. 343–347); also Jürgen Maruhn, Manfred Wilke, *Wohin treibt die SPD ? Wende oder Kontinuität sozialdemokratischer Sicherheitspolitik*, (München: Olzog 1984.)

31. Karl Kaiser, "Der Zerfall des sicherheitspolitischen Konsenses in der Bundesrepublik Deutschland: Die Entwicklung der Diskussion in den achtziger Jahren'', in: Manfred Funke, Hans-Adolf Jacobsen, Hans-Helmut Knütter, Hans-Peter Schwarz (eds.), *Demokratie und Diktatur, Geist und Gestalt politischer Herrschaft in Deutschland und Europa*, (Düsseldorf: Droste, 1987, pp. 487 f.)

32. See Karl Kaiser, "Einfrieren und Nichterstgebrauch von Kernwaffen – Wege in der Gefahr?", in *Frieden politisch fördern: Richtungsimpulse*, (Gütersloh: Rat der EKD, 1985, pp. 77 ff); McGeorge Bundy, George F. Kennan, Robert McNamara, Gerard Smith, "Nuclear Weapons and the Atlantic Alliance", *Foreign Affairs*, Spring 1982, 60:4, pp. 753–768; also Karl Kaiser, Georg Leber, Alois Mertes, Franz-Joseph Schulze, "Nuclear Weapons and the Preservation of Peace", *Foreign Affairs*, Summer 1982, 60:5, pp. 1157–1170.

33. Christoph Bertram, "Rückkehr zu alten Träumen. Die Sicherheitspolitik der SPD birgt viele Risiken", *Die Zeit*, 5 September 1986. For consequences of SPD decisions on security policy, see also: Lothar Ruehl, "In der militärischen Wirklichkeit illusorisch", *Frankfurter Allgemeine Zeitung*, 15 September 1986.

34. Friedenssicherung und westliches Bündnis in der Einschätzung der Bevölkerung 1984 bis Mitte 1986. Repräsentativerhebungen der Konrad-Adenauer-Stiftung", *Interne Studien* (KAS), 4/1986.

35. See especially Flynn/Rattinger, *op. cit.* page 365 ff.

36. Hans Rattinger, "The Federal Republic of Germany: Much ado about (almost) nothing", in *op. cit.*, p. 173.

37. A similar situation existed in the Federal Republic at the time of *Ostpolitik*, when government and opposition advocated fundamentally opposed foreign policy positions.

38. Gregory Flynn, "Öffentliche Meinung und Atlantische Verteidigung", *NATO-Brief*, no. 5/1983, p. 6. The British Labour Party, which has formed a working party with the SPD on questions of security and foreign policy, is currently in a similar situation. In a joint communique both parties affirm their support for NATO; favour the creation of a European pillar of the Alliance, which must work for a new phase of détente; fundamentally reject SDI; favour the zero option for medium-range missiles and advocate a restructuring of conventional defence; both consider the renunciation of the first use of nuclear weapons necessary. (SPD Press Statement 610/86, 14 November 1986).

39. The local elections in Hesse in April 1987, in which the Greens increased their votes at the expense of the SPD, are a good illustration. For the first time in 41 years, the SPD (who had toyed with the idea of a renewed coalition with the Greens in Hesse) was pushed into opposition by the voters in favour of a CDU/FDP coalition.

40. See David Gress, "What the West should know about German Neutralism", *Commentary*, January 1985, 26–31; Hans Peter Schwarz, "The West Germans, Western Democracy and Western Ties in the Light of Public Opinion Research", in James A. Cooney *et al.* (ed.), *The Federal Republic of Germany and the United States*, (Boulder, Co.: Westview Press 1984, 56–97); Gebhard Schweigler, "Anti-Americanism in Germany", *Washington Quarterly*, 9:1, Winter 1986, 67–84; Herff, *op. cit.*

41. Peter Graf von Kielmannsegg, "The Origins and Aims of the German Peace Movement" in Laqueur/Hunter, *op. cit.* p. 337. See also: Gerd Langguth, "Wie steht die junge Generation zur deutschen Teilung?", in *Politische Studien*, No. 289, Sept/Oct. 1986, pp. 524–542.

42. Cf. note 34.

43. Study of the Institut für Demoskopie, Allensbach. Quoted from Schweigler, *op. cit.* p. 77.

44. In this context it is interesting to note that in an American survey of opinion 35% of the British questioned and 43% of the Germans blamed President Reagan for the failure of the Reykjavik summit (Gorbachev was blamed by only 9% and 6% respectively). *The Guardian Weekly*, 9 November 1986.

45. Klaus-Peter Stratmann, *Aspekte der sicherheitspolitischen und militärstrategischen Entwicklung in den 90er Jahren*, Ebenhausen (SWP-AP 2474, June 1986, p. 14).

Chapter 3
Public Attitudes and the Defence Debate in Britain

MICHAEL CLARKE

There has been a rapid and significant shift in the defence debate in Britain. Many disagree on the extent of the shift but few would dispute the rapidity of the change or the fact that defence is a major political issue in contemporary Britain. Clearly this requires some explanation which is particular to Britain. General analyses of the evolution of the 'defence consensus' in Europe do not account for the way in which the issue has been raised, or the particular disputes which feature in the argument. To understand why it is that elections are fought on defence as much as on economic management, we must examine how the issue has become a matter of party policy for all the major political parties.

The defence debate in Britain

There are many obvious and oft-repeated features of the defence debate in Britain. It has traditionally been the case that defence has had very little salience in British politics. It has not been the stuff of day-to-day political debate, or even of General Elections prior to the 1980s. Foreign affairs in general have been thought to feature only once in an election between 1945 and 1979 – that of 1955 where the reputation of Anthony Eden as a "peacemaker" figured in the campaign. Only a little over 5% of the British public regard defence or foreign affairs as among the most important issues facing the country.[1]

This lack of salience is reinforced by a number of well-known public attitudes. Pacifism has never been a potent force in Britain. In 1939, after more than a decade of anti-war sentiment, only 60,000 people in Britain registered as conscientious objectors.[2] Even now, what Ivor Crewe describes as "radical pacifist dissent" is confined to around 10% of the population.[3] Public views of the Soviet Union remain remarkably constant: the Soviet Union is a clear and growing military threat; it is necessary to defend Britain against such a threat, and there is a strong vein of opinion – stronger than in other European states – that whatever passes for "Soviet aggression" must be resisted.[4] Such broad attitudes have created a predisposition to leave defence matters to the experts. This, in turn, has reinforced the tendency towards centralism in British government which in defence and foreign affairs has been characterised by a small political élite; "unexpectedly small" according to Dahrendorf.[5] And it is backed up by a largely consensual Press and a wide interpretation of official secrets.[6]

It is hardly surprising, therefore, that foreign and defence policy was characterised for 30 years by a high degree of bipartisanship between the major political parties. Until 1980, Parliamentary scrutiny of defence was, at best, patchily successful and the political parties' own defence committees were not powerful or influential bodies. Still less did the party conferences exercise any power in relation to the declared defence policies of the party leaderships, although they occasionally tried to do so.

All these points are fairly obvious and well-understood in analyses of the domestic roots of British defence policy. And in themselves they make it seem either surprising that the defence debate should have become so politicised; or not so surprising if we assume that the politicisation is rather superficial, a temporary departure from the norm. There are, however, some less obvious aspects of the public's attitude to defence which help us to understand not only why the debate seems to have changed but also why the extent of the change may be greater and more permanent than traditional analyses would lead us to suppose.

For one thing, British public and elite attitudes to defence have always been curiously self-contained. For a power which shouldered so many global responsibilities in 1945, Britain was slow to accept the interdependence which this created. Britain's pivotal role in the formation of NATO was never mirrored by an acceptance of European interdependence on any wider issues. The process of decolonisation perhaps created a self-image of independence. Certainly, the Anglo-American relationship, on which all else rested and without which all British defence and foreign policy lacked coherence, was a relationship interpreted in Britain as providing a unique measure of independence. Through the manipulation of the Anglo-American special relationship, Britain traditionally perceived itself as being able to remain outside embryonic European entanglements, though in reality they could hardly have been avoided and might better have been embraced more willingly at an earlier time. Nevertheless the Anglo-American relationship may have held some British defence options open for longer and it certainly created a vocabulary of independence. The British nuclear deterrent – the Polaris submarine force – is a prime example of this. It is "independent" in a technical sense, in that it is capable of being used independently. Only *in extremis*, however, could its independent use even be contemplated. For the majority of its existence the deterrent, in fact, has been an example of strategic interdependence. The missiles were supplied by the US and plans for their use – other than the most unlikely eventuality of independent use – are dictated by the Single Integrated Operational Plan. For all peacetime purposes, and almost every conceivable wartime purpose, the independence of the Polaris submarine force is simply not relevant. It is extraordinarily difficult to conceive of any circumstances where Britain would contemplate launching its missiles independently; that is, separately. Yet debate in Britain over its value, its cost and dangers, has been cast almost exclusively in terms of its "independence" rather than its contribution to Western security. Its abandonment, if we listen to the terms of the debate, would create a problem for Anglo-American relations much more than for NATO, for this would affect Britain's international standing and its conception of its role, rather than leave a hole in NATO's nuclear defences.

Discussion of British defence policy, therefore, has been an essentially insular affair; not Gaullist in trying to assert independence through action; nor, in the style of Bonn, making a virtue of interdependence. Instead, Britain has conducted a defence policy based on the implicit assumption of an independence that was scarcely justified. And just as the makers of existing defence policy have tended to assume that it could evolve without being significantly constrained by any of the allies apart from the United States, so the radical reformers who would like to shift the policy decisively in a non-nuclear direction tend to make the same assumptions; a non-nuclear defence policy would be feasible because Britain is sufficiently independent to be able to adopt and implement such a policy without being thwarted by the reactions of other NATO members.

Another less obvious feature of the traditional picture of the domestic defence consensus is more narrowly defined. It is the fact that there are no significant sub-groups in the composition of British public opinion on defence. It is usual to observe that the general decline of such a powerful defence consensus as did exist is bound to have been stimulated by a generation change within the British public. This, however, is not substantiated by opinion poll data. It seems highly plausible that generational change will have some effect on perceptions of defence, but there is no immediate evidence as to what that effect may be. On nuclear and NATO-related issues there is no discernible difference in opinions between age groups.[7] Nor is it possible to discern significant differences on the basis of gender or social class.[8] In a situation where defence has such a low salience among political issues this is not very surprising. Nevertheless, it becomes a critical factor in the situation where defence *is* on the agenda, since it allows party affiliation to become the demarcation between different views of the issue. As we shall see, the party politicisation of defence is the key to the understanding of change, and the lack of any other dimensions in past defence issues means that the current defence debate is *defined* by party loyalty, even if it is not primarily *about* party politics.

The traditional consensus, therefore, has been remarkably self-contained in the tepid arguments in which it has engaged over 30 years, and it has lacked any identifiable sub-groups of opinion save those defined by the political parties. The defence consensus was therefore in a condition to suffer a more dramatic discontinuity than could have been predicted in the late-1970s. As the political parties diverged from their tradition of bipartisanship, so the break has indeed been swift and significant.

Sources of change in the defence debate

The most significant and direct source of change has therefore been the way in which defence has become a party political issue, and hence an electoral issue. Political parties are the most obvious links between public opinion and policy and as such they both clarify and polarise opinion. For all the "fudging" which party leaders find necessary, the polarisation of opinion which is characteristic of party competition is a process which classifies intellectual issues and serves also to change them.

In the case of Britain this began in the wake of the Labour Party's defeat in 1979. Like many European socialist parties, the Labour Party moved towards its Left wing in adversity. The more activist supporters in the constituencies gained some power. The trade union movement had also devolved power away from the more centrist union leaders of the 1960s, towards active members of the rank and file. Above all, the swing towards Left-wing policies found national leadership among the party executive, ex-Cabinet Ministers and emergent leaders from the party's back benches and some centre and Rightist Labour MPs left the party to help found the SDP. A shift to the Left while in opposition was not unexpected, though the vehemence of the arguments was somewhat surprising. The anti-nuclear platform was used as a weapon by the Left of the party to try to capture control of the whole, as indeed it had been similarly used in the late 1950s. In that earlier period, however, the issue subsided with the power struggle. In the present case, the successes of the Labour Left have been turned against them, the centre-Right is back in control of the party, having used the novel constitutional weapons that the Left had invented. Left-wing activism in the constituencies and the trade unions can find little national expression and no credible parliamentary leaders around which to coalesce. Certainly, for the time being the power struggle of the 1980s is over. Yet the anti-nuclear issue is not. The Labour Party – as a party – has committed itself to a radical non-nuclear defence policy. That commitment first won a majority at the party conference in 1980 and has been reaffirmed at four successive party conferences since 1982 where it has commanded the two-thirds majority which elevates it to official policy. It has certainly been adopted by the present leadership.[9] Neither supporters nor opponents of this stand within the parliamentary party expect it to be ditched or compromised in the immediate future, notwithstanding the electoral defeat of 1987.

During the same period, the Liberal Party and the newly-founded SDP, have also evolved a defence policy which departs from the old consensus. In this respect the Liberal-SDP Alliance is having to respond to the impetus provided by the Labour Party. There is clearly a rank-and-file demand among both Liberals and SDP members for some new, possibly radical, approaches to the nuclear element in British defence policy, though it is not clear quite how strongly such a demand is made. But the reaction of the Alliance is further evidence that anti-nuclear sentiment is not restricted to the Left wing of the Labour Party; still less was it merely a tactic to gain control in intraparty struggles. The Conservative government has thus been pushed a little way to its instinctive Right. The Alliance has occupied an uncertain, agonising reformism in contrast to Labour radicalism. The Government has therefore adopted a positively non-reformist policy; it must maintain the British independent nuclear deterrent and in the light of a possible sea change at the Reykjavik summit, it has shown some reluctance to accept the arms control proposals for removing those intermediate nuclear forces from Britain which it fought so strenuously to install in 1983.

Such party manoeuvres are both cause and effect of a general polarisation of opinion in Britain. As Table 3.1 shows, there is a consistent and impressive minority of opinion in favour of even some of the more radical of the Labour Party's policies.[10] Support for NATO remains consistently high, and this has scarcely changed over the years.[11] But opposition to the first use of nuclear weapons, to cruise missiles, Trident submarines and even US nuclear bases, is high. Party political manoeuvres are a part cause of these findings, since party identification will create a series of responses across the board. But they are also part effect, since opinions are consistent and substantial, and when similar questions were asked without reference to the fact that they were Labour Party ideas, the differences in findings, according to Gallup, were "not statistically significant".[12] In the case of questions 3 and 7 a comparison can be made with a Marplan opinion poll of September 1986 (Table 3.2). In November 1986 another Gallup survey

Table 3.1   Approval of Labour's Defence Policies

Q. Here are some of the ideas from the Labour Party's defence policy. Could
you tell me whether you approve or disapprove of them?

	General public	Con	Lab	Lib/ SDP
1. Britain to continue as a member of NATO	77	86	69	81
2. Obtain an agreement from NATO not to be first to use nuclear weapons in the event of a war breaking out	67	53	75	74
3. Send cruise missiles back to the United States	50	28	67	54
4. Remove all US nuclear bases from Britain	40	16	60	42
5. Cancel the Trident submarine missiles programme	40	17	59	42
6. Press NATO to withdraw all short-range nuclear weapons from Europe	36	17	58	33
7. Britain's defence to be based on not having nuclear weapons	34	15	54	32
8. Get rid of the Polaris nuclear submarines in Britain	33	13	53	31
9. Reduce Britain's defence forces for operation outside Europe	32	15	44	34

Source: *The Gallup Survey of Britain*, 1986, p. 55.

Table 3.2   Marplan Survey of Political Attitudes

Britain is safer having its own nuclear weapons

	All			Conservative			Labour			Alliance		
	1986	1985	1984	1986	1985	1984	1986	1985	1984	1986	1985	1984
Agree	50	52	53	71	72	79	41	39	39	45	53	52
Disagree	36	35	31	18	17	14	47	50	50	42	34	37
Neither	9	9	6	9	9	5	8	7	6	11	9	6
Don't know	4	4	10	2	2	2	4	4	5	2	4	5

The Government should tell the American Government to remove its cruise missiles from
British soil

	All			Conservative			Labour			Alliance		
	1986	1985	1984	1986	1985	1984	1986	1985	1984	1986	1985	1984
Agree	54	50	48	32	29	28	73	67	72	61	50	56
Disagree	32	36	36	55	56	62	17	22	18	29	35	34
Neither	10	9	7	11	11	7	7	6	6	9	10	7
Don't know	4	5	9	3	4	3	3	5	4	1	5	3

Source: Marplan Survey of Political Attitudes, *The Guardian* 26 September 1986.

of young voters (under 30 years of age) showed significant party political differences in favour of the Labour Party, and yet revealed strik-
ingly similar findings in relation to nuclear issues. On a question which
incorporated propositions 3 and 4 in Table 3.1, 51% of young voters
were in agreement. In a similar question to proposition 5, the percentage in agreement was 42%. On a question identical with proposition 1
the proportion in agreement was somewhat lower at 66%.[13]

Though any attempt to generalise across different polls is fraught
with dangers, it does seem that what data exists supports the proposition that a relatively consistent strand of opinion has developed over
the last four years which takes a more-or-less radical view of nuclear
defence policy. Clearly, the party politicisation of defence is based on at
least a significant groundswell of opinion which is channelled, though
not created, by the parties.

What more general factors, therefore, might have created this
groundswell? After all, the peace movement was having a clear impact
on British politics in 1979 and 1980. "Disarmament" was certainly
discernible as more than a fringe issue by 1978. Yet it figured hardly at
all in the British General Election of 1979. It was, by most accounts, a
major factor in the 1983 election and again in 1987. Political parties
have therefore latched on to an issue that was at least partially
mobilised long before they recognised its significance.

There has, of course, been a decline in the general defence consensus
in Europe, and this has affected Britain no less than any other NATO
country.[14] As Flynn and Rattinger point out, "leaders can no longer
afford the luxury of statements for purely 'domestic' consumption".[15]
The defence debate is as interdependent as defence itself.

Yet accounts of the general international situation – strategic parity
and the failures of detente, divergent interests between Britain and the
United States – do not quite make the link between the general politicisation of defence and the evident polarisation of opinion in the battle
between the parties. In Britain's case, at least, there is something more
specific. For one thing there has been an increase since the 1960s in the
proportion of the population who are pessimistic about the chances of
our being able to keep the peace. This has not been a uniform increase in
concern and the overall salience of "fear of war" is still lower than
certain economic and social issues. But the general increase in concern
has leapt in the 1980s with the prominence of nuclear issues.[16] In 1963
only 16% of those polled by Gallup felt that a nuclear war could
happen. In 1980, in another Gallup poll, that figure had risen to 39%
and in 1983 it was over 61%.[17] In this respect, interestingly, there is, for
once, some generational and social difference, since the young are
markedly more pessimistic than the old; middle-class people more than
working-class, and women more pessimistic and fearful than men.[18]
This increased fear of war seems to translate into a generalised degree of
sympathy for the existence of the peace movement, even if not for its

particular policies. And the peace movement has conducted a skilful and successful series of campaigns, demolishing the public's support for British civil defence plans, pointing out the dangers of nuclear weapons and exploiting the irreconcilable conflicts in the notion of nuclear deterrence. The role of what might be termed "informed" and "middle" opinion has also been critical. The churches and professional organisations have played a role in articulating ideas and mobilising a degree of "apolitical" concern. The whole movement appealed to a commonsense instinct, which derived from the heightened fear of war, that complex weapons systems were getting beyond the point of effective political control.

Ivor Crewe has probably expressed the result better than anyone else:

. . . a quarter of the British public – the same proportion that wants a non-nuclear defence strategy – approve of both the object and tactics of the peace movement. Another quarter sympathise with their broad aims and concerns but are sceptical about their methods and would not join them. Another 40% or so reject both their objectives and tactics and do not share their concerns, and the remaining 10% have no views to speak of. That this latter figure is so small is testimony to the public impact of the peace movement . . .[19]

More significantly, it appears that there is a growing sense of "moral equivalence" between the superpowers in the eyes of the British public. There is no question but that the US is more popular in Britain than is the Soviet Union; culturally superior, more trusted, more liked. But strongly positive attitudes are not the same as opinions regarding US policy and US leadership under particular presidents. In this respect, there has been a consistent decline in confidence in US foreign policy since the time of Kennedy. Likewise, there is no question that the Soviet Union is seen as Britain's adversary; a military threat to Britain, distrusted and disliked. It is not automatic, however, that the Soviet Union is seen as the power most likely to cause a war. Rather, the super-powers tend to be seen as making up a system, or a power-politics game; and it is the system or game that is dangerous. As far as nuclear war and peace are concerned, the clear cultural and moral preference for the democratic United States does not mean approval for US policies, or confidence in American leadership of the Western alliance.[20] This selective scepticism has markedly increased during the Reagan presidency and in reaction to events such as the invasion of Grenada in 1983, the bombing of Libya and the Chernobyl accident in 1986.

Insofar as the peace movement or the unilateralists in the Labour Party have been able to portray the problem as a systemic one, they have been able to mobilise some general sympathy for their cause among a public that is not anti-American. In 1984 Henry Kissinger discerned a "barely disguised neutralism" in Western Europe.[21] This was a simplistic overstatement at the time and has gained no further credibility since. Such a misrepresentation arises from the fact that the

United States engages in a cold war contest while Western Europe does not perceive itself as having that choice. The Western Europeans are just as involved but for them the *contest* over the last 25 years poses a more immediate threat than one of the adversaries whose political threat has clearly diminished.

We may summarise the changes that have taken place in the defence debate by saying that the political parties have channelled and shaped the nature of the defence debate in the mid-1980s. They have done this by mobilising a debate which pre-dated their interest. And the fact that there was something to be mobilised and the major outlines of a radical critique of nuclear defence was due to the activities of the peace movement, which drew upon more basic public reactions to the threat of war, the systemic nature of nuclear deterrence and a certain sense of moral neutralism when it came to judging the military stance of the United States.

The defence debate is now very much within the party political arena. It is not a foregone conclusion that after the previous two elections, radical defence policies are a natural vote-loser. For one thing, elections in Britain are not normally decided on an issue such as defence. However 'good', 'bad', 'imaginative' or 'irresponsible' a Labour or Alliance non-nuclear policy is perceived to be, it will not stop a party, or a coalition, taking power if it enjoys the benefits of a natural political swing. The nuclear defence issue, moreover, is one on which there is no absolute majority of opinion. To return to Ivor Crewe's conclusions above, if opinion breaks down to; 40% pro-nuclear, 25% anti-nuclear, 25% *possibly* anti-nuclear, and 10% undecided, then clearly anything remains possible. Most important of all, however, such gross figures disguise the fact that this cross section of opinion is *unstructured*. The "consistent" 30–40% of opinion which favours the non-nuclear alternative in any given survey appears not to be the same 30–40% over time. This reflects both the complexity of the issues and the natural ambiguity of the public in wanting to be defended, but not too dangerously.[22]

This is both good and bad news for both sides of the argument, for it indicates that the gross figures are quite liable to wide fluctuations in response to general political conditions. Most importantly, it implies very strongly that the presentation of the arguments will be more than usually crucial. As Kellner points out, it is not so much the *policy* of non-nuclear defence which harms the Labour Party in public esteem but rather the *image* it presents of a party which may not be in control of the issue.[23] Thus Marplan found in December 1986 that the Conservatives were the 'most trusted' party on defence issues at 40% (Labour at 27%). Again, this was hardly an overwhelming vote of confidence at 40%. The same survey recorded a mirror image on health policy where Labour was 'most trusted' with 45% (Conservatives 22%). Defence and health policy, in other words were image-makers, more than intrinsic issues, during the election campaign.

If this, then, represents the party political arena for the defence debate, what are the particular issues being fought out within it?

Contemporary issues

It is hardly surprising that there are a number of complex issues which constantly interact to produce an array of specific arguments in the current defence debate in Britain. It is possible, however, to discern three distinct strands of argument which structure the debate. Most immediate is the issue of the independent British nuclear deterrent. This issue stands out as a barometer of anti-nuclear consensus and, typically, it has been discussed in an essentially self-contained way. It presents nuclear defence arguments in a simple context: should Britain retain a nuclear deterrent as a weapon of last resort? It is an issue over which a British government can exercise some genuine control. The present Conservative government is determined to carry through the programme to replace the Polaris submarine fleet with Trident submarines in a way that will be technically and economically unstoppable, by pushing the work ahead and agreeing contracts with generous cancellation clauses.[24] The independent deterrent also stands as a separate issue because the economic costs are calculable and attributable to a single programme. In reality, of course, it is a highly interdependent issue, but this is not how it is characteristically presented.

Thus it is that the parties present their policies on this issue with a mixture of conviction and expediency. The Government is quite clear that it is necessary (and affordable) to "remain nuclear", not just for the sake of NATO but more for the sake of Britain's own political integrity. To abandon Trident, said Mrs Thatcher, would leave Britain wide open to intimidation.[25] For good or bad this is a highly consistent position.

The Liberal/SDP Alliance, on the other hand, has struggled to bring consistency into its policy. The Alliance is caught between a powerful, though perhaps untypical, groundswell of grass roots Liberal support for a non-nuclear policy, and a more traditionalist SDP preference for a continuation of current policy, centred around the personal commitment of David Owen to a continued role. Thus Alliance policy has concentrated on the question of affordability. According to the joint Liberal/SDP statement on defence on which it fought the 1987 elections, Trident would be cancelled "at the first opportunity", though not, let it be noted, "immediately" as was proposed in an original draft.[26] Polaris would be maintained and its future replacement determined only in the light of prevailing circumstances. On the positive side, the Liberal leader, David Steel, is anxious to bring the British deterrent into the arms control process and to promote measures that could increase European security – more conventional weapons, a nuclear weapon free zone of 150 km along the front and a move away from planning for theatre nuclear war in Europe. The essence of the compromise between the Liberals and the SDP is that "A stronger 'European Pillar' should be developed within NATO".[27] This would be a proof of commitment and may even provide a vehicle for Anglo-French nuclear co-operation to provide a credible political rationale for a retained British nuclear force. This constitutes the main outlines of Alliance policy, at least as far as the leadership is concerned, though there is some doubt about the loyalty of the rank and file to it. For the future, the Alliance hopes to command general support behind a policy that would scrap Trident but retain a nuclear deterrent, at the same level of lethality of the existing Polaris force, pending an arms control agreement that would negotiate it away.

Finally, the Labour Party has an unambiguous commitment to the cancellation of the Trident programme, the scrapping of Polaris and the dismantling of other British ground, sea and air force nuclear systems. In the case of the Labour Party the rationale for this is to save money that can be spent elsewhere in the defence budget, to *exercise*, rather than relinquish, independence by taking a self-interested unilateral measure, and quite overtly to encourage the development of a process of European disarmament in which this would rank as an important first step. Like the policy of the Conservative Government, Labour's proposals on this score are consistent and firmly established. They sit at the opposite end of the spectrum from present official policy.

A second distinct issue concerns the relationship with the United States. Two factors are critically important. In the first place the steady decline over 20 years in the public's confidence in the leadership of the USA is subject to sudden fluctuations (particularly downwards) in the light of specific events. In April and then in June 1986, for the first time in Gallup's polling on these issues, more British people (57%) disapproved of the role that the United States was playing in the world than disapproved of the role of the Soviet Union (52%).[28] This is a remarkable judgement on the specifics of a battle for hearts and minds which, in other respects, is no contest.

Secondly, this judgement is expressed in particular over the issue of cruise missiles.[29] No other issue has mobilised anti-nuclear sentiment like cruise missiles. Levels of public support have fluctuated for the installation of these missiles but the Greenham Common protest and some very inept public relations on the part of the government ensured that the cruise issue was a symbol of the whole debate. And the importance of the symbol was not that cruise was a nuclear missile, but more that it was an *American* nuclear missile. Opposition has been substantial; ranging (and varying) from 36% to 53% between 1981 and 1983, and it seems now to stand at around 50%.[30] Evidence is, of course, circumstantial, but the larger rejection of cruise as opposed to any other nuclear system, plus the scepticism regarding the role of the United States, and a natural suspicion of a future mortgaged to new weapon systems, seems to indicate that it is the nationality of cruise rather than its existence which makes it unpopular.

The response of the political parties to these trends has been polarised by the rhetoric over cruise but, in some respects, is not dissimilar. And it displays again that characteristic self-containment of the defence debate in Britain. There is a certain degree of anti-Americanism in all parties. This is countered by a larger measure of opinion which values the Anglo-American relationship and fears the damage which an expression of anti-Americanism, however eccentric, could do to US perceptions of the relationship. In the Conservative Party anti-Americanism is confined to a small, Right-wing section, almost "Gaullist", who command a certain amount of curiosity but little real support. Insofar as Conservative anti-Americanism finds practical expression, it does so in relation to particular debates over defence industries such as Westland in respect of helicopters or GEC as the manufacturer of the Nimrod airborne radar system. Within the Liberal/SDP Alliance, the sentiment is expressed by many rank-and-file Liberals, and occasionally by Liberal MPs, and is opposed most strongly by the majority Liberal leadership and just about all of the SDP. In the Labour Party, however, there exists a latent and long-standing anti-American sentiment with which all Labour leaderships have to contend. This makes Labour's debate different from the other parties. The Conservatives and the Alliance argue among themselves over whether Polaris, Trident, cruise or battlefield nuclear systems are necessary, and if so, why. In the Labour Party, on the other hand, all of these weapons are rejected in themselves. The intra-party argument is over whether a future British government could *afford* to abandon these weapons and risk the damage that would be done to Anglo-American relations and the future of NATO. Yet this debate is now taking place against a curious background in which European nuclear arms control is being promoted strongly and rapidly by the United States itself. And this is one reason why it is not automatically the case that defence is a vote-loser for the Labour Party, as many on the Right in Britain seem gleefully to assume. For both good and bad reasons, the Labour Party may find itself tapping an undercurrent of scepticism about American policies and their consistency and presenting itself as the party of independence and constructive East-West detente.

Finally, there is the question of Britain's relationship with NATO. On this, there is little disagreement in principle but a good measure of dispute over specifics. There is strong and consistent public support for NATO among the British public and within the political parties. The problem for the Labour Party is not whether to be strongly in favour of NATO. The party conference has persistently voted down by a large majority resolutions that would commit a future government to withdrawal from NATO; in 1986 this majority, thanks partly to trade union bloc votes, was 5.4 million to 1 million.[31] The leadership is unanimously pro-NATO, and the policy document on defence reaffirms Labour's commitment to the NATO Alliance.[32] The problem for Labour, rather, is to be believed.

Opponents of the Labour Party's policy are convinced that a non-nuclear defence policy would do irreparable harm to NATO in both political and military terms; and once implemented, the policy would be delivered effectively into the hands of the Leftist minority in the party who are anti-EEC, anti-American and anti-NATO. Labour's policy would quickly become CND's policy. This, certainly, is the line of attack taken by the Conservative Party, the Liberals and the SDP. The Labour leadership's task is to convince the public that this is not the case. There are two general approaches to this problem.

First, the Labour Party cannot back away from a commitment to negotiate with the United States over the future of US nuclear bases in Britain, with a view to their removal. This cannot be anything other than a major problem for NATO. The only way in which the inherent conflict involved in this could possibly be mitigated is for the Labour leadership to work hard to prepare the ground in America and to foster as much European support as possible among opposition parties who may be in, or near to, power themselves at the same time. This may make the problem easier to handle among NATO policy-makers and may increase public sympathy for this aspect of Labour's strategy. Neil Kinnock, after touring the United States in December 1986, might count as a victory the *Washington Post* editorial which said, "Mr Kinnock is doubtless right in thinking that, at least in the short run, nothing very dramatic would happen if he came to power and carried out Labour's promises. But he would be quite wrong to assume that a Britain moving toward unilateral nuclear disarmament would mean a safer and more stable Europe".[33] This constitutes one of the more influential moderate reactions from within the United States. Mr Kinnock might also take comfort from the fact that in the autumn of 1986 the 40% of the British public who approved of the removal of US nuclear bases from Britain had not diminished, according to Gallup.[34] Nevertheless, there is no escape from the fact that it will still be a very delicate issue indeed. And there is a contradiction in prevailing British public sympathies. It may be possible to exploit doubts about the wisdom of having American bases in Britain, just as there are obvious doubts about the siting of American cruise missiles; but these doubts are accompanied by a strong faith in NATO, as an alliance, and by the general popularity of America, if not of some of its policies at the present time.

The second strand, therefore, concerns how the Labour Party, and to a lesser extent the Liberal/SDP Alliance, can demonstrate their NATO commitment at a time when they advocate some important symbolic changes in its strategy. The way all three parties approach this is to support a strengthening of the conventional military component of NATO strategy. A more robust conventional defence, in particular a strengthened and streamlined BAOR it is said, would at least raise the nuclear threshold, show resolve and be a positive contribution to moving NATO in a new direction. As a policy of the opposition parties, this also has the advantage of making the present government seem neglectful of our real defence needs. The opposition can portray itself supporting real defence with a reallocation of resources saved on the cancellation of Trident.

This approach is intellectually appealing, though the economic costs and technical problems of improving conventional forces are much more considerable than even the informed public seems to assume. It is impossible to predict, however, how this approach will be received by a broader public. It may appear to be a sensible and prudent trade-off in the interests of NATO. More likely, however, since the public (mis)perception is of an overwhelmingly strong and growing Soviet Union, it will be greeted with scepticism. Typical of the British debate, however, this trade-off in the face of NATO interdependence has been up for discussion within the Labour Party since 1984, and since 1986 has featured in Alliance policy also. But it has been all but ignored in the face of a much more independent sort of debate over whether Britain should or should not remain as a nuclear power.

All of these issues, therefore, are likely to cut in different ways and it is not clear how they will appeal to public opinion in an era in which both nuclear arms control and nuclear force modernisation are moving ahead rapidly. There are too many ironies and contradictions in the contemporary situation for the present, conservative defence policy to be taken for granted, by the government, or by anyone else.

Notes

1. David Capitanchik and Richard C. Eichenberg, *Defence and Public Opinion* (London, Routledge and Kegan Paul and Royal Institute for International Affairs, 1983, p. 18).
2. Arthur Marwick, *Britain in the Century of Total War* (Middlesex, Penguin Books, 1970, p. 293).
3. Ivor Crewe "Britain: Two and a Half Cheers for the Atlantic Alliance" in Gregory Flynn and Hans Rattinger, eds., *The Public and Atlantic Defense* (London, Croom Helm, 1985, p. 29).
4. *Ibid.*, pp. 14–16, 27; Capitanchik and Eichenberg, *op. cit.*, pp. 16–17.
5. Andrew J. Pierre, ed., *A Widening Atlantic? Domestic Change and Foreign Policy*, New York, Council on Foreign Relations, 1986, p. 51.
6. William Wallace, *The Foreign Policy Process in Britain* (London, George Allen and Unwin, 1977, pp. 114–7): Kenneth Newton, "Mass Media", in Henry Drucker *et al.*, eds., *Developments in British Politics 2* (London, Macmillan, 1986, pp. 314–20).
7. Crewe, *op. cit.*, p. 52: Capitanchik and Eichenberg, *op. cit.*, pp. 83–4.
8. *Ibid.*, pp. 48–58.

9. See, Labour Party, *Defence and Security for Britain*, London, 1984.
10. Gordon Heald and Robert Wybrow, *The Gallup Survey of Britain, 1986* (London, Croom Helm, 1986). For more historical comparison, see one of the earlier versions, such as Norman Webb and Robert Wybrow, *The Gallup Report: Your Opinions in 1981* (London, Sphere Books, 1982).
11. Gregory Flynn, "Public Opinion and Atlantic Defence", *NATO Review* 31, 5 1983, p. 10. See also, Flynn and Rattinger, *op. cit.*, p. 375.
12. Heald and Wybrow, *op. cit.*, p. 54.
13. *Daily Telegraph*, 4 November 1986, p. 11.
14. Philip A.G. Sabin, "Reassurance, Consensus and Controversy: The Domestic Dilemmas of European Defense" in Stephen J. Flanagan and Fen Osler Hampson, eds., *Securing Europe's Future*, (London, Croom Helm, 1986, pp. 136–62.) See also International Institute for Strategic Studies, *Defence and Consensus: The Domestic Aspects of Western Security*, (Adelphi Papers 182, 183, 184, London, IISS, 1983).
15. Flynn and Rattinger, *op. cit.*, p. 387.
16. Gregory Flynn, "Images of Security: Deterrence and Deliverance", in Gregory Flynn *et al.*, *Public Images of Western Security*, (Paris, Atlantic Institute, 1985, p. 60).
17. Crewe, *op. cit.*, pp. 22–3: Capitanchik and Eichenberg, *op. cit.*, pp. 21–2.
18. D. Lipsey, 'What Do We Think About the Nuclear Threat?' *New Society*, 25 September 1980.
19. Crewe, *op. cit.*, p. 32.
20. *Gallup Survey of Britain, 1986, op. cit.*
21. Richard Gwyn, "A New Neutralism", *World Press Review* 31, September 1984, p. 38.
22. Hugh B. Berrington, "British Public Opinion and Nuclear Weapons" in Cathy Marsh and Colin Fraser, eds., *Public Opinion and Nuclear Defence*, (London, Macmillan 1988). See also, Patrick Dunleavy and Christopher Husbands, *British Democracy at the Crossroads*, (London, George Allen and Unwin, 1985, pp. 160–4, 178–80).
23. Peter Kellner, "The Truth Behind Party Dressing", *The Independent* 15 December 1986, p. 14.
24. Peter Davenport "Why Trident Might Never Be Scrapped", *The Times*, 8 October 1986, p. 6.
25. *The Times* 4 December 1986, p. 2.
26. Liberal Party, *Defence and Disarmament: Report of the Joint SDP-Liberal Alliance Commission*, London, 1986, p. 29.
27. *Ibid.*, p. 44.
28. *Gallup Political Index* No. 310, June 1986, p. 37.
29. Crewe, *op. cit.*, pp. 46–7.
30. Heald and Wybrow, *op. cit.*, p. 52: Crewe, *op. cit.*, Table 2.19, p. 39; Capitanchik and Eichenberg, *op. cit.*, p. 23.
31. "Labour Settles for Non-Nuclear Defence", *The Guardian* 3 October 1986, p. 4.
32. Labour Party, *op. cit.*, p. 4.
33. "A Hard Job for Kinnock", *Washington Post*, 1 December 1986, p. 6.
34. *Gallup Political Index* No. 314, October 1986, p. 27.

Chapter 4
The Military Balance – and its Implications for NATO

STUART CROFT and PHIL WILLIAMS

The nature of the debate

Discussion in Britain about the conventional military balance in Europe is desultory, sporadic and haphazard, and hardly warrants the term debate. This is not to suggest that the balance is ignored. It is simply that there is little systematic analysis and rigorous argument, at least in the public domain. There are three major reasons for this: geography, perceptions of stability and a preoccupation with other issues. All three factors have contributed to a sense of relative detachment about the military balance in Central Europe.

Geopolitical considerations explain a great deal: Britain enjoys the luxury of being in the rear of the European theatre, and it is hardly surprising, therefore, that there is little preoccupation with the minutiae of the conventional or nuclear balance in the Central Region. For the Federal Republic of Germany, which is not only on the front line of the East-West struggle but is the potential battleground should deterrence fail, such detachment is impossible.

The second reason for the lack of debate over the military balance in Europe stems from a fairly widespread belief that the situation in Europe is relatively stable. Indeed, the predominant assessment of East-West relations in Europe is one which critics on both the Right and Left, for very different reasons, regard as overly complacent. Many on the Left contend that the military standoff between the blocs is inherently more volatile than is often assumed, while critics on the Right argue that the danger is not of ignoring instability but of under-estimating the Soviet threat. Nevertheless, the dominant view is that the

Soviet Union, whatever its long-term aspirations, is prudent in its behaviour and is unlikely to take the very high risks of escalation that would be attendant on any military action against NATO forces in Germany so long as the United States is firmly committed to Western Europe. In a sense, defence policy makers and planners in Britain adhere to a political conception of deterrence in Europe rather than a military one. Consequently, the precise balance between NATO and Warsaw Pact forces in Central Europe is not deemed to be crucial to Western European security – although it is acknowledged that the disparity between East and West cannot be allowed to become too marked. This conception of European security, of course, has the added convenience that it helps to provide a rationale for the British strategic nuclear deterrent which, it is argued by the Thatcher government, provides a second centre of nuclear decision-making and therefore an additional element of risk and uncertainty in Soviet calculations.

A third reason why there has been little debate over the military balance as such is that there has been a preoccupation with other things, and especially whether Britain should or should not acquire a strategic nuclear capability to replace Polaris. There is only so much which can be placed on the agenda of public debate, and in Britain nuclear issues have had pride of place. Connections have naturally been made between the costs of acquiring Trident and the difficulties this might cause for Britain's attempts to maintain its existing conventional forces in West Germany and the north-east Atlantic. Indeed, concern over the opportunity costs of Trident was evident in the debate over defence priorities which both preceded and followed John Nott's defence review in the early 1980s. Yet that debate mainly took the form of a battle between the advocates of the "continental commitment" and the proponents of a predominantly maritime role, and did little more than allude to the military balance in Europe. Supporters of the maritime strategy based their case partly on arguments concerning the increasingly global nature of the Soviet threat and the need for Europeans to be less parochial in their approach to security. But their case was also dependent upon the possibility that the conventional phase of hostilities in Europe would be protracted, thereby making resupply and reinforcement by sea crucially important. For their part, those who wanted to maintain BAOR at existing levels pointed to the likely political effects in Washington of a reduction in the strength of the British contingent in Germany. They also contended that weakening British forces in Germany would make it more likely that a conventional war in Europe would be short, either because the Soviet Union would win a quick victory or because NATO would have to resort to the early use of nuclear weapons. In these circumstances sea-borne resupply and reinforcement would be rendered irrelevant. Although the debate, in some ways, revolved around assumptions about the military balance in

Europe, these were rarely made explicit and were certainly not subject to any systematic analysis. The conventional balance in Europe has been a key element in the hidden agenda of the defence debate, but has rarely come into the open.

To some extent this may be changing. The British defence debate of the mid and late 1980s is one in which more explicit attention is being given to the conventional balance in Europe. This is not wholly surprising. Britain cannot be oblivious to the debate about the balance taking place in other NATO countries. Indeed, there have always been echoes in Britain of both the German and, more especially, the American debates. In the late 1970s, for example, Senators Sam Nunn and Dewey Bartlett issued an influential report entitled *The New Soviet Threat* which suggested that the big problem for NATO was the possibility of a Soviet attack from a standing start. Some of these issues were then introduced into the discussion in the United Kingdom with the publication of a study on *Warning and Response* by Conservative MP Julian Critchley which, like the Nunn report, pointed to the need for increases in NATO preparedness.[1]

As the debate elsewhere has become more intense, however, so there has been an increased interest in Britain in the military balance and ways in which it might be improved. The impulse for strengthening conventional forces has come from several sources. One of the most important of these is the peace movement, which has been anxious to minimise if not eliminate NATO's reliance on nuclear weapons. This desire to downgrade the role of nuclear weapons has become enshrined in the policy of the Labour Party which emphasises that the acquisition of Trident will lead inexorably to a diminution in Britain's conventional contribution to NATO. There are some who go further and propose a fundamental restructuring of Britain's military posture which abandons the current strategy in favour of some form of territorial defence based on a Swiss, Yugoslav, or Swedish model. Such a strategy, however, would require not only reshaping Britain's military forces but also British society. Consequently, these more radical proposals have found little favour in Britain. Nevertheless, the pressure for moves towards a non-nuclear defence policy has evoked some reaction from the defence establishment. The desire to contain the protests and provide reassurance to the domestic public as well as deterrence of the Soviet Union has encouraged a growth of interest within the policy-making community in strategies which emphasise delayed first use rather than "no first use".

The second source of pressure to increase conventional strength was less surprising. General Rogers, when Supreme Allied Commander Europe, consistently argued that with the current balance of forces in Central Europe, NATO would have to use nuclear weapons within a few days of any major Warsaw Pact incursion into Western Europe. He also suggested that this could be avoided if NATO countries increased their defence spending not by the 3% per annum agreed in 1977 and 1978 but by 4% or 5% per annum. Similar recommendations were made by *The Economist* in 1982, when it claimed that an addition of about 1%–1½% per year in NATO defence budgets would allow the Allies to resist a Soviet conventional incursion for a month. Although *The Economist* recognised the difficulties in finding the additional money in a period of sluggish economic growth, it claimed that "for anyone who wants to reduce the West's present dependence on nuclear arms, this modest rearmament for the sake of practicable denuclearisation should now become the centre pieces of the defence debate".[2] In other words, a middle ground was being mapped out by those who did not believe in a non-nuclear posture but were nevertheless prepared to consider ways in which dependence on nuclear weapons might be lessened.

The issue also became bound up with the growing interest in Emerging Technologies (ET) which seemed to provide unprecedented opportunities to improve conventional defence. This interest was stimulated in large part by the report of an international study group known as ESECS (European Security Study) which suggested that development in technologies such as sensors and information-processing was leading to considerable advances in the capacity for target acquisition, precision guidance, and discrimination and lethality at far greater distances than hitherto. Once again this found a response in the British debate with a 1984 report issued by the British Atlantic Committee and entitled *Diminishing the Nuclear Threat*. Prepared by a group of former high-ranking officials and military officers, the report suggested that new technology offered unprecedented opportunity for NATO to reduce its reliance on nuclear weapons. At the same time there was a clear recognition that this would not be cheap and that NATO members, including Britain, would have to make some very hard decisions about priorities.

Both the proponents of new technology and the advocates of higher spending on defence have been delineating what is essentially a reformist posture within NATO, seeking to diminish the West's reliance on nuclear weapons. Certainly some of the new weapons systems such as the Multi-Launch Rocket System can substitute for short-range nuclear artillery. Less reliance on nuclear weapons, however, is not the same as a completely non-nuclear strategy. A greater capacity for sustained conventional resistance will not eliminate the need for some battlefield nuclear weapons to deter the use of these systems by the Soviet Union. The possibility of nuclear escalation will remain a key element in NATO strategy, although the reformers hope that this would not be forced upon the Alliance by the lack of non-nuclear options.

This, of course, still does not go far enough for many members of the peace movement who advocate a totally non-nuclear defence. This was invariably dismissed as unrealistic until the Summit between President

Reagan and Mr Gorbachev at Reykjavik in October 1986. Although this meeting failed to produce a comprehensive agreement, progress was made towards more radical arms control agreements than had been envisaged by the West European allies. As well as agreeing on the elimination of all long-range theatre nuclear forces from Europe – the zero-zero option – President Reagan also seemed willing to contemplate the abolition of all strategic ballistic missiles. How serious the negotiating process actually was at Reykjavik was not entirely clear. As the scope of the potential agreements became clear, however, it sent shock waves through West European governments and defence establishments which have traditionally relied upon the American nuclear guarantee as the ultimate basis for their security. Since then Washington has backed away from the President's goal of eliminating all ballistic missiles. Nevertheless, the very fact that such far-reaching agreement was contemplated has had a profound psychological impact in Western Europe. Yet in one sense Reykjavik merely highlighted the existing tendency by the United States to de-emphasise nuclear weapons. This tendency had previously been manifested most obviously in President Reagan's Strategic Defense Initiative (SDI) but had also been evident in demands by former Secretary of Defense Robert McNamara that NATO adopt a "no first use" posture and in claims by former Secretary of State Henry Kissinger that the American nuclear guarantee was incredible. The way in which European interests were so obviously disregarded at Reykjavik, however, gave old fears a new intensity. In response several European governments, including that of Mrs Thatcher, emphasised that drastic cuts in nuclear arsenals should not take place unless accompanied by significant reductions in conventional forces in Europe. Without parallel progress on conventional arms reductions, it was argued, NATO would be placed at a major disadvantage. Whether or not Reykjavik leads to the far-reaching agreements beyond the INF agreement, the very fact that such radical measures could be placed on the agenda has already contributed to a sharper focus on the conventional balance between NATO and the Warsaw Pact.

The Thatcher government, of course, claimed that the only way of remedying the imbalance in favour of the Warsaw Pact was through asymmetrical force reductions. Unilateral force increases by the NATO allies will be insufficient to offset the Warsaw Pact advantage. This is in marked contrast to the assessments offered by the nuclear disarmers. Although they are the most pessimistic about the dangers of the current strategy, the nuclear disarmers are, in many cases, also the most optimistic about the ability of NATO to resist conventionally. Those not in the neutralist wing of the movement want changes in strategy and force structure which they believe will rectify NATO's deficiencies and improve the balance. All this highlights another element in the British discussion about the balance – the fact that assumptions tend to be made selectively in a way which is politically most convenient. To some extent, of course, this is inevitable in that the balance is not something which can be measured precisely.

Assessing the military balance: the dominance of politics

The difficulties inherent in attempts to assess the military balance in Europe have increasingly been acknowledged in the annual British *Statements on the Defence Estimates*. In fact, there has been a remarkable increase in the sophistication of these documents. From simply presenting a picture of increased Warsaw Pact capabilities, the Statements have graduated to a more thorough appraisal of the balance which acknowledges the inherent difficulties in any attempt to provide a comprehensive assessment. The 1986 *Statement* not only acknowledged that "all accounts of the military balance are . . . necessarily incomplete" but also admitted that "there is so much scope for the exercise of judgement and opinion . . . that the outcome is bound to be controversial".[3] At the most basic level there are problems in deciding which forces to count, in categorising weapon systems, and in the reliability of counting. When an attempt is made to move from quantitative indicators and to take into account qualitative factors, the problems become even greater. The different equipment characteristics of the two forces, the differences in preparedness and reinforcement capability and factors such as surprise, training and morale all enter the equation. If the French are counted into NATO force levels, for example, the balance can be made to look less unfavourable to the West. Similarly, it is possible to cast doubt on the reliability of the armies of several members of the Warsaw Pact. It is also possible to make widely differing judgements about what level of superiority is required for an offensive to penetrate the defence. The implication of all this is that the balance can be made to look as good or as bad as is politically convenient for those who make the assessment.

Without being too cynical, it can be argued that those who are more-or-less content with the *status quo* and with existing NATO strategy tend to see the conventional balance as clearly in favour of the Warsaw Pact; that the military reformers tend to see it as adverse but also as something which can be corrected with a considerable but manageable commitment of effort and resources; and that the nuclear disarmers tend to see it as being far less asymmetrical than is usually assumed. Inevitably this arouses some suspicion that the assessments of the military balance are not the starting point of the analysis but the end point and have almost as much to do with political rationalisations as with strategic rationales.

There is nothing novel or unique to Britain in this. In the 1960s US

Secretary of Defense Robert McNamara and his civilian systems analysts challenged the conventional wisdom that NATO was massively outnumbered in Europe because it faced 175 Soviet divisions. By introducing new forms of assessment they demonstrated that Soviet superiority was far less pronounced than had hitherto been believed. Soviet divisions were considered to be far smaller and much less combat-effective than those of the United States and its NATO allies. In the light of this reassessment, it appeared that the imbalance in Europe had been greatly exaggerated. Although such a reappraisal was long overdue, and in some ways very persuasive, it had clear political purposes. The rewriting of the conventional balance justified the American move to a strategy of flexible response and gave credibility to McNamara's exhortations to the Allies to spend more on conventional defence and move away from the trip-wire strategy. The Europeans at that time were reluctant to go too far in this direction – partly because of their distaste for any notion of fighting a large-scale but limited conventional war in Europe, but also because of the resource implications. Ironically, the most powerful critique of the McNamara strategy was presented by Denis Healey who argued very strongly that the Warsaw Pact had a number of distinct advantages which made it impossible for the Alliance to dispense completely with reliance on nuclear weapons. The large number of tanks available to the Warsaw Pact, together with the possibility of surprise and the fact that the attacker had the initiative in terms of the time and place for the offensive, made it impossible for NATO to contemplate sustained conventional resistance.

What makes this ironic is that Denis Healey has been one of the leading figures in a party which has increasingly become committed to non-nuclear defence and which justifies this not only in terms of its desirability but also in terms of its feasibility. The Labour Party's National Executive Committee presented to the annual conference in 1984 a statement on defence and security which claimed that there was a rough conventional balance in Europe between NATO and the Warsaw Pact, with NATO having superiority in some categories and the Warsaw Pact in others.[4] For Labour, such an assessment of the balance is the only means of resolving the dilemma stemming from the party's aversion to nuclear weapons on the one side and NATO's need to rely upon them on the other. In a sense, therefore, the conventional debate is very much a subsidiary of the nuclear debate.

This is not to deny, however, that there is much merit in the Labour Party's proposals for strengthening conventional defence. Furthermore, the party is on strong ground when it argues that the Trident acquisition, as currently projected by the Conservative government, will require further cuts in conventional forces. If there are high levels of economic growth, of course, such cuts need not occur as there would be more resources for all purposes, public and private. With more money available for public expenditure the pressure on defence would be eased and the government would be able to procure Trident without sacrifices in other areas of the defence budget. If the economy does not perform well, however, the pressures on the defence budget could become intense. In these circumstances, another defence review could be unavoidable. If so, there are two broad strategies which could be adopted. One is to inflict equal misery across the board and impose a degree of stringency on all the armed services by stretching out new equipment programmes and cutting back on operations and maintenance. The other is to attempt to establish a clear hierarchy of roles, missions and capabilities. In the event that the government does not take the easy way out and establishes a clear set of priorities, the navy, which was saved from the most severe effects of John Nott's "Way Forward" by the Falklands War, may once again have to take the brunt of the economies. By cancelling Trident (and Britain's out-of-area role), it is argued, a Labour Government, if it had been elected in 1987, would have avoided (at least in the short and medium term) the need for a defence review. Indeed, it seems likely that such a Labour Government would have maintained, and possibly even enhanced, the British contribution to NATO's capacity for conventional defence in Europe as well as the maritime contribution to resupply and reinforcement.

The Labour Party at the 1987 election proposed to try to move NATO strategy towards "no first use". The revulsion against nuclear weapons, however, has not led to blanket endorsement by the Labour Party of all initiatives in the conventional field. Although the party fully supports military reform and greater reliance on conventional forces, it is discriminating in which reforms it supports. The emphasis is not only on non-nuclear defence but also on non-provocative defence. It does not subscribe to "deep strike" strategies. Although it has singled out the Air Land Battle concept for particular criticism (partly because of its emphasis on integrating conventional, nuclear and chemical weapons) it has also been highly critical of General Rogers' idea of Follow-on Forces-Attack (FOFA). Any strategy which aims to seize Warsaw Pact territory is also anathema.

Within these guidelines or constraints, however, the Labour Party emphasises its unequivocal support for conventional defence. Among its proposals for enhancing NATO's capacity to resist is a redeployment of NATO forces near the border, greater reliance on obstacles and barriers which could be rapidly emplaced in times of crisis, the exploitation of "precision guided munitions", and a move away from large and expensive weapons platforms. In addition, the Royal Air Force would be restructured away from offensive and towards defensive roles (for example, deploying RAF Tornados in the Air Defence Variant rather than for interdiction).

Most of these proposals are unexceptionable. The idea of greater reliance on barriers in particular has much to recommend it. Not only would it reduce the gap between NATO's peacetime status and its wartime dispositions, and thereby make it slightly less vulnerable to surprise and deception, but it would also enhance crisis stability because it is so clearly defensive. The idea of terrain modification, to include landscaping and prepared defensive positions, all designed to slow down, halt or canalise a Warsaw Pact advance has considerable – although far from unanimous – support in military circles. General Rogers regarded this as an area where considerable improvement could be made and went a lot further in initiating such measures than is generally appreciated. The problem, though, is West German sensitivity to anything which appears to solidify the divisions between East and West. In addition, there is considerable opposition from local farmers to any idea of preplaced explosives. The suggestion, for example, that NATO could emplace pipes in the ground which, in a crisis, could very rapidly be filled with liquid explosives, aroused considerable opposition in the Federal Republic. Yet this idea has recently been enthusiastically advocated by Denis Healey as something which would provide an effective barrier to a rapid tank advance.

At the same time, aspirations to move towards on all defensive defence encounter several difficulties. Arguments against deep attack with conventional missiles are persuasive, given the problems that the Soviet Union might have in the fog of battle in discriminating these from nuclear systems. It does not make much sense to reduce NATO's need for deliberate escalation through strategies which increase the probability of inadvertent escalation. Nevertheless, rigid insistence on this would place NATO at a considerable disadvantage in any war in Europe. This could be a considerable handicap if NATO had already taken steps to reduce further its reliance on nuclear weapons. The presence of these weapons in the NATO order of battle poses enormous problems for Warsaw Pact planners: the more that Pact forces are concentrated for a decisive breakthrough, for example, the more vulnerable they become to nuclear attack. If NATO not only denied itself the option of resorting to nuclear weapons but also ruled out certain conventional options (such as interdiction, which has always been part of the military repertoire and which may be necessary to prevent reinforcing echelons of Warsaw Pact forces reaching the battle area) it would be placing itself at a major disadvantage. It is one thing to suggest that the conventional balance in Europe is not nearly as unfavourable to NATO as it is often portrayed; it is quite another to imply that it is sufficiently good or could be made so in order to allow the Alliance to fight with a series of self-imposed inhibitions. Such a proposition would certainly find little support from those who have to implement the strategy.

The major thrust of Labour's non-nuclear defence policy, however, is not military but political. In many ways it represents an attempt to reimpose the dominance of politics over defence policy. The focus is not on how to improve defence: it is on how to use defence to improve political relations with the Soviet Union and Eastern Europe. The argument put forward in the 1987 election was that although a Labour Government would attempt to provide for a credible conventional defence, this would be only one element in a more comprehensive approach which focuses on security rather than simply deterrence and defence. Underlying Labour's defence policy is a set of assumptions and purposes relating to the future evolution of East-West relations in Europe. It is hoped that a non-nuclear defence policy would facilitate an improved political relationship between the two blocs and encourage measures to dismantle the institutionalised military confrontation that has dominated Europe since the early 1950s. This is seen as the best means of enhancing British security, West European security and the security of the Soviet Union. In a sense, the Labour Party would attempt to revive détente in Europe through measures designed to enhance the security of all.

An all-conventional denial strategy would not only help to promote common or reciprocal security but would provide necessary insurance in case such an approach failed. For all its attractions, however, there are problems in moving towards a non-nuclear posture. There is a large gap between the aspiration to render reliance on nuclear weapons either minimal or non-existent and the provision of the conventional forces necessary to make this anything like a feasible proposition. Furthermore, this gap may well be widening, with the result that consolidating the gains of the last few years may take precedence over further improvements. Indeed, governments may find it increasingly difficult to maintain the quantity and quality of their conventional forces. Resource allocation dilemmas will confront all governments, but would have been particularly acute for a Labour Government committed to increased public spending on a wide range of social welfare provisions. Hence in resource terms at least, non-nuclear defence may be an idea whose time has passed.

Current trends in the military balance

NATO has periodically gone through phases in which reducing reliance on conventional weapons and developing a capacity for sustained conventional resistance have been prominent on its agenda. The outbreak of the Korean War in 1950 provided the impulse for the first major effort at conventional rearmament. Even as the Lisbon Goals were being agreed upon in 1952, however, Alliance members were beginning to stretch out their defence efforts and to increase reliance on nuclear weapons. The second big drive took place in the 1960s as the United States tried to impose its conception of flexible response upon reluctant allies who were unwilling to go so far so fast. During the late 1970s and the early 1980s there was another attempt to establish a stalwart conventional capability through the Long Term Defence Programme and the agreement to increase defence budgets by 3% per annum. Although the 3% has fallen by the wayside, the Alliance has established a Conceptual Military Framework within which it hopes to exploit new technology. Nevertheless, it seems likely that once again member nations will lack either the willingness or the ability to make available the necessary resources. The early 1980s were relatively good years for the Alliance in terms of increased defence spending. Although much will depend on the level of economic growth, the late 1980s and the early 1990s could be a period of famine, in which the battle for resources will be acute both within governments and within defence ministries.

This concern over the scarcity of resources has been evident in the British response to the growing interest in both the United States and West Germany in Anti-Tactical Ballistic Missiles (ATBMs) whether as part of "extended air defence" or as the European component of the Strategic Defence Initiative. Although the Ministry of Defence accepts that Soviet missiles armed with conventional warheads could pose a potential threat, it remains somewhat sceptical about the severity of that threat. And even if it does materialise, it is far from being self-evident, in the British view, that ATBM is the most appropriate response. Greater emphasis on hardening and mobility might be more cost-effective and more palatable to Europeans reluctant to do anything which associates them too closely with President Reagan's SDI. At the very least proposals for ATBM deployment will be carefully scrutinised to assess just how vital these defensive systems are. Furthermore, in a period of scarce resources, systems which are not central to the roles and missions of any of the military services are unlikely to fare well in the budgetary battles.

Although London has been far more sceptical on the ATBM issue than either Bonn or Washington, anxieties over the availability of resources are evident throughout the Alliance. The United States, for example, faces acute problems as it attempts to reduce the overall budget deficit and meet increasingly onerous defence commitments. Indeed, it seems likely that the United States defence budget will be squeezed from both ends. The overall level of resources available is almost certain to decline, while the demands from the services for the fulfillment of force goals and the provision of resources necessary to implement ambitious goals and missions will remain intense. In this competition the navy could be very well placed as a result of John Lehman's political skill in getting the keels laid down for the 600 ship target. If the navy is to have the aircraft and manpower necessary to turn the 600 ship force into more than a notional entity, however, its budget will have to increase by around 2%–3% a year. In this event, something else in the defence budget will have to give. Unless there are major arms reduction agreements along the lines discussed at Reykjavik there is unlikely to be a marked change in the investment for strategic offensive forces. SDI, of course, adds an extra burden on the budget, although it seems likely that President Reagan will find that the funding for the SDI programme authorised by a Democrat-controlled Congress well below the level he requests. If SDI is one probable casualty of the concern over the budget deficit, another more immediate one will almost certainly be operations and maintenance. There is no guarantee, however, that sufficient reductions can be made in this area to avoid the necessity of more fundamental cuts in capability. Should this be necessary, an obvious target is the military presence in Western Europe, together with the forces earmarked for reinforcement of NATO deployed in the United States itself.

Such reductions are all the more likely in the event of transatlantic squabbles over defence becoming more intense or more frequent. Certainly this cannot be ruled out. There has been mutual disenchantment on both sides of the Atlantic because of differing threat perceptions and divergent attitudes on out-of-area issues such as the American raid on Libya. There have also been serious differences over arms control. The Reagan administration, from being somewhat diffident about arms control, embraced a much more cavalier approach at Reykjavik which alarmed several governments in Europe. At the same time these governments are hostile to the decision to abandon SALT II limits and are firmly committed to the maintenance of the ABM Treaty. These differences are another source of irritation to governments on both sides of the Atlantic and could prove a further source of frustration, misunderstanding and resentment. Should tensions in Atlantic relations again come to the fore this could have direct consequences on the way in which resource allocation choices are made in Washington. In an atmosphere poisoned by recriminations it is unlikely that maintaining the American military presence in Europe will find effective champions either in the executive branch or the Congress. It is certainly not inconceivable, therefore, that there will be a significant reduction of American troops in Europe over the next five to ten years. Although it is difficult to place a precise figure on this, a reduction of between 50,000 and 100,000 is not out of the question.

In this event, the United States would almost certainly demand that the Europeans provide the necessary compensation. This would be all the more difficult because the Europeans face resource dilemmas similar to those in Washington. France, for example, is finding it extremely hard to modernise its strategic nuclear forces and maintain the desired level of conventional forces, while the Federal Republic of Germany faces not only budgetary strains but acute manpower shortages as a result of demographic trends. The only possibility for adequate compensation by the Europeans would be from increased co-operation in the development and acquisition of weaponry and the rationalisation of forces. Consequently, reliance on nuclear weapons would be increased rather than reduced. This could be disturbing not only to many Europeans but also to many Americans who might look upon Western Europe not as a source of additional security but as a source of unacceptable risk – a possibility which becomes less remote if Americans are made more aware of their vulnerability as a result of the discussions over SDI. This sentiment was evident in the 1984 debate on the Nunn Amendment, which attempted to establish the conditions on which American troops would stay in Europe. Although the Amendment was defeated, the impulse to reduce the nuclear risk to the United States of its commitment to Western Europe – in some interpretations at least – was also evident at Reykjavik and in the INF agreement, and could become increasingly powerful. One result of such a trend could be that American troop reductions might take on their own momentum.

A possible worst case scenario would arise if the United States concluded that reliance on a trip-wire strategy was too dangerous and that disengagement was preferable. The risk with this, of course, is that it could undermine the whole framework of security which, for all its imperfections, may be preferable to any other framework which currently seems feasible. The American presence in Europe acts not only as a counterweight to the Soviet Union but also as a pacifier on what has historically been an extremely turbulent and war-torn continent.[5] Furthermore, in view of Soviet fears about resurgent German power, alternative arrangements in which the Federal Republic looms large could prove more destabilising than the existing situation.

There is nothing inevitable about this worst case, but it seems at least as plausible an outcome as the creation of a viable non-nuclear defence. It would be even more likely if a Labour Government had been elected in 1987 and had implemented its plans to evict American cruise missiles and nuclear bases from Britain. In the autumn of 1986 Denis Healey attempted to give a future Labour Government some room for manoeuvre by questioning the certainty of Labour carrying out this part of its programme. Furthermore, even in the Labour Party's official document on defence, *Modern Britain in a Modern World*, there was no clear time-table for such a programme.

Perhaps the most likely outcome of all is that the Western Alliance, in the absence of massive shocks, will continue to muddle through as it has always done. It has long learned to live with a conventional imbalance in favour of the Warsaw Pact. Although this is far from satisfactory, it is unlikely that the asymmetries will reach the point where the Soviet Union might be tempted into adventurism. To ensure that this remains the case NATO will continue with its efforts to exploit "emerging technologies" and make incremental improvements in its defences. While such measures will not radically shift the balance in NATO's favour they should at least slow down the deterioration in its position. Moreover, there are several initiatives which could make better use of existing resources. Some of the more ambitious ideas associated with deep strike, for example, could be moderated so that the focus is on hitting shallow rather than hitting deep. Not only would this be easier and less expensive than deep attack but it would also have a more immediate effect on the battlefield. Similarly, some reallocation of resources away from expensive aircraft designed to penetrate deep into well-defended Warsaw Pact territory might be appropriate, even though this would mean impinging upon well-established and deeply cherished roles and missions of NATO air forces. The military assets that are freed from these tasks could be channelled into air defence of key NATO installations and close air support for ground operations. Other concepts of operations require equally careful scrutiny to ensure that they are as effective and efficient as possible. Furthermore, some of the improvements are relatively straightforward, if somewhat lacking in glamour. It has been suggested, for example, that the provision of a number of air-refuelling tankers would have far-reaching benefits in terms of sustainability of NATO air power.[6]

Not all the improvements are associated with air forces. Changes in established procedures and concepts of operations for the land battle are already being made in an attempt to maximise combat effectiveness. In 1985, for example, a number of modifications were made in the organisation and tactics of the Northern Army Group as a result of initiatives by General Bagnall, the Commander of the Group. The essence of these changes was that the four national corps which make up NORTHAG would fight in a more integrated fashion. Not only has more emphasis been placed on manoeuvrability but the scheme allows for the use of an operational reserve of up to three divisions which could engage Warsaw Pact forces in any of the Corps areas as necessary.[7]

It is clear from this that a "business as usual" approach to maintaining the military balance in Europe is no longer deemed adequate. However, there is also a limit to what can be achieved through reform and rationalisation. Faced with a budgetary squeeze and the prospects of a balance in which the trend may once again become increasingly adverse to the Alliance, therefore, there could well be a revival of interest in conventional arms control in Europe. This would be neither novel nor unprecedented. The MBFR talks which began in Vienna in 1973 were designed primarily to contain Congressional demands for unilateral American troop reductions in Western Europe. Their very existence was enough to stem what had appeared at times to be inexorable demands for a smaller American military presence in Western Europe.

Another attempt in the late 1980s to use arms control as a means of compensating for military weakness and preventing a growing imbalance of conventional power, however, is unlikely to work. Such a strategy is dependent upon a coincidence of interests between the West and the Soviet Union – and it is not clear that there is sufficient convergence to render it feasible. The economic incentives for Moscow to reduce military manpower are not very great. This is in marked contrast to the strategic level, where the Soviet Union is concerned with slowing down the technological competition with the United States to release energy and resources for industrial and economic reform. Furthermore, the political incentives are negligible given that the West has little with which to bargain. There is no reason why Moscow should engage in conventional force reductions in a period when NATO is likely to confront increasing difficulties in maintaining its order of battle. At the end of the day, therefore, it will be difficult for NATO to avoid continued reliance on nuclear weapons. The conventional balance may not be as bad as some worst case thinking suggests, but neither is it as good as some best case thinking implies. In these circumstances, the maintenance of flexible response may well be deemed vital. Although flexible response is politically attractive because it is capable of flexible interpretation, it is also capable of flexible implementation. In the event of hostilities – which are the only infallible way of determining the validity of assessments of the military balance in Europe – flexible response provides for a variety of possible answers. A military strategy could hardly be asked to do more.

Notes

1. J. Critchley, *Warning and Response* (London: Leo Cooper, 1978).
2. "Without the bomb" *The Economist* 31 July, 1982 pp. 11–12. See also pp. 30–32.
3. *Statement on the Defence Estimates 1986 1* Cmnd. 9763-1 (London: HMSO, 1986, pp. 58–59).
4. *Defence and Security for Britain* Statement to the 1984 Labour Party Annual Conference by the National Executive Committee.
5. J. Joffe, "Europe's American Pacifier" *Foreign Policy* No. 54 Spring 1984 pp. 64–82.
6. See "NATO's Central Front" *The Economist* 30 August 1986, *Survey* p. 21.
7. See R. Cowton, "NATO makes big changes in plans to counter Soviet attack" *The Times* 14 June, 1985.

Chapter 5
Arms Control and the Military Balance: The West German Debate

K. PETER STRATMANN

It is difficult to separate the debate in the Federal Republic of Germany about the military balance from the general debate about defence policy. This is because the standards applied to the former are to a great extent a function of the latter, *ie* they reflect political and military strategic preconceptions arising out of a certain world view as well as practical concerns of current politics. For this reason it is necessary to sketch some of the structural aspects which are particularly relevant to the evolution and direction of this defence political debate in the Federal Republic.

Structural aspects of the debate about defence policy

The debate in the Federal Republic about the military situation and its implications for defence policy reveals a complicated interaction of a multiplicity of changes. This process has not merely involved the interested public and the political opposition, but also the official defence policy. Its causes lie in several areas.

An important external factor is the fundamental shift in the military balance of forces between East and West since the 1960s, in particular in the nuclear realm. This change in the military strategic boundary conditions of Western security policy has to be seen in the light of the evolution of East-West relations from a phase of a perceived détente and hopes for arms control at the beginning of the 1970s to sharp political antagonism in the late 1970s and early 1980s characterised by a strong military emphasis.

These external influences have made it more difficult for the Federal Republic to pursue the objectives of its security policy to combine a credible military deterrence within the framework of the North Atlantic Alliance with an *Ostpolitik* which would contribute to a reduction of tension and a policy of arms control. Contrary pressures from the Soviet Union and the United States threatened to create contradictions between the different components of this policy. They sharpened the security dilemma of the Federal Republic as a dependent country in a militarily particularly exposed position and led to a domestic political polarisation which was bound to destroy the hitherto existing consensus with regard to foreign and defence policy.

An important internal cause for this change in German defence policy arose from the fact that official policy failed for too long to accept the reasons for and consequences of NATO's change of strategy from the doctrine of massive retaliation to flexible response in 1968, and to explain it to the public so as to ensure its domestic political acceptance. Instead officials continued to explain the new strategic concept, despite its requirement for a flexible defence capability, mostly in terms of the old, inflexible deterrence strategy and thus continued to employ the old formulations for its justification. Representatives of the Federal Government were co-operating within NATO (especially in the Nuclear Planning Group, the High Level Group and the integrated military structure) to develop and implement the new strategic concept in terms of its military conception and operational planning, but this took place on a confidential basis, even if under the political control of the minister concerned, and it did not seem to have a perceptible effect on the level of information and the awareness of the problems in the Cabinet and the Bundestag, the political parties, the armed forces or the general public. Thus a gap developed between the official German military policy within the Alliance, which was formulated and implemented by a small circle of civilian and military experts, and an information policy for the Government and the public which had in many ways quite a different content, clinging as it did to a continuity of the hitherto valid strategic rationale.

The problematic nature of this institutional and conceptual dichotomy came rapidly to the surface when the government was unexpectedly confronted with the "democratisation" of defence policy by the controversies surrounding the neutron weapon and the dual-track decision.[1] In these circumstances it was relatively easy for "opposing experts"[2], who rejected the Atlantic security policy of the Federal Republic, to cast doubt on the logic and credibility of official policy by demonstrating its contradictions.

Without encountering effective political opposition these "opposing experts" succeeded in convincing a population gripped by a deep fear of war that the deployment of American medium-range missiles in Western Europe constituted a fundamental change in the valid military strategy of NATO, which would lead to the outbreak of nuclear war in the near future, resulting in the complete annihilation of the Federal Republic. That these claims struck a chord with many in the population is demonstrated not merely in the rise of the anti-nuclear peace movement and the growth of the Green Party, but also in a far-reaching reorientation of social democratic defence policy, the final result of which cannot yet be estimated.

The gap between the official, active policy of the Federal Republic in the development of military doctrine and military planning in the Alliance and the presentation and justification of this policy to the public does not appear to have closed despite the change of government in Bonn and the political success in deploying INF. On the contrary, the bitter experiences with the INF controversy have led those in government, in response to public pressure for some steps towards nuclear disarmament, to avoid discussing the dilemmas of nuclear strategy which are particularly difficult for the Federal Republic. The response of the government to the revived proposal of a "zero option" for American and Soviet INF in Europe indicates that the original military strategic reasons for deployment are still given little political weight. Public statements emphasise the value of negotiated solutions, while not making clear that Western negotiation must take into account the military strategy and operational criteria of current NATO planning.

Further indications of the differences between the way in which the government itself analyses problems and its public presentation have for some time been discernible in the field of negotiations about conventional arms control. In the public presentation, for example, there has been a consistently positive evaluation of the MBFR negotiations as an important political element in the East-West dialogue and a means to stabilise the military situation. Internally, however, at least among the military, the predominant concern has been that a possible agreement along the lines of the Western negotiating concept would endanger the stability of NATO's forward defence instead of strengthening it. A similar dichotomy between the publicly emphasised positive contribution to détente and internal concerns from defence political and strategic perspectives had earlier characterised the policy of the then Federal Government with regard to the evolution of the American negotiating position in SALT II.

Another internal cause of the deep-rooted change in the defence political configuration in the Federal Republic lies in the fact that parties, educational establishments, the media, trade unions and church organisations are now in the hands of a generation whose political socialisation was strongly influenced by the protest against the

American war in Vietnam and the triumph of the "New Left" in the student movement. The neo-Marxist and anti-military orientation of this movement implied necessarily a fundamental rejection and critique of established Western defence policy. By means of a revisionist reinterpretation of Cold War history and the rejection of anti-Communism, the strategy of the Soviet Union ceased to be a threat. Thus the United States was given prime responsibility for the militarisation of the East-West conflict and the development of the arms race. We cannot investigate here in which areas of debate and by what steps such views, following the "march through the institutions", have influenced the mass consciousness. Nevertheless, it is beyond question that during the 1970s in the universities and peace research institutes of the Federal Republic a fundamental opposition developed. It had at its disposal an effective media infrastructure and developed a systematic body of arguments directed at the tensions within NATO strategy and the security dilemmas of the Federal Republic and made them the object of political agitation. The criticism of these "opposing experts" of the deterrence system, of NATO's nuclear doctrine which in their view involved suicidal risks, of the reduced sovereignty of the Federal Republic on questions involving its very existence, (namely the American decisions about the use of nuclear weapons), of the allegedly anti-democratic orientation of the Bundeswehr and its offensive and revanchist indoctrination, (as well as of the alleged manipulation of the existing military East-West balance in official threat analyses by NATO and the Federal Government) encountered an emotionally and intellectually sympathetic public of former co-students whose influence and multiplier effect was the greater, the higher their professional and social standing.

The latent potential for political change contained in these developments was first demonstrated by the controversy about the dual-track decision and the turn-around in the defence policy of the Social Democratic Party which followed within a few years, as well as the astonishing degree of approval for demands for an "alternative strategy", not merely among intellectuals but also in religiously and socially-involved circles of the population.

In fact it can be said that in the Federal Republic discussion about detailed aspects of strategy and operational concepts or evaluations of the military balance are determined by fundamentally different philosophical views about what the security problem of the Federal Republic is in political and military terms. Consequently there can be no agreed set of criteria to evaluate the political and military objectives of security policy. Furthermore these fundamental divergences in political outlook lead to a politicisation of defence political issues, *ie* they become tactical instruments in the interests of various internal domestic and foreign policy interests. It is not possible to give a detailed and comprehensive analysis of the interaction of such factors on the basis of overt tactics regarding the evaluation of the military balance in the Federal Republic. Instead we shall simply compare the official evaluation of the military balance with that of opponents of the government's security policy. This, of course, cannot be truly representative of the entire spectrum of opinions on this issue. Nonetheless it provides an insight into important typical characteristics of this debate.

Evaluations of the military balance

The significance of the conventional military balance

The official evaluation of the conventional balance between NATO and the Warsaw Pact does not merely reflect the increased strength of the armed forces in the East. It is also based on a changed evaluation of the strategic and political significance of NATO's conventional defence capability for the Federal Republic. This change, therefore, also affects the criteria according to which the conventional balance of forces is established and evaluated.

Particular emphasis is put on the result of Soviet efforts to create a purely conventional strategic offensive option for central and northern Europe. This is designed to allow the Soviet leadership, in case of conflict, to achieve their military and political objectives without having recourse to the use of nuclear weapons while at the same time undermining NATO's ability to resort to nuclear response. It is not necessarily assumed that the Soviet motive underlying the development of their strategic concept is a desire to engage in aggression. But it is clear that the Soviet Union, with its politically offensive goals, is aiming not only to exacerbate NATO's nuclear dilemmas but also further to constrain the strategic options of the Western Alliance in the area of conventional defence.

Critical factors in the development of Warsaw Pact conventional capabilities are:

— first, the comprehensive strengthening of Soviet land forces of the first echelon stationed at the periphery of the Warsaw Pact territories with regard to their mobility (in particular the development of an air mechanised combat capability), flexibility (by enabling restructured regiments to engage in combined arms combat and improved leadership), firepower, armour and logistical reach;
— secondly, the development of a powerful modern air strike component, which, given the support of its highly capable air defence system, could attack the ground-based air defence and the NATO air forces on their own territory, in order to gain air dominance in critical areas and operational stages.

Both developments call into question what used to be regarded as areas of NATO advantage, whereby for a long time the Alliance had hoped to compensate for its quantitative inferiority in conventional forces: *ie* superior material quality in armaments and equipment as well as superior air forces, which could not only secure NATO's own air space but also actively support the operations of NATO's land forces by attacks on the enemy air force as well as engaging in interdiction strikes and providing close air support. Particularly worrying in view of these changes is the increasing capability of the Warsaw Pact to start a conventional offensive with strategic objectives with very little warning time, for example, without deploying reinforcements from the western military districts of the Soviet Union. Given the comparatively long period of time needed by NATO to achieve full strength for its active forces after the decision to mobilise, the need to move forces over long distances into the combat area and prepare them for the defence, as well as transport reinforcements of air and land forces from the United States, the possibility of a successful operational surprise can no longer be excluded. NATO's forward defence might collapse quite rapidly if an attack were to occur before defence preparations were complete and the defence had to take place with reduced units, overstretched front-line and without the availability of local and operational reserves.

In this context the official analysis emphasises the Soviet interest in the concept of a conventional strike, which would precede the attack by the land forces and be designed to eliminate key components of the NATO air defence system, command and control etc. in a surprise attack. To execute this conventional first strike, which substantially complicates the problem of a surprise attack and the possibility of decisive initial operations, the Soviets might not only use aircraft and precision-guided air-to-ground missiles, but in the 1990s probably also improved ballistic missiles with conventional warheads, against which there is at present no defence. For this reason the Ministry of Defence is demonstrating strong interest in the development of an "extended air defence" system in Central Europe with an ATM/ATBM capability.

Official concern about this orientation of operational thought and the complementary developments in the armed forces of the Warsaw Pact is increased by negative trends in the defence policy of Western countries. Financial and demographic problems suggest that the number of forces deployed in Central Europe will be reduced, while their dependence on mobilisation will increase. NATO's anti-tank capability will be considerably reduced by the introduction of improved armour by the other side. The present modernisation of NATO's air defence system could be neutralised before the programme has been completed. The implementation of the FOFA concept is hindered *inter alia* by the fact that so far only inadequate means have been made available.

Thus it cannot be excluded that in future NATO's conventional capability to respond to an attack with short warning time will be reduced. This would not only call into question the value of the investment in improving NATO's capability to hold out in a conventional conflict, but would, more importantly, make dependence on a very early use of nuclear weapons a military necessity. This would strongly contradict the often proclaimed Western aim to "raise the nuclear threshold" and would further undermine the still existing political support for NATO strategy.

Under the pressure of the anti-nuclear protest movement and because of strong and long-standing German reservations about the use of nuclear battlefield weapons, the Federal Government – or anyway the Ministry of Defence – has revised earlier views about the mission and requirements for the conventional defence of NATO. After a long shadowy existence, strategic operational criteria for the evaluation of the military threat, the determination of Germany's own force requirements and the development of the NATO operational concept in Central Europe have received increased attention in the last years. To put it in simple terms, the top leadership of the Bundeswehr has thus come closer to the original American interpretation of the strategy of flexible response.

In effect then, the concept whereby the purpose of force comparisons and operationally oriented military strategic situation evaluations were reduced *ad absurdum* by the paradox that NATO viewed a conventional inferiority as a strengthening of nuclear deterrence, while an effective conventional defence capability was seen as endangering this deterrence is no longer valid. Weakness was interpreted to be strength, strength to be weakness. It is therefore no longer regarded as a convincing argument that the need to resort to early nuclear escalation owing to NATO's inadequate conventional defences would exclude, from the Soviet viewpoint, the possibility of a purely conventional war in Europe and would thus strengthen the overall war-preventing effect of deterrence in general. Even the *Hardthöhe* now considers the mission of NATO's conventional defence in Central Europe to be that, in the face of aggression, it should destroy (or at least defend against) the first strategic echelon of the Warsaw Pact with the aim of delaying and weakening the follow-on forces until the reserves and reinforcements from the Western side, which have to be mobilised and transported to the combat area, can maintain a balance of forces sufficient to defend Western Europe over a longer period of time. The evaluation of the military balance of forces and the strategic situation as well as the military requirements for force planning should be based on this strategic plan and its operational implementation.

This shift in the strategic perspective could have several practical consequences. One of these may be an improvement in the quality of threat analyses. Perhaps in future there will be greater interest in developing insights into the potential and limitations of success for a conventional defence of Western Europe by means of a systematic gathering and analysis of all relevant data about the Eastern and Western force postures based on advanced wargaming, instead of assuming its hopelessness, illustrated by methodically simple numerical force comparisons which tell us very little. More appropriate evaluation procedures refined by operational analysis would presumably make available insights into the evaluation of the military strategic situation by the other side which would rest on a more secure foundation. Furthermore, it would yield indications of what measures would most effectively influence this evaluation of the situation in terms of a risk perception that would discourage the other side from initiating a war. Such an operational analysis of the data furnished by the intelligence services could also have highly desirable effects on the rationalisation of NATO's force and operational planning and contribute to a more realistic assessment of the military threat.

Western arms control policy would also no doubt benefit from a clear analysis of NATO's conventional requirements based on their role and operational needs and thus invested with real political weight, instead of the definition of the well-worn formula of "sufficient forces" without strict reference to a concept of military stability. It is, however, by no means certain that these positive consequences of a revised interpretation of strategy will occur. The suggested revision could remain confined to the thinking of military staffs and thus politically without effect on future budget decisions, procurement practice and negotiation guidelines.

It must be remembered that since the 1950s nearly all aspects of defence, *ie* objective, conditions and requirements of military operations in case of war, have been fundamentally eradicated from the security consciousness of the West German population. This eradication was an understandable political reflex in view of the fact that the Federal Republic can expect to be secure only if war is entirely prevented. Confronted with the conventional and nuclear offensive and destructive potential of the Soviet Union, it would be meaningless for this tiny, densely-populated and highly-industrialised country, which might be the potential battlefield, to seek security in the capability for a successful defence. The NATO doctrine of war prevention by total nuclear deterrence helped to defuse this dilemma. The integration of Bundeswehr units in NATO's structure of command required and permitted the delegation of operational military problems to the integrated staffs, which remain outside the immediate spheres of interest and influence of national politics.

Under these circumstances there was the gradual development of a studied amilitary, *ie* purely political, understanding of security policy. The interpretation of NATO strategy as a political means to avoid war by the threat of nuclear retaliation was portrayed positively in contrast to "war-fighting strategies", which were declared to be out-of-date in the nuclear age and were rejected because they cast some doubt on the effectiveness of the deterrent and because of their effect on the arms race. In the popular version of this argument, the mission of the Bundeswehr would be seen to have failed as soon as the first shot was fired.

Because this view of security policy has deep historical roots and, furthermore, a psychopolitically stabilising effect, it would require determined political leadership and good public relations to convince the West German population of the need for and the benefit of efforts to enhance NATO's conventional defence. However even the governing conservative-liberal coalition does not seem to be inclined to invest political capital in such an effort. On this subject it merely continues the policies of the previous government which had increased the defence budget in real terms and initiated a comprehensive modernisation programme for the armed forces. But a primary concern of its political rhetoric was to avoid a reaction in military terms to the evident erosion of the foundations of the German interpretation of NATO strategy as a purely political nuclear deterrent strategy and instead point primarily to the need and possibility of détente and arms control in Europe as a political strategy to secure the peace. As the political security guarantee based on deterrence was becoming increasingly problematic, it was to be superseded by another political strategy based on the relaxation of tension. It is true that the often quoted Harmel formula suggested that military measures for security and diplomatic efforts to achieve détente should be viewed as complementary but there was no consistent attempt publicly to defend, on political and military grounds, an adaptation of the defence mission and the conventional force requirement of NATO to the changed strategic boundary conditions. The objective of arms control policy did not seem to lie so much in achieving military stability by reducing the offensive capabilities on the basis of operational strategic criteria, but rather in altering the political motivation and interests of the other side to achieve higher political stability through confidence-building. The arms control process or dialogue, which was mostly understood in terms of a policy of détente, did not affect the separation of the new German security philosophy from operational military problems and requirements in any way, but rather gave it a new formulation and justification. The pattern of a dichotomy of a positively-viewed political and a negatively-viewed military understanding of security remained.

The significance of the regional nuclear force balance in Europe

Official German evaluation of the nuclear force balance in Europe has been characterised since the beginning of the 1960s by a dichotomous attitude toward the role of theatre nuclear forces (TNF) in NATO strategy. The deployment of these weapons systems and the planning of their possible use were regarded as vital for an effective nuclear deterrence. Nuclear battlefield systems were designed to exclude any possibility of the Soviet side considering a limited conventional aggression. NATO aircraft with continental range were likewise to exclude the rational possibility of a geographically limited nuclear war in Europe in which the territory of the Soviet Union would remain an invulnerable sanctuary. In short, TNF's were designed to remove any gaps in the spectrum of escalation between conventional defence and a general strategic nuclear war.

In the German view this function of TNF in the process of escalation did not require a balance of regional nuclear forces between the Warsaw Pact and NATO. The purpose of American nuclear weapons in Europe was merely the coupling of the regional defence with the US strategic nuclear forces which were considered to constitute the sole essential factor. From the strategic point of view there was, therefore, no reason to construct a nuclear balance of forces for TNF in Europe which would have to be artificially divorced from the entire strategic balance between East and West, or to assign to such a theoretical comparison any particular significance.

This position was also an expression of the German conviction that TNF must not be understood to be weapons of war-fighting. Their essential purpose did not lie in their military effect on the battlefield in the sense of tactical or operational objectives, but rather in their political effect in confronting the strategic risk calculus of the Soviet leadership with the real possibility of escalation. In this analysis it would in fact be damaging to try to establish a quantitatively and qualitatively optimal force structure of TNF based on operational war-fighting criteria. Such a policy could unwittingly signal to the opposite side a preparedness by NATO to limit a potential nuclear confrontation geographically and thus endanger the effect of extended strategic deterrence.

We shall not discuss in more detail the dilemmas of the German attitude to nuclear doctrine (especially with regard to the function of battlefield weapons, the intensive use of which would lead to self-destruction or the problem of escalation control). In effect, the Federal Republic was primarily interested in those elements of the TNF posture which supported and elucidated the concept of escalation and most of all that of strategic coupling. American proposals to develop a real nuclear war-fighting capability to compensate for the allegedly diminishing credibility of the coupling to Europe were categorically rejected. Like the approach to the political and strategic evaluation of the conventional force balance, NATO's weaknesses and disadvantages in a comparison of regional nuclear capabilities in

Europe on the basis of military operational criteria (target coverage, vulnerability etc) did not seem to diminish the effectiveness of overall deterrence, but instead to enhance it. From the Soviet point of view, the argument went, the probability of a strategic reaction by the American leadership must be greater if the flexibility for the successful conduct of a theatre nuclear war in Europe were reduced.

It is characteristic that the question of the regional nuclear force balance did not gain political significance in the Federal Republic until considerations and criteria based on the politics of arms control replaced this strategic approach. With the dual-track decision the question of which side had more medium-range systems of certain categories (plus their respective warheads) than the other suddenly became significant. Thus the concept of parity as the goal of negotiations became paramount, even though NATO's deployment decision involved, for the reasons given, a disparity, *ie* a smaller number of weapons (Pershing II and cruise missiles) than the expected growth in SS-20 deployments.

It is also characteristic that the chosen approach to arms control eventually led to the proposal of a "zero option", *ie* the renunciation of the modernisation of NATO's INF component which, especially from the German perspective, possessed a strategically critical significance with regard to the 'nexus of escalation'. The demand for numerical symmetry thus resulted in a willingness to put on the negotiation table a system which was of great structural significance for NATO's entire nuclear system.

As a result of the painful debate about the deployment of cruise and Pershing II, numerical notions of parity play a less significant role at present. Without causing any disquiet, NATO is reducing its TNF arsenal in Europe by about one third, while the Warsaw pact has increased its stock of nuclear-capable artillery and has modernised its quantitatively superior arsenal of TNF as a kind of "response" to NATO's response. By contrast the question of whether NATO will modernise its equivalent missiles of the Lance and Pershing Ia type is not clear.

The possible consequences of these developments for the nuclear options and the defence planning of NATO do not figure in the debate about defence policy in the Federal Republic. This can be explained by the fact that the existence of Soviet TNF nuclear options have always been ignored, because otherwise consideration would need to be given to the issue of nuclear war-fighting or of which nuclear operational capability NATO needs to maintain a credible deterrent. The German dogma, according to which nuclear weapons are generally political weapons, but under no circumstances war-fighting weapons, would come under pressure.

A further explanation may be, that the only purpose for which nuclear weapons now figure in the programmes of all German parties is their function as objects of the demand or hope for disarmament. Even Federal Government spokesmen argue in favour of an INF "zero option" – not on the grounds of military strategy with reference to the requirements of a valid Alliance doctrine but from the point of view of détente and the positive implications of such a result as indication for a fundamental change in Soviet *Westpolitik*.

In this political climate the judgement of one's own inferiority in the regional nuclear balance has the primary function of proving how far one's own side has already moved towards the desired dismantling of nuclear weapons in terms of unilateral positive steps. Force comparisons have the purpose of supporting the political demand of an equivalent reduction on the other side. Internally within the Alliance such numerical balances are designed to support the demand for an equitable distribution of the contingents which are to be dismantled over the countries in which they are deployed, in order to avoid the Federal Republic being "singled out". If the trend continues (without taking into account the nuclear capabilities essential for the implementation of NATO strategy in Europe), it would probably have to be rationalised officially on the basis that the implementation of the concepts of deliberate nuclear escalation would increasingly become the task of the national nuclear forces of the United States stationed outside Europe (assuming that such a justification would still be necessary). This fall-back position however should not conceal the risks which would arise with the erosion of the role of West European countries in NATO's system of nuclear-sharing.

The nuclear strategic balance

Even for the official German evaluation of the intercontinental force balance, operational aspects of first strike vulnerability, target coverage, the required employment options and so on, have never been very important. American controversies about the state of the strategic balance, which were fought over with complex models of counterforce nuclear exchanges, have not penetrated much into the defence and political consciousness of German governments. The view predominated that the American leadership knew best which nuclear strategic capabilities it would have to maintain against the USSR in order to fulfil its obligations to the Alliance. Specifically German criteria regarding the material prerequisites for securing an "extended strategic deterrence" under conditions of strategic nuclear parity (for example, the quantitative and qualitative aspects of the American capability to execute selected strategic options) have never been published. The strategic interest of German governments has been directed primarily to the declaratory and symbolic manifestation of the American will to be strategically coupled.

The fact that there is a contradiction between a strategically operational conception of stability, based on the possibility of actual employment of strategic nuclear weapons, and a political concept of stability which is directed towards non-usability – and that this contradiction is of central concern to NATO's nuclear doctrine – has mostly remained unmentioned in public discussion. The official reaction of the Federal Government to the codification of Soviet-American parity in SALT I and SALT II described it as a stabilising success of the policy of détente. In view of the size of the remaining arsenals, no adverse consequences for the effectiveness of the American protective umbrella for Western Europe were recognised. On the contrary, for many years there have been increasing admonitions from official quarters that the superpowers should engage in further nuclear disarmament in accordance with their obligations as a result of the Non-Proliferation Treaty.

Opposition views

It is not possible to make general statements about the numerous divergent streams in the political opposition on defence in the SPD, Green Party, Communists and other groupings in the peace movement. The specific differences between them are too great. However, a large proportion of these opposition groups can be excluded from this discussion: first, the orthodox Communists and any associated organisations, who take the view that peace will be enhanced if the strength of socialism (and hence socialist countries) increases, secondly, those (mostly supporters of the so-called non-dogmatic Left and pacifist religious people), who are fundamentally opposed to any military defence policy for the Federal Republic, who reject any military security thinking on principle as "deterrence thinking" and attempt to weaken and displace the strategy, armed forces and military integration of NATO by means of a new "peace culture".

The political effect of such views should not be underestimated. They find an echo in church organisations, determine the official line of the Greens and find support also within the SPD. But for an analysis of the debate about the military situation this "fundamental opposition" is of little interest because it rejects the goals, means and criteria for the evaluation of any military security policy as completely misguided.[3] As a result there is no serious consideration of the problems of the military balance of forces and the military-strategic posture of NATO and the Warsaw Pact in this political movement which has grown out of "critical peace research". Standards of the official military and arms control policy which are primarily based on the concepts of stability and equilibrium are dismissed as tactical means of the state which are allegedly used in an arbitrary manner to legitimise a continuation of the arms race, block genuine détente and disarmament and secure the domestic stability of conservative rule.

Positions within the SPD

The evolution of the positions within the SPD on security policy deserves particular attention for several reasons;

1. The leadership of the SPD is concerned on the one hand to distinguish itself from the "fundamental opposition" by maintaining elements of continuity with its previous policies as a party in government. It emphasises, for example, the usefulness of NATO membership, demands an increased Western European voice in the security policy of the Atlantic Alliance, relies on the instrument of arms control negotiations and insists on the need for military stability on the basis of an assured defence capability which can expose any potential aggressor to "an unacceptable military risk".[4] At the same time the SPD decisively rejects the current military strategy of NATO and demands that it should be fundamentally changed. It gives highest priority to disarmament efforts and takes as its point of departure a fundamental revision of the political and military basis of the established Western threat evaluation. The declared goal of this policy is to reduce the military confrontation in Europe, in a step-by-step process in co-operation with the Warsaw Pact countries and without risking destabilisation.
2. However one may view the analytical foundations and the inherent ambivalences of this political perspective of a "security partnership", or its risks or chances of success, it is remarkable insofar as it attempts to set constructive long-term political aims and military conditions of security into a systematic context.
3. This perspective may in certain circumstances offer the possibility of winning back support from parts, of the current fundamental opposition for a wider and more stable consensus in security policy.

It is, however, not surprising, that the present positions of the SPD on security policy have provoked criticism. They involve a far-reaching reorientation: as an opposition party the SPD has the advantage of being able to ignore the constraints of practical feasibility imposed on the government. It is also subject to the need to unite opposing trends within the Party and remain an electoral option for voters from more radical and more conservative sections of the electorate at the same time. In such circumstances one could not primarily expect logical coherence and linguistic precision; one would rather look for the design of an ideal security policy, which would promise to resolve all problems and contradictions.

Such a synthesis would of course require a certain degree of trust. But with some goodwill the public might, for example, indeed accept the paradoxical assurance that the denuclearisation of Europe would strengthen (instead of removing) the coupling of Western Europe to the strategic nuclear protection of the United States. One might, for example, also consider, that the decisions of the Essen SPD conference are also realistic. They envisage that modern conventional weapons systems can and should be substituted for nuclear weapons on the battlefield and for long-range interdiction.[5] On the other hand this option has been practically excluded by the decision of the Nuremberg party conference since it rejected all NATO's long-range conventional weapons systems because of their potentially destabilising, "offensive" characteristics. This obvious contradiction is resolved in a simple manner: the military task of the interdiction of follow-on echelons (as well as offensive counter air missions) are declared to be unnecessary. Conventional defence and fire support of NATO forces at short range are to be developed to such a degree of effectiveness, that any "deep strike" missions would no longer be required.[6].

The shift in SPD security policy

It is not possible to give a detailed account of how the security policy of the SPD evolved from its earlier positions until the late 1970s to its present rejection of the strategy of flexible response, and the now sacrosanct criteria of "structural inability to attack" and "security partnership" with the countries of the Warsaw Pact. Probably the most important factor was the conflict with American policy towards the Soviet Union, which began under Jimmy Carter and sharpened considerably under Ronald Reagan. Deep mistrust of American intentions was indicated by such assertions as:

— NATO arms procurement serves primarily an American strategy, to engage the Soviet Union in an arms race which is designed to bring about the political and economic collapse of the Soviet Union
— Under American influence, NATO's strategy is developing into an offensive war-fighting strategy; the development of offensive operations deep within East European territory is designed to prevent Soviet military involvements in the Third World by threatening "horizontal escalation".
— The deployment of American medium-range missiles in Europe, in particular Pershing II, serves to threaten the political and military leadership of the Soviet Union with "decapitation" and at the same time prevent a possible nuclear counterstrike on the continental United States, thus limiting nuclear war to Europe.
— The thesis of an alleged orientation of NATO towards a first

strike with the intention of disarming the opponent in turn supports the assertion that in a crisis the Soviet Union would be forced to seek to destroy the American medium-range weapons in Europe, which constitute a critical threat to the Soviet Union, by means of a pre-emptive nuclear strike. The consequence of this is that NATO strategy in Europe endangers crisis stability, that is, it constitutes a factor which could actively lead to the outbreak of war. The use of nuclear weapons would be virtually automatic and, as a result, as if drawn by a magnet, massive Soviet nuclear strikes would fall on the territory of the Federal Republic.

— This alarming scenario was supplemented by the assertion, that NATO was engaged in "conventionalising" and "militarising" nuclear weapons, *ie* eliminating the threshold between conventional and nuclear warfare – again as a result of American influence. The release and use of nuclear battlefield weapons would thus no longer be under political but under military control. Military commanders would be under pressure to use the weapons because of their short range and hence (alleged) high vulnerability ("use them or lose them"). Faced with this situation both superpowers would (in their own national interests) endeavour to limit nuclear warfare to the European theatre.

Without discussing the controversies about neutron weapons, PD 59, the NATO dual-track decision, "horizontal escalation", the Air Land Battle doctrine and the FOFA concept,[7] which are relevant in this context, I would simply wish to point out that this overdramatic critique is mostly misleading and unjustified. It misrepresents fundamentally the determinative political and military boundary conditions of NATO strategy and operational planning. It also ignores the existing military balance of forces and its strategic consequences. Furthermore, it does not engage in a realistic analysis of American strategic interests and actual American behaviour within the Alliance.

As a result of political zeal and calculations this extreme form of strategic critique has been endorsed by the leadership of the SPD, despite its obvious contradictions and factual inaccuracies. Thus, for example, the following erroneous views have found currency in the SPD:

— Western insistence on an "offensive" force posture is the main cause of the stagnation of arms control efforts in the framework of MBFR; the strategy of "flexible response" requires a continuous arms race and results in a growing stockpile of new and increasingly dangerous nuclear weapons in Europe; furthermore, NATO strategy, with its dependence on the early use of nuclear weapons, could provoke the pre-emptive use of nuclear weapons by the Soviets during a crisis or a limited conventional confrontation; it is therefore extremely destabilising and endangers successful crisis management.

The fact that these easily-refuted assertions were adopted by the SPD without much opposition was to a significant extent the consequence of political rivalry between the "government wing" in the Cabinet and Parliament and the Party leadership "in the barracks". The latter consistently cut itself off from military and military-political expertise in the ministries and the Bundeswehr and based itself instead on academic "opposition experts" from the peace research institutes and the developing peace movement.

The currently significant emphasis on the preconceptions of security policy and military strategy and guiding principles of the SPD still reflect this background of the role of the strategic debate in foreign and domestic policy in the late 1970s and early 1980s. They can only be satisfactorily explained if account is taken of the exaggerations as well as the one-sided and polemical simplifications which accompanied the politicization of the debate at the time. This relates in particular to the astonishing radical nature of the alternative concepts demanded by the SPD compared to the security and defence policies of the West as conducted hitherto. The same applies to the "fundamental opposition" to American policy which is considered to be a most dangerous threat to peace. It is to be countered by the "self-assertion of Europe" (whereby the differing views of the French and British governments are discreetly ignored). It also applies to the SPD emphasis on "German national interests" for its rejection of NATO strategy (and ironically especially for its critique of those elements of the doctrine of flexible response which were strongly influenced by earlier German governments, including in particular those led by the SPD). The notion that NATO strategy increases the danger of an unwanted war in Europe, that it could be perceived in the East as an offensive threat and fuels the arms race can only be understood as arising from the politicisation of the debate at the time. But such assessments shape the actual demands by the SPD to restructure and equip NATO forces in an unmistakably defensive manner and limit them to an exclusively conventional defence.

The SPD and its security policy principles

The debate among security policy experts in the SPD is characterised above all by the enumeration of guiding principles for a security policy designed to produce stability.[8] Interesting and convincing as these guiding principles may be in themselves, it has so far not been possible to translate them into guidelines for political practice or combine them into a practicable strategy. The conflicts between objectives and means inherent in the criteria developed by the guiding principles would have to be analytically worked through and political decisions taken as a result. This task has so far not been seriously undertaken. The inter-relationship between the various principles and guidelines and the degree of priority assigned to them remains largely unclarified. The practical consequences of this conceptual vagueness can be illustrated by the following example.

At its conference in Nuremberg in 1986 the SPD established the following as one of the criteria of a NATO strategy of war prevention:

> The structure and equipment of the armed forces must result in a credible capability to engage in forward defence; this means that the armed forces must confront any potential aggressor with an unacceptable military risk.[9]

The force requirements, which result from the implementation of this criterion were defined in the following terms:

> The peacetime strength [of the Bundeswehr] must enable coverage near the border, which effectively protects against surprise attacks or prevents *faits accomplis*; it must be sufficient to secure the reinforcement by Allied armed forces.[10]

If one takes these tasks for forward defence seriously, the existing NATO forces would undoubtedly have to be strengthened and improved to be able to respond to surprise attack and sustain its position. However, the SPD conference decided, in stark contrast to these requirements,

— to reduce large parts of the armed forces to cadres
— to reject the extension of the period of military service
— to reject the recruitment of women for the Bundeswehr
— to reduce the defence budget
— to cancel the agreement with the United States about wartime host nation support of American reinforcements.[11]

What is not clear so far are the additional restrictions which might result for force and operational planning from the implementation of the following criterion:

> The Alliance must take into account the political and military concerns of our Eastern neighbours. It must therefore demonstrate in a particular way the defensive character of its strategy by its emphasis on the defence near the border.[12]

If one also considers the SPD demand to make conscientious objection to military service easier, its negative view of any measures of civil defence or other areas of emergency planning, the questions must be asked: how much significance is attached to the postulated conventional stability and the unacceptability of military risk with which a potential aggressor is to be confronted *in practice*? There is no doubt; however, that the SPD conference decisions can be easily justified by further guiding principles and criteria of social democratic security policy. According to the Nuremberg conference, for example, NATO forces should be evaluated according to the "principle of sufficiency" and offer no incentive to the arms race. It is also stated that within a strategic situation "generally perceived to be stable . . . partial superiorities and inferiorities" could be tolerated. Furthermore the costs of defence must not place excessive demands on the social and economic resources of Alliance members and must not undermine social and economic stability.

SPD evaluations of the military balance and the military strategic situation

The fact that the security debate within the SPD centres more on a general programme than specific measures facilitates the avoidance of controversial commitment for the present by emphasising future expectations and general postulations. Of particular significance are prognoses which foresee major breakthroughs in European arms control as well as a major increase in the efficiency of Western defence.

With regard to expectations for arms control, there is a discernible tendency in the SPD, as a result of wholesale rejection of the "arms race", to ignore defence political alternatives to progress in arms control. Thus SPD spokesmen have rejected the development of a Western air defence system with ATM/ATBM capabilities on the basis of the argument that security cannot be gained by technical means and rearmament, but only politically, by negotiating away the threat. The other side of the coin is that far-reaching concessions in disarmament have to be required not only of the West, but also of the Soviet leadership. Thus for example it is demanded, that the Soviet Union should renounce its offensive strategy in Europe and transform its armed forces according to the principles of "structural inability to attack". Already during the most intensive phase of the controversy about the dual-track decision it could be seen that within the SPD and the peace movement the dangers of war and visions of nuclear holocaust were proclaimed most vociferously by those opposition experts and politicians who consistently denied the possibility of a calculated aggression by the Soviet Union. They saw the cause of war not so much in political developments as in the mechanics of the nuclear weapons build-up, possible technical failures and the loss of political control as a result of the predomination of military logic and require-ments in times of crisis, which could, for example, arise through out-of-area conflicts of the superpowers and spill over into the European arena. The responsibility for both risk factors were primarily assigned to the sharpened American policy of "neo-containment", the "new

American strategies" and the allegedly negative effects of NATO strategy. One might therefore say that the source of threat was now perceived as coming from the opposite direction.

The tendency in the SPD, to distance itself fundamentally from military-strategic criteria and perspectives of security policy by insisting on the "primacy of politics" and the need for a "realistic threat analysis" may turn the political demand for conventional stability and effective defence into an empty formula. Military strategy necessarily orientates itself according to the hypothetical case of conflict. It has to deal with the question of how the armed forces could and would operationally carry out their politically defined task against the military forces and options of the other side. If, as is currently the case in the SPD, this very question is discredited as alleged military worst case thinking and the military analysis of the situation is placed in opposition to the political analysis instead of treating the former as an integral part of the latter, security policy will lose its orientation with regard to the military situation. As a result the defence and arms control policies of the Federal Republic would then be conducted exclusively on the basis of diplomatic or domestic usefulness or opportunities, without regard to the military balance of forces or defence requirements. However, it should be noted that this development in the thinking of the SPD about security policy represents an extreme manifestation of the traditional West German attitude to security issues, ie the repression of the question concerning military operational prerequisites of a stable forward defence and credible nuclear deterrence from public consciousness.

Particularly well-known proponents of the "realistic threat analysis" demanded by the SPD are Christian Krause of the Friedrich Ebert Foundation and the Bundestag member Andreas von Bülow.[13] Both make no bones about the political motives for their attempts to correct the analysis of the military balance currently prevailing in NATO. Both conduct their arguments on the basis of political assumptions about the foreign and military policy interests and goals of the Soviet Union and other Warsaw Pact countries, which in the long term imply little inclination to get involved in conflict and thus a corresponding unwillingness by the Soviet Union to take risks. As a result it is relatively easy for NATO to confront any aggressor with an "unacceptable risk". It would be able to do this even from a position of unambiguous strategic inferiority. However, the proponents of this analysis do not believe that such a situation is currently prevailing. Indeed, they believe that the effectiveness of nuclear deterrence is given so long as NATO possesses any kind of nuclear potential, no matter how small, which by "demonstrating" NATO's willingness to use nuclear weapons could effect the escalation to the strategic level, as long as the second strike capability of the United States *vis-à-vis* the Soviet Union remains beyond doubt.

Thus the SPD extends the line of thinking in the official German understanding to its logical extreme, according to which nuclear weapons, as "political weapons", should be limited to the function of demonstrating to the Soviet Union the risk of a general nuclear war. The United States is expected to continue to protect Western Europe by threatening "massive retaliation" against the Soviet Union on the basis of an assured "minimum deterrent".

However, issues of nuclear strategy play merely a subsidiary role in the alternative threat analyses presented by Krause and von Bülow. Their prime interest lies in refuting the thesis of a Warsaw Pact conventional superiority over NATO. In this way it is to be shown that the alleged dependence of Western strategy on the concept of nuclear first use and deliberate escalation is a fiction. Thus the most important obstacle to the path of nuclear disarmament would be removed. In Krause's words:

> The self-deception as regards the conventional superiority of the Warsaw Pact is one of the greatest obstacles on the path to a change in thinking about security policy. Criticism of NATO's threat analysis is therefore not a matter of wanting to be right, but rather a political necessity.[14]

We cannot at this point discuss in detail the data, scenarios and analyses with which von Bülow and Krause support their thesis that there exists a stable conventional equilibrium between the Warsaw Pact in NATO; a detailed critique can be found elsewhere.[15] Suffice it to say that both fail to present adequate documentation of the present force posture. They also systematically ignore the qualitative and structural improvements of Soviet land and air forces which have taken place since the early 1970s and confront NATO with new critical problems of defence. The result is essentially prejudged by their assumptions that:

— the non-Soviet Warsaw Pact forces are generally considered unreliable and therefore little (if any) account is taken of them in the military balance;
— the 33 Soviet divisions of the second strategic echelon in the western military districts which have to be mobilised and excluded from the balance of forces in Western Europe;
— numerical troop strength is treated as the ultimately decisive factor of combat strength;
— "Western divisions" are assigned greater combat strength than "Eastern divisions" (without taking into account the considerable differences between them);
— the equipment and weapons of Western forces are deemed to be generally qualitatively superior;
— the extraordinary difficulties which face the implementation of the NATO concept of forward defence as a result of the growing

capability of Warsaw Pact forces to launch an attack without prior reinforcements are ignored.

Conclusion

In general, there is a discernible trend of increasing conceptual incoherence in the security policy of the Federal Republic. A combination of factors, constraints and utilitarian arguments would lead one to believe that Bonn's role in critical decision-making with regard to NATO's military policy will decline in future. Such relative passivity in the military arena may, however, be accompanied by increased activity in putting pressure on the Alliance in arms control negotiations, since only by easing the political burden of the security relationship with the Soviet Union could the pressure on the Federal Government resulting from the conflicts between domestic and foreign policy goals of security policy in West Germany be reduced. How critical these developments will prove to be will depend on the extent to which those observers who believe the Soviet Union is already on the way to a real "security partnership" in Europe, or those who interpret the foreign policy dimension of Gorbachev's new political thinking as an instrument in the service of old ambitions of power politics, turn out to be correct.

Notes

1. For a more detailed discussion see the contribution by Angelika Volle in this volume.
2. See Studiengruppe Militärpolitik (eds.), *Aufrüsten um Abzurüsten? Informationen zur Lage. Friedensforscher reagieren auf die internationale Krise* (Reinbek 1980); Horst Afheldt, *Defensive Verteidigung* (Reinbek 1983); Dieter S. Lutz, *Weltkrieg wider Willen?* Die Nuklearwaffen in und für Europa, (Reinbek 1981); Ulrich Albrecht, *Kündigt den Nachrüstungsbeschluss*, Frankfurt 1981; Wilhelm Bittorf (ed.), *Nachrüstung, Der Atomkrieg rückt näher*, (Reinbek 1981).
3. With regard to the controversy between representatives of the SPD and the Greens on this issue, see Torsten Lange *et al.*, "Einseitige Abrüstung ist kein Selbstzweck, über mögliche Gemeinsamkeiten in der Friedens- und Sicherheitspolitik von SPD und Grünen, Eine Replik auf Karsten D. Voigt", in *Frankfurter Rundschau*, 25 August 1986, p. 14; Karsten D. Voigt, "SPD-Reformen und Grüner Fundi-Anspruch", *Vorwärts*, No. 1, 3 January 1987, pp. 30–31. Deeper insight into the view of the Greens can be found in Volker Böge *et al.*, *Angriff als Verteidigungs – AirLand Battle, AirLand Battle 2000, Rogers-Plan, Bonn/Hamburg* 1984; Böge *et al.*, *Euro-militarismus. Zur Bedeutung der "Europäisierung der Sicherheitspolitik"*, Köln/Bonn, 1985. An influential earlier work is Komitee für Grundrechte und Demokratie (eds.), *Frieden mit anderen Waffen, fünf Vorschläge zu einer alternativen Sicherheitspolitik* (Reinbek 1981).
4. Resolution of the Nuremberg SPD Party Conference 1986 on peace and security policy. See *Parteitag der SPD in Nürnberg*, 25–29, 8, 1986. Übersicht über die Beschlüsse des Parteitags in Nürnberg, Part 7, Paragraph IV 4 (published by the SPD Party Executive Bonn).

5. Resolutions of the Essen Party Conference of the SPD about peace policy, in *Politik – Aktuelle Informationen der SPD*, No. 5, June 1984, Paragraph VII.7.

6. This assertion is remarkable as only a few years ago two influential authors from the SPD, Christian Krause and Andreas von Bülow emphasised in their analyses of the threat NATO's alleged capability of an effective interdiction of the second strategic echelon of the Warsaw Pact forces. This assertion served to support the thesis, that the more than 30 Soviet divisions in the Western military districts of the USSR were of no significance for the situation in Central Europe, thus leading to the conclusion that with regard to a regional conventional force comparison NATO was even enjoying a superiority over the Warsaw Pact! See Christian Krause, *Vom militärischen Kräftevergleich zur sicherheitspolitischen Lagebeurteilung*. Forschungsinstitut der Friedrich-Ebert-Stiftung, May 1981, p. 21 f.; also Krause, "Plus/Minus dreiundreissig Divisionen, Stimmt der militärische Kräftevergleich?", *Die neue Gessellschaft*, No. 11, 1982, pp. 1076–1081; Andreas von Bülow, *Alpträume West gegen Alpträume Ost. Ein Beitrag zur Bedrohungsanalyse*, Bonn (SPD Party Executive, Press and Information Department) 1985, p.21.

7. See K.-Peter Stratmann, *Modernisierung und Dislozierung nuklearer Waffen in Europa. Mögliche Funktionen vereinbarter Beschränkungen bei der Stabilisierung der Abschreckung*, Ebenhausen (SWP-AP 2337), September 1982. A shortened version was published as chapter 15 in Uwe Nerlich (ed.), *Soviet Power and Western Negotiating Policies*, Vol. 2 [The Western Panacea. Constraining Soviet Power through Negotiation], Cambridge, MA, 1983; K.-Peter Stratmann, "Zur politischen Bewertung des nuklearen Kräfteverhältnisses, in Erhard Forndran", Gert Krell (eds.), *Kernwaffen im Ost-West Vergleich. Zur Beurteilung militärischer Potentialte und Fähigkeiten*, Baden-Baden 1984; Stratmann, " 'AirLand Battle' – Zerrbild und Wirklichkeit", *APZ*, B 48/1984, 1 December 1984, pp. 19–30; see also "Kommentar und Replik", *APZ*, B 7-8, 1985, 16 February 1985, pp. 33–37; Stratmann, "Gefährdung westlicher Sicherheit, Entwicklungsperspektiven der NATO und Aspekte der deutsch-amerikanischen Sicherheitsbeziehung", in Uwe Nerlich, James A. Thomson (eds.). *The Soviet Problem in American-German Relations*, New York 1985, pp. 273–305.

8. For a general survey see Franz U. Borkenhagen. "Aspekte der sicherheitspolitischen Diskussion in der Bundesrepublik Deutschland. Aus dem Blickpunkt der SPD", *Österreichische Militärische Zeitschrift*, No. 2, 1987, pp. 138–145; also Borkenhagen, "Kriterien für einen militärischen Strategie- und Strukturwandel", APZ, B 43/1986, 25 October 1986, p. 15–24.

9. See Note 4.

10. *ibid.*, Paragraph VI 2.

11. *ibid.*, Paragraph VI 3, 4, 6, Paragraph VII.

12. *ibid.*, Paragraph IV 9.

13. See especially Christian Krause, *Vom militärischen Kräftevergleich zur sicherheitspolitischen Lagebeurteilung, op. cit.*; Krause, Plus/Minus dreiundreissig Divisionen, *op. cit.* Krause, "Konventionelle überlegenheit als Argument der Sicherheitspolitik"; *Neue Gesellschaft/Frankfurter Hefte*, No. 7, 1986, pp. 627–629; Andreas von Bülow, *Alpträume West gegen Alpträume Ost, op. cit.*

14. Krause, "Konventionelle Überlegenheit", *op. cit.*, p. 629.

15. See Hans-Joachim Schmidt, *Alpträume über Alpträume – Stellungnahme, Zur Studie von Andreas von Bülow: Alpträume West gegen Alpträume Ost. Ein Beitrag zur Bedrohungsanalyse*, Hessische Stiftung für Friedens- und Konfliktforschung: Frankfurt, March 1986; K. Peter Stratmann, *Anmerkungen zu Andreas von Bülow, Alpträume West gegen Alpträume Ost – Ein Beitrag zur Bedrohungsanalyse*, Ebenhausen (SWP-LN 2445), August 1985, reprinted in *Frankfurter Rundschau*, 12 and 14 October 1985 p. 10 and 10 f.; Klaus Arnhold, *Zur Problematik eines Vergleichs der konventionellen Landstreitkräfte von NATO und Warschauer Pakt in Europa, Kritische Anmerkungen zu einer Studie der Friedrich-Ebert-Stiftung*, Ebenhausen (SWP-AP 2372), September 1983.

Chapter 6

Conventional and Nuclear Forces and their Interaction in the Defence of Europe

FRANZ-JOSEPH SCHULZE

The principal objective: prevention of war

The principal objective of the Alliance is the prevention of war, conventional as well as nuclear war. One cannot be deemed more important than the other. It is often stated that even a conventional war would nowadays, given the enormous destructive capability of modern conventional weapons, cause untold casualties to one's own population which would approach the scale expected in a nuclear war. This argument, however, blurs the fundamental qualitative change in a war brought about by the use of any nuclear weapon. It also ignores the fact that the development of conventional weapons systems in recent decades has led to increasing accuracy. This results not merely in a reduction of the necessary scale of destructive capability, but allows also – in contrast to the area bombardments of World War II – the discrimination between combatants and non-combatants.

There cannot be a preference between preventing a nuclear rather than a conventional war, for one main reason: the probability of a nuclear war would rise considerably if any armed conflict was to break out between nuclear powers. Of all conceivable causes of a nuclear war – technical malfunctions, errors, miscalculation – the most probable is a conventional war between nuclear powers. The decisive threshold is not between conventional and nuclear war, but between war and no war.

The efforts of the Alliance to reduce political tensions and engage in arms control are one means of this war prevention policy; a secure defence capability and political solidarity are, in the words of the 1967 Harmel Report, "the necessary prerequisites for an effective policy directed at greater relaxation of tension".

Deterrence as a means of securing peace

The strategic means of securing peace is deterrence. It is designed to indicate to a potential attacker that the possible gains that could result from the use of violence bear no relation to the risks incurred. It therefore depends on the perception and evaluation by a potential aggressor of the defender's capability and determination to defend. The effectiveness of this concept of deterrence depends on three conditions being met:

1. The political determination of all member states, to resist all aggression collectively by the use of force or the threat of its use;
2. the availability of balanced, sufficiently strong and immediately deployable armed forces, which could be strengthened rapidly by mobilisation and reinforcements from overseas.
3. The possibility, to choose between the various available military options in such a way, that NATO's reaction and thus the aggressor's risks remain incalculable.[1]

At stake is not only the deterrence of war. The enormous efforts of the Soviet Union to build up its military potential across the board does not imply that it is planning to launch an attack across our borders. Superior military power achieves its political effect in a much more subtle manner.

In the Soviets' view, their military potential is one of the principal tools of Soviet foreign policy, whose purpose in peacetime is to underline political demands by the mere demonstration of superior force.

Superior military force is designed to undermine the confidence of the people of the Atlantic Alliance in both the character and the adequacy of their own defence. The lack of confidence in the capability to defend paralyses political will and the determination of those in government in times of crisis. European history is full of examples when nations, out of fear of a more powerful neighbour, and out of a real or even merely imagined inability to defend themselves, have sought to seek their salvation in a preventive display of good behaviour towards the threatening neighbour and a policy of increasing appeasement.

The military potential of the Alliance must therefore be such that it strengthens or restores the confidence of those in government and their populations in the capability to deter or defend. Deterrence of a potential aggressor and the preservation of the confidence of one's own population in the capability of defence are equally important goals of security policy. The military planning of the Alliance must therefore be directed towards both objectives.[2]

Deterrence is credible only if it is backed by a visible capability and by an unmistakable determination to defend one's freedom and independence. Whoever subordinates the preservation of freedom to the maintenance of peace destroys the effectiveness of deterrence.

Deterrence presupposes that the defender is prepared to fight. It must always be geared towards war-fighting in order to be an effective means of war-prevention. The distinction that is frequently made between "deterrent capability" and "war-fighting capability" is misleading. It is true, however, that the aspects of deterrence and war-fighting can at times result in different conclusions with regard to operational planning.

But there are no weapons that exclusively serve deterrence, no "exclusively political weapons". Military force as a whole and in all its parts is a political instrument. It is the unalterable paradox of a deterrent strategy that the determination to use any weapon, up to and including nuclear weapons, has to be made credible in order to prevent any war, and not only nuclear war.

Collective defence

One of the central elements of deterrence and defence in Europe is the principle of collective defence. The deployment of land and air forces from six different nations in the Federal Republic of Germany and their command structure are a convincing expression of this principle.

The deployment pattern of the eight army corps is chosen in such a manner that every corps has formations of other allied nations as its neighbours. Behind this "layer-cake" of the army corps, air defence units of different nations are deployed in two belts. This deployment structure ensures that any attack against the allied forces in the Central Front will always be met immediately by forces of several nations. It makes it impossible for the aggressor to direct this attack in such a way that only the forces of selected nations would be affected.

The North Atlantic Treaty involves no automatic commitment to come to the aid of a member state subject to external aggression. The stationing of allied troops on German soil, their deployment and command structure ensure, however, the immediate collective reaction against aggression. This guarantees an optimum of deterrence. If deterrence, *ie* the prevention of war, is the foremost task of the Alliance, this deployment and command structure have to be maintained, even if other solutions might seem to be more attractive to some military planners.

Forward defence

Forward defence is a corollary of collective security. For the Federal Republic of Germany it was and remains an essential precondition of a German contribution to collective defence. How could there be a will to defend and resist aggression if the strategic concept of the Alliance is based on giving up German territory and its population with the objective of wearing out the attacking forces or of winning time for later counter-attacks to restore territorial integrity?

This is true not only for the Federal Republic of Germany, but in the same way for all its European neighbours. Nobody should maintain the hope of being able to mount a determined defence on the Rhine after the attacking armies have succeeded in penetrating deep into West Germany. It must be the objective of the defence to thwart the opponent's plan of attack at its most vulnerable point, *ie* before the attack has gathered momentum.

Determined and forceful forward defence is at the same time an essential element of deterrence. Only if the opponent has to reckon with determined opposition right from the beginning, denying him the rapid seizure of strategically important objectives, like the North Sea and Channel ports, will the defender achieve a deterrent effect. "Area defence" concepts, aimed at wearing the aggressor down within one's own territory, which imply a willingness to sacrifice one's own territory and population, are not very likely to convince the attacker of one's own determination to defend, and thus to deter.

Forward defence cannot be a static defence, and we should not try to make it that. There is no lack of proposals for the erection of field fortifications, barrier-lines along which to slow the enemy down; even continuous border fortifications along the German border have been discussed. Such proposals engender a Maginot line philosophy. They bind forces. They lead to the loss of tactical and operational mobility. Forward defence does, however, demand a maximum of agility and initiative down to the lowest levels of command.

The NATO triad

Nuclear weapons are an indispensable element of deterrence. In peace and war they have the greatest deterrent effect. Their enormous destructive potential confronts every attacker with the risk of self-annihilation. The longest period of peace in European history would have been unthinkable without the war-preventing effect of nuclear weapons. The destructive potential of these weapons has forced the political leaders of the nuclear weapons states to engage in careful first evaluations to an extent hitherto unknown.[3]

The loss of the nuclear component of our deterrent potential, even in the form of a renunciation of the first use of nuclear weapons by NATO, would increase the probability of conventional war. The attacker's forces would no longer face the danger of the nuclear weapons of the defender and his conventional superiority could be fully brought to bear. The defender would even be confronted by a completely different conventional threat, since not only could the attacking divisions (which would no longer be forced to disperse as widely on the battlefield) concentrate at any time and place to achieve a massive breakthrough, but also the follow-on echelons could be maintained at a relatively close distance to exploit the successes of the first attacking echelon rapidly and decisively.[4]

The Soviet Union itself would be relieved of any existential risk. Its own territory would not be endangered in any way. With the removal of this risk, however, the so far effective obstacle to the Soviets' use of military force to secure their political goals in Europe would be removed.

The backbone of deterrence is the close and indissoluble linkage between conventional and nuclear forces on the continent of Europe with the intercontinental nuclear potential of the United States. The coupling of these three elements of the NATO triad confronts the Soviet Union with an incalculable risk that any military conflict between the two alliances could escalate to a large-scale nuclear exchange.

The NATO "dual-track" decision and the subsequent stationing of long-range theatre nuclear forces was based on the realisation that in the age of strategic nuclear parity the imbalances within this triad, that is, the gaps and weaknesses of the nuclear weapons stationed in Europe, have gained greater importance. It was the argument of a closer coupling of the components of the NATO triad which played a central part in the NATO decision of December 1979. The deployment of long-range theatre nuclear forces (LRTNF) has indeed coupled NATO's conventional and nuclear forces on the continent of Europe more closely than ever before with the strategic arsenal of the United States.

Some aspects of the public discussion in the West could lead the Soviets to miscalculate dangerously. On the other hand, however the Soviet leadership assesses the likelihood of a first use of nuclear weapons by NATO, the deployment of long-range theatre nuclear weapons capable of reaching the Soviet Union itself from that territory against which their attack is directed, makes the risks incurred by such an attack obvious.

There is no doubt that by deploying these weapon systems the United States has accepted new risks regarding a direct Soviet retaliation against American territory, and it has done so in the interests of European security and at the urging of Europeans. "Extended deterrence" embodies the principle of the strategic unity of the territory of the Alliance.

The arms control perspectives of the summit at Reykjavik and in particular the "zero option" have raised a number of serious questions for the Alliance with regard to the future significance of the nuclear component of its deterrence posture.

The deterrent link between conventional and nuclear forces in Europe and the strategic nuclear arsenal of the United States would be weakened if all long-range theatre nuclear forces were withdrawn. A new gap would be created between the remaining American short-range nuclear weapons and the strategic arsenal of the United States. In the words of the then Supreme Allied Commander Europe, General B. Rogers, "to confine arms reduction to medium-range weapons throws us back to the year 1977".[5]

Professor Karl Kaiser, in his lecture on the occasion of receiving the 1986 Atlantic Award, stated quite correctly that the complete withdrawal of Pershing II and Cruise missiles, ie those weapons which can reach Soviet territory, would significantly influence Soviet risk calculations with regard to an attack on Western Europe. "The dual-track decision was passed on the principle that an attacker cannot be deterred by risks for his Allies, but only by risks to his own territory."[6] Whatever the shape of all the alternative solutions currently being discussed which are designed to ensure that the Alliance retains the capability to reach Soviet territory in case of a Soviet attack on Europe, they can hardly have the same deterrent effect as weapons stationed on the territory under attack.

The nuclear threat against the Federal Republic of Germany would remain unaffected by the implementation of the "zero option". All important targets currently covered by the SS20 can, after their withdrawal, be reached by Soviet short-range missiles which are not matched by any systems currently deployed by NATO. The almost complete superiority of the Warsaw Pact in this area would substantially reduce the flexibility of a NATO response.[7] Hopes for the elimination of this imbalance, be it by one-sided Soviet concessions in negotiations or by additional NATO deployments up to agreed ceilings, are not supported by historical experience.

Strengthening conventional forces

With regard to the conventional component of the NATO triad, corrective measures are more urgent than ever. The Warsaw Pact has always enjoyed a considerable conventional superiority over the North Atlantic Alliance. This superiority has been subject to continuous quantitative, and in recent times also increasingly qualitative, improvement. The arms build-up of the Warsaw Pact since the mid-1960s has exhibited with increasing clarity its offensive character and the intention to achieve the capability of a short-warning attack.[8]

The build-up of the Warsaw Pact's military posture is designed increasingly to reduce NATO's capabilities to respond, and thus to rob NATO's strategy of flexible response of its central element, namely that of flexibility. Thus the Soviet Union is acquiring in increasing measure not merely new military options, but, as NATO's military ability to react decreases, new possibilities of achieving its political goals.

The North Atlantic Alliance must regain a position where it can implement its strategic concept. Stronger conventional forces are the *sine qua non* of flexibility in the response of the Alliance.

With regard to this question, there seems to be a wide-ranging consensus within the Alliance. But despite a whole series of special efforts undertaken by the Alliance in the 1970s to improve its conventional capabilities, General B. Rogers, when Supreme Allied Commander Europe, concluded: "Although Allied Forces in Europe increase their capabilities every year, the gap between the conventional potential of NATO and the Warsaw Pact increase every year."[9] He warned member states again and again that "the conventional strength of NATO is today clearly insufficient to meet the growing conventional threat by the Warsaw Pact", and that this insufficiency could create a situation in which we might have to rely on a very early use of nuclear weapons for our defence.

We have to ask ourselves whether this dependence on an early use of nuclear weapons contributes to the undermining of the dual goal of the Alliance of credible deterrence and the preservation of the self-confidence of our peoples. Only a strong conventional capability can restore people's trust in the adequacy and the character of their defence. It should therefore be a matter of high political priority for our countries to reduce the dependence on the first use and in particular early first use of nuclear weapons.[10]

Deliberate escalation

The objective should be to reduce NATO's present dependence on the early use of nuclear weapons and not "raising the nuclear threshold", even though these terms are often used synonymously. An essential element of the current military strategic concept of flexible response is deliberate escalation. This means the carefully considered, intentional escalation of a conflict onto another level of intensity. It is designed to signal to the attacker that continued aggression will pose an existential risk to himself. In the interest of terminating the conflict quickly, the defender has to keep open the possibility of confronting the aggressor with this risk a very early stage. The notion of raising the nuclear threshold could be interpreted by a potential aggressor as the intention of the defender to keep the conflict under all circumstances on the conventional level. This would endanger the effective deterrent link between conventional and nuclear forces.

Undermining NATO's nuclear options has a high priority in Soviet efforts to reduce the effectiveness of the strategy of "flexible response". Experts estimate that the Soviet Union might be capable of providing a missile defence against the short- and medium-range missiles already in the 1990s. Deployment of such a defensive system would have grave consequences for NATO's strategy of "flexible response". One of its central elements would be more or less neutralised, depending on the effectiveness of the Soviet defensive system. The constraint or even neutralisation of the selective strike option for NATO's long-range theatre nuclear missiles, ie the Pershing II and Cruise missiles, would impose particular restraints on NATO, since they are uniquely suited to demonstrate to the Soviets that their territory will not remain a sanctuary. However, NATO's selective strike options would be neutralised far more effectively by the withdrawal of its long-range theatre nuclear forces than by Soviet missile defence systems.

The conventionalisation of deterrence?

As long as nuclear weapons exist, it is not possible to replace nuclear by conventional deterrence. The history of mankind is one single story of futile attempts to provide conventional deterrence. Furthermore, efforts to establish conventional balance between NATO and the Warsaw Pact would face insurmountable political, economic and human obstacles. The demographic developments in all member states of the Alliance alone make the notion of a possible quantitative increase in armed forces purely illusory. On the other hand, the hope of achieving a conventional balance in Europe by means of arms control agreement becomes the less realistic the more the other side gains the impression that the nations of the Western Alliance lack the strength to implement effective measures for improving their conventional forces.

NATO does not need to match the Warsaw Pact plane by plane, tank by tank or artillery piece by artillery piece. What is needed is the conventional capability to deny the Warsaw Pact those operational options on which the Pact bases its confidence of a rapid success, which is demanded by its strategic doctrine and to which its operational concepts have been adapted.[11]

NATO can strengthen its conventional forces considerably by making better use of its technological superiority and by employing modern technologies for certain key tasks.[12] Its technological superiority is always praised. Unfortunately, it often does not go beyond the research laboratories and development centres, while the Soviet Union has deployed new weapons systems with increasing frequency. Results emerging from SDI research could make a substantial contribution to the rapid development and deployment of modern conventional systems.

Attack with little preparation

Should the Soviet Union ever decide to seek a military solution to the conflict with Western free societies, the objective of Soviet strategy would be the rapid defeat of NATO in a short conventional *blitzkrieg* with the maximum exploitation of surprise.[13]

One of the most serious consequences of the quantitative and qualitative improvements of the Warsaw Pact armed forces lies in their growing capability to mount an attack with little preparation, *ie* with short warning-time for NATO. The offensive capabilities of Warsaw Pact air power, which have grown immensely, strengthened by a steadily growing fleet of battle helicopters, have contributed to this capability in the same way as the structural reforms of the land forces and their growing ability to fight a combined arms battle and to drive deep into NATO's rear.

Should the Warsaw Pact succeed in mounting its offensive before the NATO forces can be deployed and prepare their defences, NATO would face the dilemma of a nuclear decision at a very early stage. One of the most important tasks in NATO's conventional force improvements must therefore be to minimise the probability and the consequences of a surprise attack. That requires more than an increase in warning-time. Nearly all military conflicts since (and including) World War II show that surprise with all its advantages could be achieved even when there was no lack of warning and ample warning-time.

Improvements in all-weather, day-and-night reconnaissance, in particular target acquisition, are extremely urgent. It is also necessary to co-ordinate national and NATO reconnaissance efforts, data interpretation and near real time transmission. But such improvements will not suffice. To minimise the impact of a possible surprise attack it is necessary that at least part of the armed forces are in a high state of readiness; it requires rapid political decisions and the quasi-automatic implementation of certain planned countermeasures. These would include measures to block and slow the rate of advance of the attacker, to force the attacker to disperse his land and air forces, but also actions of direct defence. Furthermore, our armed forces must be given an improved capability for meeting engagements even in conditions of a surprise attack. This, in turn, means again an improved reconnaissance and target acquisition capability.

The Soviet Union is in the process of adding a new dimension to the option of a short-notice attack. The follow-on systems of nuclear short-

and medium-range missiles, which are integrated on the level of divisions, armies and fronts, have a greater range and a considerably improved accuracy. These capabilities increase the nuclear threat against Western Europe; the militarily decisive fact is that, with an improved accuracy of these ballistic missile systems, their deployment in a conventional configuration becomes possible and thus opens up to the Soviet Union a qualitatively new conventional option.

The extension of European air defence to neutralise the new offensive options of the Warsaw Pact has acquired particular urgency. It is necessary, independently of whether or not and when the US Strategic Defense Initiative is realised.

Follow-on forces attack

Maintaining the momentum of the attack and rapid penetration into the defender's rear are the basic requirements of Soviet operational doctrines. Their realisation depends decisively on two factors:

— the capability for a combined arms combat, *ie* the close and effective cooperation between air and land forces and their arms;
— the continuous, rapid and unimpeded flow of follow-on echelons to relieve the battle-weary formations at the right time and in the appropriate sector.

It is therefore paramount to deny the aggressor these operational possibilities and destroy the cohesion of his concept of operations. NATO must develop this capability not only to be able to defeat the offensive, but also to undermine the Soviet Union's confidence in its ability to achieve its objectives and thus deter aggression.

Blunting the first echelon of attack and striking deep to wear out follow-on forces or to erode the aggressor's air power are not alternatives to be pursued at the expense of each other. They are complementary tasks which have to be accomplished simultaneously in order to mount a successful defence.

Of course these operational objectives of eroding the enemy air superiority and striking the follow-on echelons would lose their operational significance if the defence does not succeed in holding the first echelon of attack. To that extent, countering the first wave of attack has first priority, of course. But it is also true that the defender would not be able to hold out long against the front-line attack if he does not succeed in eroding the enemy air superiority and in interdicting the constant flow of fresh follow-on forces.

NATO has to find a different way of determining its priorities – priorities not between, but within the operational areas described, priorities of measures where the effort promises a high return, where certain elements of the attack can be neutralised and thus the cohesion of the attacker's operations disrupted.

To give just one example: the improvement in target acquisition and data processing. Here lies one of the greatest weaknesses in NATO. All improvements in artillery firepower – and this is also true for air attack – are meaningless if they are not accompanied by a decisive improvement in target acquisition and rapid data transmission. Today's target acquisition capabilities do not even permit the effective use of existing firepower.

Extending the battlefield into the enemy territory constitutes no new military strategic concept. It does not imply giving up the principle of a defensive defence. It remains one and the same forward defence, whether we are talking about defeating the first echelon of the attack, striking the follow-on forces, eroding the enemy air force on the ground or paralysing the enemy command and control structure. All these tasks have been integral elements of the strategy of flexible response from the beginning and are a well-established part of NATO's operation plans. But the means available to carry them out have always been inadequate; with the shift in the correlation of forces they have steadily become more so.

The need to extend the combat zone into the enemy's territory does not merely arise from Soviet operational principles. It is also a political imperative. The emphasis on the defensive character of the Alliance must not be taken to the point at which the other side gains the impression that the victims of aggression are willing to bear the devastations and the destruction of the war alone. This, however, would be the result if NATO were to concentrate all its efforts solely on defeating the front line of the attack.

The aggressor has to be aware that his territory will not be a sanctuary. To make this clear is not merely an essential element of *deterrence*, that is, the effective discouragement of the opponent to resort to war, but also of *reassurance*, that is, the preservation of public confidence in the Alliance countries in the capability of effective defence. Nothing could better encourage an aggressor to continue his attack and discourage one's own population in its will to resist than the limitation of combat to one's own territory.

The extension of the combat zone into the enemy's territory requires new weapons systems. Let me give just one example: the attack on the enemy air force on the ground will be most effective if the first attacks on the main bases of Warsaw Pact air forces occur in immediate response to the enemy attack, so that the returning aircraft of the first wave of the attack are forced to divert to other air bases. This is the way to achieve the maximum reduction in the attack rate of the enemy's tactical air forces. But this requirement for fast reaction can be satisfied only by ballistic missiles.

This analysis leads some commentators to fear that the implementation of such proposals for the improvement of conventional capabilities would virtually provoke the Soviet Union to destroy the improved capabilities of the defender by a pre-emptive strike. However, if one interprets the improved conventional capability to meet the aggressor at the point where his attack is launched, supplied and supported, to be a provocation of the aggressor, one must in consequence renounce any improvement of NATO defence capabilities.

Fear that such improvements in the conventional defence should induce the Soviet Union to engage in a preventive nuclear strike misjudges Soviet awareness of risks, which until now has always been clearly evident, and presupposes an intensity of aggressive will which cannot be influenced by any measures of deterrence. Furthermore, this argument overlooks the supreme priority given by the Soviet Union to the integrity of its own territory. As long as the conflict can be maintained on the conventional level, the integrity of the Soviet Union is not at risk. To keep it at that level, and thus avoid nuclear escalation, is therefore in the Soviet Union's greatest interest.

The yardstick whereby all measures to increase the effectiveness of the West's defence ought to be measured is its capability to deprive the option for the Soviet Union to resort to violence, in moments of crises, of any attraction whatsoever. To achieve this, the Alliance must be able to meet any recognisable threat in a way which does not weaken the firm stance of any of its governments and peoples or provoke a resort to war by others.[14] The proposals for an improvement of NATO's conventional capabilities satisfy this criterion.

Strengthening the conventional capabilities of the Alliance requires carefully considered, possibly difficult, decisions and sacrifices. If one believes that the member nations of the Alliance are not able to bear this burden, one must not hide from the consequences – the continued dependence on the early use of nuclear weapons in case of conflict and the growing instability of our own security.

Notes

1. Karl Kaiser/Georg Leber/Alois Mertes/Franz-Joseph Schulze, "Nuclear Weapons and the Preservation of Peace". *Foreign Affairs*, 60.5 Summer 1982, 1157–1170.
2. European Security Study (ESECS), *Wege zur Stärkung der konventionellen Abschreckung in Europa* (Nomos Verlagsgesellschaft, Baden-Baden 1983, p. 12).
3. Kaiser/Leber/Mertes/Schulze, *op. cit.*, p. 1157.
4. *ibid*, p. 1159.
5. General Bernard W. Rogers, 'Die Atomwaffen bleiben unser Trumpf', *Rheinischer Merkur/Christ und Welt*, No. 50, 5 December 1986, p. 3.
6. Karl Kaiser, "Die Diskussion über die NATO-Strategie nach dem Gipfeltreffen von Reykjavik", *NATO-Brief*, No. 6/1986, Brussels.
7. Karl Kaiser, *op. cit.*

8. Ministry of Defence White Paper 1983, Bonn.
9. General Bernard W. Rogers, *"Das Atlantische Bündnis, Rezepte für ein schwieriges Jahrzehnt"*, *Europa-Archiv*, 12/1982, pp. 369 ff.
10. Kaiser/Leber/Mertes/Schulze, *op. cit.*, p. 1169.
11. ESECS, *op. cit.*, p. 18.
12. European Security Study (ESECS II), *Stärkung der konventionellen Abschreckung in Europa, Zweiter Bericht* (Nomos Verlagsgesellschaft, Baden-Baden 1985, p. 15).
13. ESECS II, *op. cit.*, p. 16.
14. ESECS II, *op. cit.*, p. 13.

Chapter 7
Flexible Response and Nuclear Weapons: A British View

HUGH BEACH

"Let it be clearly understood that we in this island are resolved to maintain armed forces on the continent of Europe for as long as is necessary."
Anthony Eden, 5 February 1952

When Anthony Eden gave this undertaking, and two years later cast it in categoric form as the price of West German entry into the Western Alliance, he meant it in sincerity. Prescient as he was, he can hardly have foreseen that more than 30 years later the necessity for British forces in Germany would promise to be as long-lived as ever. These forces consist of some 150,000 men and women (including the resident families) spread across a swathe of territory some 50 miles wide from the eastern to the western borders of the Federal Republic. They live in over 40 different towns. Three-quarters of the them are under 30. They run over 90 schools, 70 churches, six hospitals, their own television and radio networks, live entertainment, a youth training scheme and innumerable voluntary and welfare organisations. About one in three of the marriages are to German girls. Local defence expenditure in *Deutschmarks* is approaching £1,000m a year. All this represents a British investment in collective security without precedent.

It also represents by far the greater part of the British armed forces world-wide. The British Army of the Rhine (BAOR) comprises a major combat force, 1 British Corps, and the means of supplying that Corps with full logistic back-up. The Corps would take its place in war alongside Dutch, German, and Belgian Corps, under HQ's Northern Army Group, with an American Corps planned to act as Army Group reserve. 1 British Corps consists of three armoured divisions and an air-mobile brigade, supported by a reconnaissance brigade and strong artillery assets. On mobilisation, it would be reinforced with regular and reserve forces from the United Kingdom up to a total of 150,000 troops – a difficult operation which was triumphantly demonstrated in Exercise Lionheart in the autumn of 1984.

RAF Germany forms part of 2 Allied Tactical Air Force, alongside units of the United States Air Force together with elements of the German, Netherlands and Belgian air forces operating from bases in their own countries. It is being built up to a force of eight squadrons of Tornado, two of Harrier, and two of Phantom, with two squadrons of support helicopters – one Puma and one Chinook – and forces for the protection of their own airfields.

These forces see themselves, and are seen by the British people, as their first line of defence against a possible invasion from the East – as if to say that "Our frontier is on the Elbe", And this in a sense is true. What is not true, however, is that such an invasion is in any sense likely. So long as the Western Alliance exists in more-or-less its present form, few contingencies seem less likely. The true purpose of British forces in Germany is rather different, and politically crucial. It is to play its part, at one remove, in maintaining the cohesion, self-confidence and self-respect of the free nations of Western Europe, in face of the huge military preponderance of the Soviet Union. In Britain the Soviet Union, whose political system and society are near-to-universally rejected, is regarded as aggressive and expansionist, and as a clear potential threat (though not an immediate danger) to the West. Its professed good intentions on disarmament elicit a sceptical response. The United States is therefore seen as an indispensable counterpoise. It is the object of widespread if diffuse goodwill and regarded as by far and away Britain's most dependable ally, whose good intentions towards Britain's security are not in doubt. Its good judgement and effectiveness in global relations is another matter.

So the important thing is to maintain the commitment of the United States Congress and people to practical support for collective security. The United States military presence in Western Europe amounts to some 500,000 souls, including wives and families; a huge hostage presence whose existence ties the United States into the European security system indissolubly (so long as they remain) on the principle of the "finger in the mangle". The price of keeping them, as is clearly understood in Western Europe even had Senators Mansfield, Nunn and others not provided periodic sharp reminders, is that the countries of Western Europe themselves show sufficient investment in their own defence. This has to take the form of forces in being; of the necessary arrangements for their reinforcement and supply, including the transatlantic link; and of credible doctrines, training and exercises for their use in war. This paper tackles mainly the doctrinal issues.

The concept underlying all preparations by the Western Alliance is that of prevention. That nuclear war must be prevented goes without saying. The Chernobyl reactor is reported as having emitted only one-tenth of the radioactivity of the Nagasaki bomb, yet the Russian estimate of eventual deaths is 6,530; 18,000 were referred to clinics and hospitals for scrutiny; 5,000 doctors and nurses were drafted in and 100,000 people were evacuated. Scaled up for the number of Nagasaki-equivalent bombs in the theatre stockpiles of the opposing forces in the West (say 10,000), the potential destruction and dislocation in a future nuclear war becomes almost unimaginable. What is equally well realised, at least in Germany, is that a future war between East and West, even if conducted solely with non-nuclear weapons, could result in a scale of casualties not seen since the Black Death or the Thirty Years War. There is no conceivable sense in which "the defence of Western values" could be served by such an undertaking. The difference between such a post-war world and the present would exceed by an order of magnitude the differences between Eastern and Western society today. It follows that the objective is the prevention of *all* war.

Given that the incentive for any Russian military intervention or incursion into Western Europe is low (and space does not allow further discussion of this), what is needed for prevention is that the Soviet Union should have no military options to which the West can offer literally no effective response: no prospect of quick and easy gains, no free ride, no *faits-accomplis*. Given, secondly, that an effective equivalence subsists at the level of strategic nuclear capability, and that NATO Europe can quite certainly muster sufficient forces to repulse any local and small-scale invasion – a sudden snatch on Lübeck or Hamburg – even if staged late on a Friday afternoon, it emerges that the most difficult contingency is that of a massive rolling advance across the inter-German border.

This might be carried out with, or without, prior mobilisation on the part of the Soviet Union. If extensive mobilisation were attempted (no doubt under the disguise of some training manoeuvres, as in 1968) NATO could rely upon some warning, whether or not it took advantage of it. More likely, perhaps, would be an assault with the bare minimum of visible preparation, in which case NATO might have no more than 48 hours in which to prepare for battle. However improbable, this would be so harsh a test of the entire Western system as to provide the norm against which the adequacy of NATO military plans and provisions have inevitably to be judged.

The question of the military balance in Western Europe is complex, and the subject of separate studies within this book. It must suffice that, on certain conventional assumptions concerning the respective stages of mobilization and build-up reached by the two sides, the fidelity of Allies, states of training and the nature of military doctrine, it is generally accepted that in such a war the West would be out-numbered by two or two-and-a-half to one in such factors as tanks, guns and military aircraft. It is further assumed that, since NATO is a defensive alliance "and will never fire the first shot, regardless of provocation", the military initiative must lie with the Soviet Union. While NATO is obliged to cover all avenues of approach, the Soviets can manoeuvre, mass and reinforce at the places and times of their choosing. Thirdly, it is assessed in consequence, that under such an assault the defensive system of the West would lose coherence and face defeat, if not within days then at most within a week or so and long before the full reinforcing potential of the United States could be brought to bear. It is regarded as impossible that NATO should acquire conventional capabilities strong enough to guarantee success against any type of (albeit non-nuclear) attack anywhere in the Alliance area. The prospect could thus be of the Federal Republic being over-run, at least to the Ruhrgebiet or the Rhine if not to the Channel ports, within the timescale of a short war. This has been the perceived situation for the past 30 years, and so remains today.

The balancing factor, enabling the Western Allies to sustain their self-confidence, cohesion and self-respect in face of this uninviting prospect, has been the *deus ex machina* of battlefield nuclear weapons. Under the so-called strategy of Flexible Response, current since the late 1960s, the military policy of the Alliance in face of attack would pass through three successive stages:

— Direct defence, to defeat an attack or place the burden of raising the stakes on the aggressor. This is regarded as the "preferred response".
— "Deliberate escalation" on NATO's part, to include possibly the first use of theatre nuclear weapons.
— "General nuclear response", seen as the ultimate guarantor of Alliance deterrence.

Thus the key factor in this strategy is the readiness and ability of NATO to *initiate* a nuclear strike against the assailant if there were no other way of stopping him.

It must be conceded that in its primary aim, enabling the Western European nations to keep their nerve in face of the military overhang from the East, this policy has been successful. It has allowed the diversion, to socially more useful purposes, of the vast amounts of money and resources which might otherwise have been needed to match the Warsaw Pact more closely in military terms. There is no indication whatever that its utility in this regard is waning. Nevertheless, it is becoming increasingly recognised that, if seen not as simply a vital ingredient in the general panoply of deterrence but as a programme for action in the event of deterrence failing, the concept of "deliberate escalation" makes almost no sense at all. The question is, when the moment came that defences were faltering and coherence being lost, if application were made for the "release" of nuclear weapons, what would actually occur? The answer is, of course, that no one can possibly know. It is conventionally assumed that NATO, after clear and adequate warning, would use one or more nuclear weapons to cripple Warsaw Pact reserves east of the inter-German border or some other target designed to make continuance of the offensive unacceptable to them.

Intermediate nuclear forces (INF), with their ability to threaten targets within the Soviet Union itself, might be the most appropriate delivery means, bearing in mind the deterrent object of the exercise. In their absence the job could be done by longer range battlefield systems, for example Tornado in the strike/attack mode, or indeed by strategic systems. It is argued that, in these circumstances, retaliation could not be in the Russians' interest, serving only to destroy the territories that they were bent upon possessing. Rather they would be brought to see the true enormity of the enterprise they were engaged upon, and would be compelled by horror and shock to desist and, in due course, to withdraw. Such an outcome is certainly conceivable, and a military policy producing that result would have proved itself to be both rational, moral and practical. But an alternative outcome can equally clearly be discerned, whereby the Russians (whose motive, in the first instance, *need* not have been simple territorial aggrandisement) would repay like with like, and nuclear "first use" by the West would prove to be but the first stage of escalation in its literal sense. The metaphor is that of the moving staircase: once place a foot upon the lowest tread and there is no running back, no emergency stop button; one is carried willy–nilly to the top. A policy which had this outcome would be both the most irrational and the most immoral that it is possible to conceive. Between these two extremes, complete military success on the one hand and the self-destruction of Western civilisation on the other, lies an indefinite spectrum of other possible outcomes. To speak of *relative probabilities* in the context of contingencies for which there is no precedent (and to which there might effectively be no sequel) is probably nonsense. But at the very least it would be grossly irresponsible not to recognise the *possibility* of some more or less catastrophic upshots.

From these reflections a number of consequences follow. The first concerns the likelihood of ever obtaining governmental agreement to nuclear release in such circumstances. The Americans (and to a small degree the British) would, in theory, be able to go it alone but it is hard to think of any conceivable circumstances when it might be in their interests to do so. It has proved hard enough to persuade governments to co-ordinate policies for gas pipelines or Olympic boycotts, let alone issues where the very survival of nations is at stake. For a concept of flexible response the necessity of timely release is crucial, and the likelihood of obtaining it is regarded in military circles with scepticism.

A second consequence concerns the military outcome of any

encounter involving more-or-less equal numbers of nuclear weapons on either side. For a number of reasons this could not be of any military benefit to the West – as war games and trials have repeatedly attested. At the simplest, nuclear weapons increase the rate of attrition; and high attrition benefits the big battalions. A third area of concern is moral. There is nothing to choose between first use and retaliation *per se*: everything hinges on the outcome, whether it be to stop the war in its tracks or crank up the ratchet of escalation by one more rung. But there is moral incoherence in a policy which purports to deter a nuclear conflict by threatening to initiate one. This was the logic, however dimly perceived, behind the General Synod of the Church of England in its resolution (carried by an overwhelming majority) that Britain should "forswear" first use. The military are no less sensitive to these considerations.

The dilemma is therefore quite plain. There is a need on the one hand to preserve the doctrine of flexible response for its undoubted utility in the context of deterrence and (paradoxically) in the preservation of confidence. A large, if not overwhelming, majority of the British public accept the necessity for a nuclear element in defence. A resigned awareness of the possibility of nuclear war, and the poor prospects of personal or national survival in such event, does not add up to a fatalistic willingness to submit to military blackmail. A public avowal of "no first use" is, therefore, exactly the wrong kind of arms control policy to pursue. It is by its very nature unverifiable. Since some nuclear weapons able to be used at theatre level (if not stationed necessarily in continental Europe) will be needed to deter first use by the Soviets, nothing would change in the real world. Nevertheless a formal pledge of "no first use" would be taken seriously by Western public opinion and might be held in the Federal Republic to have the force of law. To the extent that these facts served to diminish uncertainty in the minds of Soviet policy-makers, they could be held to undermine deterrence. ·

On the other hand the utility of "first use" as an operational policy is close to vanishing. Thus it is no surprise that NATO Ministers collectively declare "undue reliance on the early use of nuclear weapons" to be an "unacceptable situation that we are determined to avoid".[1] It is no surprise when the Supreme Allied Commander in Europe believes that "credible deterrence requires NATO to attain a conventional capability that would give us a reasonable prospect of frustrating a non-nuclear attack by conventional means".[2] It is no surprise when two successive Commanders-in-Chief of the Northern Army Group, in public lectures about their operational policies, use the word "nuclear" only in the context of something to be avoided almost at all costs![3]

This is the context which has led to discussion of "raising the nuclear threshold" – a concept which in many instances lacks precision. If, following the Reykjavik summit, agreement were reached on the removal of all INF systems from Europe even more importance would attach to measures for improvement of the conventional balance.

It is absurdly perverse to argue that measures to improve conventional defences could in some way be inimical to deterrence, which is to say make war more likely. The Supreme Commander has discerned the real issue. "The problem is not," he says, "that our forces will not perform admirably at their General Defensive Positions (if appropriate advantage has been taken of warning times); they will. The problem is they cannot fight long enough through lack of adequate sustainment. . . . Primarily it is as a result of our inability to sustain our forces adequately with trained manpower, ammunition and war reserve material."[4] He spells out the consequent requirements in three main areas. The first is to bring those forces already committed to the Alliance up to the required standards for "manning, equipping, training, sustaining and maintaining". The second is to modernise weapons systems, and in particular the means of deep interdiction of enemy follow-up echelons. The third is to add to the force structure a further element of "trained mobilisable reserves". These are the eminently practical and attainable prerequisites for credible deterrence through the "reasonable prospect of frustrating a non-nuclear attack by conventional means". This formula matches, as closely as need be. Professor Freedman's proposed criterion for future NATO planning, that it be based on the presumption that "nuclear forces will not be used and should not be needed".[5] One could not ask for more.

Two classes of practical consequence appear to follow. The first is to downgrade provision for battlefield nuclear weapons. For the British, the implications are slight. The nuclear delivery means provided in Western Germany consist of the Tornado squadrons of RAF Germany, one regiment of Lance missiles and five regiments of artillery. The Tornado nuclear bombs are British and few in number (say 100); missile warheads and artillery shells are American and a proportion of them (perhaps 300) would be made available for British use in war. All but the Lance missile regiment have a primary non-nuclear role, and a conventional warhead for the Lance missile is also in the offing. So de-emphasing provision of tactical nuclear warheads need involve no more than the routine back-loading of obsolescent material and its replacement in smaller numbers. When the deployment of Pershing II and Tomahawk is complete, the American tactical nuclear stockpile in Europe is supposed to number some 4,400, ranging in yield from 1–2 kilotons upwards. It appears to be the intention of the British Labour Party, when next in office, to press for the removal of all battlefield (as well as intermediate) nuclear weapons from Europe in the interests of a less-nuclear policy. This is to travel too far too fast. Nor is there great logic in the suggestion of the Palme Commission, adopted by the joint SDP-Liberal Commission, to ban all short-range nuclear weapons from a zone on either side of the East-West divide to a depth of 150 km.

As the Soviet member of the Palme Commission observed, nuclear munitions could be quickly reintroduced into the proscribed area, so this measure would be of small military significance and could create an unfounded impression of enhanced security.[6] All that is needed in the immediate future is a further reduction in the *number* of warheads provided, which could be both immediate, unilateral and drastic.

In due course this might be extended to the successive abolition of further classes of battlefield nuclear weapons. In past years it has been decided progressively to forego nuclear warheads for mortar bombs (Davy Crockett), land mines (Atomic Demolition Munitions) and surface- to-air guided missiles (Nike Hercules). Similarly in future it could be decided to discontinue nuclear provision for artillery and for the Lance missile. On military grounds the argument for so doing is strong. The political implications would be difficult to manage – the more so if INF were in process of reduction to zero – and would constitute a major subject for negotiation within the Alliance.

As to conventional force improvements, great progress has undoubtedly been made in all the areas picked out by the Supreme Commander, under the NATO regime of 3% annual growth in real resources devoted to defence, which has been in force since the late 1970s. Although this undertaking has not been honoured in full by all the European members, Britain and Germany both maintained it up to 1987.

The regime of real growth is now at an end, at least so far as the British are concerned. An analysis of the 1986 Defence White Paper suggests that in the current year allocations for land and air defence equipment are down by 10% and 5% respectively.[7] As matters stand there is provision for no more than half the armoured regiments to be equipped with modern tanks in this century, and for only half the infantry armoured personnel-carriers to be renewed, while plans for replacing obsolescent 105mm guns continue to languish. In the air force's case, financial provision for the new European Fighter Aircraft provides a major problem. The squeeze can only grow tighter and in the near future will be made worse by the reduction (by more than 25%) in the numbers of young people in the relevant age groups available for recruitment. The actual prospect, therefore, is more likely to be of further withdrawals from the front line, and more exiguous logistic provision, rather than the type of enhancement that policy would demand. This is the real context for the doctrinal debate of the future.

The opposition political parties in Britain have all shown signs of having thoroughly grasped this point and their published policy documents contain specific undertakings to do what they can, within the existing financial ceiling, to prevent such a decline. They pin their hopes upon savings from the cancellation of Trident and reductions in overseas garrisons, notably the Falklands. The present government, for obvious reasons, is utterly opposed to both these measures and affect to believe that the problem of conventional decline does not exist. The dismal truth is that even the cancellation of Trident and *a fortiori* reductions in the Falklands will only postpone the evil day when front line strengths have to be reduced again, as they were in the late 1950s, and for the same reason. No one has yet proposed a credible doctrine to meet this contingency. We return to it briefly at the end.

Meanwhile there remains the question of how the defensive battle is to be fought, given the commitment of the Alliance to a principle of Forward Defence. Since the founding purpose of the Alliance is to affirm that an attack upon any one member is treated as an attack against all, no strategy is viable which fails to affirm the integrity of the territory of every member. We are here concerned with the Federal Republic of Germany, a narrow country in the East-West sense and lacking a hinterland since the defection of the French from the military structures of NATO. It is both politically and practically quite inappropriate to plan on yielding large tracts of territory in the interests of gaining time or concentrating forces. This is one reason why the plans of the late 1940s for main defences on the Rhine shortly gave place to a Weser strategy, and this in turn was supplanted, during the 1960s, by the present concept whereby the forward edge of the main battle zone lies (in the British case) along the River Leine between Hanover and Northeim. Excellent defensive terrain is afforded by the wooded ridges which stretch north-west from the Harz Mountains, the gaps at Springe, Coppenbrugge and Sibesse, the "pin-table" of villages around Braunschweig, and the spurs leading southwards off the Mittelland Kanal. To use it makes excellent military sense.

The political directive is to fight the battle as far to the east as is possible, but this is not to be taken, as apparently it has sometimes been, to mean trying to defend statically and right up to the inter-German border. The key to resolving this apparent contradiction lies in the concept of the Covering Force, a perfectly normal and orthodox military arrangement. The Covering Force consists of mobile units deployed, very early in any alert period, into the area between the inter-German border and the forward edge of the main battle zone, an area which varies in depth (in the British case) from 6–60 km. Their task, in the first instance, is to cover the deployment of the main body. Thereafter they are tasked to observe, harass, delay and call down fire upon the advancing enemy for as long as it is militarily sound to do so. They are then withdrawn through the main defensive positions, regrouped and refurbished to play their part among the reserves for use later in the battle. None of this is in any sense controversial.

Where the main defensive battle is concerned all the national corps have been given their own area within which to conduct operations, according to the terrain and their own tactical concepts, with until recently little co-ordination save for a line behind which they must not withdraw without authority. The British, for example, giving a somewhat static interpretation to the concept of forward defence, have tended to enmesh themselves in minefields. The Germans, lacking a sufficient notion of offensive action, have had no minefield-breaching capacity. It has been the outstanding achievement of the previous Commander-in-Chief (now British Chief of General Staff) General Sir Nigel Bagnall, to have secured the agreement of his German, Dutch and Belgian colleagues to a fresh and, at least on paper, a unified concept for the main defensive battle. This places much more emphasis upon mobility rather than any rigid defensive system. It capitalises upon the capacity to manoeuvre inherent in the highly mechanised forces now provided throughout the Alliance. It looks to the air to keep the enemy's air force off the army's back; to support the land battle directly when presented with a specially appropriate and lucrative target, and to impose the greatest possible delay on selected Soviet follow-up forces. The aim is to allow concentration of forces at critical points with the aim of forcing local tactical successes, seizing the initiative, capitalising on mistakes by the other side and, if all goes well, to provide the where-withal for a locally decisive counterstroke involving reserves of at least one or more armoured divisions acting in concert. It is a bold and attractive vision, doubtless long overdue.

There is a clear indication of danger, and one not infrequently seen, when dissonance arises between political objectives, strategic doctrine and tactical concepts. The picture presented in General Bagnall's paper is one of a rare harmony, with the political aspirations of the British people for security pulling in close harness with NATO doctrines of (increasingly non-nuclear) flexible response and the Northern Army Group intention greatly to extend its conventional defence capability by means of the tactical concepts just explained.[8] The danger lies in the future and its causes are the ever-mounting cost of equipment, and the impending shortage of recruitable manpower. Ironically, (since there is no significant constituency in Britain which favours reducing the forces in Germany), the shortage of resources is bound to impose reductions. This is the more pressing to the extent that the British insist in continuing to line up behind the Americans and the French as a third independent centre of strategic nuclear decision. But even if Trident were cancelled it is hard to see how the BAOR can exceed much more than two divisions (say 35,000 men) by the turn of the century. It is to be hoped that this will be accomplished within the context of agreed and verified force reductions on both sides. The inevitability of such reductions can be held to make such agreement either more or less likely – according to taste. But the real difficulty in these reduced circumstances is how to reconcile flexibility in response with forward defence: the necessity to cover the whole front, while maintaining reserves; and the need to harness new technology in the process of downgrading still further the nuclear component in the direct defence of the inter-German border. The next Defence Review, might contribute to a solution but could not in itself find one. There is need for yet more radical fresh ideas and the sad prospect is that it may take crises if not major upheavals to induce their delivery. But the time for conception is now.

Notes

1. Press Communique. M-DPC-1(85)10. para 7.
2. General Bernard W. Rogers. "NATO's Strategy. An Undervalued Currency." Paper given to the IISS Annual Conference, 12–14 September 1985. *Adelphi Paper* 205. IISS London. Spring 1986. p. 6.
3. General Sir Nigel Bagnall. "Concepts of Land/Air Operations in the Central Region I". A lecture given at the RUSI on 23 May 1984. RUSI September 1984 pp. 59–62. General Sir Martin Farndale. "Counterstroke. Future Requirements." A lecture given at the RUSI on 15 October 1985. *RUSI Journal*, December 1985. pp. 6–9.
4. General Rogers. *Loc. cit*. p. 7.
5. Lawrence Freedman. "US Nuclear Weapons in Europe. Symbols Strategy and Force Structures", in *Nuclear Weapons in Europe*. Andrew Pierre (ed.) Council on Foreign Relations. New York. 1984. p. 68.
6. Georgi Arbatov, quoted in "Common Security." The report of the Palme Commission (Pan World Affairs. London. 1982. Footnote to p. 142).
7. *The Economist*. 17 May 1986. p. 36.
8. General Bagnall. *Loc. cit*. p. 62.

Chapter 8
British Defence Choices in the 1990s and the Implications for Germany

JONATHAN ALFORD*

It is a fundamental truth that Britain's interest in defending Germany is always going to be somewhat less than Germany's. It is another that Britain sees, more vividly than does the FRG, additional threats to its security beyond those deriving from a land attack across Central Europe. And it is a third that the overall cost per deployed unit is rising in real terms while budgets are not.

One should not draw the conclusion that Britain's contribution to the defence of the Central Front is seen as a charitable act. It clearly serves British interests to provide for deterrence and defence on the inner German border and, given the state of political relations between East and West, this is necessary. As a symbol of resolve and unavoidable commitment, substantial British forces deployed in West Germany, in the form of the British Army of the Rhine (BAOR) and Royal Air Force, Germany (RAF[G]) are explicitly intended to share risk, to deter (by nuclear linkage) and to defend as far forward as possible if war breaks out.

Yet the British, for rather obvious reasons, do not regard this as the

* This chapter was one of the last pieces of work prepared by Colonel Jonathan Alford, Deputy Director of the International Institute for Strategic Studies, before his sad death in July 1986. It has been left in the form in which he wrote it, although obviously some parts have changed during the passage of time since his death.

only commitment, although it is the only one to specify levels of forces. This has had the effect of tying Britain's hands in any review of what might be a sensible disposition of its military capabilities. Historically, it is clear that the effect of a binding commitment to the Central Front has been for that commitment to take up a rising proportion of Britain's diminishing numbers. In 1966, the strength of the British Army was 218,000; in 1986 it was 163,000. As a proportion of the whole, therefore, BAOR (at 55,000) has risen in 20 years from 25% to 34%. In terms of reinforcements earmarked for the Central Front in war, the commitment is proportionately greater, for the bulk of Britain's Army reserves are now intended to strengthen BAOR, raising its numbers to some 150,000. Thus the *relative* burden of Britain's commitment to defence in Germany has increased significantly and is beginning to impose rather painful choices as the resources which can be devoted to other missions also judged critical to Britain's security, are more and more affected. Often this is portrayed – rather simplistically – as competition between the "continental" and the "maritime". Yet there is an element of truth in the dichotomy because maintaining the strength of BAOR and RAF[G] can cost (is costing) the Navy ships; it is no distortion to portray the 1981 Defence Programme Review (Cmd. 8288) in this way. But there are at least two other major programme elements (defence of the home base and maintenance of the nuclear deterrent) that absorb substantial funds and can be affected by – and affect – the Continental commitment.

It is obvious that the national interests of both Britain and West Germany will not be the same. Britain will continue to urge some irreducible priority for the other three areas; Germany will naturally see a strong defence of the Central Front as its highest priority. In the best of all possible worlds it would be helpful, politically, if the Alliance were able to pass judgement on what it would be most useful for Britain to do for collective defence but we have to recognise that it is unlikely to do that. We have to recognise too that, even if a collective view were possible on that issue, it cannot be imposed on either party if the decision ran clearly against the national instincts and interests of either – as it surely would. Thus the question of what Britain should do will involve the reconciliation of domestic politics and instincts with Alliance – and especially European – politics. The British public cannot reasonably be asked to support an allocation of defence resources which runs dramatically counter to instinct based on geography and historical experience. While educated over many years to believe that the deployment of substantial forces in West Germany in peacetime is a necessary cost contributing importantly to Western security, it is not difficult to mobilise political support for the Royal Navy, defence of the home base and (although now with a greater degree of controversy) nuclear deterrence. It seems likely that there is a limit to tolerance and we may be close to it. If, as seems probable, the

Ministry of Defence judges that its resources are insufficient to maintain current force levels and future programmes, another Defence Review seems certain not long after the next General Election. It also seems likely that the issues and choices posed in such a review will, in their fundamentals, be no different from 1981: whether to keep BAOR at 55,000 and cut elsewhere; or to include BAOR in across-the-board reductions; or (depending critically upon the outcome of that election) to abandon the plans to renew the British nuclear deterrent, redistributing the money notionally saved to conventional account.

The cancellation of Trident [*which at the time of writing seemed probable in all electoral outcomes other than Conservative victory*] would certainly postpone the problem, provided that the money saved thereby (maybe £6bn) were redistributed to other programmes. That is not a safe assumption and it becomes spectacularly unsafe if Labour were to resurrect its ambition to bring Britain's defence expenditure (as a proportion of GNP) "into line with that of our major European Allies". This would imply reducing from (now) 5.2% to (say) 3.3% – the current FRG figure. On a budget of £18bn, that would mean reducing by over £6bn per year, far beyond what would be saved by moving out of the nuclear field – and some three times more than even pessimistic assumptions about the extent of the "funding gap" in 1990 would calculate.

Thus, it seems right to hoist warning signals now. While the extent of this gap can be debated, hardly anyone believes that there will not be one – and one sufficiently large to demand remedial action by the end of the decade. Hence the assertion about the need for another of Britain's periodic defence reviews. What is particularly disconcerting is that a review is necessary despite defence spending being at a post-war high in real terms, as a result of a steady addition of funds from 1979 to 1986 which raised inputs in real terms by about 24%. What gives added point to the assertion is that the defence budget is set to decline in real terms by between 4.72% (MOD) and some 7% (House of Commons Defence Committee) from 1986–7 to 1988–9.

I would not care to guess how things will turn out, beyond saying that many will not think it right under these distressing (and depressing) circumstances to leave BAOR untouched and cut elsewhere. The estimated attributable costs of BAOR and RAF(G) (excluding Berlin) are assessed at £3.447bn (1986–87), a figure which excludes procurement. This figure does, however, cover reinforcements and infrastructure, including TA (Territorial Army) earmarked for BAOR. It is not possible to allocate procurement costs on account of BAOR, RAF(G) and reinforcements but the total for land equipment procurement was £1.487bn and £2.803bn for air force equipment in 1986–7.

An arbitrary judgment might allocate half the Army's procurement (by value) to BAOR and one quarter of air force procurement to RAF(G) – depending upon the direction of major programmes. Thus

£743m and £700m respectively might be added on equipment account to give a total burden in 1986-7 of the Central Front commitment of about £4.89bn (or 26.5% of the defence budget).

Trimming that figure would again involve wholly arbitrary assumptions about fractional costs – and one would have to assume also the disbandment of most of the forces withdrawn if money was to be saved. I can imagine one of the options presented to Ministers for consideration being the removal of a division, divisional slice and supporting air power. Given that there are three divisions in BAOR (with a fourth earmarked in UK), a figure for savings of about £1bn might be cited – a good deal less than *pro rata* and also rather less than the projected underfunding of defence by 1990 on current trends. Depending critically upon consequent reorganisation of supporting services and infrastructure, a divisional slice might be as high as 15,000. BAOR would reduce to 40,000 under such an option.

Two questions arise. Could West German (or other) forces "fill the gap" caused by a reduction of frontage of one division in the British corps? And what would be the political consequences? The answer to the first question is almost certainly "no" and "yes". "No" because the Bundeswehr is likely to be suffering a contraction of its own at this time due to demographic constraints; "yes" if the Bundeswehr had by then undertaken to incorporate a larger fraction of mobilisable reserves than is currently planned. This would be part of a wider debate on the role of reserve forces in NATO. While few would wish to increase the size of the problem by asking the Federal Republic to fill in for a British division as well as solving their own difficulties, the fact remains that the "British problem" is likely to present difficulties which are of a lesser order of magnitude than the German problem. Furthermore, it is at least possible that an SPD Government might actively pursue the ideas of "defensive defence" which they have been flirting with in opposition; they ought then logically to approve a restructuring of BAOR.

Britain, too, faces a demographic shortfall and manning problems are likely to arise for all the services in the next few years. Unlike the Federal Republic, which maintains universal conscription, Britain's volunteer forces must work in the market place and the Services must offer remuneration and conditions of service which will first attract and then retain individuals against the rewards of other forms of employment. Given that the demographic shift in Britain will cause the services to need to attract one out of every eight 18-year-olds, instead of one out of 12, there may have to be some adjustments in pay to compete with industry (pushing up the manpower bill) but this will depend on the general state of the labour market at the time. While somewhat less easy to fill the ranks, and somewhat more costly, manpower constraints seem unlikely to affect volunteer forces to anything like the same extent as conscripted forces, where the link to the size of the 18-year-old manpower pool is direct.

With regard to the politics of possible reductions in BAOR, it is necessary to go back to Article IV of Protocol No. II on Forces of Western European Union, dated 23 October, 1954. This article, devoted exclusively (and uniquely) to British forces, states *inter alia* that Britain will "continue to maintain on the mainland of Europe, including Germany, the effective strength of the United Kingdom forces which are now assigned to SACEUR, that is to say four divisions and the Second Tactical Air Force, or such other forces as SACEUR regards as having equivalent fighting capacity". There is a clause within the Article which permits Britain to "invite the North Atlantic Council to review the financial conditions" if there is "too great a strain on the external finances of the UK". It has always been the Brussels Treaty which binds Britain to 55,000 men and, presumably, this is the commitment which would have to be renegotiated if the British Government decided that it no longer wished to devote an increasing proportion of its total forces to the Central Front but rather to check or reduce the proportion. It is, after all, a very different world from 1954, not least because in peacetime there now exists a Bundeswehr of 495,000 which did not exist at all in 1954. Moreover, it was recognised in 1954 that the British commitment under the Brussels Treaty was a precondition to satisfy France before the French Government would agree to German rearmament.

Whether or not Britain chooses to make the case for reductions on the Central Front on financial grounds remains to be seen. If it does so, it is likely to be opposed by the Federal Republic (and other members of the Alliance) both on the grounds that Germany cannot make good the resulting shortfall and on the grounds that Britain's attempt to renegotiate the commitment would be likely to cause others – especially perhaps the United States – to follow suit. It may well be that the British government will again decide not to pick a fight with the FRG over this issue and will try to balance its books in other ways. However, it is also quite possible that a future government may decide to press forward on the issue. If it does so, it is likely to make its case on the basis of two linked notions. The first is that Britain serves the collective interest in also attending to the Eastern Atlantic and defence of the home base (and, it may argue, in providing nuclear deterrent forces). Britain also provides reinforcements for Northern Norway and Denmark/Schleswig Holstein which is in the interest of those nations and of the Alliance. The second is that the military situation in each of these areas is relatively more precarious than it was, whereas the position on the Central Front has changed little – at least in terms of numbers – over many years. This is not an argument that can be resolved because the priorities to be given to various missions is somewhat scenario-dependent. Two major developments in particular give substance to the assertion that greater attention should be paid to these other claims on Britain's resources. The first is the reach and power of the Soviet Northern Fleet; the second is the range, payload and penetration of Soviet frontal aviation. Both expose the United Kingdom to attack from new directions; the former at least raises questions about transatlantic reinforcement; the latter gives a peculiar importance to the airfields of North Norway whose loss to NATO would greatly increase the air threat from that direction.

To reduce still further Britain's ability to contest maritime control of northern waters and defend itself (and the critical reinforcing base that Britain provides for the US) would seem to many (particularly in Britain) to make little strategic sense. Those who argue for no reduction in BAOR and RAF(G) as an irreducible priority have to make the case on political grounds or on the grounds that, if the centre breaks, the rest hardly matters. The balancing argument is that, if the centre holds initially and the rest collapses, the centre will collapse too. I do not intend to resolve the argument here, simply to rehearse the arguments that seem likely to be used – and to warn that economic pressures on Britain's defence budget are likely to force a revisitation of old battle lines at some point in the not-too-distant future.

While there is, in my view, very considerable validity to the essentially symbolic argument (BAOR and RAF[G] are symbols of commitment to collective security since Britain, unlike France, has committed itself inextricably to Germany's defence), this does not, *prima facie*, lead one to conclude that the symbol has to consist of 55,000 men in BAOR (together with RAF[G]) no more and no less. Some other "significant" figure might do equally well but politically this will be hard to sell, for redefining what is an adequate symbol will be taken to mean that the extent of the commitment has been redefined – which is on hardly anyone's mind at present.

Are there other ways out of the box? In 1981, the Defence Programme Review asserted that there was at least one other way. It argued that Britain did not need a surface fleet of the size and shape then possessed, adequately to perform the maritime mission in the Eastern Atlantic. It would have substituted a combination of submarines and maritime patrol aircraft for frigates and destroyers in ASW operations. That conclusion was hotly contested then and, however illogically, even more hotly after the war in the South Atlantic in 1982. Indeed, that war more or less sank the Nott Review. Retirements planned did not take place and the savings which might have been applied to the maintenance of the continental commitment did not accrue. Indeed the navy's portion of the Defence Budget has *risen* from 13.5% in 1980–1 to 14.2% in 1986–7 (Navy General Purpose Combat Forces).

It is reasonable to ask whether a future review might not reach the same conclusion as in 1981. All one can say is that it seems unlikely for reasons which are less than logical and will involve a good deal of rationalisation. One group will base their arguments on a technical re-evaluation which will emphasise the promise in ASW of towed-array and variable depth (VD) sonars and helicopters, both of which need surface platforms. Another will (unashamedly) exploit the sentiment generated by the 1982 Falklands war. A third will argue the new-found importance of light carriers with VSTOL Sea Harriers for air defence of the fleet. And a fourth will use the need to maintain a true amphibious capability (specifically for the Northern Flank but also for the "unforeseen" and to provide "flexibility"). All these constituencies taken together will make it hard for a future Secretary of State for Defence, whatever his own instincts, to savage the surface navy as Sir John Nott did in 1981.

The only other way to turn is towards the nuclear deterrent. For reasons given earlier, the Trident programme must be regarded as vulnerable under some political outcomes. If it were to be scrapped without alternative, as the Labour Party now suggests, a sum around £6bn might be released which could, on an annual basis, for a time defer all or most of the pressure to reduce either BAOR or the Royal Navy. What is not entirely clear is how Britain's allies would react to such a decision – or the electorate. Taking the British electorate first, a poll conducted by *The Times* on 13 December 1985 showed a total of 68% answering affirmatively to the question "Do you think that Britain should or should not keep an up-to-date nuclear deterrent so long as the Soviet Union continues to possess nuclear weapons?" Among those declaring themselves to be Labour supporters, the figure was still 52% for and only 38% against the proposition. If that level of support held up, a future Labour Government might find the room for manoeuvre against its own Left wing which would permit it to reverse its current stance on Trident.

However, our allies might see things differently. Caring little whether or not Britain can protect itself against nuclear threats (and many in Europe do see Britain's deterrent in that light) while caring deeply about the levels of conventional forces that Britain can maintain, Britain's European allies might well make clear that they would prefer Britain to get out of the box in which it finds itself by cancelling Trident. It is not even certain that the United States would make a different choice. Thus the political climate – and the consensus – could change over time if the consequences of sticking with Trident came to be portrayed in starker terms than hitherto. It is even conceivable that the Conservative Party without Mrs Thatcher could change its mind on Trident – but circumstances would have to be dire indeed for that to happen.

It is not quite clear where the Ministry of Defence stands on Emerging Technologies (ET) although there is little evidence that it believes that technology can "solve the problem" if the problem is defined as how significantly to raise the nuclear threshold. This is in part because there would appear to be a quite healthy scepticism about what technologists can deliver (in terms of performance) and in part because of absolute certainty that the cost of incorporation will be high – and higher than anyone now estimates it to be. On the other hand, the British Services will not reject technological opportunity and will point to a fair record of achievement (together with a few disasters, such as Nimrod) in keeping close to moving technological barriers and the Services will say that the rate of technology change in Warsaw Pact forces will permit no relaxation. When asked to say how Britain intends to respond to NATO ET initiatives, the Ministry of Defence is quick to say that a large number of its funded programmes can already be fitted into that initiative without significant distortion (Tornado, EFA, MLRS Phase III, Trigat, EH 101, Ptarmigan). Indeed, it is only with regard to some of the more fanciful brainchildren of US industry that MoD would seem to be drawing the line – such as anti-Theatre Ballistic Missiles (ATBM) and BOSS AXE. Thus Britain has no principled objection to FOFA (preferring to call it by its old name of interdiction) or to air defence or to airbase denial but seems not at all anxious to invest in exotica. Being by instinct conservative, the British military authorities would prefer to invest the money available in doing rather better what they are trying to do anyway – and they think that desirable improvements will be in any case incremental, marginal and expensive.

If one listens to the Labour Left in opposition, one might be led to believe that a Labour government would favour "non-provocative defence" and thus come into collision with the services who would have rather grave misgivings about proceeding in that direction. It is worth noting that a Labour government could in any case proceed only rather slowly to implement such a policy, given the stock of equipment in hand. The impact would be felt, if at all, in new programmes. Labour might, for example, cut tank programmes in favour of anti-tank missiles and strike aircraft in favour of ground-based air defence. It seems rather unlikely that the impact of such changes, if implemented, would be felt this century and it would seem best to discount them for the time being.

The same kind of caution would apply to ATBM. It seems to be the case that Britain is likely at best to be a reluctant supporter of Manfred Woerner's notions of an extended air defence (EAD) which would embrace ATBMs. Partly this is because Britain itself is beyond the kind of conventional short-range ballistic missile (SRBM) threat that Dr Woerner is imagining, partly because that particular threat is taken rather less seriously and partly because Britain has no plans to buy a new medium-level SAM which might be given an ATBM capability. All one can report is that there seems at present to be no evidence of enthusiasm for ATBM in Whitehall. It is the conventional threat posed by Soviet tactical and frontal aviation to airfields in Germany and in Britain which is taken very seriously indeed but this demands other solutions which involve hardening, dispersal, air defence (AD) radars, airborne early warning and AD fighters with effective avionics and air-to-air missiles.

Conclusions

This paper has tried to eschew both advocacy and undue pessimism. Yet, forced by my remit to peer into an opaque future, the unavoidable conclusion is that another review of defence commitments and resources will be forced upon a reluctant Ministry of Defence not later than the early 1990s. All the old arguments will be revisited. Options for bringing resources and commitments into line will have to be considered and evaluated by Ministers. One of these options seems certain to be some reduction in numbers of forces based in West Germany in peacetime. I do not say that it will be the option chosen but I do suggest that it will be a closer call than ever before because strategic and emotional considerations will press in the direction that it would be wrong to continue cutting other sorts of forces in order to preserve Rhine Army intact. There are other things that can be done and I have suggested some which might enable Britain to finesse the hardest question of all and the one with the most potent political consequences. I have not suggested that Britain goes cap-in-hand to West Germany looking for offset of £1bn per year for I do not think that any future government would dare to do that, however justifiable it might seem.

However it is worth saying, by way of conclusion, that the most likely outcome is quite different – and the least satisfactory in many ways. The political instinct, as so often in the past, will be to decide not to decide. Programmes will be reviewed in the light of available resources and trimmed with no sense of strategic priorities. Everything will suffer a bit of pain and every commitment then be fulfilled inadequately. Translating that into the context of this discussion, BAOR and RAF[G] will be kept at current levels and kept on very short commons – if not actually starved. The men will be kept in place to satisfy the Treaty obligation but they will be under-equipped or equipped only with obsolete or obsolescent material. Their morale will fall; 1 (BR) Corps will become again the object of pity as it struggles to keep old equipment on the road; RAF[G] will be the poor relation of 2 ATAF. That is one future that I would prefer to avoid and would take almost any other road to avoid.

Chapter 9
Constraints on German Defence Policies in the 1990s

HARALD RÜDDENKLAU

The current situation

When one looks at the expected pattern of the threat to Western Europe in the 1990s and thus considers what consequences result from this for the defence policies of the Federal Republic and Britain, one important aspect which should not be forgotten is the fact that the British-German defence relationship over the last decade has been and continues to be in the present relatively free from problems. The governments in both countries are very close in their estimates of the military force balance in Central Europe; as regards defence policy they are, right down to operational principles and strategic considerations, much closer than, for example, the Federal Republic and France. One should also draw attention to the fact that there are no problems in Anglo-German defence relations with regard to the question of forward defence, the planning for the deployment of tactical nuclear weapons or the compatibility of force structures. Many and varied military and social contacts, joint exercises and planning bear witness to the excellent military co-operation and at the same time reflect the great significance which the Federal Republic accords to the presence of British forces in West Germany.

This is in stark contrast to relations with France. Merely the announcement of joint manoeuvres between the French and Germans creates new headlines about the German-Franco defence relationship. Compared with the problems which confront the Federal Republic with regard to French defence policy, any differences with Britain are virtually neligible. The true order of magnitude of differences between

Germany and Britain and possible problem areas must therefore be kept in mind with regard to what follows.

This however, it should also be said, is only true with regard to defence relations at government level. If one included the domestic political debate about defence issues in Britain and the Federal Republic, a completely different picture would emerge: there are hardly any areas of consensus, not even between political groupings in the two countries which are close to each other on the political spectrum, like the Social Democratic Party in West Germany and the British Labour Party. Such differences could already be discerned at times in past decades, but they were less pronounced and certainly less antagonistic. The phenomenon of principally unbridgeable, mutually exclusive positions in defence questions has become the mark of the general political evolution of many member states of the North Atlantic Alliance. It can be observed since the end of the 1970s, catalysed by the Soviet arms build up and the NATO response (*Nachrüstung*). If certain political tendencies were capable of attracting electoral majorities, this would have very grave consequences for German-British defence relations; this is true for Germany as well as for Britain. At present, however, inter-governmental defence relations are based on the security policy consensus of parliamentary majorities in London and Bonn. Hence we are justified in concentrating on the official policy of the governments. What would happen if a particular grouping with a certain different view of defence policy came into government cannot be predicted in any event; the influence of parliamentary minorities on government policy is so insignificant that it can be neglected.

Elements of the threat

In order to determine the requirements and options for the German-British defence policy in the 1990s, it is necessary briefly to consider the changed threat scenario in Central Europe, seen from today's perspective, as it could emerge towards the end of the 1980s and the beginning of the 1990s. In order to judge it correctly, it is necessary to remind oneself of the following principles of Soviet military doctrine:

1. War remains a means of politics;
2. The military battle has to be decided on the opponent's territory;
3. The most essential objective in war is to achieve victory;
4. The element of surprise has to be exploited to the full;
5. One's own armed forces have to be prepared for any possible form of warfare.[1]

In the conventional realm, the main objective must therefore consist in denying the Warsaw Pact the option of a preventive attack with the expectation of a quick victory. Previous experience with regard to continuous quantitative as well as qualitative improvements in the deployment of Warsaw Pact forces consistent with this objective and the principles of Soviet military doctrine suggests that the East will seek to maximise its political options in future.

With regard to the structure of the Warsaw Pact force posture, the introduction of so-called Operational Manoeuvre Groups (OMG) constitute a tactical refinement of the Warsaw Pact concept of attack. Their purpose is to enable strong troop formations to get behind NATO forces deployed near the border as part of a "bold thrust forward", in order to bring about the conditions for the collapse of forward defence.[2]

This concept of attack results in a shortening of NATO's warning time and is designed optimally to exploit the element of surprise. NATO forces are to be prevented from properly deploying their forces for defence in the first place. In addition, following the introduction of new tank models the older types were not repatriated to the Soviet Union but were rather used to beef up the motorised artillery regiments or to increase the stock of military hardware of the first strategic echelon. The result of these structural changes has been that, despite the withdrawal of one tank division from the Soviet Forces in Germany in October 1979, there has been a marked increase in the capabilities of forward deployed Soviet tank forces. Other measures were added, such as the equipment of tank regiments with an infantry and an artillery component, in order to create the capability of "combined arms combat" at regiment level. Motorised artillery regiments were improved in an equivalent fashion.

The qualitative improvements of Soviet air strike forces facilitate the support of the attacking land forces and at the same time the attack of targets deep within NATO territory. One of the consequences is that these capabilities tie up an increasing number of NATO air forces, and hence the means of interdiction are reduced. The quantitative improvement of Soviet artillery capabilities is particularly notable. They consist today for the most part of mobile and at least partly hardened artillery pieces (armoured howitzers). Their mobility has increased, and it has become more difficult to take them out. The forward deployed Soviet divisions have now more than twice the number of artillery pieces of a NATO division.[3] Of particular concern to NATO is the observation that about 7,800 Warsaw Pact tanks are no longer vulnerable to tank defence weapons (TOW, MILAN and HOT) owing to additional armour-plating.

New short-range missiles – particularly the SS21 and SS23 – are so accurate that they can also be armed with conventional warheads. In this weapons category the Warsaw Pact enjoys a superiority of 9 to 1.[4] The capability to execute a conventional surprise attack with artillery, missiles and air forces in combination with an increased ability to execute forward thrusts by the land forces far exceeds defence needs or even the capabilities required merely to justify the claim to be a superpower.

Problems facing West German forces

Thus we have delineated the most important challenges which the North Atlantic Alliance will have to face in the 1990s for the defence of Central Europe in a time of increasing scarcity of resources. The financial situation and the evolution of the political culture in the Western nations – in addition to the demographic problems – do not permit simple and tidy solutions which are only directed towards the military requirements.

Apart from the threat scenario, the solution of personnel and structural problems in the Bundeswehr will determine in the 1990s, which of the alternative defence policies will have a future in the Federal Republic. Therefore, it is necessary to consider different approaches to the solution of these problems which are a matter of deep controversy between government and opposition.

In order to maintain a peacetime level of 495,000 men, the Bundeswehr now needs 225,000 fit recruits annually. Already at the beginning of the 1970s one could see that at the end of the 1980s the number of recruitable young men would sink below this limit. By 1988 there will be a shortfall of 25,000, increasing to 100,000 by 1994, unless effective countermeasures are taken. Bundeswehr planners consider a strength of 495,000 men to be necessary in the future, because otherwise the armed forces will not be able to fulfil their mission at the onset of conflict, even if it is possible to increase the size of the armed forces to 1.34 million men in a reasonably short period of time. The following measures are designed, in the view of the government, to prevent the reduction in the peacetime manpower level of the Bundeswehr from 1989 onwards:

— an increase in the number of short-service soldiers as well as the period of their commitment to serve in the armed forces
— an increase in the core of professional soldiers;
— recruitment of women to the Bundeswehr
— the relaxation of the entry conditions;
— the reduction of other obstacles to the draft;
— the reduction in the number of those freed from military service;
— an increase in the period of basic military service;
— an increase in the number of military training camps;
— the improvement of the alert status;
— the elimination of the deployment problems.[5]

The criticism of the opposition is directed against maintaining the peacetime level of 495,000 men and the underlying assumption that a

Warsaw Pact attack could occur suddenly and with very little warning time. The defence experts of the opposition conclude that there would be sufficient time prior to an attack for mobilisation.[6] Basing their opinion on the result of the defence structure commission created by the then Chancellor Brandt in 1970, they come to the view that the peace-time level requirements for the Bundeswehr have been set too high; they are no longer relevant at this time. This would allow for a greater development of combat brigades into cadres. It thus does not matter if the peacetime level of the Bundeswehr were reduced to 300,000, if the level of the available forces after mobilisation could be kept at 1.34 million men.[7] The government, as well as the opposition, have recognised the increased significance of the reservists. Both political camps have for years been conscious of the obvious shortcomings of the existing conception for the exploitation of this potential: there are too few exercise grounds, no systematic after-training for the officer corps of the reservists, and inadequate data about reservists in the framework of plans for rapid mobilisation, to mention just a few of the problems. Since 1983 a new concept with regard to reservists is being developed. A solution is to be presented by the end of 1987, which should give the basis for a proper use of the greatly increased number of exercise grounds planned for 1989 to enhance the viability of the Bundeswehr as the defence capablity of the Federal Republic of Germany.[8]

In particular, because of the problems of personnel and personnel structure in the Bundeswehr of the 1990s the Federal government has great interest in maintaining a substantial British troop contingent in the FRG. Apart from the question of the number of troops, it is vital for NATO in Central Europe that British forces are equipped and armed with the most modern technology. If it is a correct evaluation of the threat scenario for the 1990s that the increasing conventional superi-ority of the Warsaw Pact forces can only be compensated for by extend-ing the combat zone deep into the territory of the adversary, Britain's contribution to the defence of Central Europe will be even more important than hitherto. It will be absolutely necessary to:

— increase the capabilities of NATO with regard to the initial phase of hostilities, even given very short warning times;
— improve the ability to mobilise quickly and achieve full combat strength;
— strengthen FRG air defence as well as the capability to destroy enemy air forces on the ground.

Furthermore it is vital to strengthen NATO's combat strength against the first and the second echelon of Warsaw pact forces as well as to improve the capability to defend against enemy attack forces in the Baltic, given the need for a fast response.[9]

Bundeswehr procurement plans

As far as the Bundeswehr is concerned, the planning for the 1990s envisages an improvement of defensive capabilities, a greater emphasis of command and control, reconnaissance capability and electronic warfare. Furthermore, priorities are to be set on a basis wider than that of individual services. The improvements concentrate essentially on the following areas: reconnaissance, electronic warfare, munitions storage, research and development of smart munitions. Among the principal items which are currently being procured by the Bundeswehr are therefore the Multiple Launch Rocket System (MLRS), the Field howitzer 155–1, the anti-tank helicopter PAH-2 as well as a combined command structure for modern weapons systems in the army (allowing the combined deployment of area bombardment systems, the anti-tank helicopter PAH-2, armoured cars with field guns as well as guided munitions for anti-tank missions for battle tanks).[10]

The British do not judge the requirements differently. The British Defence Minister declared in the Statement of Defence Expenditures 1986:

> We plan to improve the fire-power, range, co-ordination, accuracy and survivability of 1 British Corps's artillery support; and three new systems, the Multiple-Launch Rocket System, the Phoenix remotely-piloted vehicle, and the artillery ADP system BATES, are being developed for introduction in the early 1990s.

Like the land forces, the Royal Air Force and the *Luftwaffe* base their procurement requirements on the new elements of the threat scenario described above.[11]

A large part of the weapons systems that will have to be procured is going to be developed and procured by both countries within the framework of NATO armaments co-operation. Due to the large areas of agreement with regard to strategic and operational principles, there are far fewer problems with regard to Anglo-German armaments co-operation than, for example, with joint projects between the Federal Republic and France.[12] However, while the Federal Government views these procurement plans as the commensurate response to the challenges of the Warsaw Pact, they are sharply criticised by the opposition. As with its proposals to solve the demographic problem which will affect the Bundeswehr in the 1990s, the opposition bases its analysis on a fundamentally different evaluation of the threat.

Opposition voices

Leading spokesmen of the opposition in Bonn, for example, Andreas von Bülow, judge the conventional superiority of the Warsaw Pact to be much less pronounced and therefore less threatening than the government. Indeed, some accuse the latter of irresponsible panic-mongering. In this context it is believed that the assumption of a short warning time (*ie* less than 48 hours) before a Warsaw Pact attack, as well as the strategic scenario of the qualitative improvements in the Warsaw Pact's force posture in the last years, is false or at least exaggerated. In the context of its concepts of *Entspannungspolitik* in the military field it considers not just the present structure to be misguided but particularly the procurement plans which are designed to achieve improved capabilities for penetrating into the depth of the combat zone.[13] Leading opposition defence experts have proposed an alternative concept which argues for the creation of the structural inability to engage in aggression, for the Bundeswehr and other NATO contingents deployed in the Federal Republic. This is to be achieved by a consistent deployment of defensive technology. In the view of the opposition what is needed is not so much the mobility and penetration capability of weapons systems, but rather a militia with strong infantry and equipped with anti-tank weapons, which could use its knowledge of the local geography, advantages of the terrain and fortifications to stop an attack by Warsaw Pact armies.

In the view of the opposition, modern technology, in particular the possibility of real time reconnaissance, gives so many advantages to the defender that, for example, the military capability to attack the second strategic echelon of the Warsaw Pact forces would be militarily unnecessary and politically damaging. These opposition spokesmen have therefore strongly attacked the General Rogers plan and the concept of deep strike; on the other hand they have not given very convincing answers to the question as to how the increasing firepower of the artillery, air force and the rocket troops of the Warsaw Pact could be met. This failure is particularly apparent with regard to the problem of how to meet the qualitatively new threat of conventionally armed, precision-guided short-range missiles, a large number of which can be launched simultaneously[14].

The problem of short-range missiles

Attempts seriously to get to grips with these questions does not only involve approaches based on arms control but also considerations of military countermeasures which are of an exclusively defensive character and are therefore compatible with the philosophy of strengthening defensive options. Central to this approach is the need to extend NATO air defence. At present, much thought is given in NATO circles to the question of how a defence against short-range missiles could be achieved. Here one has to distinguish between passive measures to increase the protection of possible targets and, on the other hand, capabilities to destroy these weapons before launch or by inter-ception of their trajectory. These measures are by no means mutually exclusive but rather complement each other.

A non-nuclear air defence effective against short-range missiles would be designed to protect military point targets, which are most probably objects of strategic targeting by the Soviet Union. A sufficient area defence is probably not realisable. The technical possibilities which are emerging enable NATO to decide about the introduction of defensive missiles against tactical ballistic and non-ballistic short-range systems. First of all however the following questions would have to be clarified:

— To what degree can the threat of short-range missiles be met by passive protection and the mobility of potential targets?
— Which NATO members will participate in this project, *ie* can one depend on Britain to the same degree as on the Federal Republic?
— Is there a connection, should there be a connection and if so of what kind, to the Strategic Defence Initiative?
— Would an extended air defence also be effective against cruise missiles and modern stand-off weapons systems?[15] Even now, although no decisions with regard to the extension of air defence have been taken, anti-tactical ballistic missiles (ATBM) have to be considered as a military necessity for the future.

Strengthening the will to defend

Of course it must not be forgotten that, despite all the problems, NATO still has a very good chance of fulfilling this task of defending Western Europe in the future. NATO enjoys a number of advantages over the Warsaw Pact. For example, compared with NATO, Warsaw Pact divisions suffer from a lack of personnel; their infantry is weak and their supply and logistics sections suffer from a lack of resources. NATO troops are generally better trained and their equipment has been and continues to be of better quality, so that one cannot exclude the possibility that a NATO soldier would fight for longer and more efficiently than his Warsaw Pact counterpart.[16] It should also be mentioned that the loyalty of various Warsaw Pact armies can by no means be guaranteed – think only of the Polish People's Army, and resupply from the Soviet Union will have to pass through Poland for the most part.

A balanced judgement of the military situation in Western Europe will also take note of the advantages enjoyed by NATO and thus distin-guishes itself from panic-mongering. On the other hand this must not lead to self-deception and self-satisfaction. Vigilance and a continuous development of one's own military capabilities, based on the evolution of the threat, will continue to be required in future, as we have seen in the search for answers to new elements in the threat scenario. It is on this point that all the alternative concepts offered by the opposition are weakest. One of the principal tasks of German and British defence policy, in the 1990s as now, will therefore consist in preventing a decline into irresponsibility and strengthening public awareness of military necessities without becoming discredited by panic-mongering. In other words, the domestic political conditions for a defence policy which meets the new challenges will have to be maintained in future. Only if this inner foundation remains strong and secure will the Western Alliance be able to realise the strengthening of its military force posture in future to meet the new threats.

New challenges

In conclusion, I would like to delineate a few important tasks for the future which the British and Germans are setting themselves jointly and which require a joint solution. The introduction of the OMGs (Operational Manoeuvre Group) by the Warsaw Pact requires increased mobility as well as the strengthening of present forces in the rear of the NATO corps areas. The former British Commander NORTHAG, General Bagnall, suggested that in future only part of 1 British Corps should be deployed at the front, while other brigades as well as airborne and battle helicopter regiments are kept deep within NATO territory in order to deal with successful breakthroughs and meet the adversary at the flanks.[17] His successor, General Farndale, implemented this concept in detail after consultation with the commanders of neighbouring forces. This concept also received particular emphasis in the British Defence White Paper. If the implementation of this concept turns out to be successful, the great vulnerability of NATO in the rear would be reduced at least in the area where the BAOR is deployed. Such a concept is also important because the threat emanates not merely from the operational manoeuvre groups of the Warsaw Pact but also from Soviet or East German *Spetsnaz* formations. Their mission (and hence their threat to NATO) consists in rapidly escalating covert combat in the rear with the purpose of hindering the mobilisation and deployment of NATO forces. Such a threat can assume strategic proportions.

One has to assume that *Spetsnaz* contingents will be deployed from the air in NATO areas even before or, at the latest, simultaneously with an attack by Warsaw Pact armies so as to hinder or prevent the development of combined warfare by NATO forces. The earlier they are deployed, the greater the chance of a Soviet military success. In order to be able to meet this particular threat, the territorial army of the Bundeswehr must be able to be deployed quickly and with sufficient forces at the focus of events. A decisive prerequisite will therefore be a comprehensive and fast reconnaissance capability.

While there has been an improvement in vehicles and heavy armoury in recent years, the urgently-needed helicopters are simply not available. But much more important, in the face of this threat, would be to make the necessary means for command control available to the territorial army. At present the territorial army depends on using the public telephone system for communications. It has to be assumed that the telephone system will be one of the primary targets in the event of an attack in the rear. In the event of a situation of tension and crisis sufficient protection will have to be given to such targets in co-operation with civil authorities and institutions so as to limit as much as possible the damage that can be done by *Spetsnaz* troops.

While the British have recognised the increasing threat to the rear and have offered a contribution to the solution of these problems by their new concept of forward defence, there is still much to be done by West Germany as well as by Belgium and the Netherlands.

Examples of joint initiatives

Of enormous importance for a successful forward defence is the maintenance of an air attack capability by NATO sufficient in quality and quantity to deny loss of air superiority or even air dominance to the other side. Only then will it be possible to provide sufficient air support for NATO's own land forces and successfully to execute interdiction operations in the depth of the opponent's territory. This is not just a problem facing the Alliance in general, but one in which there are particular problems which could be solved by joint German-British initiatives. It has been pointed out repeatedly that one simple and cost-effective measure to enhance NATO's air strike capability would be the procurement of about a dozen refuelling planes. Such an increase in the in-flight refuelling capabilities would allow NATO strike forces to remain in the air for longer periods and would thus provide them with the opportunity to deploy their weapons more efficiently than is currently the case. By staying in the air longer they are also less vulnerable to attacks on their bases.[18]

A fleet of tanker planes might be organised and deployed in the manner of AWACS. Naturally such a project could not take place on a purely Anglo-German basis, but would have to be supported by other NATO partners, in particular the Americans. But perhaps the Federal Republic and Britain could provide the initial impulse for such a project.

The comparatively frictionless co-operation between the British and the Germans in the defence of NATO's central front in past decades justifies the hope that the necessary improvements in military capabilities can be tackled and realised on a co-operative basis in future. The fact that differences (not to mention problems) between Britain and Germany with regard to security policy are hardly known is not a matter for concern; it is rather evidence that such problems do not exist. It is also an indication of how well both NATO states approach joint tasks in NATO's central area. The present positions and discussions about future solutions both in Britain in Germany are not indications of future difficulties and problems in the defence relationship between the two countries. On the contrary, one can assume that the relations between these two NATO allies, at least as far as defence policy is concerned, will continue to be an asset to the Alliance.

Notes

1. Situation Report by the Inspector General of the Bundeswehr in *Frankfurter Allgemeine Zeitung*, 20 June 1986.
2. Heinz Magenheimer, *"Rogers Plan*, 'Airland battle', und die Vorneverteidigung der NATO"*, APZ B* 48/1984, p. 7 and Philipp A. Karber, "Ein Plädoyer für die Vorneverteidigung", in *Pro Pace*, Deutsches Strategieforum, Bonn 1984, p. 15.
3. Siegfried Thielbeer, "Immer mehr und immer modernere Panzer. Fünf sowjetische Armeen mit neunzehn Divisionen in der DDR", *Frankfurter Allgemeine Zeitung*, 29 August 1986.
4. Thomas Enders, "Eine neue Option Moskaus: Drohung mit Kurzstrecken-Raketen", *Europäische Wehrkunde/WWR*, 6/1986, pp. 330–336.
5. Weissbuch 1985, Ministry of Defence, Bonn 1984, pp. 339 ff.
6. Christian Krause, "Warnzeit und Präsenz in der Bundeswehrplanung für die neunziger Jahre", *Die Neue Gesellschaft*, 2/1986, pp. 151–154.
7. Andreas von Bülow, "Skizzen einer Bundeswehrstruktur der neunziger Jahre", (SPD-Parteivorstand, Bonn 1984); see also Fritz Ulrich Fack, "Eine Partei kippt", *Frankfurter Allgemeine Zeitung*, 2 September 1986.
8. Stichworte zur Sicherheitspolitik, published by the Press and Information Office of the Federal Government, 4/86, Bonn 1986, pp. 22–27.
9. Weissbuch 1985, *op. cit.*, p. 39 f.
10. Weissbuch, *op. cit.*, p. 344–347.
11. See Weissbuch 1985, *op. cit.*, p. 346, and also *Statement on the Defence Estimates 1986*, Cmnd 9673-I, HMSO, London 1986, p. 32.
12. George Younger, "Dem Schutz Europas bleibt das Hauptgewicht", *Europäische Wehrkunde/WWR*, 7/1986, p. 387.
13. Andreas von Bülow, "Alpträume West gegen Alpträume Ost. Ein Beitrag zur Bedrohungsanalyse", (SPD-Parteivorstand, Bonn 1984); Christian Krause, "Worst-Case-Denken als Motiv westlicher Sicherheitspolitik", in Wilhelm Bruns *et al.* (ed.), *Sicherheit durch Abrüstung, Orientierende Beiträge zum Imperativ unserer Zeit*, (Bonn 1984, pp. 29–66).
14. About the issue of short-range missiles see also Enders, *op. cit.*
15. Manfred Wörner, "A Missile Defense for NATO-Europe", *Strategic Review*, Winter 1986, pp. 13–19; Pete Wilson, "A Missile Defence for NATO. We must respond to the challenge", *Strategic Review*, Spring 1986, pp. 9–15.
16. Siegfried Thielbeer, *op. cit.*, p. 5.

17. Siegfried Thielbeer, "Die Briten und die Vorneverteidigung. Farndale: Flexibel operieren", *Frankfurte Allgemeine Zeitung*, 8 September 1986, p. 5.
18. James Meacham, "NATO's Central Front", *The Economist*, 30 August–5 September 1986, p. 21.

Chapter 10

European Security: Is There a Case for New Structures?

WERNER WEIDENFELD

The President of the Federal Republic, Richard von Weizsäcker, accurately described the core of the problem:

> European security interests do not always coincide with American security interests. The United States is a world power; the Europeans are not. In Europe there are conventional weapons systems, short-range missiles, which have no application other than in a European theatre. Space technology and strategic weapons are primarily of importance to the leading powers of the alliances. There is an asymmetry between the partners of the Warsaw Pact on the one hand and those in the Atlantic Alliance on the other.[1]

The dilemma of Western European thinking about security policy is a result of the specific combination of convergences and divergences in European and American security interests. The management of asymmetries in security policies demands an effective correction of Western Europe's security political architecture. On the one hand, the transatlantic relationship is the *sine qua non* of European security policy; on the other hand, there is the danger that Western Europe becomes a dependent variable in the calculations and arrangements of the world powers, with limited relevance. How can one increase the identity of a European security policy while at the same time strengthening the domestic political consensus on security issues? The dialectic between these two aspects of security policy derives from the fact that two different tasks have to be addressed simultaneously. This tension defines the framework in which the organisation of West European security policy has to be approached.

The question about the political identity of Western Europe's security has recently received greater emphasis in the German debate about the future of security in general. The phrase European "reassertion" defines the rhetorical framework. Irritations in German-American relations have given such thinking new impetus. In this context the psychological consequences of the recent summit meeting have been described as the "Reykjavik shock".[2] It has seemed that in German politics memories of the "Potsdam nightmare"[3] have been revived – the fear of world power agreement at the expense of third countries. Despite the current interest in the issue of the organisation of Western European security there is no clearly defined discussion of the subject. The contributions usually confine themselves to diffuse rhetoric: exhortations in almost identical words about "strengthening the European pillar in the Alliance".[4] Suggestions about the implementation of this concept usually go no further than general appeals for strengthening political co-operation in the Western European Union (WEU) or the improved co-ordination of political positions among the European members of NATO. The concrete proposal of the former Federal Chancellor, Helmut Schmidt, stands in marked contrast to these confused appeals. Schmidt demands a conventional military union in Western Europe which must include France and come into being on the basis of a French initiative. Within such a framework, a joint security strategy is to be developed:

> The conventional forces of France and Germany would by themselves be almost sufficient to provide a effective counterweight to the conventionally-armed forces of the Soviet Union and achieve a balance of power. The defender does not need the same number of soldiers as the aggressor. Of course this would require a French Supreme Commander; of course it would require additional budgetary allocations. But since the budgetary resources of the Federal Republic are somewhat greater than those of France, they will have to be made available.[5]

Regardless of how one judges the strategic details of these proposals, it is symptomatic of the precision and the degree of abstraction of the political debate on security that a proposal from such a distinguished source does not provoke a substantial discussion. The same applies to the far-reaching proposals of the Prime Minister of the Saar, Oskar Lafontaine[6], who demands that the Federal Republic should follow the French example and withdraw from the military structure of NATO; and the demand by the Greens[7] for a complete withdrawal from NATO, together with the rejection of any effort at Western European defence co-operation.

Although, therefore, in the German debate about the organisation of Western European security there is no lack of appeals to strengthen the European pillar of NATO, nor is there a clearly-defined debate within the framework of which the pros and cons of the operational consequences could be understood. Even the presentation of far-reaching alternative concepts has not succeeded in provoking such a discussion.

Although this subject is currently of great interest, it must not be forgotten that it derives from a decade-old tradition. The political constellations, the room for manoeuvre, the interests and negotiability of proposals can be discerned in the context of these traditional lines of development.

Various alternatives to the *status quo* of the Atlantic Alliance by means of strengthening the West European identity, its role and responsibility, have been proposed. The particular importance which has been placed on this discussion for some time is based on the fact that this perspective arises out of a number of varied motives and objectives:

— First, there is the desire to make the existing structure of NATO more effective by giving it a second focus alongside the world power of the United States by means of a European federation. The cumbersome process of decision-making is to be facilitated by allowing Europeans to arrive at a common view in advance.[8]

— At the same time there is the intention to give the growing economic and political weight of Western Europe an expression in terms of security policy.[9] The relative success of European Political Co-operation encourages the idea of extending it to security policy. The United States lacks an equal partner for a meaningful alliance.[10] The mental reservations with regard to a more independent organisation of West European security interests seem to have generally been overcome.

— Growing reservations about the rationality of American strategic thinking lead to support for strengthening an independent West European contribution to security policy within the Alliance structure.[11] The spectrum of views on this theme ranges from scepticism over whether there is sufficient American regard for European interests, to fear of a more active and dangerously adventurous American foreign policy leading finally to anti-Americanism.[12] The central motivating power seems to be the drift in divergent directions of American and European foreign policy thinking.[13]

— This runs parallel to recurring American endeavours to demand a strengthening of West European contributions to security. The demands range from increased burden-sharing[14], a re-shaping of the NATO leadership structure[15] to the withdrawal of American troops from Europe – even if only by way of shock therapy to induce the Europeans to contribute more for their own security.[16]

— It is undeniable that the question of the acceptance and legitimacy of security policy is much more acute today than in the first decades after the war. NATO lacks the necessary political structure to have an integrating effect on the subjective positions

of West European citizens. The legitimisation of security policy could be improved by an appropriate political infrastructure.[17]
— Besides the motives which aim to strengthen the West European position in order to achieve a more effective Western security policy, there are also those voices, which cannot be ignored, that seek to overcome the alliance structures in West and East as well as the domination of the superpowers in international politics under the banner of a European identity.[18] Concern about such neutralist and pacifistic tendencies has provided particular impetus for an orientation of security policy towards Europe, at least as far as France is concerned.

This large range of motivations[19] finds its common denominator in the demand for increased West European co-operation in security policy. The particular concern at the present time, however, must not be understood as a temporary phenomenon of the 1980s. It is rather part of a considerable tradition, which has seen the discussion of security policy in many cultural and political waves and movements since the end of World War II.[20] It is important to recognise that the impulse to West European integration, while not being concerned with military issues as such, involved a significant dimension of security policy. By creating a political and economic community, Western Europe should acquire new power and international influence, resulting in a strengthening of its security.[21] Those who attempt to make Europe a totally civilian power[22] overlook the significant dimension of security policy of the process of European integration. Even without a military component the European Community can be described as a security community. The military-political dimension was addressed indirectly in the early 1950s with the proposal to create a European Defence Community.[23] After the failure of this project, it was replaced by the simultaneous entry of Germany into NATO and the WEU.[24] The theme recurred in the 1960s with the Fouchet plans[25] and the proposal for the creation of a multilateral force (MLF). It was also expressed in the German-French Treaty of Friendship of 1963, which contains a defence-political emphasis.[26] In the same decade the Eurogroup was founded in the context of NATO[27], and finally the Independent European Programme Group.[28]

In recent times changes can be registered mainly in two areas. As a result of a French initiative, attempts were made in the 1980s to reactivate the WEU.[29] Apart from that the political and economic aspects of security policy were incorporated into the areas of competence of European Political Co-operation (EPC). What began with the appropriate reference in the London report of the EPC on 13 October 1981[30] and the Declaration of the Stuttgart summit on 19 June 1983,[31] has now acquired the force of treaty in the "Single European Act".[32]

The High Parties to the Treaty are of the view that a closer collaboration in questions of European security will contribute substantially to the development of a European foreign policy identity. They are prepared to co-ordinate more closely their views on political and economic aspects of security.

In summary, three main aspects of this development should be emphasised:

1. There has recently been an increased emphasis on the Western European dimension of security policy.
2. This trend will continue and increase for a number of divergent reasons.
3. The range and inherent conflict of these reasons reduce the room for manoeuvre of West European states, in developing a coherent policy.

In view of the great sensitivity of all issues related to peace, and taking into account the fundamental currents in the spectrum of opinions among the West German population, and also because of the stability of the political organisations in Western Europe, it is unlikely that future developments in the area of security policy will funda-mentally depart from the hitherto dominant traditional lines in favour of completely new and unknown points of departure. Rather it is to be expected that, in the framework of the organisations and politics of the last decades, certain aspects of European co-operation will acquire new importance and there will be certain shifts of emphasis. For closer co-operation of West European states in the field of security, three organi-sational approaches could be further developed: NATO's Eurogroup, the Western European Union and in the context of the European Community, the European Political Co-operation.

NATO's Eurogroup

The significance of Eurogroup as a focus for closer Western European co-operation lies in the close connection with European and Atlantic interests expressed in this forum. In the narrow field of military policies, Eurogroup can point to remarkable achievements with regard to the co-ordination of issues of West European concern. The principal object of Eurogroup deliberations was the issue of burden-sharing. Besides that, Eurogroup deals with all questions of practical military co-operation – training, armaments, logistics and so on. Given the overwhelming importance of NATO for Western security, and the American security guarantees which for Western Europeans are absolutely essential, Eurogroup will continue to occupy a central position in West European security policy decision-making. On the other hand, Eurogroup will hardly become the nucleus of West European security co-operation in a wider sense. There are two significant drawbacks: two members of the European Community, France and Ireland, are not members of Eurogroup. Both countries see Eurogroup as being too closely integrated into NATO to be able to participate. Furthermore, despite its military-political significance, Eurogroup was not originally envisaged as a framework for European integration. An informal approach was its original hallmark. Thus it lacks the political substructure essential for an efficient organisation.

This problem is characteristic of NATO as a whole: the North Atlantic Treaty has been reduced to the dimensions of a military organisation, which is not what was originally intended. Thus it cannot be a significant instrument for developing and formulating a joint policy; nor can it be the focus for deeper loyalty of the Western world. Over the years, NATO has become a technical agency in charge of a product called 'security'.

The Western European Union

The WEU[33] is based on the Brussels Treaty of 17 March 1948 between Belgium, France, Luxembourg, the Netherlands and the United Kingdom, which was initially directed against the threat of a possible resurgence of German aggression. The Federal Republic of Germany and Italy joined the WEU simultaneously with their entry into NATO in 1955. The primary objectives of the Brussels Treaty are consultations and the co-ordination of questions of economic policy. The mutual defence obligations in the event of armed aggression against a member state are only secondary. The WEU has two principal organs: The Council, made up of the Foreign Ministers, and the Assembly, which consists of members of parliament of the signatory states.

So far the WEU has not become the nucleus of West European defence co-operation, despite all French efforts in this direction. It has also never created its own military organisation. Initially its particular · significance resided in its function as an organisational link between the European continent and Britain, as long as the latter was still not a member of the European Community.

The prospects for a future emphasis on the Western European Union in the development of Western European security policy can be summarised in four points:

— The WEU possesses at least the rudiments of a political substructure (Council, Assembly, Secretariat), which could be further developed.
— The WEU is an organisation based on a Treaty framework virtually predestined for such an extension.

— No notable objections in principle have so far been raised against the WEU from individual West European states.

— One of the leading powers in Western Europe which for several reasons is of particular significance in security matters, France, attaches great importance to this organisation, even though the French commitment seems to have lessened somewhat recently.

However, just as with Eurogroup, there are obstacles and weaknesses. In the first place, not all EC members belong to the WEU. It also seems doubtful whether an organisation which over decades has led a rather shadowy existence can suddenly be revitalised. A political mummy cannot be resurrected at will. For these reasons the WEU will, at most, be able to play only a supportive role in the efforts to achieve a closer co-operation of security policies in Western Europe. It is significant that while the diplomatic world has exhibited great interest in the efforts to revive the WEU, such interest has not been shared by those in charge of defence policies or by military leaders.

The European Community

In the recent past a number of considerations have led to proposals for the inclusion of security matters in the framework of the European Community and European Political Co-operation.[34] Its special attraction resides no doubt in the increased political weight of the European Community and the relatively successful operation of the diplomatic instruments of the EPC. On the basis of the Treaties of Rome, the European Community initially had competence merely in matters of foreign trade policy (Articles 3 and 110–116 of the EEC Treaty) and association (Article 238). At the summit in The Hague on 1–2 December 1969 it was decided to improve co-operation in matters of foreign policy. This decision was given concrete substance by the foreign ministers on the basis of the Davignon Report[35] on 27 October 1970 which thus created in European Political Co-operation a mechanism of co-ordination and consultation, which has led to regular meetings between the foreign ministers and the heads of the political departments in the foreign ministries. In the framework of the EPC, West European states have taken a common position on many subjects which of necessity included issues with security implications: Afghanistan, Poland, Iran, the Falklands conflict, the CSCE follow-up conferences etc. Given these practical developments, it seemed obvious to attempt closer co-operation in security matters within the framework of the EPC. This was established by treaty in the Single European Act.

A strong argument in favour of the extension of co-operation on security policy in the European Community is its comparatively well-established institutional framework. Furthermore, with the European

Parliament, European parties and associations there exists a comparatively strong political infrastructure. All this has led to an extraordinary interdependence and a level of interaction between the West European states within the EC to a degree that would seem to be indispensable for co-operation in the sensitive realm of security policies. This strong foundation of comprehensive processes of opinion exchanges and decision-making on a daily basis clearly distinguishes the organisational form of the European Community from the WEU and the NATO Eurogroup. On the question of which organisation should serve as the forum for closer co-operation in security matters, the existence of this political foundation would clearly favour the European Community, although it must not be overlooked that a minority of members strictly oppose such a development.[36]

The inclusion of security issues beyond the present framework of the Single European Act can proceed by way of three steps: agreement that the European Community should concern itself with all matters of security; the creation of a European Ministerial Council of Defence Ministers; and the creation of an institutional mechanism for information and consultation about defence policies, such as exists in the form of the EPC with regard to foreign policy.

In the long term, an effective and efficient European security policy can emerge in such a framework only if there is a clearer profile of European foreign policy in general.[37] Despite all the successes of the EPC, it is quite clear that there are many areas in which the foreign policies of the EC members do not converge.

Towards a European Security Union

All three variants of proposals to deepen security co-operation are on the level of a careful pragmatism. This pragmatism can reduce the effects of the political deficiences on security, but it cannot eliminate them. It leaves the military structures basically untouched and concentrates on the dimension of political opinion formation among foreign and defence policy-makers. In the medium term it may turn out that this political pragmatism will be sufficient to enable the adaptation of political rhetoric to the formation of political will. Another scenario, however, with at least equal probability, is one in which a real restructuring of the political architecture of Western security will occur. The factors which would bring this about might include a growing dominance of world power bilateralism, a continued estrangement between the political cultures of the United States and Europe, a crisis of legitimation of European security policy, and a more independent European identity. In such a context a pragmatic approach, which mostly confines itself to dealing with the political ornaments of existing organisations, will not be sufficient. Furthermore one can identify significant obstacles to far-reaching changes in all three organisations.

Only the foundation of a new security political organisation in Western Europe, which has its own military substructure, can provide a way out of this dilemma. Undoubtedly some of the present members of the EC would belong to this new union. It could make use of the highly-developed legitimation procedures of the EC framework as well as its close political infrastructure. In this context it would be worth taking another look at the treaty for the European Defence Community.[38] This treaty involves political institutions on a parliamentary basis. Such an approach to the legitimacy of security policies seems to be now more urgent than ever. The EDC treaty also provides for an integrated European army. This now seems to be sensible from a military-political point of view. Such a model would also enable the re-integration of French forces. Furthermore the EDC treaty provides for close connection and interaction with NATO both on the political and military level. Thus, for example, Article 2 of the EDC treaty states that the community "participates in Western defence in the framework of the North Atlantic Treaty". Article 18 states: "In war the commander of the North Atlantic Treaty Organisation exercises full authority and responsibility over the respective forces such as derives from his position as supreme commander".

Even in peacetime the NATO Supreme Commander has far-reaching authority. Details are clarified by protocols to the Treaty. All this could be organised in a similar way under currently altered conditions without affecting the rest of the NATO structure. In the same way the existing decision-making and command structures for the use of French or British nuclear weapons would not be affected, even though in the long term some modifications would appear to be sensible. The EDC treaty furthermore provides for the inclusion of the EDC together with the other European communities under a political umbrella – still a sensible and realisable perspective. This far-reaching reorganisation of West European security policy could be combined with a comprehensive reform of Western decision-making in the North Atlantic Alliance, in order to reduce the lack of legitimacy and acceptance of Western security policies. Such a reorganisation of Western security could lead to either a better understanding between Europeans and Americans or to a further drifting apart. It is also possible that there will be different emphases in American and European thinking with regard to military strategy. A sharpening of European-American conflicts in the area of defence technology is also a possibility. Within the framework of discussions between a European Security Union and NATO (or the Americans) such divergences could be dealt with and rationalised much better than on the basis of the present state of the Alliance. The current drifting apart of both continents could be transformed into an agreed division of labour.

The overall evaluation of the various factors in the security political thinking of Western European states allows four conclusions:

First, the motivational structure which determines security policy, the intentions of the political actors as they have made them known and the available institutional possibilities lead one to expect a closer European political co-operation on security matters in the foreseeable future.

Secondly, particular difficulty resides in the organisational implementation of a heterogeneous political will, since all thinkable alternatives have not only advantages, but also considerable disadvantages.

Thirdly, it has to be assumed that an attempt will be made to develop the existing organisational forms in a pragmatic fashion. Eurogroup will maintain its military emphasis. The WEU can above all draw the French into a European framework of communication. The European Community will attempt to complement its weight in foreign policy by increased co-operation in security issues.

Fourthly, the boundary conditions imposed by world politics, security policy and the politics of European integration lead to an increasing probability that the pragmatic approach practised hitherto will no longer suffice; for this reason new organisational forms for European security policy will come into existence. The renewed study of the European Defence Community treaty of 27 May 1952 could be a point of departure for the corrections in the security political architecture of Western Europe. The structural models it proposes could prove useful for the future of Europe.

Notes

1. Interview with Richard von Weizsäcker, *Die Welt*, 14 January 1987, p. 1.
2. See *Frankfurter Allgemeine Zeitung*, 23 December 1986, p. 8; for a thorough analysis of the debate after Reykjavik see Karl Kaiser, "The Discussion about NATO Strategy after the Reyjkavik Summit", speech given on the occasion of the Atlantic Award, 24 November 1986 (original manuscript); see also Lothar Rühl, "Eine konventionelle Abschreckung für Europa", in *Die Welt*, 22 December 1986, p. 6.
3. For a detailed discussion of this stereotype, see Werner Weidenfeld, *Konrad Adenauer und Europa*, Bonn 1976.
4. More recently, see Manfred Wörner, "Sicherheit im Bündnis", in: Hans-Gert Pöttering (ed.), *Perspektiven europäischer Sicherheitspolitik*, Transnational 25, pp. 6–9; Volker Rühe, 'Perspektiven unserer Aussen-, Deutschland- und Sicherheitspolitik', *Sonde*, No. 3/4 1986, pp. 76–83; Hans-Gert Pöttering, "Eine neue europäische Sicherheitspolitik?", *Aussenpolitik*, Vol 36 1985, pp. 147–156; Jürgen Möllemann, 'Die sicherheitspolitische Dimension der Integration Europas', *Bulletin des Presse- und Informationsamtes der Bundesregierung*, No. 149, 4 December 1986, pp. 1245–1248; "SPD Parteitagsbeschluss", Nuremberg 25–29,8,1986, *Politik*, SPD Information Service, No. 8, September 1986; *Entwurf für ein neues Grundsatzprogramm der SPD*, Irsee, June 1986; for the long-term implications of the discussion see the chapter "Westeuropas Sicherheitspolitik" in Werner Weidenfeld/Wolfgang Wessels (eds.), *Jahrbuch der Europäischen Integration*, Bonn 1980.

168   British-German Defence Co-operation

5. Helmut Schmidt, "Europa muss sich selbst behaupten", *Die Zeit*, 21 November 1986, p. 3.
6. See Oskar Lafontaine, *Angst vor den Freunden, Die Atomwaffen-Strategie der Supermächte zerstört die Bündnisse*, Reinbek: Rowohlt 1983, pp. 81 ff. In Lafontaine's current contributions to the security debate the emphasis has, however, been somewhat different.
7. See the Greens Manifesto for the Federal election of 1987, pp. 26ff.
8. See, for example, Karl Kaiser et al., *Die Sicherheit des Westens: Neue Dimensionen und Aufgaben*, Bonn 1981. Trevor Taylor, *European Defence Co-operation*, London 1984. For a survey of difficulties in the Alliance in the relationship between Europe and the United States see among others Robert E. Hunter (ed.), *NATO: The Next Generation*, Boulder 1984; Stanley Sloan, *NATO's Future: Towards a New Transatlantic Bargain*, Washington 1985; Gregory F. Treverton, *Making the Alliance Work, The United States in Western Europe*, London 1986; Joseph I. Coffey/Françoise E. Paublant, "Ist die NATO noch zeitgemäss? Westeuropa vor neuen amerikanischen Konzepten", *Integration*, 2/86, 51–64; Andreas Oldag, *Allianzpolitische Konflikte in der NATO*, Baden-Baden 1985; Helga Haftendorn, "Atlantische Allianz: Probleme und Aussichten", in Karl Kaiser/Hans Peter Schwarz (eds.), *Weltpolitik, Strukturen – Akteure– Perspektiven*, Stuttgart 1985, 398–410.
9. For more details see Werner Weidenfeld (ed.), *Die Identität Europas*, München 1985.
10. For reflections in this context see: Ernst-Otto Czempiel, "Die Zukunft der Atlantischen Allianz", in *Aus Politik und Zeitgeschichte*, B 13/83, pp. 10–21; also Czempiel, "Diagnose der Atlantischen Gemeinschaft, Stabile Strukturen, aber unterschiedliche Konfliktbilder", *Europa Archiv*, Vol. 39 1984, 53–62.
11. See for example Horst Ehmke, "Eine Politik zur Selbstbehauptung Europas", *Europa Archiv*, Vol. 39 1984, 195–204.
12. See among others Karl-Heinz Reuband, "Antiamerikanismus – ein deutsches Problem? Konstanz und Wandel des Amerikabildes im Spiegel der Umfrageforschung", S + F, 1/85, 46–52; Ernst-Otto Czempiel, 'Amerika- Deutschland – ein besonderes Verhältnis', *Aussenpolitik*, Vol. 34, 1983 211–223; Berndt von Staden, "Deutsche und Amerikaner – Irritationen", *Aussenpolitik*, Vol. 35, 1984, 44–53.
13. See Helmut Schmidt, *Eine Strategie für den Westen*, Berlin 1986; Robert E. Hunter, *NATO, op. cit.*, see also Stanley Hoffmann, "The US and Western Europe Wait and Worry", *Foreign Affairs*, Vol. 63, 1985, 631–652.
14. See Klaus Knorr, "Burden-sharing in NATO: Aspects of U.S. Policy", *Orbis*, Vol. 29, 1985, 517–536.
15. See the proposals by Henry Kissinger, "A Plan to Re-Shape NATO", *Time*, 5 March 1984; also Gerd Schmückle, *Das Schwert am seidenen Faden, Krisenmanagement in Europa*, Stuttgart 1984.
16. See Zbigniew Brzezinski, *Game Plan – A Geostrategic Framework for the Conduct of the US-Soviet Contest*, Boston/New York 1986; Brzezinski, "Die Zukunft von Jalta", *Europa Archiv*, Vol. 39, 1984, 703–716.
17. See Werner Weidenfeld/Wolfgang Wessels (eds.), *Wege zur Europäischen Union Vom Vertrag zur Verfassung?*, Bonn 1986, pp. 28 ff.
18. Cf. among others Peter Bender, *Das Ende des ideologischen Zeitalters, Die Europäisierung Europas*, Berlin 1981; Bender, "Westeuropa oder Gesamteuropa?" in Werner Wiedenfeld (ed.), *Die Identität Europas, op. cit.*, pp. 235–254; Claude Bourdet/Alfred Mechtersheimer (eds.), *Europäisierung Europas*, Berlin 1984; Ulrich Albrecht et al. (ed.), *Deutsche Fragen – Europäische Antworten*, Berlin 1983.
19. For a closer look see Werner Weidenfeld, "Perspektiven einer engeren sicherheitspolitischen Zusammenarbeit der westeuropäischen Staaten", in *DGFK Jahrbuch 1982/83, Zur Lage Europas im globalen Spannungsfeld*, Baden-Baden 1983, pp. 467–477.

20. For a review of the historical context see Klaus Dieter Hartwig, *Verteidigungspolitik als Moment der westeuropäischen Integration*, Frankfurt 1977.
21. See especially Karl Kaiser, 'Ein unauflöslicher Zusammenhang: Sicherheit und Integration', in Werner Weidenfeld (ed.), *Die Identität Europas, op. cit.*, pp. 173–190; Heinrich Schneider, *Leitbilder der Europapolitik*, Bonn 1977; Schneider, 'Rückblick für die Zukunft, Konzeptionelle Weichenstellungen für die Europäische Einigung', *Mainzer Beiträge zur Europäischen Einigung* Vol. 7, Bonn 1986; Werner Weidenfeld, *Europa begreifen*, München 1984.
22. Cf. Max Kohnstamm/Wolfgang Hager, (eds.), *Zivilmacht Europa – Supermacht oder Partner?*, Frankfurt 1973.
23. See Paul Noack, *Das Scheitern der europäischen Verteidigungsgemeinschaft*, Bonn 1977; Arnulf Baring, *Aussenpolitik in Adenauers Kanzlerdemokratie, Bonns Beitrag zur Europäischen Verteidigungsgemeinschaft*, München/Wien 1969; Hans-Erich Volkmann/Walter Schwengler (eds.), *Die Europäische Verteidigungsgemeinschaft, Stand und Probleme der Forschung*, Boppard 1985.
24. See Klaus von Schubert, *Wiederbewaffnung und Westintegration*, Stuttgart 1970; Gerhard Wettig, *Entmilitarisierung und Wiederbewaffnung in Deutschland 1943–1955*, München 1967.
25. Thomas Jansen, *Europa; Von der Gemeinschaft zur Union*, Mainzer Beiträge zur Europäischen Einigung Vol. 6, Bonn 1982.
26. See Joseph Rovan/Werner Weidenfeld (eds.), *Europäische Zeitzeichen, Elemente eines deutsch-französischen Dialogs, Mainzer Beiträge zur Europäischen Einigung, Vol. 1*, Bonn 1982; Robert Picht (ed.), *Das Bündnis im Bündnis*, Berlin 1982; Gilbert Zieburat, *Die deutsch-französischen Beziehungen seit 1945: Mythen und Realitäten*, Pfullingen 1970.
27. Karl Carsten/Dieter Mahncke (eds.), *Westeuropäische Verteidigungskooperation*, München/Wien 1972.
28. Johan J. Holst, 'Die Unabhängige Europäische Programmgruppe', *NATO-Brief*, 29: 2, 1981, 8–11.
29. Walter Schütze, "Frankreichs Aussen- und Sicherheitspolitik unter François Mitterand', *Europa Archiv*, Vol. 37, 1982, 591–602; Konrad Seitz, "Deutsch-französische sicherheitspolitische Zusammenarbeit", *Europa Archiv*, Vol. 37, 1982, 657–664. See also the chapter on "Westeuropas Sicherheitspolitik" in *Jahrbuch der Europäischen Integration 1983*, Bonn 1984.
30. Reprinted in *Jahrbuch der Europäischen Integration 1981*, Bonn 1982, pp. 500–504.
31. Reprinted in *Jahrbuch der Europäischen Integration 1983*, Bonn 1984, pp. 417–424.
32. Reprinted in *Jahrbuch der Europäischen Integration 1985*, Bonn 1986.
33. For an up-to-date review see Peter Schmidt, *Sicherheitspolitische Entwicklungsperspektiven der Westeuropäischen Union*, SWP-AZ 2450, Ebenhausen 1985; also Schmidt, "Die WEU – Eine Union ohne Perspektive?", *Aussenpolitik*, Vol. 36, pp. 384–394.
34. Niels J. Haagerup, "Die europäische Sicherheitsdimension", *Europa Archiv*, Vol. 38, 1983, 273–278.
35. Reprinted in Reinhardt Rummel/Wolfgang Wessels (eds.), *Die Europäische Politische Zusammenarbeit. Leistungsvermögen und Struktur der EPZ*, Bonn 1978, pp. 351–356.
36. For the differences among West European countries see Peter Schmidt, *Europeanization of Defense, Prospects of Consensus?*, Santa Monica 1984.
37. Christopher Tugendhat, "Europa braucht Selbstvertrauen, Sicherheitspolitik: Eine neue Aufgabe für die Europäische Gemeinschaft", *Europa Archiv*, Vol. 37, 1982, 1–8; Joseph C. Rallo, *Defending Europe, in the 1990s, the New Divide of High Technology*, London 1986.
38. Reprinted in Jürgen Schwarz (ed.), *Der Aufbau Europas, Pläne und Dokumente 1945–1980*, Bonn 1980, pp. 161–240.

Chapter 11
Alternative Structures for European Defence Co-operation

TREVOR TAYLOR

Introduction

British involvement in the formation and operation of the institutions in the field of European defence co-operation would suggest both that Britain has long been in favour of such co-operation and that it feels the institutional context in which it takes place to be important. In 1947 Britain signed the Dunkirk Treaty, so committing itself to the defence of France, and in 1948 it played a leading part in the organisation of the Brussels Treaty. In 1954, when the European Defence Community (EDC) collapsed, it was the UK, despite its non-involvement with the EDC, which took the initiative for the formation of the Western European Union (WEU) in 1955. In 1968 Labour Defence Minister Denis Healey was closely associated with the formation of Eurogroup and Britain was centrally involved in the talks in 1975–6 which led to the Independent European Programme Group (IEPG). Moreover, Britain in various ways makes specific contributions to these bodies. The Secretary-General and the Council of the WEU are based in London, although the Assembly meets in Paris and most of the organisation's staff work there. Britain provides the secretarial support for the Eurogroup staff group at NATO and for the IEPG staff group. Lastly, it chairs the important IEPG Panel 1 which scrutinises countries' procurement plans and seeks to identify opportunities for collaborative projects.

Not revealed by this list of activities are the reasons and motives for their being undertaken. A prime British concern in supporting European co-operation in this area has been to obtain and then keep a

US commitment to the defence of Western Europe. This motive is still present, although today it also has to take account of the possibility of rejection of the United States by Europe. The West European pre-NATO alliances demonstrated to Washington that the West Europeans were ready to do something for their own defence and were thus worthy of US backing. The formation of the WEU served to allow West German and Italian rearmament and involvement in the defence of the West. Without this, not only would a credible NATO posture have been more problematic in military terms but there would also have been the problem of dealing with the "agonising reappraisal" of American commitments threatened by Dulles. By 1968, burden-sharing within the Alliance was a real issue and Eurogroup was set up in part as a means of demonstrating to the United States the dimensions of West Europe's real contribution to its own defence. As for the IEPG, while indigenous concerns to make European arms collaboration work better were a factor in its formation, it was also significant that at the time the US was pressing for more effective use of Alliance funds to secure more defensive capability[1]. Thus one role of the IEPG was to reassure Washington that the rational use of resources was receiving serious attention.

Particularly since the coming to power of President Reagan, however, the British Government, along with others in Western Europe, has had to take seriously:

— whether Europeans should not seek to work together on defence issues so as to have more influence on the shape of NATO policies in general and on the US in particular; and

— whether Europeans should not step up their defence co-operation to prepare for the day when the US presence in, and commitment to, their continent might be much reduced. Should not the British government seek some "reinsurance" in case the US commitment should be eroded or even disappear suddenly as a consequence of some crisis in NATO? The Strategic Defence Initiative (SDI) and the Reykjavik summit signalled to some that the United States was increasingly dissatisfied with living under a nuclear threat derived in part from its commitment to Europe.

Clearly, the European institutions concerned with security must be affected by changing expectations about just what they are expected to do. In Britain, interest in European defence co-operation has been driven in part by increased involvement in Western Europe in general and in part by concern about US policies. It has not, however, been stimulated by fear that West Germany might be moving towards the option of neutrality. Either because the British are too wrapped up in their own debates about defence policy, or because they believe the momentum behind current West German policy is too great to permit any drastic change in direction, or because they are simply complacent, the British have been almost totally unaffected by the French concern in the early 1980s about possible West German neutralism. Of course, there was some British satisfaction with French worries because they helped turn France into a more constructive and less awkward defence partner.

The confused structure provided by the institutions for European security co-operation constitutes a fundamental problem for those in Britain who would like to think that Western Europe could and should develop a collective defence identity. Table 4.1 highlights the fact that the institutional provision for European security co-operation was put together over decades under varying circumstances and for different reasons. It thus looks, and is, extremely awkward from a functional, managerial perspective.

The Western European Union

When Britain entered the European Community in 1973, the *raison d'être* for this organisation as far as the British government was concerned essentially disappeared. In previous years the WEU had served as a link, which included ministerial meetings, between the UK and the membership of the European Community. EC membership for Britain made this link redundant and the WEU fell into further disuse. Britain's judgements were no different from those of the rest of the membership and from 1973 the WEU Council ceased to meet at full ministerial level. Its Assembly continued to operate and the Council met in the form of junior Ministers and the members' ambassadors in London, but the organisation was largely moribund.

In the early 1980s, voices in France began to suggest a revitalisation of the WEU as part of an effort to establish a strong European pillar in NATO. France was motivated, it seems, by fear of anti-NATO trends in West Germany triggered by the cruise missile issue.

The British government was in two minds on the French ideas. On the one hand, it looked approvingly on something which would involve France more clearly in the defence of Europe. On the other hand, there was only limited respect for the WEU as an organisation. Its staff were not highly regarded in Whitehall. Also, in the early 1980s Britain was far from convinced that a independent, firm and clear European voice in NATO would be a good thing. There was a specific fear that it might persuade Washington that it was neither wanted or needed in Europe.

On balance, Britain's desire to demonstrate its European credentials prevailed and it went along with the "revitalisation" exercise[2] with many remaining rather sceptical of its worth. WEU Council ministerial meetings were started again in 1984 in a new form with both defence and foreign ministers in attendance for the twice-yearly meetings. A new structure for the WEU staff was in place by the beginning of 1986.

Table 4. Institutions relevant to European Defence Co-operation: Concerns and Membership

BODY →	WEU 1955	EUROGROUP 1968	IEPG 1976	EC/EPC 1958/70	ESA 1975	EUREKA 1985
STATUS →	IGO	INFORMAL	INFORMAL	IGO	IGO	IGO
CONCERNS →	Comprehensive range of defence concerns	Wide range of conventional defence concerns. Promotes European position in US	European and European-US arms cooperation	Economic integration in Europe. Economic and political aspects of security in European foreign policy	Co-ordination of European co-operation in space	European co-operation in civil high technology
MEMBERSHIP						
FRG	Yes	Yes	Yes	Yes	Yes	Yes
FRANCE	Yes	No	Yes	Yes	Yes	Yes
UK	Yes	Yes	Yes	Yes	Yes	Yes
ITALY	Yes	Yes	Yes	Yes	Yes	Yes
BELGIUM	Yes	Yes	Yes	Yes	Yes	Yes
NETHERLANDS	Yes	Yes	Yes	Yes	Yes	Yes
LUXEMBOURG	Yes	Yes	Yes	Yes	No	Yes
SPAIN		Yes	Yes	Yes	Yes	Yes
PORTUGAL		Yes	Yes	Yes	No	Yes
DENMARK		Yes	Yes	Yes	Yes	Yes
NORWAY		Yes	Yes	No	No a)	Yes
GREECE		Yes	Yes	Yes	No	Yes
TURKEY		Yes	Yes	No	No	Yes
IRELAND				Yes	Yes	Yes
SWEDEN					Yes	Yes
SWITZERLAND					Yes	Yes
FINLAND b)						Yes
AUSTRIA a)						Yes

a) Participates in some ESA projects
b) In process of joining ESA.

Since then, the WEU is perceived in the UK Press not to have advanced much and its efforts to consult on the SDI have been perceived, somewhat unfairly, as unfruitful. This, however, is not entirely accurate: the Council has kept its working group on the SDI in operation and has reached interim agreements which are broadly supportive of the four points agreed by President Reagan and Mrs Thatcher in Washington in December 1984[3]. Britain is, however, among those states which are content to play down the reality and significance of any consensus on SDI within the WEU because it does not believe that the appearance of a European bloc on this issue would be useful. If a European stance appeared too supportive, it might help the pro-SDI factions in Washington to gain support. If the Europeans were too sceptical, let alone hostile, their influence would be diminished by predictable descriptions of them as faint-hearted and unreliable allies by American hawks. As a junior British Minister put it, "we should avoid rushing to early or divisive conclusions"[4]. Britain was happy with the conception of the WEU Council agreed in the autumn of 1986 and reflected at the November 1986 ministerial meeting in Luxembourg that the Council should serve primarily as a forum for frank consultation and not as a means of generating distinct stances to present to another ally, the United States. Britain was also happy that the ministerial meeting brought forth similar views on Reykjavik, including increased appreciation of the significance of the independent nuclear forces in Europe.

In Britain, an important aspect of the WEU is that it is primarily a Foreign and Commonwealth Office responsibility, although there is some Ministry of Defence involvement. For several reasons, FCO officials tend to be rather more supportive of the WEU than their colleagues in the Ministry of Defence. The FCO is generally more Europe-oriented than is MoD and the WEU is a route to FCO influence on defence questions. Moreover, there is a greater readiness in the FCO than MoD to think about the possibility of the US guarantee for Europe one day disappearing. Keeping the WEU alive then becomes one of the elements in a UK "reinsurance" policy against the demise of the Atlantic Alliance. Sentiments often heard in MoD, on the other hand, stress that Europe lacks the resources and collective determination to be able to defend itself.

Next, the FCO recognises that, insofar as European Political Co-operation has not really allowed effective debate on security questions (see below), the WEU can be a forum for European consultation. "The failure, so far, to grasp in European Political Co-operation the security issues which are so vital to Europe should not be allowed to stand in the way of better European consultation and co-ordination"[5]. The British Political Director is taking part in *ad hoc* meetings of political directors which the new WEU Secretary-General, Alfred Cahen, has begun to organise in London. The MoD is now involved in these as well. Lastly there is a sense in which the fundamental expectations and attitudes of defence officials can make them less impressed with the WEU. FCO officials accept easily that discussions that drag on over a protracted period can nevertheless be useful as a means of learning about others and of securing better understanding of a position. In the MoD, in contrast, where most of the work is concerned with other British personnel in the ministry itself, in the services and industry, and where there is a massive budget to handle, meetings are expected to produce hard decisions if they are not to be considered a waste of time. WEU gatherings produce few hard decisions, even on the contents of communiqués. What all appreciate about the WEU Council, however, is that it brings the French defence minister into a collective gathering where the full range of defence questions can be discussed.

In 1985 the British Defence White Paper included a separate chapter on "The European Pillar"[6]. While there is clearly a danger of reading too much between the lines of such a document, it is interesting that the revival of the WEU was described in rather bland terms and most attention was paid not to the Council but to the Assembly, whose potential for stimulating debate on defence questions, for helping to build consensus in Europe, and for promoting European defence co-operation was noted. This was rather hearty endorsement for a body whose membership was common with the Assembly of the Council of Europe and which often was not particularly well-informed on defence. Its activities receive almost no attention in the UK media. The British governmental assessment[7] of the WEU Assembly's capacity to influence public opinion appears somewhat optimistic.

To some extent the British position on the WEU remains one of wait and see. In no sense is the UK leading the way towards strengthening the organisation. It has supported the initiatives of others in case the WEU should prove useful yet it does not want to see much WEU involvement with arms co-operation (which is reserved for the IEPG) or with arms control. One consideration is that many of the old staff of the WEU have been and are being replaced. How well their replacements will function is still to be seen and a review of the WEU's operation is scheduled by the membership for 1987. A structural weakness of the WEU is obviously its division between London and Paris. The impact of the Secretary-General is inevitably reduced by his being located away from most of his staff. Overall, in 1986 the many reservations about European defence co-operation felt by British politicians and officials meant that there was considerable wariness about giving the WEU a central role, not least because the WEU's treaty and structure give it considerable potential. Should the WEU really get going, it might prove hard to control but there were few signs of this happening.

Eurogroup

Although it is almost inconceivable that Eurogroup will be going anywhere, the 1985 Defence White Paper showed no hestitation in laying some emphasis on it as "the main multilateral forum with NATO for practical co-operation in this field" (of European defence co-operation). The operation of Eurogroup's sub-groups, of its ministerail meetings and of its publicity activities highlighting European defence efforts were all favourably if briefly described.[8]

Eurogroup's role of seeking to defuse the burden-sharing debate within the US through publicity efforts about Europe's contribution is recognised by the UK as very worthwhile, even though it is hindered by the absence of France's forces from the data. But beyond that it is hard to perceive just what the Eurogroup does beyond providing an excuse for a dinner before NATO Defence Committee meetings where European ministers can have an informal chat. Of the bodies supporting European security co-operation, Eurogroup is the most dispensable and its sub-groups' tasks could be re-allocated to a strengthened IEPG. The White Paper's positive treatment of it is attributable to two factors. First, Britain had been responsible for Eurogroup's formation in the first place and it was the UK's turn to chair it in 1984. Politically it was thus necessary to speak relatively favourably of it. Second, the UK Government as a whole is genuinely uncertain about the rate at which it wants European defence co-operation to proceed and about the channels through which it wants progress to occur. In these circumstances, the safest and least meaningful step is to be polite about each of the candidates.

The Independent European Programme Group (IEPG)

Although he was the chairman of Eurogroup in 1984, Michael Heseltine was persuaded that European progress in defence could be easiest and most effectively pursued within the area of armaments co-operation, where the IEPG had prime responsibility. Despite formal WEU concern with arms co-operation, Britain was and remains convinced that European arms co-operation efforts must be concentrated in the IEPG. This can be justified by reference to the wider IEPG membership, to the suitability of the IEPG mechanisms for identifying collaborative project opportunities, and to the IEPG's established place as a successful interlocutor for Europe with the United States. Also to be kept in mind, however, is that the IEPG is essentially controllable, having a narrow formal area of responsibility and lacking its own staff.

For whatever reasons, Britain supports the IEPG. It has always chaired its Panel 1 on members' procurement schedules. Particularly under Michael Heseltine, there was some British initiative to get more projects going and to establish more co-operation on research. More broadly, Britain supported the then chairman of the IEPG, the Dutch State Secretary Jan van Houwelingen, who tried to give the IEPG a more central place in arms procurement, in part by introducing twice-yearly meetings of full defence ministers to give European armaments co-operation more political momentum. In this they have largely succeeded[9].

Interestingly, the 1985 Defence White Paper talked about the "significant progress" in arms co-operation and it also summarised the important November 1984 Ministerial decisions[10], thus drawing attention to the importance of European armaments collaboration for Britain's defence and industry.

The European Community and European Political Co-operation (EPC)

Focus on armaments procurement and industry leads next to consideration of the European Community's role in defence. Here there are three questions (two specific, one general) which British policy has to address:

— should the EC, specifically the EC Commission, have a role in efforts to make Europe's defence industries more efficient and competitive?
— should ministers and others meeting in EPC be able in principle to discuss defence matters?
— if the US commitment to Europe cannot be taken for granted, should a start be made on turning the EC into the basic organisation for European security?

Historically, the record is that Britain demonstrated little enthusiasm for the many proposals from Spinelli, Klepsch, Fergusson and others for Commission involvement with defence industries. This stemmed, until the mid-1980s, from a belief that it would not be in Britain's interest to promote international consideration of its national defence manufacturing capabilities and from a UK reluctance to consider the EC as anything other than a civil organisation.

In the mid-1980s, however, there was a slight change of emphasis. Led by Michael Heseltine, who built on some of the conclusions of his predecessor Sir John Nott[11], there was acceptance of the need for analysis of Europe's defence industries in general. Responsibility for the initial investigatory work was allocated to the IEPG rather than to the Commission. However, the IEPG study group in question had some contact with the Commission and worked on some items with the WEU.

Like others, the British government knows that Commission involvement with defence might cause problems within the Community with Ireland, Denmark, Greece and even France. It is also concerned that the Community bureaucracy might not deal with defence industrial questions with any effectiveness. The Commission has acquired something of a reputation as a heavy-handed and cumbersome bureaucracy while there is British awareness of the dynamism being generated within IEPG by the national staffs who currently run it. Yet Britain, like the other signatories, opened the door for Commission involvement with defence industries by agreeing to Article 30 (paragraph 6) of the 1986 Single European Act[12].

As for EPC, in the past five years Britain moved from being rather neutral about the 1981 Genscher-Colombo proposals to favouring the discussion in EPC of economic and political aspects of European security. Foreign Minister Sir Geoffrey Howe has claimed British credit for the terms of the Single European Act which reinforced the Community members' view that this should happen[13]. The British government has come to recognise that Britain's voice in the world, to be effective, must often be linked to a wider European position. In this situation, it clearly does not make sense to draw an arbitrary line around foreign policy to exclude security issues. There is broad British satisfaction with the way that EPC has operated and thus readiness has grown to see its field of operations expanded. In his speech to the European Parliament, as Chairman of the Council of Ministers, Sir Geoffrey Howe almost claimed superpower status for the EC.

> The Community is one of the leading political, as well as economic, power groups in the democratic West. We should be equal partners with our American allies in sharing responsibility for upholding and protecting Western values. . . .
> If we are equal partners with the United States we are also equal interlocutors with the Soviet Union and the countries of Eastern Europe[14].

This, however, does not mean that Britain has accepted that it should promote the Community as the basis for European defence co-operation to prepare for the day when the US commitment to Europe is no longer available. Sir Geoffrey also said that the security of the West depends on a strong United States, committed to the defence of Europe. There is still widespread concern that too much European defence co-operation, in whatever forum, would bring forward the day of US withdrawal from Europe. Also, economically, the EC is at the centre of European-American rivalry and to put defence responsibilities unambiguously into its sphere of concern at this time could be viewed by the current administration as imprudent.

Eureka and the European Space Agency (ESA)

We have seen that there is growing if cautious British governmental support for European defence co-operation, especially in the armament co-operation/high technology area. This emphasis is matched by Britain's backing for the "civil" ESA and Eureka programmes. These are of importance for the defence sector because, although civil in their primary nature, many of them have strong military implications. In ESA, the European orientation of Britain's effort is not really in question, although there is some European dissatisfaction at the way Britain, or rather Rolls-Royce, has kept to itself details of its Hotol project. In ESA, the salient fact is that Britain has been a small, declining spender on space activities as a whole[15]. As for Eureka, Britain gained credit (even in France)[16], for the way in which as chairman it not only oversaw the establishment of a large number of projects but also integrated questions of technological co-operation, first, with the need to change corporate and banking attitudes to high-risk ventures in Europe and second, with the need for a genuine single European market in high technology goods unhampered by governmental restrictions and practices.

Critique and looking forward

The pattern of European defence institutions makes little functional sense, yet British policy, like that of other European governments, has been somewhat undiscriminating in that the IEPG, EPC, Eurogroup and the WEU have all received official endorsement and in most cases strengthening. The UK government has supported the idea of European defence/security co-operation while remaining wary of its dangers. Along with other governments, it has not been keen enough on such co-operation to promote a rational institutional framework in which it could take place.

Britain has tended to follow the lead of others, not wanting to be left behind, but rarely seizing the initiative. One exception to this was Michael Heseltine who as Defence Minister put a lot of effective effort into the IEPG. Thus the IEPG study of Europe's defence industries launched in November 1984 originated from a British proposal for a study of the rationalisation of Europe's defence research effort.

Further UK leadership in the IEPG appears unlikely. There was recognition that the IEPG needed time to settle after its rapid advances under van Houwelingen's chairmanship and Michael Heseltine's replacement, George Younger, was a very different personality from his predecessor. It is to be hoped that considerable guidance as to the future direction of the IEPG will come from its study on European defence industries published in December 1986[17]. In armaments, the next few years of European co-operation will see considerable stress on specific projects, and particularly on whether major schemes like the Eurofighter can avoid the cost and delay problems of previous collaborative exercises. This is bound to distract attention from institutions as such.

From British intellectuals and even politicians outside government, there have been several ideas about institutional change[18]. The European Democratic Group, the British Conservatives in the European Parliament, have been associated with several proposals[19]. Two themes recur through much of the literature. One is that, in the central sector of armaments co-operation, there needs to be both European co-ordination of arms procurement, through the IEPG or some derivative body, and of European arms development and production, most obviously through the European Community. The other is that the notion of the European Community as a purely civil body is an artificial one. As the late Hedley Bull argued, a responsibility of any community is to provide for its members' security[20]. The logic for Community involvement in defence is strengthened by the possibility that the US might not always be available as a guarantor of US security. Without a credible security system, it cannot be expected that the economic and political benefits of the European Community could long survive.

This author's emphasis would be on the value of doing some tidying up and on the current reluctance of governments to set up any new bodies. One fairly straightforward set of changes would be to abolish Eurogroup and incorporate its functions into a revamped and strengthened IEPG. EPC could become the European body most concerned with out-of-area security issues and would seek to co-ordinate European positions on non-strategic arms control matters such as CSCE and the negotiations which are based at the UN in Geneva. For its part the WEU Council would relinquish responsibility for armaments and concentrate on strategic questions including nuclear arms control and the role of nuclear weapons in Europe's defence, although this would lead to some friction with the US. The IEPG would aim at becoming a centre for the co-ordination of European procurement, ie weapons-ordering, while the EC would have a responsibility for prompting the strengthening of West Europe's defence industries so that they could meet European and, it might be hoped US orders in a timely and competitive manner. Some membership problems could be eased if Norway could be persuaded to join the European Community.

By giving Western European states an opportunity to work together on all defence issues, these institutional changes would increase the chances of effective European defence co-operation, although issues of membership of the various bodies would have to be faced, as would questions of overlap between the different organisations. At least a start would have been made on organising a sensible division of labour between the various European bodies.

Besides trying to develop some kind of division of labour among European institutions, another priority should be to devote effort specifically to improving co-ordination and contact between them. The IEPG has already made a start on trying to hold informal, low-level discussions with the Commission but has encountered some opposition from France. The basic considerations are that many of the institutions concerned with European defence, economic, technological and political co-operation have overlapping concerns and areas of expertise useful to others. Since it seems unlikely that any single European body is going to be placed in overall charge of the whole of European security-related co-operation, additional effort is necessary to keep all institutions aware of the activities of their colleague organisations.

Britain seems unlikely to take the lead in institutional reform terms. Indeed British policy towards European defence institutions is open to the criticism of sometimes lacking coherence. This is in part attributable to different perspectives from the Ministry of Defence and the Foreign & Commonwealth Office but also important are the divisions between ministers. Put simply, the relevant specialist ministers – Howe, Younger and formerly Heseltine – are more instinctively in favour of European co-operation than is the Prime Minister. Mrs Thatcher is thought to tolerate European defence co-operation as far as it is necessary but her political instincts are always to work first with the US. Her actions during the 1985–6 Westland crisis were instructive in this regard.

Also the style of British policy does not lead the UK to initiating suggestions for wide-ranging and important changes. Certainly it is hard to imagine London being the generator of proposals for yet another new institution. The British style is for pragmatic incrementalism.

The Reykjavik summit certainly did something to increase British appreciation of the value of European defence co-operation. Reykjavik was recognised in the UK as being of great significance and Britain was appreciative of being able to work afterwards with allies, in the WEU and elsewhere, to bring home to Washington the need for a nuclear dimension in Europe's defence, at least until comparative conventional force strengths are adjusted. Mrs Thatcher, with European backing, was apparently able to persuade President Reagan of this view when she visited Washington in November 1986. However, British government personnel tended not to view Reykjavik as a clear signal of US long-term disillusion with providing a nuclear umbrella for Europe.

It is significant that the other political parties in Britain, while seeing defence as a major electoral and political issue, are little concerned yet with European institutions. They are still considering the issues on which they might want to co-operate in Europe rather than the mechanisms through which co-operation is to be achieved. The Labour Party is centrally concerned with the abolition of Britain's independent nuclear deterrent and with articulating a coherent defence policy based on conventional strength. Somewhat ironically for a party which traditionally has been little impressed by the European Community, it has discovered that such a policy pushes it towards co-operating with other European states with whose conventional forces the UK must work. It has thus begun discussions with other socialist parties in Europe, but particularly the German SPD, on how to make a non-nuclear defence look viable.

For its part, the SDP-Liberal Alliance is strongly in favour of European defence co-operation in general while having said little about institutions as such. Its major policy statement, *Defence and Disarmament*, came out strongly in favour of increased European defence co-operation across a range of issues so as to strengthen the European pillar in NATO. Yet at one point it suggested that the main responsibility for developing the pillar lay with "members of the European Community" while elsewhere it focused on the duties of the European members of NATO[21]. Thus it ignored the "Norway-Ireland" issue.

The British defence community – in government, research institutes, the media and academia – has spent some years pondering over the benefits of European co-operation in the security area. Understandably, writers have been reluctant to devote too much attention to institutions until they have become sure what benefits such co-operation could bring. In the middle of the 1980s there is more confidence about the prospective benefits from such co-operation and thought must now be given to the institutional machinery which might deliver them. Hard decisions about building up some institutions and running down others need to be faced. On the other hand, if effective institutions were created, they would be likely to be able to push states along and influence their behaviour. Perhaps that is why the UK, and other European states, are content for the moment to keep control of security co-operation mainly in national governmental hands. Yet, without reasonable international institutional provision, the gains from European security co-operation are likely to prove elusive.

Notes

1. An important study was Thomas A. Callaghan, *US/European Economic Cooperation in Military and Civil Technology*, Washington DC, Center for Strategic & International Studies, Georgetown Univ, Revised Edition Sept. 1975.
2. See Lady Young's speech to the Assembly of the WEU on 3 December 1985, text supplied by Foreign & Commonwealth Office.
3. See 31st Annual Report of the Council to the Assembly on the Council's activities in 1985, Assembly of the WEU Document 1061, 32nd Ordinary Session, 1st Part, 20 May 1986.

4. Lady Young, *op. cit.*
5. *Ibid.*
6. *Statement on the Defence Estimates* (SDE) 1985, Vol. 1, Cmnd. 9430–1, London, HMSO, 1985, Ch. 3.
7. *Ibid* and Lady Young, *op. cit.*
8. SDE 1985, *op. cit.*, p. 17.
9. See the IEPG Ministrial Declaration & Decision Document, published in *NATO Review*, Vol. 32 No. 4, December 1984, pp. 26–30.
10. SDE 1985, *op. cit.*, p. 18.
11. John Nott, "Economic Constraints and British Defence", *Survival* Vol. 24 No. 2, March–April 1982, especially p. 90.
12. Text of the Single European Act, 1986 Article 30 para 6 b), London, HMSO, Cmnd 7758, 1986.
13. *Ibid*, Para 6 a) and Howe's speech to the European Parliament 8 July 1986, text supplied by FCO.
14. Howe speech *op. cit.*
15. Data in *The Times* 13 January 1986.
16. See lead story in *Le Monde* 2 July 1986.
17. *Towards a Stronger Europe*. A report by an Independent Study Team established by the Defence Ministers of Nations of the Independent European Study Group to make proposals to improve the competitiveness of Europe's defence equipment industry, in two volumes. Available from the IEPG Secretariat, UK Delegation, NATO, Brussels.
18. See *inter alia* Assembly of the WEU, Report from the Committee on Defence Questions and Armaments, Rapporteur Julian Critchley, "A European Armaments Policy", 23 Ord. Sess., 1st Part, Doc. 786, 31 October 1978; D. Greenwood, *Report on a Policy for Promoting Defence & Technological Cooperation among West European Countries*, for the Commission of the EC, Commission Doc. III–1499/80; B. Burroughs and G. Edwards, *The Defence of Western Europe*, London, Butterworth, 1982; T. Taylor, *European Defence Cooperation*, London, RIIA and Routledge and Kegan Paul, Chatham House Paper No. 24, 1984; G. L. & A. L. Williams, *The European Defence Initiative*, London, Macmillan, 1986. One American author published in the UK in 1986 a strong statement in favour of European defence and high technology cooperation, see J. C. Rallo, *Defending Europe in the 1990s: The New Divide of High Technology*, London, Frances Pinter 1986.
19. See for instance Report for the Political Committee on "Arms Procurement within a Common Industrial Policy and Arms Sales" (the Fergusson Report), Europ. Parl. Working Docs., Doc. 1455/83, 27 June 1983; H. Bull, J. Alford and D. Greenwood, "Thinking Again about European Defence", London, European Democratic Group, undated; and Sir Peter Vanneck, Niels J. Haagerup and General W. Schall, "The European Parliament and the Security of the West", Brussels, European Democratic Group, 1984.
20. Bull *op. cit.*, p. 7.
21. Report of the Joint SDP-Liberal Alliance Commission, *Defence and Disarmament*, London, SDP & Liberal Parties, June 1986.

Chapter 12
Britain's Nuclear Commitment to Germany

LAWRENCE FREEDMAN

It is remarkable how little discussion there has been of Anglo-German nuclear relations except in the NATO context. The two countries have co-operated in the Nuclear Planning Group and elsewhere in helping to shape the Alliance's nuclear policy. They have worked together to influence the position of the United States.

However, while there is considerable material on Anglo-German attitudes with regard to the American nuclear guarantee to Europe, there is very little with regard to the British guarantee. Yet as a result of the Nassau Agreement of December 1962, Britain agreed to assign its nuclear forces to NATO. Some of Britain's nuclear inventory is based in West Germany. In providing a rationale for the total nuclear inventory, successive British governments have emphasised the contribution that this force makes to NATO's nuclear deterrence. There is little evidence that this issue has been fully thought through at the strategic nuclear level, let alone at the level of battlefield nuclear weapons and medium-range bombers.

Equally, this contribution is rarely remarked upon by the German government. Peter Malone in his study of *The British Nuclear Deterrent* found that West German officials and politicians believed that "the fact that two European powers are nuclear weapons states helps maintain equilibrium". Britain's nuclear status helps offset both the German conventional and the French nuclear capability in the internal balance of European forces and, with France, overall American dominance of the Alliance. Malone also found some respect in West Germany for the idea that multiple decision-centres might strengthen deterrence, but also for the view that French forces were more important in this context for geographical, doctrinal, political and cultural reasons. He quotes a German official to the effect that "geography and the special relationship make it very unlikely" that there would be British action independent of the United States and "the Soviets know that".[1]

In Germany there is no official questioning of the American guarantee and great stress is put on its contribution. The 1985 White Paper stresses the "vital importance" of "strong US forces and the deployment of US nuclear weapons in the Federal Republic of Germany" in guaranteeing "a maximum of visible deterrence". But no mention is made of UK nuclear forces in Europe or the role that they play.[2]

In bilateral Anglo-German relations, questions of nuclear policy have not acquired the importance that they have in the relations between Britain and France, and between France and Germany. It is not difficult to understand why both countries look to France – but not to each other. The Federal Republic has a natural interest in the intentions of its neighbour and close partner. This interest was originally prompted by France's withdrawal from NATO's Integrated Military Command and the discovery that short-range systems were under development which, if kept within French borders, could only hit German targets. Bonn has therefore sought to encourage a less selfish French policy, while Paris has accepted that it must shift the balance between Gaullist independence and Alliance responsibility.

The Franco-British nuclear relationship starts from the fact that they both maintain nuclear arsenals that require a degree of political protection. It is not that other nations are hostile to these capabilities; rather they are indifferent, lukewarm as either opponents or supporters and so quite prepared to see these capabilities compromised in support of other goals, such as arms control or improved conventional forces. For internal rather than external reasons, the British nuclear force is the most vulnerable: France is worried that it could be left isolated.

In addition both countries are nervous over the long-term cost of staying in the nuclear business. This helps explain the interest in whether the two countries can move beyond a shared (and loosely co-ordinated) defensiveness with regard to their nuclear forces to an active collaboration, with co-operation expanding to include operational problems, then targeting and even joint production of delivery systems. Of course progress depends not only on the balance of technical incentives. As with Franco-German nuclear relations, it also depends on the existence of fundamental shifts in foreign policy – either a loss of the American nuclear guarantee or a British break with the United States or a French reintegration into NATO.

There are no obvious foreign policy barriers to the further development of the Anglo-German nuclear relationship. Britain has deployed nuclear forces in Germany and they are explicitly committed to NATO. It would seem that this is what Bonn would like from Paris; it is still rare that Bonn acknowledges that it has the requisite nuclear commitment from London. One reason is that it is also rare for London to acknowledge that it has made the commitment or to offer guidance on how seriously it ought to be taken.

In this paper I intend to explore the nature and extent of this nuclear commitment to Germany. The most important question relates to its true meaning. How seriously should it be taken, given its generally low political profile?

It is worth bearing in mind that the nuclear "coupling" of the United States to Europe is often said to depend on deployed military systems more than formal reassurances. Deployed systems might become involved in a battle and encourage a general nuclear engagement despite the fact that, at the time, American instincts and interests were naturally pointing in the opposite direction. This chapter is therefore relevant to the general question of whether nuclear deployments can impose their own logic on a strategic environment. In the current circumstances this question must move beyond questions of strategic logic to the political context in which this logic is being worked out. This chapter therefore concludes with a discussion of the possibile implication of shifts in the policies of Germany, Britain and the United States for the Anglo-German nuclear relationship.

The second centre of decision

Britain offers an interesting case study for the proposition that nuclear deployments as a reflection of a long-term commitment can override what might be more basic political interests during rapidly-changing political circumstances. Its German-based forces are small compared with those of the United States. Nor has London offered the sort of regular and insistent assurances to its Allies with regard to its nuclear obligations as has Washington. The USA's more substantial deployment and regular assurances ensure that this is the most critical component of the NATO deterrent posture. Any proposition on the importance of peacetime deployments in enforcing wartime engagements valid in the British case is much more likely to be valid in the more important American case.

However, should Warsaw Pact forces begin to move through Europe, London could well face its "moments of truth" at the same time as Washington. It is this prospect that British policy-makers have in the past drawn upon in elaborating the theory of the "second-centre of decision". According to this theory should the Soviet leadership "mistakenly" dismiss as bluff the US nuclear threats and assume that they will not be honoured at the crunch, they may wonder if they can so dismiss British (and French) threats as well. At the very least, because one is depending on the reactions of policy-makers at moments of extreme stress, the uncertainties grow as more decision-centres are included. In nuclear terms the level of risk does not have to be very high for deterrence to operate. Any increment of uncertainty adds to the risk.

The most sophisticated presentation of this theory was given by Francis Pym as Secretary of Defence in January 1980 as he prepared the intellectual ground for the decision to replace Polaris:

> Our strategy seeks to influence Soviet calculations fundamentally and decisively. It seeks to guard against any risk of Soviet miscalculation. The United States, by its words and deeds, has constantly made clear its total commitment to come to the aid of Europe, and to help defend Europe by whatever means are necessary, without exception. No words or deeds in advance could make that more crystal clear. But we are of course dealing with possible situations that would be without precedent in history, and of unique peril.
>
> The decision to take nuclear action, at any time, would be vastly hard for any President of the United States to take. In recent years I think that it has become harder, if that is imaginable, because of superpower nuclear parity. The British government have the greatest confidence in the weight and reality of the United States commitment. We cast no shade of doubt upon it. What matters most is not what we think but what the Russians think . . .
>
> The Russians cannot be assumed to look at the world as we do . . . In a crisis, Soviet leaders – perhaps beset by some pressures of turmoil in the Soviet empire, perhaps looking out upon a NATO Alliance passing through some temporary phase of internal difficulty – might conceivably misread American resolution. They might be tempted to gamble on United States hesitation.
>
> The nuclear decision, whether as a matter of retaliatory response or in another circumstance, would, of course, be no less agonising for the United Kingdom than for the United States. But it would be a decision of a separate and independent Power, and a Power whose survival in freedom might be more directly and closely threatened by aggression in Europe than that of the United States. This is where the fact of having to face two decision-makers instead of one is of such significance.
>
> Soviet leaders would have to assess that there was a greater chance of one of them using its nuclear capability than if there were a single decision-maker across the Atlantic. The risk to the Soviet Union would be inescapably higher and less calculable. This is just another way of saying that the deterrence of the Alliance as a whole would be the stronger, the more credible and therefore the more effective.[3]

By and large the tendency by commentators (including this author)[4] has been to dismiss this theory on two main grounds. First, in practice it has seemed something of a convenient diplomatic fiction; a means of reconciling the instinctive understanding of the national nuclear force in nationalistic terms with the need to explain it to the Alliance as a contribution to broader deterrence. Although it has never been officially endorsed, a compelling argument similar to that of France, for Britain maintaining its own nuclear capability is to preserve the British Isles as a sanctuary, free from nuclear attack. When making the speech quoted above, Mr Pym dismissed justifications for the British nuclear capability such as: "political prestige, our status in the Alliance, or a comparison with France . . . the concept of a 'Fortress Britain' – some kind of insurance policy concept, should the United States go isolationist or the Alliance collapse".[5]

It was notable that as the Trident decisions became more controversial, less emphasis was placed in official rationales on the second-centre argument and more on the idea that a national nuclear force is the "ultimate" guarantor of national security. Thus when announcing the decision to opt for the D5 version of Trident in March 1982, Pym's successor, Sir John Nott, after briefly restating the second-centre argument as the primary rationale, went on:

> The second reason for an exclusively British strategic deterrent is that, in the last resort, Great Britain must be responsible for her own defences. She cannot shuffle them off on another nuclear power. . . .
>   To renounce our own nuclear weapons and then shelter under the American umbrella would have neither moral nor political merit, and it would leave the French, our immediate neighbour, as the only European nuclear power.[6]

The assignment of the UK force to NATO under the 1962 Nassau Agreement continued the crucial qualifier "except where Her Majesty's Government may decide that supreme national interests are at stake"[7]. Nuclear forces are assigned to NATO and targeting is undertaken at Omaha, but control is kept firmly in British hands and separate target lists have been developed.

The second main reason for dismissing the theory is that discussion of this question, which has hardly been fulsome, has been dominated by strategic forces. The second decision-centre argument has been developed as a rationale for first Polaris and now Trident. It is hard to believe in a heroic London tolerating the likelihood of its own nuclear destruction when Washington was being more cautious (or even if Washington was not being cautious). Indeed, most of the criticisms of the independent British force from within the military and political establishment are based on the improbability of Britain taking nuclear action independent of the United States.[8] At best, given France's geographic and political position, its extensive nuclear capabilities and robust attitude to deterrence in peacetime, it may be felt that Britain at any rate should consider itself to be no more than a third-centre of nuclear decision-making.

But the question would not necessarily arise in terms of "what do we do with Polaris or Trident?", but more "what do we do with Lance or Tornado?" The option of doing nothing may be less easy in the second than in the first case simply because of the exigencies of the immediate military situation. What will be the most powerful influence? The need to accept the dictates of an integrated military command, or simply national determination in order to halt a Soviet breakthrough, or would it be a fear of horrific consequences of any nuclear release?

UK nuclear deployments in Germany

Although the development of Britain's strategic nuclear capability has now been thoroughly charted, this has not been the case with other types of nuclear weapons. In the 1957 Defence White Paper a cutback in conventional forces was combined with a decision to equip British forces in Germany with nuclear artillery and this immediately exercised an influence on the plans and tactics of BAOR. However, although ordered as early as 1955, it took until 1960 before Honest Johns and Corporals were brought into service. These were under a dual-key arrangement: a conscious decision had been taken not to develop ADMs or nuclear shells. However British aircraft, such as the Valiants assigned to NATO in 1960–1, did contain nuclear weapons produced and controlled by the British.

The current position is described succintly in the Statement on the Defence Estimates 1986:

> All our nuclear forces are committed to NATO. Since 1969 the Royal Navy has maintained at least one Polaris submarine on patrol at all times, providing the United Kingdom with an independent strategic nuclear force of last resort, and making a valuable contribution to the Alliance. Nine RAF strike-attack squadrons of Tornado GR1 and two of Buccaneer are based in the United Kingdom and the Federal Republic of Germany. These are capable of nuclear operations with the British free-fall bomb, as well as conventional warfare. The Royal Navy can also deliver nuclear bombs from Sea Harrier aircraft and depth bombs from ship-borne anti-submarine helicopters, and RAF Nimrod maritime patrol aircraft can deliver US depth bombs against submarines. The British Army in the Federal Republic of Germany operates one regiment of Lance surface-to-surface missiles and five regiments of artillery capable of firing nuclear warheads supplied by the United States.

An Annex to the Defence Estimates makes clear that the deployment in the Federal Republic is of seven Tornado squadrons. The other two Tornado and both Buccaneer squadrons are based in Britain.[9] It is of note that the British Jaguar aircraft are not now deployed in a nuclear role; this role was concluded in November 1985. Thus the independent UK nuclear forces in Germany essentially consists of about 70 Tornado aircraft. These are normally assumed to carry two nuclear free-fall bombs[10] of the WE-177 type, which were first delivered to the RAF in 1966. One source gives the yield of these weapons at around 20 kilotons[11]. Another source suggests a variable nuclear yield between 5 and 200 kilotons.[12]

With regard to the systems with warheads artillery and Lance, Britain operates four batteries of three Lance short-range missiles, plus 16

M110 203 mm self-propelled howitzers and 101 M109 155 mm self-propelled howitzers. Lance has a range of 130 km, and an accuracy of 0.4 to 0.45 km, with a yield ranging from 1 to 100 kilotons. The M110 can launch a shell of two kilotons to a distance of 14 km with an accuracy from 0.04 to 0.17 km depending on the range. The M109 offers a comparable accuracy and a slightly longer range with a yield of two kilotons.

Certainly, in official circles, there has been some tendency to encourage a development of Britain's nuclear forces along the lines of flexible response. In recent years this issue has arisen largely in connection with intermediate-range systems. Tornado replaces the Vulcan bombers which were based in the UK and Cyprus. After Polaris became operational in 1969 the Vulcans were assigned to NATO. They were still capable of hitting targets in the Soviet Union even though they might have difficulty in penetrating to the most heavily-protected Soviet targets. Therefore, in principle, they could be used to extend a European war into the Soviet homeland – undermining any hopes in the Politburo that the homeland could be kept as a sanctuary.

In the late 1970s it was decided to take the Vulcans out of service. This came about in 1983 (after they had been used in the Falklands). RAF Strike Command's replacement was the Tornado, also capable of carrying nuclear weapons but lacking the Vulcan's range. Because the development and production of this aircraft was shared with Germany it had been agreed to hold down its range so it could not be deemed a threat to the Soviet Union. Even based in Germany, Soviet targets could be hit but this would be at the limit of the aircraft's range and would leave little capacity for coping with active defences.

In the late 1970s and early 1980s a number of senior officials and military officers argued that there was a national requirement for a capability to attack Soviet targets related to a land war in Europe and avoiding centres of population. It was argued that the uncertainties over other centres of decision should be faced by the Soviet Union at all levels and was suggested that a UK cruise missile might meet this requirement. This argument was in the end rejected, partly because it did not carry sufficient conviction and partly because there was concern that, with the Trident programme, sufficient funds were already being devoted to nuclear forces. The matter was decided by indications from the Atomic Weapons Research Establishment at Aldermaston that it lacked the spare capacity for an additional weapons programme.[13]

Once Aldermaston had completed its testing programme for Trident in the mid-1980s, the issue was raised again. The proposal now was not to develop a UK cruise missile but a new stand-off missile for Tornado that would give it an anti-Soviet capability. This time the objection appears to have been money. A price tag of over a billion pounds deterred the Chiefs of Staff at a time when funds were becoming scarce. The issue could arise again. The gravity bombs in use by the RAF are getting old and, with Warsaw Pact air defences improving, there is a strong case for a stand-off missile. The high cost of the 1986 proposal was due to the considerable range envisaged – to give it the ability to reach Soviet territory. A more modest proposal, based on a shorter-range and dual-capable missile might gain more support.[14] If aircraft turn out to be the more durable nuclear delivery vehicles (following the latest American philosophy that seeks the elimination of ballistic missiles) then a case might be made for upgrading these vehicles. One interesting possibility might be a joint Franco-British project looking to an extended version of the French air-launched (ASMP) missile. This was looked at briefly in 1986 but rejected on grounds of inadequate range (100 km). However, the French themselves are considering a longer-range missile (300 km) which might be closer to a revised British requirement.

This would still not provide an anti-Soviet capability so, on current plans, there will be a sharp distinction in Britain's nuclear capability between the shorter and medium-range systems suitable for use on and around the European battlefield, but not against Soviet targets, and the submarine-launched ballistic missiles (SLBMs).

Shorter-range weapons and the approach to the nuclear threshold

In the Annual Defence Estimates these systems are rarely mentioned except as an afterthought, and then listed rather than explained. There has been no official explanation for their development other than a desire to contribute to all types of NATO forces.

If the SLBMs are assigned to NATO then it is only as a strategic reserve kept well away from the Central Front. They will not be caught up in the fighting. If called upon by SACEUR, it will be because the position on the Central Front has become dire. It would then be up to the government whether to accede to the request. A failure to do so would still leave the force available for a later and no doubt more urgent request, or else to serve solely national purposes. Unless large assumptions are made about breakthroughs in Soviet anti-submarine warfare (ASW) capabilities, the SLBM will be relatively unaffected by the storm on the continent.

But the availability of European-based nuclear capabilities changes the picture. These systems are more integrated into the overall force structure and so less easy to withhold. The systems and their operators would be closely involved in the land battle. Does this necessarily mean that Britain will find the pressure to "go nuclear" irresistible?

According to Paul Bracken, three factors make a threat to "go nuclear" more believable at this level than at the strategic:

(a) decentralized and delegated control of nuclear weapons once they are put on alert; (b) the ambiguity of command authority over the employment of nuclear weapons, and (c) the complexity of wartime and crisis management.[15]

The key decision would be whether to authorize release of the nuclear shells and bombs from their storage sites.[16] This would be an extremely difficult decision in that such a move would carry a fateful signal to the Soviet Union. On the other hand the longer the delay, the more unlikely nuclear release would become because of the growing operational and political problems and thus their value as a factor in intra-war deterrence would decline. The question of release for the RAF squadrons in Germany does not appear to be so pressing as the nuclear weapons are believed to be stored on the air bases.

The operation of command and control of RAF Germany is unclear. The squadrons in Germany form part of NATO's Second Tactical Air Force, along with aircraft from Belgium, Holland, Germany and the United States. The Second Tactical Air Force has been traditionally commanded by British officers although in war they would be wearing NATO hats. This raises the familiar problem of divided loyalties at a time when national and Alliance interests might be diverging. Once assigned to NATO in this way, all nuclear decisions should involve SACEUR, including a decision by the British government to take the nuclear initiative.[17]

The British short-range nuclear forces – artillery and Lance – are no different from those of other Allies in that they are dual-key and so dependent upon American delivery of the weapons and subject to an American view. They do not raise any specifically British issues and would only be used in conjunction with the rest of NATO. There are a number of reasons why NATO commanders and political leaders would be less likely to cross the nuclear threshold with these systems than the orthodox theory of flexible response would suggest.

Because the relevant systems are dual-capable, in a hard conventional battle there would be reluctance to hold them back for nuclear purposes. With short-range systems there are substantial operational problems in identifying targets that are both relevant and suitable. Intermingling of Warsaw Pact and NATO forces will make this difficult. The prospect of retaliation in kind would be another disincentive. A nuclear battlefield would soon bear no relation to a conventional battlefield. This would be a tragedy for all concerned. If either side could be said to come out on top it would be the one with the greatest manpower reserves. There would also, obviously, be the fear of the conflict escalating to something even worse. Part of the theory of flexible response, expressed in plans for initial and follow-on use of nuclear weapons, is to convey a warning to the Warsaw Pact that such escalation could take place. Short-range forces are not even suitable for this role. On the one hand, the military conditions would create pressure for any use to be on a large scale; on the other, the consequent disaster would still be some distance from the Soviet border.

None of these problems are that much different with the longer-range systems. The crossing of the nuclear threshold at any level risks such catastrophe that it is hard to imagine any circumstances in which this would seem sensible for either immediate military or broader strategic reasons. But a sufficiently ferocious conventional battle might create virtually irresistible pressures for nuclear use. All that can be said is that should nuclear use be contemplated, more possibilities are liable to be seen with the longer-range than the short-range systems. In NATO exercises military commanders are more likely to call for nuclear air strikes than nuclear artillery. It can be directed more precisely and therefore individual engagements have a greater (although still not high) chance of staying limited. Moreover, strikes to the rear of the immediate battle zone will be closer to the Soviet homeland and so will emphasise to the Politburo the need to find a basis to settle the war before further disaster.

There are aircraft (the F-111 based in Britain) and missiles (cruise and Pershing) capable of attacking military-related targets in Soviet territory. The Soviet Union has at any rate made clear that any nuclear detonations on its soil would warrant a full-blooded response against the instigator. Once one superpower had lost its sanctuary status, the other could not expect to hold on to its sanctuary status. It was to undermine any Soviet expectation of holding on to such a status that European governments encouraged, or at least accepted, the deployment of cruise and Pershing.

Without such an expectation the Soviet Union would be even less willing to go to war and so deterrence should be strengthened. Cruise and Pershing are dedicated to the nuclear role and capable of penetrating Soviet defences, and so would be more credible than F-111s. In the December 1987 Washington Summit, President Reagan and Mr Gorbachev agreed to the complete elimination of all cruise, Pershing and SS-20s, as well as shorter-range systems (500 km plus). This leaves F-111s in a more prominent position. As we have seen, since the removal of the Vulcan aircraft, Britain does not make a contribution at this level and is now unlikely to do so in the future. With the most substantial US systems removed there will be even less of a case for "signalling" an expanding nuclear threat by means of nuclear strikes; a case arising out of the exigencies of the military situation would be less affected.

Assessing the nuclear response

Because an all-out nuclear strike could not turn a land battle but only swamp it in a holocaust, it is unlikely that it would seem an appropriate response to a deteriorating military situation. It is therefore medium-range aircraft that are likely to appear as the most serious nuclear option should conventional forces be failing on the battlefield. Britain has this option independent of the United States. Under what set of circumstances is it conceivable that it might be exercised independently? One might be if the Federal Republic – and even more of West Europe – appeared to be on the verge of being lost; another might be if BAOR itself was facing complete defeat.

The latter case would only stand out if the Central Front was holding up comparatively well elsewhere. In these circumstances a unilateral Britain nuclear strike would be less than welcome by other Allies. At any rate nations have been known to abandon armies in the field before, especially when the only available action against the enemy was likely to make matters much worse. Abandoning the continental Allies would be a more fateful decision, but again hard to see as being more fateful than risking general nuclear war. The pressures to "go nuclear" would be greatest should the United States be inclined in this direction. UK forces might make a strike more militarily effective should it participate; it would make its strategic priorities explicit should it not. The existence of a comparable UK option to that of the US might force the British government to confront the true nature of its nuclear commitments to the Alliance earlier than would otherwise have been the case.

It is true that creating a potential to act unilaterally means that Soviet planners cannot wholly disregard the possibility of this potential being realised, though it is unlikely to be decisive in their calculations. However, it should be recognised that the very act of creating and maintaining during war a choice at this level of nuclear capability could force a UK government to clarify its position when it (and probably its Allies) would prefer not to. Following a decision in London to prepare for nuclear strikes in order to demonstrate NATO solidarity or simply to anticipate the worst, further developments could begin to slip out of direct control. This prospect – part of "the threat that leaves something to chance" – could enhance deterrence. However, in the absence of a NATO consensus on nuclear release the UK government may feel reluctant to continue to maintain a continental nuclear option and inclined to withdraw its air assets to the United Kingdom.

We have assumed up to now that only NATO countries could conceivably initiate nuclear war. However, Soviet use cannot be ruled out. Does the existence of UK nuclear forces in Germany help to deter such use? As the issue here would be one of response to the reality of Soviet nuclear use, although not yet directed against the United Kingdom, the calculations would be different. But again the existence of medium-range forces poses a choice. It would depend on the extent of the Soviet attack as to whether a NATO response would offer any hope of retrieving the situation. However, a response might be seen to be justified by the UK as adding credibility to its national nuclear deterrent. There would be a case for responding, if only because not to do so would encourage the Soviet Union to push on further and threaten the United Kingdom itself. Alternatively the risk of further escalation might simply encourage a horrified withdrawal. Soviet promises that the British Isles would be respected as a sanctuary would reinforce this. Nonetheless it is hard to suggest that Soviet planners would find it easier to contemplate an attack *without* NATO being able to respond in kind than *with*, and it is even possible to argue that the UK would have a slightly greater incentive to respond than the US simply because it would be most at risk if the USSR became emboldened in its nuclear threats.

The changing roles of conventional and nuclear weapons

Nevertheless one cannot dismiss lightly the British tolerance of a degree of nuclear exposure in Germany. The fact that BAOR rather than RAF Germany has been turned into the most important symbol of the British commitment does not alter the fact that the nuclear deployments do increase the risks for Britain of a European war beyond those which might be deemed prudent by British policy-makers actually confronting the reality of such a war.

Furthermore, future developments could give these deployments an even greater symbolic importance. We will leave aside the possibility of a German decision to expel nuclear bases as being both unlikely and of such fundamental importance that the implications would go well beyond the confines of this chapter. More likely but also far-reaching would be a persistent decline in the American commitment to nuclear deterrence or a British adoption of a non-nuclear policy.

There is now evidence of a secular trend in the United States away from full-blown nuclear deterrence. The incredibility of nuclear threats in the face of conventional war has been a matter of strategic concern for some three decades, with the sense of incredibility growing with the Soviet nuclear threat and the revelations of senior American officials such as Robert McNamara and Henry Kissinger, once in retirement, as to the hollow nature of past reassurances with regard to the US nuclear guarantee to Europe.

Under the Reagan administration this process has speeded up. This is not just the result of popular support for such ideas as "no-first-use" of nuclear weapons, or the Catholic Bishops Pastoral Letter, but it also follows the administration's own policies: the setting in 1981 of impossibly high standards for effective deterrence which it has since failed to meet; the non-nuclear vision informing the Strategic Defence Initiative; and the position struck at arms control negotiations, most notably at the Reykjavik summit.

At times when the American guarantee is subject to doubt, it is natural for the "European" case for the maintenance of a British nuclear capability to gain support. This can be seen in the position adopted by the Liberal-SDP alliance in Britain, although this is now being played down as a result of difficulty in explaining how this rationale could be reflected in practical policy.

Discussion of a British-French replacement for the American nuclear guarantee creates unease in both countries in that it would involve a degre of commitment and a heightened nuclear exposure that they have hitherto been unwilling to accept. It also raises the question of the German role: Bonn would have to accept a guarantee possibly less credible than the one that had just been withdrawn (with the hope that proximity would compensate for lower capability); or allow itself to become fully brought into the Franco-British arrangements (which would raise major questions of command and control); or else accept the logic of its position and develop its own nuclear capability.

In practice the problem is unlikely to arise in such a stark form. It is more a question of a tendency in American thinking than a definite shift and is generally directed most at the threat to initiate nuclear war. The key policy issue is therefore the balance between conventional and nuclear forces and the doctrine that governs their use. Concern over the implications of the long-term trends in American thinking provides an argument for holding on to a nuclear capability but not for a major re-orientation of current policy.[18] Equally, following the reductions in the warhead stockpile agreed at Montbello in 1983, there is unlikely to be major pressure for further rationalisation of short-range nuclear forces within NATO as a whole.

If there are pressures for change these are likely to come more through arms control. The fact that in the 1986 Iceland summit the Soviet and American leaders were willing even to consider a completely non-nuclear world is in itself significant but it is still unlikely that such a world could be created.

If there is one theme that runs through the Reagan Administration's position on these matters it is the focus on ballistic missiles. The most radical position admitted by the Administration is the complete elimination of strategic ballistic missiles within ten years, with the Strategic Defence Initiative serving to confirm the end of the missile age. Within Europe all intermediate- and shorter-range missiles (ballistic and cruise) will be removed in five years. The possibility has been raised of some sort of negotiation on short-range nuclear forces, again focusing largely on missiles rather than aircraft.

There are good practical reasons for concentrating on ballistic missiles rather than on aircraft. Reductions in aircraft are harder to verify and also tend to have more substantial implications for conventional capabilities. However if only aircraft and cruise missiles were deployed there would be a potential for an offence-defence arms race in that air defences are already deployed and continually under development. The West would be relying on advantages in offensive technology to counter the Soviet geographical and operational advantages in defences.

The end of strategic ballistic missiles would have substantial implications for the future of the UK nuclear deterrent. However, it is improbable that there could be general agreement in favour of such a step (with France, in particular, having an effective veto). Since Reykjavik, the American enthusiasm for this prospect also seems to have waned. Should it come about, Britain would be forced to consider either the submarine-launched cruise missile or upgrading the Tornado squadrons. The fact that the elimination of ballistic missiles could be accompanied by pressure for qualitative improvements in both the air offence and defence means that this could become very expensive (in addition to the wasted expenditure on Trident). There is no reason to believe that such measures would in themselves force Britain out of the nuclear business.

In view of the Strategic Defence Initiative it is also necessary to consider the possibility that even if Britain decided to stay with ballistic missiles these could be effectively neutralised by a Soviet SDI. However the warheads and advanced penetration aids that can be carried by Trident would allow it to saturate the sort of Soviet defences available over the coming two or three decades. Any problems with "exotic" defences will be for the next generation of UK forces; the best judgement must still be that neither side will in the end deploy comprehensive defences against ballistic missiles.

There is no reason to believe that any of the other measures currently under discussion on European systems will make it more difficult in principle for Britain to maintain its medium and short-range capabilities, although in practice there could well be political pressure to reduce. For the moment the most likely target for pressure remains the strategic forces. In the context of increasing attention to all European-based nuclear systems in a new arms control negotiation, it is quite possible that British systems would acquire a prominence that they currently lack.

Labour's policies

The lack of prominence is revealed by the neglect of the non-strategic British nuclear capabilities in Labour Party statements on defence policy, which brings us to the second of the developments that could challenge the British nuclear role in Germany. The re-evaluation of policy following the general election defeat of 1987 could lead the Labour Party to move away from its non-nuclear policy, but as yet there has been no change.

It is very difficult to forecast how any Labour Government would set about implementing a non-nuclear policy.[19] The Party programme in 1987 promised that Polaris would be decommissioned and Trident aborted and that US nuclear systems (but no other US military assets) would be asked to leave Britain. It is logical that such a policy would inevitably lead as well as to the removal of a nuclear capability from RAF Germany and BAOR. However, in the most recent Party documents (including the 1987 manifesto) no mention was made of this problem.[20] There is unfortunately no evidence that this problem has been fully addressed, even with regard to such practical measures as how British troops would exercise with the troops of other Allies that still maintain a nuclear capability.

Clarifications of the overall policy reveal that the Labour leadership accepts that NATO will continue to benefit from the US nuclear guarantee, and that the Alliance as a whole will not be converted to a non-nuclear policy overnight. Port visits from US warships would still be allowed. Indeed, the main target of the policy appears to be the threat of first-use. The difficulty is that this position, for which there is widespread sympathy on the centre-left of West European politics, has become obscured by an apparent readiness to abandon a retaliatory second-strike capability, for which there is minimum support.

In British political terms the most unpopular aspect of the Labour Party programme would be to end the "independent" nuclear capability. However in practical terms this will be the easiest part of the programme to implement, although by the next election it will have no pressing justification. Only if the parliamentary majority was very slender might a Labour government renege on this pledge. Far more difficult, though electorally (in a Gaullist sort of way) far more popular, would be moves directed against US nuclear capabilities in Britain, although again less pressing by the early 1990s with the departure of cruise.

Although the commitment that these systems should go remains, there is no firm time-table and much is being made of the importance of consultation with allies. In such a process the force of West European opinion will be extremely important (specially in the context of an attempt to gain international support for the government's economic policies). It can be presumed that the affects on American policies – with general US withdrawals from its European commitments coming either by way of retaliation or by following a British precedent – will be stressed. The probability is that these pressures will be difficult to withstand and that the future of US nuclear systems will remain a matter of consultation for many years.

What could happen would be a visible British stand in favour of no-first-use by NATO. It might be felt that this policy could be given meaning without inciting a major NATO crisis by removing the UK nuclear forces from Germany, as well as making sense in terms of the removal of the national strategic nuclear capability. Indeed it could come about as a consequence of the decommissioning of Polaris (for it would be strange to maintain a capability to enter into nuclear exchanges without the back-up of strategic nuclear forces) without much thought being given to the implications for the rest of the Alliance, and especially for West Germany. And if Bonn had shown slight interest in these systems in previous years why need much notice be taken of an interest that had been rather suddenly acquired?

As has been shown in earlier sections, the existence of medium and short-range nuclear forces based in Germany provides an Alliance dimension to Britain's nuclear policy that would otherwise be absent. A decision by Britain to reduce its nuclear exposure in Germany would be a statement as to the risks it was prepared to run on behalf of an ally. The same would be true of a decision to keep UK forces in Germany should American forces be withdrawn.

Any fundamental decisions of this sort would give these forces a prominence that they currently lack. It would then become necessary to address the basic issues raised by their current deployment in the Federal Republic. Because so little attention is directed towards them at the moment it is quite possible to disregard these basic issues. In the event of a re-think by a British Government then they will become harder to disregard, even though neither the British nor German governments has up to now has really acknowledged the existence of these systems. It would be unfortunate if the profound issues raised by British nuclear systems in Germany suddenly rushed to the fore without any prior consideration of the implications both for Anglo-German relations and NATO as a whole.

Notes

1. Peter Malone, The British Nuclear Deterrent, (London: Croom Helm, 1984), pp.175–8.
2. The Federal Minister of Defence, White Paper 1985: "The Situation and the development of the Federal Armed Forces", para 74.
3. House of Commons Official Report., Vol 977. cols. 678–9 (24 January 1980).
4. Lawrence Freedman, Britain and Nuclear Weapons (London: Macmillan, 1980), Chapter 12.
5. House of Commons Official Report, 24 January 1980, Col. 678.
6. Ibid., 29 March 1982, col. 25.
7. The Nassau Agreement: Statement on Nuclear Defence Systems – 21 December 1962, Clause 8. Reprinted in Andrew Pierre, Nuclear Politics: The British Experience with an Independent Strategic force, 1939–1970, (London: Oxford University Press, 1970), pp. 346–7.
8. See for example Field Marshal Lord Carver, A Policy for Peace (London: Faber & Faber, 1982).
9. Statement on the Defence Estimates 1986, Cmnd 9763-I. para 404.
10. Statement on the Defence Estimates The Military Balance 1986–1987.
11. Shaun Gregory, The Command and Control of British Nuclear Weapons (University

of Bradford School of Peace Studies, Peace Research Report Number 13, December 1986), p.12.

12. Lawrence Freedman, "Britain's Other Nuclear Weapons", *The Independent* (2 January 1988).

13. Lawrence Freedman "Britain and France", in Richard Betts (ed) Cruise Missiles (Brookings Institution: 1981).

14. Mark Urban, "RAF urges new missile to beat Soviet defences", *The Independent* (10 November 1986). The simplest option may be to modify the *Sea Eagle* anti-ship missile.

15. Paul Bracken, The Command and Control of Nuclear forces, (Yale University Press, 1983), p.165.

16. Although SACEUR does not formally require such authorization it is generally assumed that he would seek it.

17. See Gregory, *op. cit* p.12.

18. If this concern had been more pressing in the late 1970s when UK officials were addressing the future of the strategic nuclear forces then there might have been a greater interest in a more self-sufficient nuclear capability. See Colin McInnes, Trident: The Only Option (London: Brassey's, 1986), Chapter 4.

19. For an attempt to assess the future prospects for British defence policy see Lawrence Freedman, "Defence Policy after the Next Election", *Political Quarterly*, Vol. 57; No.4 (Oct–Dec 1986).

20. The Labour Party, Modern Britain in a Modern World: The Power to Defend our Country (The Labour Party: London, December 1986). The Labour Party Manifesto (May 1987).

Chapter 13
Britain's Nuclear Weapons and West German Security

CHRISTOPH BERTRAM

I

The Soviet-American Summit at Reykjavik in October 1986 was, according to Horst Teltschik, Chancellor Kohl's foreign policy adviser, a "healthy shock" for the Europeans. A shock it was certainly – to experience the cavalier way in which an American President was prepared to sacrifice America's ballistic missile arsenal for the sake of an unproven, futuristic and – at best – imperfect strategic defence option. Whether it will turn out to be a healthy shock, however, remains to be seen: too little time has passed to judge if, at last, West European governments have realised that they now need to formulate a common position on their strategic requirements which is more than the usual reflex of American fashions.

The challenge, of course, is clear enough. Once again a supreme representative of the United States has demonstrated a profound uneasiness over the integration of the United States into the seamless spectrum of nuclear deterrence. America, understandably, does not want to see its survival at stake in the event of a war in Europe, particularly a nuclear war. And Ronald Reagan has not been the first and will not be the last American president to try to escape from a Nato doctrine which suggests otherwise: massive retaliation (Eisenhower), flexible response (Kennedy, Johnson), limited nuclear options (Nixon, Carter) and the vision of strategic defence which would render nuclear missiles "impotent and obsolete" – these are all examples of the recurrent desire of American leaders to avoid involvement in a theatre conflict of which they cannot control the limits.

It is possible that, as this author believes, these attempts will always be frustrated. As long as the United States remains committed to the security of Western Europe with all its military potential, all efforts to introduce additional fire-breaks on the slope of escalation once the central fire-break, that of the passage of deterrence to nuclear use, has been crossed are likely to be futile. Only if the United States should ever become convinced that its security is confined to the integrity of the national territory of the Western hemisphere, will it escape from the consequences of extending deterrence to other regions. As a world power America does not have this choice.

Yet, objective factors are one thing, intentions are quite another. That the United States would like to disentangle itself from the automaticity of its nuclear alliance is not in doubt. Hence there is a need for America's allies, whether nuclear or non-nuclear, to consider efforts that would render the American burden somewhat easier and, at the same time, provide themselves with a counter-weight against the consequences of recurrent American attempts to opt out of the realities of the nuclear age.

It is in this context that the British (and French) strategic nuclear forces have gained increasing relevance for the security establishment in the Federal Republic. Not so long ago, West Germans tended to play down, even ridicule, the attempts at nuclear status with which their chief European allies were involved. More recently, during the Euro-missile debates and faced with repeated Soviets attempts to restrict, with an INF agreement, the size of the British and French nuclear forces, West German opinion clearly resented insistence by France and Britain to enlarge and modernise their forces; this was seen as an unjustified obstacle to possible compromise.

Yet today, while there is still not much strategic enthusiasm for the British and French deterrent forces, not least because it is increasingly difficult to maintain them without cutting into the resources for conventional forces, a more supportive attitude is gaining ground in West Germany. Might the British nuclear deterrent (and for that matter, the French) not also strengthen deterrence against an attack on Western Europe, particularly its strategic corner-stone, West Germany? Could it reinforce now, or even replace in a distant future, the American "nuclear guarantee" for West European security?

This paper will discuss these questions in two parts. The first seeks to define the nature of nuclear forces in general and the British nuclear forces in particular. The second will look at the impact that these forces might have on the evolution of European security.

II

In his excellent chapter, Lawrence Freedman reflects a certain British frustration that, in contrast to France's *force de frappe*, the – more sizeable – British nuclear forces do not seem to receive much notice in the West German security debate. But while that frustration is understandable, it is also irrelevant. The nature and the limitations of these nuclear forces are essentially identical, whatever the difference in presentation and attention may suggest.

The difference between the strategic forces of the two European nuclear weapon states is more apparent than real. While the French have a truly "independent" deterrence in the sense that, at least at present, they are able to manufacture all its elements, the British have been dependent on the supply of American missiles since the Nassau Agreement of 1962. Their decision to modernise their force has been determined, as again demonstrated in the government's Trident II commitment, by the modernisation decisions of the United States.

Yet both countries have an independent deterrent in the sense that they alone decide whether their forces will ever be fired in anger. Britain's total dependence on American strategic delivery systems gives the United States leverage in the supply of spare parts, but not in the ultimate decision of use. It is true that, in contrast to France, British strategic forces are part of the NATO strike plan. When the British Prime Minister is faced, *in extremis*, with the decision to release nuclear strategic forces, this cannot be other than an autonomous decision, just as in the case of France. Britain will never decide to launch a strategic attack on the Soviet Union because her Allies want it but only because she feels that her own, ultimate security cannot be safeguarded in any other way NATO rules cannot change what is, after all, the elementary rule of nuclear military power: it is a political, not a military decision, and it is one you take only for yourself, not on behalf of another power because its consequences concern your own very survival.

This is true for all nuclear forces. It is even more so for the "minimum deterrence" force of Britain and France. The only reason why there is an element of credibility in the American "nuclear guarantee", as opposed to that of Britain and France, is the sheer size of the American arsenal. When a power has so much nuclear ammunition, it is a bit more probable that it may employ some of it for the sake of its extended security interests. But even there, doubts have been persistent. In 1979, Henry Kissinger caused dismay when he declared that the allies of the United States could no longer rely on American nuclear forces for the deterrence of a Soviet conventional attack – because of the attainment of strategic parity by the Soviet Union! Even with the currently envisaged modernisation of their forces, Britain and France will remain, forever, in the position of marked inferiority to the strategic forces of the Soviet Union.

As François de Rose has pointed out[1], France's nuclear arsenal may not even be enough to deter conventional attacks on French territory. "It is even more legitimate to enquire about the credibility, in the eyes of an adversary, of a declaration which announced our resolution to unleash this process [the use of nuclear weapons] if the Elbe river were crossed by Warsaw Pact forces which did not use nuclear or chemical weapons." To expect Britain and France to provide any degree of extended deterrence means to misunderstand profoundly the limitation of minimum deterrence forces, even in their credibility to deter threats to the core national interest.

For this reason, Lawrence Freedman's discussion in this volume of Britain's tactical nuclear systems (he calls them significantly "European-based") which, because they are integrated into the force structure, might increase the pressure on Britain to "go nuclear" is both intriguing and misleading. Freedman rightly points out that these systems are all too often neglected in any discussion of theatre forces in general and Britain's nuclear contribution in particular. But the reason for the neglect is the sheer conceptual difficulty of providing a consistent task for the tactical nuclear weapons of small nuclear powers. They are rightly forgotten because they do not make any sense.

The strategic forces of small nuclear powers have a clear function, namely to deter a nuclear enemy from attack on the country's territory with nuclear weapons and, perhaps, from attack with massive conventional forces. This is a task that is credible, since the immediate survival of the nation is at stake. But it is very difficult to provide a distinct rationale for the non-strategic forces of such countries, as exemplified by the semantic fuzziness with which they have been treated in the past. Are they "tactical" as opposed to strategic weapons – and what does this mean since their separate use – separate from the use of the strategic forces of such countries – is difficult, if not impossible to contemplate? The latest French label as "pre-strategic" weapons is more to the point but even this emphasises rather than diminishes the basic contradiction: there is no pre-strategic use for the nuclear forces of a minimum deterrent power; every use is strategic. In contrast to the nuclear superpowers, small nuclear weapon states can use nuclear weapons only as a means of the last, desperate resort, because only then the threat to fire them is credible. There is no room here for less-than-all-out options. The link between the first – pre-strategic – use and strategic obliteration is so direct for small nuclear forces, that every use puts national survival on the line.

If the British "theatre" systems in Europe do not, on the surface, fall into this category, is is solely because they are part of the NATO structure. Their credibility is not underpinned by the British Polaris missiles but by the full range of the US nuclear arsenal. Take that away and there is no credible, separate function for them to perform.

III

What follows from the nature of the British nuclear forces for the security of Western Germany? In the purely military sense very little, the British nuclear forces make sense only for the narrowest objective possible: British survival against nuclear or major conventional attacks in case of a major, unprecedented world conflict.

This must come as a disappointment to those who think that European forces might somehow make up for defects in the American posture or doctrine. Thus Uwe Nerlich[2] has argued that, if US intermediate nuclear forces were withdrawn from Europe as the result of the ''zero option'', the French and British nuclear forces would have to take over the function of ''more flexible deployment''. The nuclear strategic systems of France and Britain are seen as part of the overall deterrence spectrum; they are supposed to be able to fill the gap left by American nuclear withdrawals from Europe.

But this is simply not the case. It is because the decision to order the release of French nuclear forces lies with the French President alone, that these forces are credible in their limited way. If somehow they were integrated into a chain of escalation (and hence of command), reaching from the European battleground to the American President, the French nuclear forces never would have been built, and the threat of their use never believed. It is their independent nature which is their sole *raison d'être*; there can be no ''continuum of deterrence'' resulting from the combination of several independent forces.

The same applies to the British nuclear forces. It is true that they are allocated to NATO and their use is at the request of SACEUR. But this can only be a contingent arrangement, applying only as long as the British Prime Minister is convinced that Britain's security cannot be safeguarded better by withholding British nuclear forces. This he can do unilaterally at any time.

This does not mean, however, that the nuclear forces of the three Western nuclear weapons states coexist in complete isolation from each other. The most elementary impact is that the potential enemy has to face, and plan for accordingly, three nuclear arsenals instead of one. The question is whether, from a military-strategic point of view, any other, more subtle enhancements of deterrence follow from the existence of several Allied nuclear forces and several ''centres of decision-making''.

The answer will be different for the nuclear and the non-nuclear members of the Western Alliance. For the former, the fact that the nuclear forces of their Allies complicate the task of Soviet planners to deal with each nuclear force individually will be a welcome bonus. For the French strategic planner to be able to calculate that only a fraction of the Soviet strategic arsenal is likely to be deployed against French targets, while the bulk has to deal with American and, to a lesser extent, British targets, means that the odds are not all against him, and the same will apply to his British colleague.

There have been, it is true, considerable American doubts in the past over the desirability of nuclear diversity within the Western Alliance.

The strategy, at times professed, of smaller nuclear powers to "tear an arm off" the Soviet Union and thus drag the United States into a nuclear conflict has, understandably, not been greeted with enthusiasm by Europe's American protector. Yet, significantly, these concerns never seem to have been strong enough to overcome both the general American conviction that several Western nuclear deterrent forces are, above all, a problem for the Soviets, and the more specific American confidence as expressed in the transfer of nuclear missiles to Britain. A United States more worried about the strategic implications of third countries' deterrent forces would also have been more reluctant about supplying them with central nuclear technologies. Clearly, the proliferation, within limits, of minimum deterrence forces among allies has been seen, in the United States, as more conducive to strengthening rather than to weakening overall deterrence of Soviet offensive intentions.

But this is no more than the obvious: it is better to have a multitude of nuclear allies than a multitude of nuclear enemies. It is difficult to push the implication much further. Since there can be no organic link between the Western deterrence forces, their impact upon each other is indirect and relative, rather than direct and absolute.

This is even more pronounced in the case of the non-nuclear members of the Alliance. From the perspective of extended deterrence in Europe, as pointed out above, what matters are the nuclear capabilities of the United States, not those of Britain and France. It is true that the Western Alliance has officially welcomed the existence of these smaller forces, and recently one of West Germany's most knowledgeable officials, Lothar Ruehl, State Secretary in the Ministry of Defence, declared: "The British and French nuclear forces continue to play their role of deterrence in Europe, to the advantage of Western Europe and the Federal Republic".[3] But what exactly "their role" is supposed to be, no one has yet defined with any precision. The direct impact of the British nuclear forces for West Germany's security remains obscure.

One might even argue that – from the point of view of the non-nuclear members of the Alliance – the indulgence of European powers in costly nuclear programmes is a very mixed blessing. For one thing, as the French – not, to their credit, the British – have demonstrated repeatedly over the years, nuclear weapon states in the Alliance are tempted to claim that political consequences should follow from their exalted status – a seat in an Alliance directorate, for instance, a greater role in East-West relations, a condescending posture towards the non-nuclear states in general and West Germany in particular. Usually, such an attitude has not facilitated but complicated co-operation within Western Europe and the Alliance on security matters.

For another thing, not even superpowers, much less European middle-powers, have the means to provide adequate funds to all military tasks. They have to set priorities. For France and Britain, maintaining and modernising a national nuclear deterrent force has meant, quite naturally, that less money could be devoted to conventional forces. It is true that the actual cost for the purchase and upkeep of the British nuclear forces has been moderate to-date (much more so than for their French equivalent). But these costs will rise very substantially with the introduction of the Trident II system, while at the same time British defence expenditure is experiencing a decline in real terms. Whatever the merits of nuclear forces, there is no question that they absorb funds which otherwise might be available for conventional forces. And these are the forces which are relevant, above all for the security of West Europe's non-nuclear states, not the limited size of an *in extremis* nuclear arsenal.

This German prejudice for conventional rather than nuclear forces will be even more pronounced in the 1990s. As a result of demographic trends and financial pressure or both, conventional forces in NATO are bound to shrink. It is difficult to imagine that the Bundeswehr, which depends for roughly 50% of its manpower on conscripts, can maintain its present size when the annual cohort drops by 50%. It is equally difficult to imagine that the United States which in the years of defence plenty has entered into a series of major, long-term procurement commitments that are costly to revoke will, in the years of defence penury, resist the temptation to cut personnel and reduce the number of American conventional forces in Europe. When the two major contributors to conventional strength in NATO are forced to cut the size of their forces, their partners will not be far behind – not least since "the Soviet threat" will appear much less formidable than in earlier periods of post-war history.

In this situation of conventional drain, the decision of the European nuclear weapon states to invest scarce resources in forces which are of only indirect relevance to the security of their allies in Western Europe, at the expense of forces which are of direct importance, will not be widely welcomed by the non-nuclear NATO members. If the British Labour Party's programme of denuclearisation had any redeeming features at all, it was the pledge to devote the funds saved from cancelling Trident (if there are any) to improving Britain's conventional forces.

Yet this highly sceptical assessment of the value of British nuclear forces for the security of West Germany depends on one crucial element: the continuing credibility of the American nuclear commitment to Western Europe. While it lasts, the priority is clear: Alliance-wide deterrence is to be assured by the United States, while the other Allies should concentrate on conventional defence. The unsettling question, of course, is: what if it does not last?

At this stage, such concerns seem highly premature. Even if uncertainty set in after the "Summit of Dreams" in Reykjavik, Western Europe has no interest whatsoever in precipitating a development which might never occur by pretending that it is imminent. Moreover, the question is somewhat beside the point because it suggests that until America's nuclear commitment is in doubt there is no need for West European governments to work out for themselves, and together, the significance of nuclear weapons and strategies for their common security.

But the need exists today, not just in a distant future, for two reasons. First, the abrupt changes in US strategic policies over the past ten years have contributed to a weakening of the respectability of nuclear deterrence in Europe. Because European governments were unprepared to engage in a strategic debate with their major ally, Europe often seemed, in the eyes of many of its citizens, the helpless victim rather that the main beneficiary of America's extended deterrent. But a nuclear alliance of sovereign states – and the combination of both factors is the outstanding characteristic of the North Atlantic Pact – cannot endure if the common strategy is no more than the appendix of various, and varying, nuclear doctrines emerging from the fertile American debate. For the health and vitality of the West, Europe has to become, even in the complex field of nuclear forces and philosophies, a respected partner for the dialogue with the United States.

Significantly, neither nuclear nor non-nuclear European allies qualify so far in this respect. The British experience with the United States on an issue so central to the survival of British strategic nuclear forces as SDI has underlined that point. Only if there is a common West European position can America's allies on the old continent hope to take part in shaping what is, after all, a common Alliance strategy.[4]

The other reason why Western Europe needs to involve itself with developing a strategic perspective of its own is different, but related: only then is it possible to imagine that a politically coherent Western Europe will ever emerge from the Common Market framework.

So far, hopes that this goal – if indeed it is still shared among British and West German élites today – could be reached through other avenues have been disappointed. These was, once, the notion that economic integration would spill over into political integration. But, on the contrary, the lack of political will also slowed down the momentum for economic cohesion. Then there was the idea that political co-operation in foreign policy (POCO) would somehow provide Western Europe with the ability to speak with one voice and thus give political clout to the economic club. But POCO, however valuable in co-ordinating the positions of governments on matters not central to their foreign policy such as the Middle East, South Africa or ASEAN, has shied away from addressing the really central ones – Alliance matters and East-West relations. It has given to the Community the semblance of cohesion in foreign policy, while, in reality, often no more than covering up for political inaction.

Thus there is much to suggest that the easy ways to West European political unity are also the ways that will not lead there. The indirect strategy that followed the collapse of the European Defence Community in the early 1950s did not work. The lesson of the past three decades is the opposite: if Europe wants to continue to avoid the toughest challenge, that of continental security, it will not come about at all.

Of course, developing a common European perspective will not be a matter of months but of years. What is important for the context of the British (and French) nuclear deterrence forces, however, is that such an effort now must include nuclear issues as well. David Owen is right: "Britain's political disposition to work together with France and West Germany on issues of a European nuclear strategy would provide a certain firmness to the road on which Europe is approaching the United States".[5] But it will also provide a certain firmness to the political basis on which Western Europe itself can be built.

The answer to the question asked at the beginning of this chapter is, therefore, more circumstantial than the renewed West German interest in the nuclear forces of Britain and France would suggest. The direct impact of these forces, whether strategic or "pre-strategic" on West European and West German security is marginal. They do not provide deterrence beyond the narrowest definition of British and French national security. Indeed, they may even weaken deterrence for Western Europe as a whole since they absorb precious resources which otherwise might be available for conventional defence.

But by their very existence the British (and French) nuclear forces allow and force European governments – provided they are willing to go down that road – to evolve a common perspective of their strategic needs in a nuclear world; to introduce this effectively into the Alliance debate with the United States and, through the process of continuing debate and refinement, to promote a European political personality as well. Without the British and French nuclear forces, the training ground on which a coherent European security policy might evolve would lack realism. Because they challenge European governments to take nuclear matters seriously and not leave them entirely to the United States, they allow Western Europe, if it wants to, to be ready if, some time in the distant future, the present arrangements for its security should no longer hold.

Notes

1. "La force de dissuasion nucléaire française et la sécurité de la République Féderale d'Allemagne", in Karl Kaiser and Pierre Lellouche: *Le Couple Franco-Allemand et la Défense de l'Europe*, Paris 1986, S. 191.
2. Kaiser and Lellouche, *op. cit*. S. 187.
3. *Le Monde*, March 7, 1987: "La position de Bonn reste prudente malgré l'optimisme de M. Genscher," p. 6.
4. See David Owen, "Europas Strategie der nuklearen Abschreckung," *Europa-Archiv* 1986, p. 375.
5. *Ibid*.

Chapter 14
The Security Problems of NATO's Northern Flank

CLIVE ARCHER

United Kingdom-Federal German defence co-operation in the maritime and Northern Flank areas of NATO has to be seen in a multilateral context, that of the Atlantic Alliance. It is limited when compared with the UK-FRG relationship on the continent of Europe and the scope for its development depends to a great extent on the policies and posture of third countries, especially the United States and the Scandinavian members of NATO.

This chapter will define the areas under consideration and evaluate their importance, examine the defence forces in the two regions, look at the defence roles of the United Kingdom and the Federal Republic, and offer some conclusions.

The areas defined

The maritime and Northern Flank areas can be defined in NATO terms. From the European perspective the maritime area can best be limited to the EASTLANT Command area.[1] The Channel Command relates more to the United Kingdom's continental commitments. The Northern Flank is most sensibly defined as the area covered by the Northern Command of NATO. Its defence is significantly tied to the EASTLANT maritime area. The two areas – the maritime and the Northern Flank – can be considered from different perspectives, each of which has consequences for their security significance.

The maritime area can be seen in a wider NATO context, when the most important element is the broad strategic balance between the Warsaw Treaty forces – air, seaborne and submarine – and their Atlantic Alliance equivalents. Whilst the "bean count" is of relevance, it is also necessary to know something about the maritime strategies of the respective powers. Reference here can be made to current works on these topics: a resumé of the message they contain would be that the Soviet maritime presence has steadily increased in this area over the last 20 years whilst the United States' response to this expansion has been somewhat varied. After appearing to accept a sort of "perimeter defence" at the Greenland-Iceland-United Kingdom (GIUK) gap in the mid-1970s, it has now become more bold in the deployment of a Forward Maritime Strategy which seeks to deny the Soviet Union possible control of the Norwegian Sea and to reassert the right of a US naval presence in the Barents and Baltic Seas.[2]

The maritime area can also be seen as the more limited zone of the eastern part of Supreme Allied Commander Atlantic's (SACLANT) command where the action has been concentrated over the past few years. Increasingly this part of the ocean has been seen as an area in which the naval strategies of the USSR and the USA overlap in peace and which would be very important in terms of submarine activity, sea control and denial, and aerial superiority.

Restricting the zone of interest even further, special emphasis can be placed on the Soviet-Norwegian maritime boundary area because of its strategic significance as the doorstep to the Kola Peninsula and its utility as a submarine bastion, and because of the disputed nature of the maritime border in the offshore domain.[3]

The Northern Flank's importance can also be understood from differing perspectives. Perhaps the most common view is that which emphasises the "flank" element. In other words, the AFNORTH Command is seen in the context of what is needed on the Central Front – in time of peace, crisis and war – and the greatest importance thereby attaches to the Baltic Approaches, Denmark and Schleswig-Holstein. This view emphasises the importance of ground and air forces; whilst the naval aspects centre mainly on the control of the Danish straits and on support to amphibious operations.

Another way of looking at the Northern Flank is to see all of the AFNORTH Command as being the northern third of the dividing line between east and west which stretches from the North Cape down to the mountainous Soviet-Turkish frontier, albeit with some neutral buffers in between. In this case, the region is seen as less of a flank and more as an equal section of a continuous broad front line.

A more concentrated perspective looks at the northernmost part of the East-West divide, placing the spotlight on the Soviet-Norwegian border and the three northern counties of Norway. The military interest in this area is one of air superiority, amphibious operations, a tight Norwegian defence around the Tröms region, and a strong dependence by the Norwegians on internal and external reinforcements.

A final view includes both the maritime area and the Northern Flank and sees the zone as an approach and a shoreline to the Arctic Ocean. Emphasis is placed on the northern islands of Greenland and Svalbard and on the possible use of the polar seas as submarine-operating sanctuaries, primarily for Soviet SSBNs based in the Kola peninsula.

These various perspectives point to three general aspects of the strategic significance of the maritime area and Northern Flank. The first is that these areas cannot be seen in isolation; they have to be considered in the wider context of the East-West balance. In military terms they form a link between North America and Western Europe (especially the maritime area) and are closely connected with the Central Front. However, both areas have certain characteristics that mark them out in military terms as different from other areas of NATO responsibility.

Secondly, the point needs to be made that whilst a NATO-Warsaw Pact conventional war can scarcely by won on the Northern Flank, let alone in the maritime domain, it could be lost there.[4] This is particularly the case for a war enduring at the conventional level for a period of more than a few days, by which time the reinforcement of Europe from North America is likely to have become crucial. Not only would loss of the maritime region affect NATO's ability to reinforce, but the loss of important land areas of the Northern Flank could seriously undermine air cover for the Central Region and allow its flank to be turned.

Finally, the changing importance of the maritime/Northern Flank area should be noted. Twenty-five years ago, a major concern in the Northern Flank was one of a limited Soviet "grab" of some North Norwegian territory[5], and the defence of the North Atlantic mainly involved preventing Soviet conventionally-powered submarines from disrupting the Atlantic sea lines of communications. Limited action against North Norway is now seen as a most unlikely option for the Soviets, and the emphasis is more on defending the AFNORTH region in the context of a determined Warsaw Pact onslaught on Western Europe as a whole. Even more important, perhaps, is deterring such an attack. In ensuring deterrence, NATO forces in the North Atlantic have had, over the years, to face the reality of the growth of the Soviet Northern Fleet as well as the substantial expansion of the Kola Peninsula as a Soviet maritime base with a major strategic significance.

Defence forces

The maritime area and the Northern Flank provide base and operating facilities for sections of both the NATO and Warsaw Treaty Organisation's defence forces. An examination of the military strength in the zone thus provides an indication of its strategic significance.

The Soviet forces have built up considerably in the past decade and assessments of their strength can be found in the IISS *Military Balance*, in particular the version published for the Norwegian Atlantic Committee. Other information can be found in an RMA Sandhurst Consultant Report entitled *Soviet Amphibious Warfare and War on the Northern Flank* (1984), in Tomas Ries's *The Nordic Dilemma in the '80s: Maintaining Regional Stability under New Strategic Conditions* (1982), and in Harald W. Støren's paper for the Institute of Political Science, Oslo.[6] (An outline of Soviet and WTO forces in the area can be seen in Table 14.1).

What is the significance of these forces? The most important aspect of the Kola Peninsula is the base it provides for the Soviet Northern Fleet with its surface, submarine and amphibious elements. Because the most modern Soviet sea-launched ballistic missiles can reach North America when fired from the Barents Sea and the Arctic Ocean, Soviet SSBNs no longer have to move out into patrol areas in the North Atlantic or Norwegian Sea. The new Typhoon class of Soviet submarine can operate under the Arctic ice, making it less vulnerable both to surveillance and to many anti-submarine warfare measures. Sizeable elements in the Northern Fleet are devoted to the protection of the SSBN operating areas. These include long-range maritime attack aircraft (Badger, Backfire), cruise missile-carrying submarines (SSGNs) such as the Charlie and Echo type and surface vessels such as the 'Kresta II' and 'Krivak' class ships. Another important activity would be to attack elements of any NATO aircraft-carrier battle group (CVBG), or indeed individual surface ships and submarines that might form the "forward edge" of NATO's maritime deployments in Northern Waters. Further to the south and west, a task for the Soviet forces would be to attack NATO's sea lanes of Atlantic communication, principally with their nuclear attack submarines. The Northern Fleet could also be expected to intercept NATO reinforcements close to home in the seas approaching Norway and Denmark. Its amphibious capability allows a naval infantry brigade to be moved from the Kola to the Norwegian coast; and there is also a back-up of commercial shipping to support such landings. The air defence aircraft on the Kola Peninsula would have the tasks of safeguarding Soviet territory against Western aircraft and cruise missile attack; and of extending air cover over amphibious landing areas in Norway.

The Sandhurst study suggests that certainly Denmark, the Kattegat and the Skagerrak, and most likely Sweden and Southern Central Norway, are included in the Soviet's Western Central Theatre of Operations (TVD). Its authors conclude: "The Baltic littoral, we believe, is seen as the flank for the central front, both in attack and defence."[8]

The Soviet and other Warsaw Pact countries have important maritime forces in the Baltic as well as supporting base and port facilities. The IISS Norwegian supplement identifies the primary function of these forces as "to gain control of the Baltic and carry out operations to

Table 14.1

Soviet and WTO Forces in the Northern Theatre 1984

	Northern Fleet	Baltic Fleet
Sea Forces		
Submarines:		
Ballistic, nuclear-powered (SSBN)	40	0
Ballistic, diesel-powered (SSB)	1	6
Cruise missile, nuclear-powered (SSGN)	27	0
Cruise missile, diesel-powered (SSG)	5	5
Nuclear-powered attack (SSN)	46	0
Diesel-powered (SS)	50	22
Total	169	33
Principal Surface Combatants		
Kirov, Kresta, Kynda	9	3
Sverdlov	2	1
Sovremenny	3	0
Others	63	40
Minor Surface Combatants	62	149
Minelayers and Minesweepers	65	138
Amphibious ships	16	52

Air Forces

Northern Fleet Naval Aviation: LRMP-attack	95
Backfire	30
ASW-LRMP	65
PVO Strany, North LMD + Arkhangelsk ADD: Interceptors	240
13. TAC AA, North LMD: recce	30
13. TAC AA, South LMD: FGA	130
PVO Strany, South LMD: Interceptors	100
30. TAC AA + Baltic Fleet and Polish naval aviation:	
Interceptors	100
FGA	182
recce	50
PVO Strany, Baltic MD Interceptors	100
Poland: Interceptors	143
FGA	220
Baltap (WTO): Interceptors	231
FGA	159
recce	40

Troops

Kola Peninsula: 2 motorised infantry divisions   1 mobilisation division
                1 missile brigade   1 airborne battalion
                1 naval infantry brigade
Southern Leningrad Military District: 7 motorised infantry divisions
                                      1 airborne division
                                      1 missile brigade

Sources: IISS, Ries and Støren, as note 6.

open the exits from that area".[9] If successful, this would allow the Soviets to use their considerable base and repair capacity in the Baltic to support the Northern Fleet. The Sandhurst study stresses the importance of air defence in the Baltic for the Russian homeland. The authors consider that, should the Soviet Union be unable to turn the Baltic into a *mare sovieticum* in wartime, NATO would be able to threaten the USSR with air strikes and outflanking amphibious actions. It would therefore seem likely that the Soviet's secondary aim in war would be to prevent NATO use of the Baltic. On land, the Soviet forces would thrust to the south of Hamburg with subsidiary axes north to South Jutland and to Bremerhaven-Wesermunde. Warsaw Treaty troops might undertake short- and long-range landings in order to knock out enemy assets and tie up NATO forces.[10] It can be concluded that whilst the USSR would prefer to have control of the Danish Straits and keep them open in wartime, it is more likely that, faced with stout NATO opposition, they might prefer the Straits to be closed to all shipping.

The Western forces in the North Norway and Baltic areas are to a great extent responding to expected Soviet deployments, both in the case of indigenous forces and outside reinforcements. The peacetime "in-place" forces of Norway and Denmark are scarcely sufficient to hold a determined surprise attack from the east. They should, however, be able to resist an attack and delay its progress for long enough to permit mobilisation and reinforcement to take place. Once its reserve forces have been mobilised, each country presents a considerable obstacle to any opponent's further advance, and so increases the chances of the timely arrival of overseas reinforcements. These outside forces would come mainly from the United States and Britain and although the early deployment of the ACE Mobile Force would bring to the area contingents from other NATO European countries.

Norway's own armed forces are deployed to facilitate the "resist and reinforce" response to a Soviet attack. They are not, of course, helped by the proximity of North Norway to Soviet bases in the Kola Peninsula, nor by Norway's demography, with most of the population concentrated in the south-east, away from the northern frontline. The Norwegian aim is to have enough standing forces in the north which, together with reinforcement plans, will provide a credible defence for the area, without giving the Soviets cause to complain that their strategic elements in the Kola are being threatened. There is also a need for Norway to do enough for its own defence so that its allies will be encouraged to provide reinforcements whilst not, at the same time, giving the impression that North Norway might be used as a springboard for an attack on the Soviet Union.

The bulk of Norway's standing land forces are stationed in North Norway with an infantry battalion in South Varanger and a battalion group in Porsanger in Finnmark. The Tröms area has a standing brigade of some 5,000 men (Brigade North). These standing units serve as readiness forces alerted to resist sudden attack, and also perform the task of training Norwegian soldiers in the field and preparing them for subsequent service in the mobilisation force.[11] The maritime approaches to the Tröms area are protected by coastal artillery, torpedo stations and minefields as well as by ships. These include minelayers, mine counter-measure vessels, landing-craft, coastal submarines, fast patrol boats and frigates, all of which contribute to the task of delaying and eroding any enemy seaborne invasion. North Norway has five military airfields, some with a ready anti-aircraft defence system. In peacetime there are two squadrons of F-16 fighters stationed there to protect the airfields and other reinforcement installations. They may also have a limited anti-shipping role. One maritime reconnaissance squadron of Orion, a helicopter squadron of UH-1B, a search and rescue (SAR) squadron of Sea King helicopters and the planned deployment of additional F-16 and F-5 aircraft from South Norway completes the air picture in North Norway.[12]

The ground forces in the north can be rapidly reinforced from the south of the country. Mobilisation can be undertaken within 24–48 hours with two additional brigades being added to the Tröms and Nordland strength. Within five to seven days the north can be reinforced with some 80,000 Norwegian troops, representing five Army brigades as well as navy, airforce and Home Guard personnel.

All this is impressive for a country of some four million people but would scarcely be enough to counter, let alone repel, a sustained attack by the Soviet Union. National mobilisation and reinforcement of the North must be seen as a holding operation to prevent a quick victory by an aggressor whilst it prepares to receive allied reinforcements. The Canadian Air/Sea Transportable Brigade Group (CAST BG) had North Norway as its sole commitment until this task was scrapped in 1987. The US marine amphibious brigade (MAB) may take up to 20 days to arrive. It consists of about 5,000 men plus two air defence squadrons, two close air support squadrons and other support aircraft and helicopters. A British and Dutch Commando Group forms part of the United Kingdom/Netherlands Amphibious Force (UK/NL AF) assigned to SACLANT, and could be moved to North Norway, an area where they exercise each year, within a few days if moved by sea, or more quickly by air. The Allied Command Europe Mobile Force (AMF), composed of light forces from the US, the UK, Canada, the Federal Republic of Germany, Italy and the Netherlands, also exercises regularly in North Norway and could be deployed there in time of crisis, thereby displaying alliance solidarity with Norway. Plans for the reinforcement of Norway have been improved over the last few years by a combination of better host nation support and by some prepositioning of equipment and supplies.

The Collocated Operating Bases (COB) agreements with the United States provide for the preparation of airfields to receive US air strength in time of crisis or war.[13] A recent study of the reception capability of

Norwegian airfields has shown that about two-thirds of the bases available for the reception of US aircraft are in the south of the country and that "there is a need to expand some of the additional airfields available in northern Norway".[14] Air support for North Norway could also be provided by US Naval Aircraft operating from aircraft carriers of SACLANT's Striking Fleet Atlantic.

Increased prepositioning of material has been undertaken. To hold crucial northern areas against enemy attack, it is vital to have there "formations capable of sustained operations"; with equipment and supplies prepositioned for allied and national forces alike.[15] This reduces deployment time and frees transport for other uses. Snow-mobiles and winter equipment for the UK/NL amphibious forces and equipment for one battalion group of the CAST BG is prestocked in North Norway, and there was some discussion about whether the same should be done for the US MAB. In the end, political sensitivities over prepositioning US supplies on the doorstep of the Kola, together with an operational need to maintain flexibility, led to the January 1981 decision that the MAB should prestock its material in the Trøndelag area.[16] However, it was decided to preposition the equipment for an extra Norwegian brigade in North Norway.[17]

Host Nation Support (HNS) is seen as a crucial method of cutting down the development time of Allied reinforcement. Improvements in HNS can be seen in new infrastructure projects to provide storage for supplies and equipment and in transportation, POL, engineering and medical support.[18]

The defence posture of the Danes is much more tied to the Central Front than that of Norway, though many of the political constraints exercised by Norway are also applied by Denmark. Like Norway, Denmark does not allow nuclear weapons on its territory in peacetime, nor does it permit the permanent basing of foreign troops on its soil (with the exception of two US defence areas in Greenland). The Danish defence posture provides for a mixture of national self-defence capability and outside reinforcement.

First, in examining the defence of the Baltic Exits, South Norway should be considered. The standing forces there are one reduced infantry battalion, one tank squadron, one field artillery battery and one rifle company plus tank platoons at some airfields. There is a mobilization potential up to a total of ten brigades and command, support and logistic units.[19]

The Danish land forces consist of the Jutland Division with divisional troops and three armoured infantry brigades plus one combat group with three battalions in Jutland. Zealand has two armoured infantry brigades and three combat groups, each of two infantry battalions and one artillery battalion. On Lolland-Falster there is a combat group of one infantry battalion; and one artillery battalion can be activated. The Bornholm Region has a reduced infantry brigade equivalent.

The Regional Defence Force has a variety of infantry and artillery battalions, tank destroyer squadrons, pioneer companies and guard units, as well as some 24,000 men. The Home Guard has 60,400 men and women, most with a good knowledge of their local area.[20]

The Danish Air Force has four squadrons of F-16 fighters and two of F-35 Draken together with some transport, training and SAR units. These are six batteries of Improved-HAWK missiles on Zealand, two of which are an extension of the air defence chain of the Central Region.[21]

The Danish Navy operates primarily in the Baltic Approaches and the Baltic Sea. It has five frigates with Sea Sparrow SAM and Harpoon SSM and five fishery protection vessels, some of which operate in Greenland and the Faroes for part of the year. There are also ten Fast Attack Craft of the 'Willemoes' type, 22 large patrol craft and five coastal patrol vessels, seven minelayers, six minesweepers, four submarines, two coastal forts and seven Lynx helicopters.[22] All this produces a fairly defensive naval profile with the emphasis on coastal activity.

It should be remembered that the AFNORTH Command area includes the Federal Republic *Land* of Schleswig-Holstein. Its defence is connected with that of Jutland and is undertaken by the West German Sixth Armoured Infantry Division and the Danish Jutland Division, assisted by the West German Home Guard unit, (HSB 51), with about 5,000 men and 50 tanks. The Federal Republic's airforce has one wing of 36 Alphajets to provide close support in Schleswig-Holstein. The German Navy has more than 100 Tornado aircraft deployed in the anti surface ship role.[23] The surface combat units of the West German Navy are also substantial and include seven destroyers and nine frigates which could be asked to help counter Soviet surface forces in the Baltic and North Sea Areas.

Clearly, Danish forces by themselves would be unable to protect their crucial land and maritime areas from determined onslaught by Warsaw Pact powers. The successful defence of Denmark – and the areas it guards – has to be undertaken in concert with NATO allies. As with Norway, there is a judicious mix between reinforcement, prestocking and host nation support.

The main allied reinforcement for the Baltic Command is the UK Mobile Force, part of SACEUR's strategic reserve (SSR). This consists of an infantry brigade, support units and a supply group. Close air support is provided by a squadron of Jaguars; and helicopter air-lift by two squadrons of Pumas. Also part of SSR is an American infantry division of some 16,000 men and about 100 tanks. Whether this would be deployed in the BALTAP area would depend on SACEUR's priorities; as would the deployment of further RAF and USAF squadrons and the introduction of elite units such as the 82nd Airborne Division and 101st Air Assault Division.[24] US Marine amphibious forces also provide a mobile strategic reserve which can be deployed to BALTAP, as can the UK/NL AF, provided it is not operating in North Norway.[25] The AMF may also operate in Denmark, in Zealand.[26] It is also possible that the BALTAP region could receive air support from the aircraft carriers of SACLANT's Strike Fleet Atlantic. The American Strategic Air Command's B-52s could also be used in the area. Finally further reserves can be brought into the area from the United Kingdom and the United States.[27]

The question of prestocking is less essential for forces in Denmark than for those going into Norway, since the country is much closer to the central theatre of operations and does not suffer from Norway's difficulties of transportation. However, some prestocking of material in Denmark has been undertaken – indeed equipment and supplies for about five US air squadrons are kept there. The United States has COB agreements with Denmark but the maintenance of reception facilities for outside forces is the responsibility of the Danes in their own country and of the West Germans in Schleswig-Holstein. There is some debate as to whether the POMCUS system of prestocking should be introduced into the BALTAP area.[28]

The importance of the maritime area off north Norway and in the Norwegian Sea and North Sea has been discussed; but the largely coastal nature of the Danish navies needs to be noted. Only the West German Navy provides escorts for duties in the EASTLANT area. The main responsibility for action against the Soviet Navy in this area lies with the United States, United Kingdom and Dutch Naval forces.

The United States Second Fleet is part of the US Atlantic Fleet. In war, it provides SACLANT's Atlantic Striking Fleet. The number of ships and aircraft under the control of the Commander, Second Fleet, will vary but average figures would be about 70 ships and 300 aircraft. Of course by no means all of these would be assigned to operations in the maritime areas off the Northern Flank. The Standing Naval Force Atlantic (STANAVFORLANT), which consists of between five and nine destroyers or frigates from the participating NATO countries, is a force under the operational control of SACLANT in peacetime. Its ships may be dispersed to other forces in war. The Striking Fleet consists of up to four aircraft carriers with some 150–360 combat aircraft and could be deployed in the Atlantic area or the Norwegian Sea. SACLANT's amphibious forces include the UK/NL AF and the US MAF.[29] The Royal Navy has three ASW carriers, 15 destroyers and 39 frigates which are assigned to SACLANT for use in the EASTLANT area. Its two assault ships form the basis of the specialised amphibious lift provided to the UK/NL AF.

There has been some recent debate about the new US Maritime Strategy revealed at the end of 1985. It is not intended to rehearse the various arguments here but it is appropriate to mention the consequences of that strategy for America's European allies.[30]

The Maritime Strategy affects the Northern Waters and Northern Flank in peacetime, in transition to war and in time of conflict. In peacetime, the US seeks to deploy its naval forces well up into the Norwegian Sea (in 1985 the US took one of its carriers into the Norwegian fjords). In a period of confrontation, the US fleet could be moved to forward positions with marine amphibious forces embarked and sea-based air power deployed. This pattern of forward deployment would not be confined to North Atlantic sea areas. After the outbreak of war, US maritime forces would seize the initiative to apply early and direct pressure on the Soviets. The aim of operations of this phase has been stated thus:

> to defeat Soviet maritime strength in all its dimensions, including base support. That converts to classic Navy tasks of anti-submarine warfare, anti-surface warfare, counter-command and control, strike operations, anti-air warfare, mine warfare special operations, amphibious operations and sealift.[31]

In a third phase, the US force would carry the fight to the enemy, seeking war termination on favourable terms. ASW would continue to destroy Soviet submarines including their SSBNs. This would be done in combination with America's allies worldwide.[32]

Clearly the US Navy's Strategy has important consequences for NATO's North European Allies even if one does not accept the critical approach to it shown by some commentators.[33] Although it has much in common with NATO's concept of maritime operations (CONMAROPs), these consequences are, nevertheless, ambiguous. On the one hand an enhanced peacetime naval presence by the US in Northern Waters is a guarantee of the US commitment to the defence of that part of the world and to the securing of the Northern Flank for the following reasons:

> Control of Norwegian territory to the North, and in particular the airfields, is also important for an effective defence of the sea lines of communication across the Atlantic and in the Norwegian Sea, as well as for the defence of Iceland. . . . the use of Norwegian territory will be important for early warning, air defence over sea areas, attacks on surface warships and anti-submarine operations, *so for these reasons alone it is an Allied interest to reinforce Norway.*[34] [emphasis added]

This could suggest that the European Allies might be able to leave the forward maritime operations in the Norwegian Sea to the United States which might carry out such tasks as reinforcement and air support in its own interests. The Europeans would only have to see to their own coastal defences, make sure that ground attacks were held off until the Americans arrived, and help reinforce the Norwegian mainland. This broad division of maritime labour rules out large involvement in high seas operations by the West Europeans.

On the other hand, it might be argued that the US maritime strategy demands just such an involvement – as a West European interest. Of course, the strategy itself calls for Allied assistance, and as General Huitfeldt has pointed out, there are good *Allied* reasons for reinforcing Norway. It can be argued that there are equally good reasons for the NATO European countries to maintain a maritime presence in the north. If the Americans are left to develop the maritime strategy them-selves, uninfluenced by their NATO allies, they are more likely to pro-duce an outcome about which the Europeans have qualms. These qualms have been recognised by Admiral Watkins, the US Chief of Naval Operations, who proclaimed that the strategy "does not imply an immediate 'Charge of the Light Brigade' attack on the Kola Peninsula or any other specific target".[35] It would be important, therefore, that in a period of crisis, the first forward maritime movement in the Norwegian Sea was not made by a US carrier battle group – with all the implications that has for direct superpower confrontation – but by a NATO force, such as STANAVFORLANT. The continued effective-ness of STANAVFORLANT in this site calls for a continued North West European maritime capability beyond the coastal areas of the North Sea.

Britain and Germany

From what has been said, it should be clear that neither Britain nor West Germany provide the main Allied defence effort in the maritime and Northern Flank areas; and that these areas are not the most import-ant in their military reckoning. However, the areas are nonetheless of importance to both countries, more so for the United Kingdom than for the Federal Republic.

The United Kingdom has commitments to the reinforcement of Norway and Denmark with options for deploying the UKMF, the UK/NL AF, the AMF, as well as in the provision of forces. Further-more, there is an option for deploying RAF aircraft in the defence of Norway and Denmark. The Royal Navy deploys its ships in the defence of the EASTLANT area, and in the Channel Command area. Its 50-escort navy aims to fill the variety of tasks that are required, includ-ing anti-submarine warfare, anti-aircraft defence, surface warfare, minelaying and mine counter measures and amphibious operations. What the Royal Navy lacks for such a vast area is size; and it is likely to see its numbers further depleted in the coming decade.[36] This can be seen particularly in the question of its now ageing LPDs, *Fearless* and *Intrepid*. These only escaped being removed from the operational fleet because of the Falklands War; and it may be that the Treasury will achieve what the Argentinians failed to do. Should the Royal Navy's specialised amphibious striking capability not be retained, the role of the Royal Marines in Northern Europe must be in doubt, putting at risk an important reinforcement element.

The Federal Republic's navy, with some 24 submarines and 16 escort vessels, is much smaller than the Royal Navy and has a larger coastal element for Baltic operations. There are five corvettes, 40 guided-missile fast attack craft, 57 MCMVs and 50 various landing craft. The naval air arm has three squadrons of maritime attack aircraft, one squadron of reconnaissance aircraft, one squadron of maritime reconnaissance and one each of search and rescue and of ASW helicopters.[37] Most of the duties of the German Navy will be in the Baltic, where they already operate a division of labour in mining and MCM with the Danes, and in the North Sea. Air and ground forces are supplied for the defence of Denmark and a contribution is made to the AMF but the principal effort of West German forces is, of necessity, directed towards the Central Front.

There is close co-operation between British and West German forces in the maritime area and Northern Flank – in STANAVFORLANT, AMF, air support in BALTAP – all of which activity takes place in the NATO context.

Conclusions

Despite the relatively modest nature of United Kingdom and West Germany forces assigned to the defence of the two areas under discussion when compared with the potential US contribution, their input is nevertheless important in military and political terms.

Both countries may have to face two major challenges – apart from that of the Soviet Union – to their existing presence in the northern areas of NATO. The response to each situation should be considered in an Alliance context and may require closer defence co-operation between Britain and West Germany.

The first challenge is already on the way. It is the depletion of both countries' defence equipment through the funding gap between what is voted to the defence budget and what it costs to continue to undertake tasks as before. The case of *Fearless* and *Intrepid* has already been mentioned and the Royal Navy is likely to face a further diminution of its surface fleet in the 1990s. Despite its increased responsibilities, the West German Navy will find that by 1989 it will only have eight of the 12 frigates planned in 1976 and, in the case of the replacement for MCMV and minehunters, there will be fewer new vessels than the numbers they replace. More money buys less and it does so across the board in NATO. Denmark's frigates were reduced to nucleus crews in 1986, the Royal Netherlands Navy's escorts were cut by two and their sub-marines by the same number. The Norwegian Navy's plea for three more frigates is likely to be rejected for lack of money, Belgium's new fast patrol vessels have been delayed.[38] The danger is that the opera-tional requirements of the navies of northern Europe will be determined not by the threat that is faced or by considerations of the appropriate NATO response, but by the vagaries of the budgetary axe. The NATO frigate (NFR-90) may be a suitable answer – or it may become a sea camel, designed by a committee, that nobody really wants. The Norwegians have already turned it down. Perhaps now is the time for the Allies – with Britain and West Germany in the lead – to consider what the NATO maritime profile should be by the end of the century and what each country can best contribute towards its achievement.

The second challenge is more problematic but must be considered. It is that of a possible American withdrawal from Europe. Since the foundation of NATO there have been fears of American isolationism leading to a US administration removing its troops from Europe. Whilst the Reagan administration has not issued such threats itself, there are indications that American opinion – reflected in Con-gress – is more prepared to take such action; and there seems to be a long-term weakening in the ties that bind the United States to its defence commitment of Western Europe. It is not necessary to over-stress the danger, but it is possible that within the next 10–15 years the USA could withdraw most, if not all, of its troops and its ground-based missiles from Europe. (It should be added that this could be done after an agreement was reached with the Soviet Union.) The Americans may also decide to keep a certain residual presence in and around Europe, such as co-located bases, prestocked material and the facilities for rapid reinforcement, together with a strong maritime presence off the Atlan-tic coasts of Europe. In other words, Western Europe could be "Norwegianised".

What then would the European members of NATO do? It they still felt that they were military and politically threatened from the east, they would have to reconfigure their defence forces to make them more effective, to allow them to maintain their deterrent value and to make reinforcement from the USA more likely. Such a re-evaluation process would affect the maritime role of NATO Europe states. Clearly the Central Front would have to be reinforced and there would be military and political pressure on the United Kingdom not to renounce its Con-tinental commitment. Yet in the long term it may make more sense for the British to concentrate on those tasks they have traditionally done well – the naval ones – and to persuade the Federal Republic not to press its navy out into the blue waters. If indeed such a division of labour was, after careful study, found to be sensible *in extremis*, should not consideration be given to its paler shadow now at a time of renewed budgetary pressure?

Notes

1. NATO Information Service *The North Atlantic Treaty Organisation. Fact and Figures* (Brussels: NATO Information Service, 1983 (Tenth Edition), p. 110).
2. See Admiral James D. Watkins, "The Maritime Strategy" *US Naval Institute Proceedings*, January 1986, supplement pp. 4–15; Jahn Otto Johansen *Sovjetunionen og Norden. Konfrontasjon eller naboskap?* (Oslo: Cappelen, 1986); Lars B. Wallin (ed) *Proceedings of a Symposium on the Northern Flank in a Central European War, Stockholm, November 4–5 1980*, (Stockholm: The Swedish National Defence Research Institute, 1982); Johan Jørgen Holst, Kenneth Hunt and Anders C, Sjaarstad *Deterrence and Defence in the North* (Oslo: Norwegian University Press, 1985, especially chapters 1, 4, 7 and 8).
3. Nils Morten Udgaard *Northern Areas – Oil and Politics*, (Oslo: The Norwegian Atlantic Committee, Security Policy Library No. 5 – 1986); Willy Østreng *Soviet i Nordlige Farvann*, (Oslo: Gyldendal, 1982); Clive Archer and David Scrivener "Rising Stakes in Northern Waters", in Captain John Moore (ed) *Jane's Naval Review* (London: Jane's 1986, pp. 157–165).
4. Robert Weinland "Northern Waters: their Strategic Significance" in David Scrivener (ed) *Northern Waters: Resources and Security Issues* (Aberdeen: Centre for Defence Studies, 1981, p.A.56).
5. Nils Ørvik *Europe's Northern Cap and the Soviet Union* (Cambridge Mass: Harvard, Center for International Affairs, Occasional Paper No.6, 1963).
6. The full references are: The Norwegian Atlantic Committee for the International Institute for Strategic Studies *Militaerbalansen 1985–1986*, (Oslo: Norwegian Atlantic Committee, 1985); C.N. Donnelly *et al.*, *Soviet Amphibious Warfare and War on the Northern Flank* (The Hague: Soviet Studies Research Centre, RMA Sandhurst, December 1984); Tomas Ries *The Nordic Dilemma in the 80's: Maintaining Regional Stability Under New Strategic Conditions*, (Geneva: PSIS Occasional Papers No.1, 1982); Harald W. Støren *Problemer og muligheter ved kombinering av avskrekking og beroligelse i forholdet mellom Norge og Sovjetunionen. Virklighetsoppfatninger, prinsipper, målsetninger og valg av virkemedler*, (Oslo: Institutt for Statsvitenskap, 1985).
7. See *Militaerbalansen 1985–1986* pp. 128–9, *op. cit.*
8. Donnelly *et al.*, *op. cit*, p. 143.
9. As note 7, p. 129.
10. As note 8, pp. 147, 151–2.
11. Tønne Huitfeld "Options and Constraints in the Planning of Reinforcements: A Norwegian Perspective" in Holst, Hunt and Sjaastad (eds), as note 2, p. 175 and *Militaerbalansen 1985–1986*, *op. cit.*, p. 129.
12. *Militaerbalansen 1985–1986*, *op. cit.*, p. 130.
13. Nils Petter Gleditsch "COD og Invictus" *PR10 Inform*, No.13, 1984.
14. Michael Leonard "Options and Constraints in the Planning of Reinforcements: An American Perspective" in Holst, Hunt and Sjaastad (eds), as note 2, p. 166.
15. Huitfeld, *op. cit.*, pp. 177.
16. Huitfeldt, *op. cit.*, pp. 186–190; Leonard, *op. cit.*, pp.168–9 and Johan Jørgen Holst, Hunt and Sjaastad (eds), *op. cit.*, pp. 218–9.
17. Huitfeld, *op. cit.*, pp. 186–189.
18. Leonard, *op. cit.*, pp. 163, 167–9.
19. As note 12, p.132.
20. *Ibid*, pp. 133 and 47.
21. *Ibid*, pp. 47–8.
22. *Ibid*, p. 47.
23. *Ibid*, p. 133.
24. Bjarne F. Lindhardt *Allierede Forstaerkninger til Danmark* (Copenhagen: Samfundsvidenskabeligt Forlag, Dansk Udenrigspolitisk Institut Forskningsrapport nr.5, 1981, pp. 84).

25. *Ibid*, pp. 88–92.
26. Flemming Schroll Nielsen *AMF - NATO's Crisis Force*, (Copenhagen: The Information and Welfare Services of the Danish Defence, 1982, pp. 25–6).
27. As note 24, pp. 92–5.
28. *Ibid*, pp. 137–9.
29. As note 12, pp. 136–7.
30. See, for example, Admiral James D. Watkins, as note 2, and *US Naval Institute Proceedings*, January 1986, Supplement pp. 41–47 for a full bibliography on the subject by Captain Peter M. Swartz.
31. Watkins, *op. cit.*, p. 11.
32. *Ibid*, p. 13.
33. For example see John M. Collins "The Maritime Strategy", *US Naval Institute Proceedings*, March 1986, p. 18. A recent trenchant criticism of the strategy is John Mearsheimer "A Strategic Misstep - The Maritime Strategy and Deterrence in Europe", *International Security*, Fall 1986.
34. Huitfeldt, *op. cit.*, p. 180.
35. Watkins, *op. cit.*, p. 10.
36. See David Greenwood "Younger's Budget Brew", *Defence Minister and Chief of Staff*, No.2 1986, pp. 5–12; Norman Friedman, "Western European and NATO Navies", *US Naval Institute Proceedings*, March 1986.
37. *Militaerbalansen 1985–1986*, *op. cit.*, pp. 49–50.
38. Friedman, *op. cit.*

Chapter 15
British and German Defence Co-operation at Sea and on the Northern Flank

FRANK KUPFERSCHMIDT

Among the European allies, Britain and the Federal Republic of Germany contribute the lion's share to NATO's defence forces. Some 66,000 British troops stationed on German territory stand for their country's commitment to common security and represent a clear and essential link between these two countries which "maintain the most comprehensive and most intense contacts of the whole of Europe on security and defence matters", as George Younger, Secretary of Defence recently put it.[1]

Regular staff talks at Ministerial level and frequent contacts between the services of both sides have laid the basis for much practical co-operation. Exchange programmes for officers have been established and are being extended with the aim of further improving mutual understanding and common operations. An important number of German officers and other ranks of all three services were and are still trained in Britain. Ships' crews carry out operational sea training with the Royal Navy and more than 40 ship visits are paid to UK ports every year. Distinct maritime and Northern Flank dimensions of this bilateral co-operation, however, are less well developed. The roles of both Britain and the Federal Republic in the defence of these areas, which need to be seen within the wider framework of NATO, are different; and they depend on the policies and posture of other countries in the region as well as historical developments.

Based on Clive Archer's description of the overall strategic situation and the Soviet threat to northern Europe and adjacent sea areas in the preceeding chapter, this essay examines in more detail the context in which the forces of Britain and Federal Germany would be employed, their roles in the defence of NATO's Northern Flank and their contributions to the Allied posture; finally it looks at possible future developments.

The requirement for exterior reinforcements

The overall aim of NATO's defence strategy is to prevent war through deterrence. On the Northern Flank this requires the Alliance to demonstrate the ability to retain (or if lost, regain) control of key positions in Norway and Denmark and to deny the Warsaw Pact control of the Norwegian and North Seas as well as the Baltic. However, whilst the national in-place land and air forces on the Northern Flank play a vital role in deterrence, they are not, by themselves, sufficient to defeat a Soviet attack if deterrence should fail.[2] Moreover, increasing concern is voiced in other NATO countries over the reduced peacetime manning of land units, the declining number of ships and aircraft, and the growing obsolescence of equipment in the military services of Norway and Denmark[3].

The Norwegian Chief of Defence has himself stated that the 1986 Norwegian defence budget is inadequate and presents certain risks.[4] Although the country has NATO's second highest defence expenditure *per capita* after the United States[5], it needs to spend more on defence and to increase its annual budget by 6.7% at least until the year 2000. In real terms, however, the rate will only be 3.5%. Other high-ranking Norwegian officers, too, openly speak of the necessity of improving the country's conventional defence. Norway has standing forces of 37,000 men, most of which are deployed in the Northern provinces. After the reserves have been called up, 8% of the population would be under arms, thus increasing the number of troops to 325,000, a considerable achievement when compared to the much lower degree of mobilisation achieved in other Allied countries. But even these forces would only be able to halt the Soviet advance for a short time.[6]

In Denmark, owing to lack of funds, the services had to cut back manpower to 29,600 men overall. As a result, ships and aircraft have had to be taken out of service. Danish Social Democrats have proposed reducing the contribution to forward defence even further.[7]

Questions are already being openly asked as to the minimum a member country is allowed to contribute to common defence without endangering the solidarity of its partners.[8] From an Alliance point of view, the trend towards further reductions of force contributions needs to be reversed; and, in the special case of the Baltic, it is important that the Federal German Navy should not eventually find itself providing the only NATO maritime contingent. It is for this reason that the

Table 15.1   NATO-Armed Forces on the Northern Flank

NORWAY

Introduction: One of the founding signatories of the NATO alliance in 1949, Norway has the smallest population of all the Scandinavian countries with 4,150,000 people. Norway spent a total of $1.598 bn on defence in 1985. The total Armed Forces strength is 37,000 regulars (23,200 conscripts). Additionally, there are 201,000 reservists and about 80,000 home defence.

Army: 20,000 (13,000 of this total are conscripts). There are two operational, five regional and 16 operational territorial commands. Manpower forms one brigade, one all-arms group, two border garrison battalions, an infantry battalion as well as independent armoured squadrons and artillery regiments.

Navy: 7,600 including 1,000 coast artillery (5,000 conscripts). Personnel based at Horten, Haakonsvern, Ramsund and Olasvern (Tromso). Naval forces consist of 14 submarines, five frigates, two corvettes, 38 fast attack craft, two MCMV, five amphibious craft, 23 support ships and one helicopter squadron consisting of six Lynx aircraft for SAR/reconnaissance duties.

Air Force: 9,400 (5,200 conscripts). There are five squadrons of ground attack fighter aircraft, one squadron of maritime reconnaissance aircraft, two transport squadrons, one SAR helo squadron. For air defence purposes, there are four artillery battalions and one SAM battalion.

DENMARK

Introduction: Has a population of 5,150,000 and in 1985 her defence expenditure was $1.007 bn. The Armed Forces personnel total 29,600 (with 9,900 conscripts) and a reservist strength of 162,200.

Army: 17,000 (with 8,100 conscripts). Standing force is 8,500. There are two divisional headquarters (consisting of five mechanised infantry brigades and six regimental combat teams), eight independent infantry battalions and one army aviation unit.

Navy: 5,700 personnel (1,100 conscripts) based at Copenhagen, Korsor and Frederikshavn. Naval forces consist of four submarines, 10 frigates, 16 fast attack craft, 27 patrol craft, 13 MCMVs and eight Lynx helicopters.

Air Force: 6,900 personnel (700 conscripts). Tactical Air Command consists of 3 Squadrons of Ground Attack Fighters, one squadron of Air Defence Fighter aircraft, one Reconnaissance Squadron. The Air Defence Group has one SAM battalion and, additionally, there is one transport Squadron and one SAR Squadron.

GERMANY – (Northern Flank only)

Army: about 30,000 personnel (including conscripts and mobilised home defence brigade)

Field Army:
One armoured infantry division consisting of two armoured infantry brigades, one armoured brigade (equipped with Leopard 1 tanks and Marder) and one home defence brigade (with M 48 tanks).

Territorial Army:
One home defence brigade fully dependent on mobilisation (with M 48 tanks)

Air Force:
Two squadrons reconnaissance aircraft RF4-F
two squadrons fighter-bomber Alphajet
one wing transport aircraft C-160
one Air Defence regiment with NIKE and HAWK batteries

Navy: 36,200 including naval air arm (10,000 conscripts)
24 conventional submarines, seven destroyers, nine frigates, five corvettes, 40
guided missile attack craft, 59 mine counter-measure vessels, 34 support ships
including tankers, 30 small landing craft.

Naval Air Arm:
Three squadrons with Fighter bomber Tornado
one squadron with reconnaissance aircraft RF-104G
two squadron with MPA Breguet Atlantic
one squadron with ASW helicopter Sea Lynx
one squadron with SAR helicopter Sea King to be converted to ASVW
helicopters.

Bases:
North Sea: Wilhelmshaven, Borkum, Nordholz (Naval Air)
Baltic: Flensburg, Olpenitz, Ecknernförde, Kiel, Neustadt, Schleswig
                    (Naval Air), Eggebek (Naval Air), Kiel-Holtenau (Naval Air)

---

government in Bonn is concerned that Denmark maintains the level and
composition of her naval forces.

The unsatisfactory situation is further complicated since, for political reasons, Norway and Denmark do not permit foreign combat
troops to be stationed on their territory in peacetime.[9] Thus, both are
critically dependent on comprehensive and early outside reinforcements in times of crisis and in war.

The role of the US Strike Fleet on the Northern Flank

To appreciate the role of the British and German forces in the defence
of the Northern Flank, it is first necessary to understand the role of the
most important allied contingent in this theatre, the United States
forces; and to examine the operational framework within which these
forces are employed.

The possibility of an early move of the US Strike Fleet into the
Norwegian Sea is one of the West's key elements for achieving sea control in the Northern Flank area and for protecting an unconstrained
flow of reinforcements to support both the battle in the Northern
Region and on the Central Front. With its far-reaching capability to
project sea and air power deep into the Barents Sea and into the Soviet

Table 15.2   NATO-Reinforcements for the Northern Flank

LAND REINFORCEMENTS

---

1. ACE Mobile Force (AMF).   This is a multi-national, brigade sized force combined with a number of air squadrons which is intended for rapid deployment early in a period of tension to demonstrate NATO solidarity and, if necessary, to fight alongside theatre troops. It has several deployments options, two of which are in the Northern Region, so its presence on the Northern Flank cannot be guaranteed.

2. Second Marine Amphibious Force (II MAF).   The United States provides II MAF for the defence of the Northern Region. This divisional size force firstly deploys 4 MAB, a brigade sized force with integral air support, to North Norway and then follows with the remainder staging through the UK to the area within the Region which is most in need of support.

3. Canadian Air Sea Transported Brigade Group (CAST).   The CAST is a light brigade group which is dedicated to the defence of North Norway. It is moved partly by air and partly by sea.

4. The UK/NL Amphibious Force (UK/NL AF).   This mainly regular brigade sized force comprises of three British and one Dutch battalion equivalents with organic combat, helicopter and logistic support. It is assigned to SACLANT who has agreed with SACEUR that the force may be employed in support of the Northern Region to make best use of its Mountain and Arctic Warfare capability.

5. United Kingdom Mobile Force (UKMF).   This brigade sized force has deployment options in Zealand and Schleswig-Holstein. It consists of four infantry battalions with armoured reconnaissance, medium, artillery, engineer and a large logistic support group.

6. SACEUR's Strategic Reserve Land (SSR(L)).   The United States Ninth Infantry Division is a modern, well equipped force which has options for deployment in the Northern Region. It is retained in the UK for use by SACEUR as part of his land reserves.

AIR REINFORCEMENTS

---

7. Regional Air Reinforcements.   Six squadrons, one of which is British, reinforce Norway and up to seven squadrons, two of which are British, reinforce Denmark. The three British squadrons are all Jaguars.

8. SACEUR's Strategic Reserves Air (SSR(A)).   Twelve squadrons, which includes three UK tornado and one UK Harrier squadrons, are retained in UK for use by SACEUR. All or part of this force could be available in the Northern Region.

(Compiled by King's College London for the Northern Flank Conference in London in May 1986)

homeland, the US Strike Fleet provides a major contribution to the defence of NATO's northernmost member country, which cannot be replaced by any European navy. The large US carriers operate an air-group of 86 fixed wing aircraft, 24 of which are usually fighters, approximately 34 are attack aircraft, and the remainder are for air-borne early warning, electronic countermeasures and ASW protection. Four of these carriers, if deployed to the Northern Flank, would nearly quadruple the Allied in-place air forces.

For some time, the question of whether and when US Carrier Battle Groups (CVBG) would be dispatched to the Norwegian Sea has been a matter of public discussion. If support were too little, or too late, far more effort would be needed to regain lost territory than if it had been successfully defended from the start. A major problem, however, has been that other US commitments, such as in the Pacific and the Mediterranean, have made it particularly difficult to guarantee the availability of sufficient carriers for the Northern Flank tasks. This situation has now been improved by the additional battle groups which are part of the 600-ship navy.[10] Yet, during the transition period before the naval build-up is completed, the US would inevitably find it diffi-cult to concentrate the navy's efforts on the European theatre to the extent that would be desirable.

The projected increase in US naval power is supplemented by a new maritime strategy in which the US navy sets itself a task of "contain-ing" the Soviet Northern fleet as close to its bases as possible.[11] "By making it clear at the outset that Soviet SSBNs will be at risk in a conventional war, the strategy alters Soviet correlation of forces calculations and thus enhances deterrence".[12] Furthermore, the threat to their strategic assets is aimed at discouraging the Soviets from early forward deployment and forcing them to withhold sufficient general-purpose forces to protect their SSBNs.

Some Western strategists, however, believe that this concept could lead to destabilisation and add to the risk of escalation[13]. But their alter-native approach might, it is argued, lead to ceding the Norwegian Sea to the Soviets early in the conflict. This, in turn, would restrict CVBG operations to the south-west of the Greenland-Iceland-UK gap, with· serious consequences for the defence of Northern Norway. It has been widely assumed in the public debate, that former Supreme Allied Com-manders Atlantic (SACLANT) had assessed the deployment into the Norwegian Sea as too risky for their carriers, and that the new US Mari-time Forward Strategy constituted an important change of policy. This, in fact, is not the case. Although, in practice, different SACLANTs might have held different views, the decision as to whether carriers should be deployed further north or retained south of the gaps has not been subject to formal changes in NATO policy but depends solely on the military situation. The current US maritime strategy is based on the use of early and vigorous forward deployment of maritime power to

Table 15.3 British and US Naval Forces

UNITED KINGDOM

Navy 70,600 personnel (including Royal Marines.)
Bases at Devonport, Faslane, Portland, Portsmouth, Rosyth.
Strategic forces consists of 4 SSBN.
Naval forces comprise 14 nuclear powered, 15 conventional submarines, three anti-submarine-warfare-carriers, two amphibious assault ships, 15 destroyers, 41 frigates, 39 mine counter-measure vessels, 32 patrol vessels and seven land-ing ships. The Fleet Air Arm consists of 32 Sea Harrier, 107 Sea King Heli-copters (87-ASW, 20 Commando) 32 Wasp (22 ASW, 10 training), 41 Wessex (21 commando, 10 training, 20 SAR).

ROYAL FLEET AUXILIARY (RFA) 2,600 personnel, naval vessels, civilian crews
14 tankers and 4 replenishment ships

ROYAL MARINES 7,800 personnel
The one commando brigade composed of three cdo groups, one cdo artillery regiment, one battery (Army), two cdo engineer squadrons (one regular, one reserve), one logistic regiment (with Army), one light helicopter squadron and support units.
One Special Boat Squadron, three assault squadrons.

UNITED STATES

Navy: SECOND FLEET (ATLANTIC) NATO assigned: 14,850 personnel
Bases: Norfolk, Va (HQ), Mayport, Roosevelt Roads (Puerto Rico), Charles-ton, New London, Newport, New York (Staten Island), Boston, New Orleans, Bangor, Kings Bay.
Average strength: 34 SSBN, 50 nuclear powered attack submarines, four car-riers, 93 principal surface combatants, 24 amphibious ships. As one of the four major fleets in the United States Navy, the Second Fleet remains ready to con-trol assigned ocean areas, defend the US from attack through the Atlantic, deny the use of ocean area to an enemy, and support adjacent theatre commanders, particularly those in Europe.
The composition of Second Fleet reflects its wide capabilities as the major bat-tle force in the Atlantic. This battle force consists of a balanced mix of func-tional task forces, the attack carrier force, the sea control and surveillance force, the amphibious force and the mobile logistic support force.

---

demonstrate that the Soviets will not be able to cut the sea lanes from the United States to Europe.[14] As it takes some seven days to move forces from the US across the Atlantic into the Norwegian Sea, early warning and appropriate reaction are preconditions for such timely deployments. But these are uncertainties to which any concept is sub-ject. Thus, initially, the European navies may have to contain the Soviets with their own forces. Contingency plans have been set up to deal with such a situation, to which Britain and the Federal Republic of Germany, among others, have assigned naval forces.

But the US Navy also has a peacetime role on the Northern Flank which is often not fully recognised. By exercising in areas which would be of strategic importance in war, NATO demonstrates its commitment to a common defence and is thus enhancing deterrence. In the last 10 years US carriers have only operated for 33 days in the Norwegian Sea.[15] Hence the demand for an increased American presence in North European waters, which is also supported by the former Norwegian Prime Minister, Kare Willoch, and by senior military representatives.[16] However, the present government in Oslo does not appear fully to share this view. It believes that too frequent and too massive American deployments to the Northern Flank are counterproductive and compromise Norway's security policy, which is a "trade-off between deterrence and reassurance", and which so far, is said to have worked well.[17]

The operational framework

As the inventory of NATO's naval forces has reduced and that of the Soviets has increased, NATO has had to ensure that the best use is made of its scarce assets. At the operational level, the "TRI-Major NATO Commanders' Concept of Maritime Operations"[18] is an important contribution in ensuring that there is an agreed maritime doctrine for the Alliance. British and German naval forces are deployed in accordance with its principles.

The numerical superiority of the enemy afloat in the Northern Flank area requires that full use is made of the depth of the area to engage his forces early and repeatedly. Consequently, the principles set out in the concept of operations are:

- containment, including tying down Warsaw Pact forces in defensive tasks by creating Allied threats from the sea against the enemy's coastal areas;
- defence in depth, including striking enemy bases and facilities which support his forces at sea as well as amphibious landings as required in the high north; and most importantly,
- keeping the initiative; because distances are too great in the region for maritime forces to be deployed in time to prevent critical damage being done by the Soviets were NATO solely to "chase after" events.[19]

There is an obvious and close relationship between the US forward maritime strategy and the principles of the "TRI-MNC Concept of Maritime Operations". The principles of containment and defence in depth correspond to the forward element in the maritime strategy, whereas keeping the initiative complies with the demand for early deployment to the Norwegian Sea.

Improved co-ordination of operational planning and procedures would be a further promising approach to enhance NATO's defence on the Northern Flank, particularly in the regions where the boundaries of all three major NATO commands meet. As these boundaries cannot be removed, problems of Command and Control which they generate have to be overcome by appropriate agreements to ease cross-boundary operations. The conclusion of the "TRI-MNC-Agreement on Maritime Operations in the North Sea and Adjacent Waters" was a first step in this direction and marked a milestone within the field of operational planning. Since then, several new operational plans have been developed and tested in Allied exercises.

The British contribution

The UK defence budget for 1986–7 amounts to £18,479 billion, "higher in absolute terms than that of any other ally, except the United States",[20] and third in the Alliance in expenditure *per capita*.[21] Ninety-five percent of the provisions are dedicated to NATO tasks. Expenditure on running the naval and air general-purpose forces as well as European Theatre Ground forces accounts for 49% of the defence budget. Although the United Kingdom contributes substantially from its own forces to the defence of the Northern Flank area, and acts in some circumstances as a staging area for US reinforcements, Britain also has major tasks on the Central Front and in the Atlantic. The Norwegian Sea and North Sea, however, are direct maritime approaches to the British Isles and a first line of their defence.

Britain supports the Northern Flank with her fleet, with Royal Marine Commandos as well as with army and air force units. Its naval contribution on the defence of the Northern Flank and maritime area is by far the greatest of the north-west Europeans[22]. At present, the Royal Navy provides about 60% of the standing forces available to NATO in the East Atlantic and Northern Flank Area[23]. Up to three ASW carriers (CVS) of the battle-proven *Invincible* class with their air groups, 14 destroyers and 34 frigates as well as 17 nuclear-powered submarines and four squadrons of RAF maritime patrol aircraft could be made available for operations. However, a number of these ships will be assigned to the Channel Command and others may be needed in the South-Western approaches, another sea area which is crucially important to the West for reinforcement and resupply shipping.

In an early stage of war, British forces, together with other north-west European navies, would be called upon to contain Soviet naval power until US CVBGs arrive.

The largest single contribution to NATO maritime forces is that made by the

United States, but the availability of US ships in the Eastern Atlantic at the outbreak of hostilities cannot be assumed. European navies, and in particular the Royal Navy, must therefore be ready to play a leading role in initial operations.[24]

The first and most important task would be to assert sea control for the Alliance in combined naval and air operations. Enemy forces must be denied the opportunity for full deployment and breaking through to the Atlantic and Southern North Sea and this means Western forces operating as far north and close to Soviet bases as possible. There, carriers, destroyers and frigates, helicopters with hull-mounted and towed array sonars, surface-to-surface and surface-to-air missiles would have to operate in a multithreat environment. Once the US Strike fleet has arrived, a number of additional Royal Navy units may be tasked to its protection and support.

Since ships operating in the Eastern Atlantic are subject to the permanent threat of Soviet air attack, air defence for those units is a very high priority defensive task. The updated programme for the Sea Harrier is a significant step towards meeting the requirement for increasing the effectiveness of air defence in the British surface fleet, as is the introduction of the vertical-launch Sea Wolf.

British submarines would be deployed in barrier operations against Soviet submarines on their passage through the Norwegian Sea and the Greenland-Iceland-United Kingdom gap. Nimrod maritime patrol aircraft will add to their detection and fighting capacity. They are equipped with the new Stingray torpedo and later will be fitted with Harpoon anti-ship missiles, giving them a new capability against surface units. Closer to its home base, the Royal Navy has to engage in mine countermeasures, an often underestimated but nevertheless important complementary task. Mine countermeasure vessels will have to operate around the British coasts, clearing and maintaining access routes for surface warships and submarines and those to be used by reinforcement and resupply shipping.

The combined British-Netherlands (UK/NL) amphibious force would be the first reinforcement to arrive in Northern Norway and therefore plays a decisive role. It would be ferried by sea, which would take up to seven days or, if the situation demanded it, by air, without its heavy equipment. The British element of the force consists of 3 Commando Brigade Royal Marines supplemented by the necessary specialist amphibious shipping, which includes the 20-year-old assault ships *Fearless* and *Intrepid*. Their replacement is due in the mid-1990s. For some time, there have been doubts as to whether the Royal Navy would retain this type of ship or at least an equivalent.[25] Under policies laid down in the 1981 Defence White Paper the assault ships should already have been scrapped but the Falklands campaign changed the situation drastically and they were reprieved. In December 1986 the UK government announced its intention of retaining an amphibious lift capacity in the long term, thus reversing earlier plans.[26]

With the scrapping of the commando carrier *Bulwark* in 1984, and the sale of the support carrier *Hermes* to India in 1986, the Royal Marines lost their dedicated seaborne helicopter landing capability. Although the three CVS can be deployed in a commando role this is only a secondary task for them and their availability for it depends on the overall military situation. The British government has initiated work on an additional aviation support ship able to operate troop-carrying helicopters.[27] For the moment though, according to the Ministry of Defence "the UK/NL amphibious force has sufficient helicopters and landing craft at its disposal to land directly from its own shipping across and over the beaches and to establish an initial lodgment ashore".[28] Most of the landing force trains in Norway each winter to prepare in the environment in which they would have to fight. To afford the force more flexibility and to speed up reinforcement, some heavy specialist stocks like snowmobiles have been pre-stocked in the most likely area of operations. While at sea, the UK/NL amphibious force needs protection against air, surface and subsurface threats. This would commit quite a number of Royal Navy escorts, including perhaps one CVS.

The only land reinforcement force dedicated exclusively to the Baltic Approaches (BALTAP) area is provided by the United Kingdom Mobile Force (UKMF). This formation of near divisional size comprises the first Infantry Brigade with armoured reconnaissance, medium artillery, engineers and a large logistic support group – 14,000 men in all. The Royal Air Force contributes the necessary airlift capacity[29]. Deployment options lie in Zealand and in Schleswig-Holstein. "By having UKMF designated as our BALTAP Reinforcing Force the UK has accepted that the defence of the BALTAP area is to be considered as 'Forward Defence for the UK' ", General Otto K. Lind, then Chief of Defence Denmark, stated in February 1985.[30]

Since in January 1987 London indicated "it was considering possible changes" to the deployment of the force[31], Danish politicians and military authorities have expressed concern. They fear the considerable consequences that a withdrawal, or even a reduction, of this force would bring for Danish security policy and posture. What particularly concerns them is the fact that they have done much in providing host nation support for this force so as to increase its deterrence value by making it "work better and better"[32].

On the other hand, Danish defence spending has been frozen at 2% of its gross national product for some years, less than half the British figure. Some observers, therefore, see the discussion of the UKMF deployment as an attempt to step up pressure on Denmark's politicians to increase funds for defence.[33] However, from the British government's point of view, it is part of a process in improving the overall effectiveness of the deployment of its armed forces. Moreover, any decisions on the redeployment, or possible changes in structure, of UKMF will only be taken in close co-operation with the NATO Commands concerned.

The third and last of the land reinforcements which Britain provides is her contribution to the ACE Mobile Force. It is available to SACEUR for deployment on NATO's Northern or Southern Flanks. An infantry battalion and other force troops, including armoured reconnaissance, artillery, helicopters and logistic support, form the British share of this contingent.

Apart from NATO's shortage of in-place land forces, its position on the Northern flank is also weak in air assets. "Air reinforcements are particularly important . . Plans and preparations for rapid transfer of Allied aerial combat forces are therefore an important part of Norway's deterrence policy".[34]

Six squadrons, including one from the Royal Air Force, are assigned to reinforce Norway. A further seven are planned to go to Denmark and here Britain contributes two squadrons. There are also four additional UK based squadrons belonging to SACEUR's Strategic Reserves (Air) which could be rapidly deployed to the Northern region. The Royal Air Force operates two squadrons of Buccaneer aircraft from northern Scotland in the maritime role. These aircraft are soon to be fitted with Sea Eagle air-to-ship missiles. A certain number of UK fighter squadrons is also dedicated to air defence of the maritime region.

For deterrence to be credible it is necessary to be seen to train where one would have to fight. British forces do this by taking part in many exercises on the Northern Flank, on national, bilateral and NATO-wide levels. Overall, Britain's considerable contribution to the defence of the maritime area and Northern Flank is second only to US efforts[35] but that could change in the not too distant future. Against the background of declining funds for defence and the cost of programmes such as Trident, priorities may have to be reviewed. Will there be a second cutback for the Royal Navy to follow that of the 1981 Defence Review? Officially, the government stands firmly by its target of a surface fleet of about 50 destroyers and frigates but looking at the funding and building rate of new ships, it seems doubtful whether this number will be maintained throughout.

During parliamentary debates earlier in 1986[36], MPs on both sides of the House criticised the gap between the Royal Navy's tasks and resources allocated to accomplish them. Once again, specialisation within NATO, the sharing of roles between member countries and a reduction of the British contribution to the Central Front were urged.

In a financially difficult situation for defence, the conflict in priorities between Britain's maritime role in NATO and her commitments on the Central Front receives particular attention.[37] On the one hand cuts to the strength of BAOR would ease the strain on the Royal Navy, allowing more resources to be devoted to the maritime role and thus making it possible to match commitments to resources. On the other hand, this would substantially damage NATO's posture in the Central Region and give a totally wrong signal, not only to the Warsaw Pact but possibly also to other partners in the Alliance. What is even more important, the reduction of British forces on the Central European Front would conflict with binding Western European Union agreements on the British force levels to be maintained on German soil. However important the Northern Flank may be for the Alliance, to make cuts in BOAR to help the Royal Navy would be a development which Germany least of all would wish to see. An alternative would be to abandon Trident. But the government is convinced that the British strategic nuclear deterrent is indispensable; a position with which most European governments would agree.

The German contribution

In 1986, the Federal Republic of Germany spent DM50.3 billion (£16.22 billion)[38] on defence, 19.1% of the country's total budget and roughly 3.3% of the Gross Domestic Product. With the reduction of the number of personnel or ships in other Allied navies[39], the relative weight of Germany's contribution increases. Its share within the maritime defence posture of the six north-west European navies amounts to roughly one-third. In the Baltic it carries the main burden of the maritime defence, providing approximately three-quarters of the naval forces and all the naval air power there[40].

However, the German contribution to the defence of the Northern Flank is not exclusively maritime. Army and air force, too, are committed to the defence of Schleswig-Holstein and the Baltic Approaches. Assigned to COMBALTAPs forces, both would have to defend as far east as possible, attacking amphibious and air landings executed in conjunction with the advance of Warsaw Pact land forces. For this task the army provides a heavy armoured division and a home defence brigade, 30,000 men in all, equipped with 332 Leopard 1 battle tanks and 300 mechanised infantry fighting vehicles.

On the air side, the defence of the BALTAP area is seen as a forward protective barrier for southern Norway; and also to some extent for the UK Air Defence Region, against the air threat emanating from the East. The German air force contributes two squadrons each of reconnaissance and fighter bomber aircraft. In addition, there are sizable ground-based air defence forces operating in Schleswig-Holstein under command and control of 2ATAF. While for the moment the air defence continues to rely heavily upon NIKE and HAWK systems, the way has been paved for an important change in the late 1980s. Then, Patriot and HAWK will form an overlapping area defence system against all levels of air attack, complemented by Roland-systems for point defence.

The Soviet naval build-up over the last two decades led to a change in threat assessment and had therefore great influence on Federal Germany's naval conceptual planning. In the late 1950s and during the 1960s, in the face of a Soviet fleet more-or-less bound to coastal waters, the country's naval contribution to the Allied defence concentrated on the Baltic Approaches. But gradually the perspective had to be changed. With the growing potential of both the surface ships and submarines of the Soviet Northern Fleet, the defensive tasks in the North Sea and the Baltic demanded similar priorities. To defend the "front door" to the Baltic Approaches, whilst leaving its "back door" unguarded did not seem a sound policy. Eventually, the defence of the Northern Flank area as a whole was to receive more attention.[41]

In June 1980 the Federal Security Council lifted self-imposed national restrictions for German naval forces in Allied operations. Without affecting the maritime posture in the Baltic, ships based in the North Sea were given greater freedom for manoeuvre in exercises. Since then, they have been deployed more often beyond 61° North (Bergen-Shetland line) and the Dover-Calais line. This decision was based on the assessment of the Northern Flank area as a single strategic and operational entity. It also took into account the inherent flexibility of naval assets and their envisaged employment as set out in the Defence Policy Guidelines and the Federal German White Paper of 1979[42].

In the light of the Soviet naval expansion, the invasion of Afghanistan, and the resulting commitments of US naval forces to regions outside the NATO treaty area, the German move won wide support. It was seen as a contribution to enhanced Allied flexibility.

In the Baltic, the Federal Navy operates a layered defence system. The concept of operations to the east of Bornholm is to weaken the Warsaw Pact's offensive capabilities by making it difficult for hostile forces to use this sea area for initial deployment and as a supply route. This task can only be fulfilled by those naval units which are capable of either operating undetected or penetrating strong enemy defences. Accordingly, Germany's defence in depth is based on a substantial number of small, silent patrol submarines, equipped with modern wire-guided torpedos and a considerable mine-laying capacity, and four fighter bomber squadrons of the Naval Air Arm with up to four Kormoran air-to-surface missiles each. In the Baltic Approaches area, the routes to and from the Atlantic must be secured for allied operations and denied to the enemy. Friendly forces, exposed to a permanent air threat, must be capable of repelling enemy amphibious forces, of landing raiding parties, and of carrying out mining and mine countermeasures operations. Small, agile combat units capable of taking advantage of the numerous islands, bays and straits to avoid detection and to use their weapons for surprise attacks are best suited for this purpose under the conditions prevailing in this area. Naval fighter bombers, fast patrol boats, both with anti-ship missiles, small mine countermeasure vessels, and helicopters with air-to-surface missiles have these capabilities. Mine-warfare units ensure that sea lines and harbour approaches are kept navigable while medium and small landing-craft contribute their share to operational mobility of Allied land forces within the area.

Nearly all Federal German ships are prepared for defensive minelaying to block off hostile amphibious landings and other surface forces, should these have penetrated the forward defence lines.

In the North and Norwegian Seas enemy forces must be repelled and contained as far north and close to their bases as possible. The German escort fleet of 16 destroyers and frigates, with auxiliaries and helicopters, new submarines, ASW and long-range maritime patrol aircraft and naval fighter bombers are provided for the common defence of this sea area. Destroyers and frigates could be employed in multipurpose task groups in escort or area operations supported by Tornado aircraft in reconnaissance and attack missions, while submarines and MPA could take part in barrier operations. The Federal Republic has steadily increased its contribution to the defence of NATO's Northern Flank during the last 15 years and further improvements are planned.

On the personnel side the reduction in numbers of young men eligible for military service has been tackled by the extension of military service from 15 to 18 months and by keeping more reserve personnel under training. This will ensure peacetime manning on as high a level as possible.

The scope for closer Anglo-German co-operation

The Soviet Union's maritime expansion will, it is believed, continue for some time, supporting the country's claim of having become not only a global power but a maritime power as well. As before, the United States will have to carry the main burden of the Alliance's defence posture in meeting this challenge. Against the background of the strengthened US American naval construction programme it can be argued that the US Navy could shoulder an increased share in attempting to redress the maritime balance in northern Europe; and that British and Federal German maritime forces need not necessarily maintain their present strength. After all, the number of US escort ships (cruisers, destroyers and frigates) increased from 178 to 219 between 1980 and 1987 and will reach a total of 238 units in 1990.[43]

This argument both misses the point and disregards the American mood. For years, successive Supreme Allied Commanders Atlantic have criticised the shortage of escorts, whose numbers have continued to drop despite the Soviet naval build-up. With its 600-ship navy, the United States aims to secure on a global scale its lead over the adversary's maritime power. This is crucial to the West because its sea lines of communication are not confined to the NATO area and are vital to Western interest whilst the Soviet sea lines of communication are not vital to Soviet interests. The US Navy has therefore to make up for deficiencies in the allied naval presence out of area. Consequently, there is no case at all for a cutback in European naval forces; indeed, rather the opposite is true. Allied navies are already stretched to their limits with their present commitments and further demands, as a result of Soviet naval expansion, may be in the offing.

Deterrence can be reinforced by an increased allied naval presence in Northern waters as a means of demonstrating more clearly NATO's interest in the freedom of the seas in this area. British and American ships are said to have operated there more frequently 15 years ago than they do today[44]. In the Baltic, clearly visible Allied naval deployments, including those from countries not neighbouring these waters, are a valuable means of signalling to the Soviet Union the international status of this sea, and that any attempt to create a Soviet *Mare Clausum* would be opposed.

A multinational "Standing Force" or "On-Call-Force" for the Northern Flank could meet both these requirements, and at the same time diminish Norwegian misgivings by turning away from an exclusively US–USSR confrontation to a more broadly-based demonstration of Allied resolve. Moreover, the activation of such a force and its deployment to specific areas close to the Soviet homeland could be a useful instrument in a crisis management context. It is believed that this idea was studied by NATO some years ago and rejected on the grounds of reduced operational flexibility and the amount of additional planning that would be generated. Some military authorities argue that in fact contingency plans provide the same political and military results as NATO standing or on-call forces would do. Nevertheless, it seems to me necessary to look into this question again as the military balance on the Northern Flank shows a continuing shift to the disadvantage of the West.

Britain and Federal Germany, providing the two biggest north-west European navies, although different is size, composition and options, already play an important and significant role in the defence of the Northern Flank. Given the extent of their mutual interests in the area, there is a good case for still closer co-operation between the two navies within the general framework of the NATO Alliance. Bilateral exercises and closely co-ordinated naval presence in the northern seas and an exchange of ships, starting with minesweepers, each to operate within the national task forces of the other (a common feature of Franco-German relations), would also reinforce a "European" element in naval co-operation. British and Federal German ships, together with Norwegian units, could constitute the core of a "Standing Naval Force" or "Naval On Call Force" for the Northern Flank. With British officers assigned as NATO Commanders of the maritime and North

European areas of operations (Commander-in-Chief Northern Europe, Commander-in-Chief Channel and Commander-in-Chief Eastern Atlantic) closer bilateral co-ordination of strategic policy and operational matters could be used to increase further the effectiveness of Allied naval and air assets. However, both partners are well aware that in the end there is no substitute for men and the necessary hardware such as ships, tanks and aircraft.

Let us return briefly to the question of role specialisation[45] which was addressed in the House of Commons debate mentioned earlier. The aim of specialisation is an increase in capabilities and efficiency at constant costs. To some extent, NATO's forces are already specialised, adjusting their weaponry to the prevailing characteristics of their particular areas of operations. Thus Britain does not operate small missile craft which Baltic operations require, and the Federal Navy has no ASW aircraft carriers which are important to Eastern Atlantic operations. Further specialisation, however, such as axing whole services or significant parts of them, could be dangerous and would probably prove counter-productive. Even in peacetime, role specialisation would lead to greater dependence on other countries' decisions. If a state were to abandon its maritime forces, for example, it would *de facto* be without the means to implement sovereign policy decisions related to territorial waters, exclusive economic zones, fishery protection and environmental questions. As a result of specialisation, countries would have to drop specific commitments. In these areas the principle of multi-nationality as a clearly visible expression of Allied solidarity and preparedness to fight together would be weakened. This subject has already been touched upon in considering the Danish naval contribution to defence in the Baltic. Furthermore, it is at least uncertain whether reductions in specific areas of armed forces in one country would really be offset by significant increases in capabilities in the other, as decisions on procurement are taken nationally and depend very much on the internal situation of member states. In the end, therefore, it could well be that specialisation would come to be seen as a way of reducing one's contribution to the common defence, thus diminishing NATO's overall capabilities. A more promising approach to improved efficiency is certainly further to boost co-operation in procurement, ensure inter-operability and standardise as far as possible.

Arms control talks on conventional forces could also bring some relief for national defence budgets. But these negotiations do not yet cover navies and this will probably not change in the near future. The question how far Allied naval forces could profit from reduction of ground and air forces, if agreed, is also open to speculation.

These considerations apart, it seems however that the situation on the Northern Flank is bound to change anyway. Notwithstanding possible changes to the deployment options of the UKMF, the reinforcement programme could be dealt a serious blow if, as has been forecast,

Canada were to drop her commitment to send 5,000 troops of the Canadian Air Sea Transportable Brigade supported by two fighter squadrons.[46] The government White Paper published in June 1987 announced the decision to abandon this Canadian commitment. Who would replace this contingent? Could the UK take over the Canadian role? Decisions have yet to be taken. But they could bring about substantial changes in the military situation in Norway and Denmark with serious implications for the defence posture as a whole.

Overall, the picture of the military situation and the state of preparations for defence on the Northern Flank is not improving. The United States is determined to make a great effort to redress the balance by increasing the strength of its naval forces, in combination with the new maritime strategy. On the European side, the United Kingdom and the Federal Republic of Germany are making the biggest contributions to the defence of this theatre of operations. For the future, one is left with the hope that co-operation in procurement may finally pay off in the form of more equipment at lower prices, that further efforts in standardisation and inter-operability will reduce running costs, and that above all the economic recovery in the West will permit all North European members of the Alliance to invest more in their defence.

Britain and Germany, however, should use the room that is available for further co-operation in defence, and more particularly related to their roles on the Northern Flank, thus strengthening the European element within NATO.

Notes

1. George Younger, (translation) "Dem Schutz Europas bleibt das Hauptgewicht in Europäische Wehrkunde" *WWR* 7/86 p. 385.
2. See Table 15.1.
3. John Berg, "Norwegian army 'too weak' on Northern flank", *Jane's Defence Weekly*, 15 March 1986 p. 456; Vizeadmiral Helmut Kampe, "Die Ostseezugänge sind eine strategische Schlüsselposition", *Marineforum* 1 February 1986, p. 13; Alexander Szander, "Technik und Prestige", *Süddeutsche Zeitung*, 24 July 1986; Egbert Thomer, "Dänemarks Streitkräfte magern ab", *Kieler Nachrichten*, 3 June 1986; Helmut Hubel, "Die eigenwilligen Nordeuropäer: Dänemark und Norwegen", in *Beilage der Wochenzeitung Das Parlament* B 37/82, 18. September 1982, pp. 18–19.
4. Peter Howard, "Peace, but not at any price", *Jane's Defence Weekly*, 12 April 1986, p. 657.
5. Statement on the Defence Estimates 1986, HMSO, Cmnd 9763-I, p. 41.
6. For the concept of total defence see Rolf Hallerbach, "Norwegens Verteidigung, Flankenschutz für die NATO", *Europäische Wehrkunde* 5/86, pp. 277–278.
7. Vizeadmiral Ansgar Bethge, "Die Nordflanke, ein Gebiet höchster Priorität", *Marineforum* 10/1986, p. 338.
8. Hubel, *op. cit.*, pp. 18–19. Colonel Jonathan Alford, "The Current Military Position in the Northern Flank", Paper for the Northern Flank Conference 7–8 May 1986 London, p. 8.
9. This policy is an important condition for the so-called "Northern Balance", a system of mutual restraint. For further information on this subject see Johan Jörgen

Holst, "Das Nordische Gleichgewicht und die Nordflanke, eine Betrachtung aus norwegischer Sicht", in *Nordeuropa, Ausfalltor der Sowjetunion zu den Weltmeeren*, (Herford 1985, pp. 83–84 and 86–87); Nils Andren, "Gegenwärtige Sicherheitsprobleme in Nordeuropa, Das 'Nordische Gleichgewicht' und seine Bedingungen", *Beilage zur Wochenzeitung Das Parlament B* 37/82, 18 September 1982, pp. 3–13; Katarina Brodin, "Die Nordflanke Europas aus schwedischer Sicht", in *Nordeuropa, Ausfalltor der Sowjetunion zu den Weltmeeren*, pp. 105–107; Sir Peter Whiteley, "Die Nordflanke der NATO, *Nauticus* 1980 (Herford 1979 pp. 124).

10. Stefan Terzibaschitsch, "Washingtons, Seerüstung, Wiedergeburt der Weltmachtflotte", *Europäische Wehrkunde* 6/86, pp. 348–351: 20–40 strategic submarines and support vessels; 15 aircraft carriers; 4 battleships; 238 surface escort vessels (cruisers, destroyers, frigates); 100 nuclear attack submarines; 14 mine warfare vessels; 75 amphibious ships; 6 guardships; 65 fleet support and replenishment ships; 60–65 other auxiliaries.

11. See Admiral J.D. Watkins, USN, and others, "The Maritime Strategy", US Naval Institute Proceedings, January 1986, Supplement.

12. Linton, F. Brooks, "Naval Power and National Security: The Case for the Maritime Strategy", *International Security*, Fall 1986 (Vol. 11, No. 2), pp. 70–71.

13. J.F. Erickson, "Der Kriegsschauplatz Nord und die sowjetischen Optionen", in *Nordeuropa, Ausfalltor der Sowjetunion zu den Weltmeeren*, p. 48; Tony Samstag, "Kola: the Reason NATO looks North", in *The Times*, 3 September 1986 referring to the Study of the Norwegian Foreign Policy Institute; John J. Mearsheimer, "A Strategic Misstep, The Maritime Strategy and Deterrence in Europe", *International Security*, Fall 1986 (Vol. 11, No. 2) pp. 3–37.

14. Brooks, *op. cit.* pp. 58–70.

15. Kampe *op. cit.*, p. 10. See also Vizeadmiral Rolf Steinhaus, "NATO und die maritime Herausforderung", *Marineforum* 9/86, p. 291 and Günter Gillessen, "Mehr Aufmerksamkeit für die Norwegen-See", *Frankfurter Allgemeine Zeitung*, 7 July 1986.

16. Kare Willoch, "Norwegens Sicherheitspolitik, Bedingungen für Stabilität: Stärkung im Hohen Norden", *Europäische Wehrkunde* 9/86, p. 499; Lieutenant General Tønne Huitfeldt, "The Threat from the North-Defence of Scandinavia", *NATO's Sixteen Nations*, October 1986, pp. 26 and 29.

17. Holst, *op. cit.*, p. 92–93; Brodin, *op. cit.*, p. 128; Bethge, *op. cit.*, p. 336.

18. The concept was agreed between Supreme Allied Commander Europe, Supreme Allied Commander Atlantic and the Commander-in-Chief Channel.

19. Admiral H.C. Mustin, USN, "The Role of the Navy and Marines in the Norwegian Sea", *Naval War College Review*, March–April 1986 pp. 5–6.

20. as note 5, p. 40.

21. *ibid.* p. 41.

22. Belgium, Denmark, Germany, Britain, The Netherlands and Norway.

23. as note 5, p. 16.

24. *ibid.* p. 60 para 7; Michael Meyer-Sach, "Der TVD Nordeuropa", *Marine-Bundschau* 6/1986, p. 336; Admiral Sir William Stavely, GCB, ADC, *RUSI Journal*; Vol. 131, No. 2, June 1986, p. 12.

25. *Jane's Fighting Ships 1986/87*, Foreword, p. 117; Alford, *op. cit.*, p. 9 Simon O'Dwyer-Russell, "UK's amphibious dilemma"; *Jane's Defence Weekly*, 12 April 1986 pp. 660–661; "UK Amphibious Forces", *RUSI News-Brief*, May 1986.

26. *Daily Telegraph*, 10 December 1986, p. 1; *The Times*, 10 December 1986; *Jane's Defence Weekly*, 20 December 1986, p. 1439. For earlier plans see "The Way Forward", HMG Defence Review 1981.

27. *Daily Telegraph, The Times, Jane's Defence Weekly, op. cit.*

28. as note 5, p. 34.

29. For further information on UKMF see *Armed Forces*, January 1987, pp. 27–29.

30. *RUSI Journal*, Vol. 130, No. 2, June 1985, p. 11.

31. Christopher Follett, *The Times*, 12 January 1987.
32. *RUSI Journal, op. cit.*
33. Follett, *op. cit.*
34. Johan Jörgen Holst, "The Norwegian Industry's Role in the Defence of Norway and the Alliance", *NATO's Sixteen Nations*, December 1986, p. 52.
35. The US contribution comprises: Three or four Carrier Battle Groups (depending on the overall military situation); 2 Marine Amphibious Force (divisional size); 9th Infantry Division (SACEUR's Strategic Reserve Land, can be deployed elsewhere if the situation demands); 18 air squadrons (all or part could be available in the Northern region) see also Table 15.2.
36. House of Commons Debate on the Royal Navy, 6 February 1986, Hansard.
37. See Captain Brian Longworth "The Case for a Maritime Strategy", *Defence*, February 1983, p. 89. Admiral Sir James Eberle sees the balance between Continental and Atlantic commitments in jeopardy in "The Atlantic Connection", *Naval Forces* No. IV/1985, Vol. VI, p. 7. In his foreword to *Jane's Fighting Ships 1986–87* Captain Moore even speaks of a "maritime mess". (p. 113).
38. At an 1986 average exchange rate of DM3.10 German marks to the £1.
39. Denmark's frigates will be reduced in personnel. The Netherlands' Navy will lose two escort vessels and two submarines. New fast patrol vessels for the Belgian Navy are delayed.
40. Federal Minister of Defence, White Paper 1985, p. 111.
41. Compare Federal Minister of Defence, White Paper 1970, p. 39, para 64, White Paper 1979, pp. 176–177 and White Paper 1985, pp. 213–218.
42. White Paper 1979, p. 176, para 224.
43. Terzibaschitsch, *op. cit.*
44. Willoch *op. cit.*, Huitfeldt, *op. cit.*, p. 32.
45. For more on this subject see David Greenwood, "Towards Role Specialization in NATO"; *NATO's Sixteen Nations*, July 1986, pp. 44–49; Vizeadmiral Dieter Wellershoff, "Spezialisierung und Multinationalität als Teil der Abschreckung der NATO"; *Marineforum* 9/1986, pp. 286–288. Also published in *NATO's Sixteen Nations* January 1986.
46. Tønne Huitfeldt and Sharon Hobson, "Canada may ditch CAST commitment to Norway", *Jane's Defence Weekly*, 20 December 1986, p. 1427. For more information on CAST see Sharon Hobson, "The CAST commitment", *Jane's Defence Weekly* 18 October 1986, pp. 893–897.

Chapter 16
Collaboration in Arms Production: A German View

TIMM R. MEYER

Armaments co-operation has been one of the objectives of the Alliance ever since its foundation. At the beginning, the mutual military advantage of common, *ie* standardised or at least inter-operable weapon systems was the main concern. Today the emphasis is on the most efficient use of the Allied partners' financial and technological resources. From one generation of weapon systems and equipment to the next, the costs rise by approximately 5% annually in real terms.[1] With an average real increase of no more than 2%–3%, the national defence budgets in recent years have not kept pace with these cost developments. In the years ahead, even these modest rates of increase will not be attained. If conventional defence is to be secured at a level commensurate with the outside threat, a major effort will have to be made to reduce or at least stabilise armaments costs through comprehensive and systematic armaments co-operation.

The European partners of the Alliance, in particular, are confronted with this problem. Due to its size, the US armaments market allows great production runs with correspondingly low unit costs. The European market, on the contrary, is characterised by fragmented production structures. They have only been able to persist due to occasional armaments co-operation, exports to Third World countries and, above all, because governments have considered the maintenance of national development and production capacities for the adequate equipment of their own armed forces, to be desirable from the defence policy point of view and have, therefore, deliberately accepted the costs involved. These conditions are currently changing, however. The export markets outside the Alliance are shrinking due to financial problems and the build-up of national defence industries in Third World countries, some of which are beginning to export their own armaments production, thereby exposing the Europeans to severe competition with "cheap offers". The capacity utilisation problems resulting from shrinking export markets coincide with those caused by the increasing time scales for the planning, development and introduction of new weapon systems in all European countries. These problems will alter the foundations of defence procurements in Europe in the long run. Developments unmistakably point in the direction of an integrated European armaments market. This may still sound unfamiliar to many. It must be borne in mind, however, that in this way the armaments market would only be catching up on a development process that the European Community's civil market has almost completed by now.

Foundations of Anglo-German armaments co-operation

Armaments co-operation in the sense of close collaboration in the planning, development, production and use of defence equipment requires convergent security policy and military and defence industry interests. In the relationship between Britain and the Federal Republic of Germany, this convergence of interests arises from their political and military involvement in NATO. Whereas Britain, according to its own data, devotes 95% of its defence budget to NATO purposes, the German defence budget is entirely spent on tasks within the Alliance. A part of the British armed forces is integrated into the frontline defence of Central Europe on German territory. British Forces Germany includes the British Army of the Rhine (BAOR) with 55,000 men, 600 tanks and about 3,000 other armoured combat vehicles, as well as Royal Air Force Germany (RAFG) with 10,000 men and 155 fighter aircraft. BAOR comprises 124 units and formations in the so-called "British rear combat zone" as logistic support for the combat formations, as well as army units in Antwerp, the supply base and transit port for reinforcements from the UK. Here, mention should also be made of the British Forces' Berlin Brigade with 3,000 men which, however, does not belong to Britain's NATO units. Table 16.1 depicts the noticeable volume of the British and German contributions to the Alliance. It must be noted that the outstanding contribution of British Forces Germany towards defence on the border of the Federal Republic has always played a major role in German considerations regarding possibilities of mutual co-operation.

The operational concept and the resulting tactical and technical requirements of the German and British armed forces have been converging over time and today are largely identical in many areas.

Table 16.1   British and German share of NATO forces in Central Europe and
the Northern Flank

Forces	UK	GERMANY
Land Forces	20%	50%
Main Battle Tanks	10%	60%
Anti-Tank Weapons	9%	38%
Artillery	7%	43%
Armoured Vehicles	4%	38%
Ground Air Defences	6%	60%
Combat Aircraft	25%	30%
Naval Forces	33%	30%

Thus the conditions are right for the expansion of Anglo-German armaments co-operation.

It must not be overlooked, however, that procurements for the British forces involve a number of special factors that tend to impede joint armaments projects in individual cases. For Britain's land and naval forces, overseas commitments have always been of great importance. More recent examples are Britain's military engagement on the Falklands and its presence in Hong Kong. Mention must also be made of its increased involvement in the AFNORTH area. These obligations can only be fulfilled with armed forces equipped for expeditionary missions. Furthermore, the organisation and equipment of the British land and naval forces are also determined by the military requirements of operational concepts geared to Britain's position as an island. Another special feature is Britain's status as a nuclear power and the resulting appropriation of funds for the planned modernisation of its nuclear potential, *ie* the replacement of the Polaris rockets with the successor Trident II system. The expenditure of £14 bn envisaged for this purpose will place a heavy burden on the British defence budget from the mid-1990s onwards and may, in fact, restrict the financial scope for new conventional armaments projects. Future budget trends will be a decisive element in this context. As matters now stand, a substantial increase in budget means cannot be reckoned with; the defence budget 1986–7 was the first not to show any real increase in appropriations as against the previous year.

Joint development

After the Federal Republic of Germany joined the Alliance in the mid-1950s, a national defence industry began to emerge very slowly. The lack of technological know-how at the time only allowed the build-

Table 16.2 Collaboration

Projects	Status — Initial study or development stage	Status — In-service	No. of partner nations	Participating nations
AIRCRAFT & HELICOPTERS				
(i) UK & WEST GERMANY				
Tornado (C)		✓	3	UK, WG, Italy
Eurofighter (C)	✓		4	UK, WG, Italy, Spain
NH 90 (HC)	✓		5	France, Italy, Neth, UK, WG.
(ii) UK or W. GERMANY & OTHERS				
Jaguar (C)		✓	2	France, UK
Harrier II (C)		✓	2	UK, USA
Goshawk (T)	✓		2	UK, USA
Gazelle (HC)		✓	2	France, UK
Lynx (HC)		✓	2	France, UK
Puma (HC)		✓	2	France, UK
EH 101 (HC)	✓		2	Italy, UK
A 129 (HC)	✓		4	Italy, UK, Neth, Spain
Alpha Jet (T)		✓	2	France, WG
Transall (TR)		✓	2	France, WG
PAH 2 (HC)	✓		2	France, WG
MISSILES				
(i) UK & WEST GERMANY				
Trigat (AT)	✓		3	France, UK, WG
ASRAAM (AA)	✓		3	UK, WG, Norway
Short-range anti-radar	✓		7	Belgium, Canada, It., Neth, UK, USA, WG
(ii) UK or W. GERMANY & OTHERS				
LRSOM (LR)	✓		3	UK, USA, WG
Martel (AS)		✓	2	France, UK

Table 16.2 Continued

Projects	Status — Initial study or development stage	Status — In-service	No. of partner nations	Participating nations
ANS (S)	✓		2	France, WG
Roland (SA)		✓	3	France, USA, WG
HOT (AT)		✓	2	France, WG
Milan (AT)		✓	2	France, WG
LAND EQUIPMENT				
Multiple Launch Rocket System (MLRS)				
– Phase I	✓		5	France, Italy, UK, WG, USA
– Phase III	✓		4	France, UK, WG, USA
FH 70 Howitzer	✓	✓	3	Italy, UK, WG
SP 70 Howitzer	✓		3	Italy, UK, WG
NAVAL EQUIPMENT				
NATO Frigate Replacement	✓		8	Canada, France, Italy, Neth, Spain, UK, USA, WG
PARIS Sonar		✓	3	France, Neth, UK
Sea Gnat Decoy System	✓		3	Denmark, UK, USA
OTHER EQUIPMENT				
Midge Drone		✓	3	Canada, UK, WG
Midge Post-Design Services	✓		3	France, UK, WG

Notes: (i) C = combat aircraft; HC = helicopter; T = trainer; TR = transport
(ii) AA = air-to-air missile; AS = air-surface missile; AT = anti-tank missile; LR = long-range stand-off missile; S = anti-ship missile; SA = surface-to-air missile.
(iii) B = Belgium; C = Canada; D = Denmark; F = France; It = Italy; Neth. = Netherlands; Nor. = Norway; Sp = Spain; UK = United Kingdom; USA = United States of America; WG = West Germany
(iv) Data based on 1985–86.

Sources: Cmnd 9430 (1985), Pretty (1984); Taylor (1985).

up of maintenance capacities. Within a relatively short time, however, the necessary framework was created for the German defence industry to take in orders for the licensed production of sub-systems and components. Since the mid-1960s, the knowledge and capabilities acquired in the process have enabled it to start its own development work for new weapons systems and equipment. During this build-up of the German defence industry, Anglo-German relations in the armaments sector were of necessity of a unilateral nature, *ie* they were essentially limited to procurements in Britain for the Bundeswehr. The first Anglo-German joint projects included the studies for a vertical take-off aircraft which, however, did not lead to joint development and production. In the Federal Republic, work on this aircraft was continued up to the stage of flight tests with a prototype. Britain used the results of the studies for the subsequent development of the RAF Harrier. There was at the time no further intensification of bilateral co-operation. The Federal Republic concentrated its efforts on participation in multilateral co-operative projects within the Alliance. Bilateral co-operation was only enhanced within the special relationship of French-German reconciliation after the Second World War, on the basis of the Franco-German Treaty of Friendship, concluded in 1963 by President Charles de Gaulle and Federal Chancellor Konrad Adenauer, which expressly provides for armaments co-operation. Similarly, Britain maintains bilateral armaments relations with the United States for historical reasons. For a long time, Britain's interests were mainly focussed on national development and production of weapon systems and military equipment. This was due to its international commitments, its efficient and diversified defence industry and its desire to remain independent in armaments exports. The possibilities of independent British armaments production have, however, been gradually eroded by increasing financial problems such as are faced by all members of the Alliance, and by severe crowding-out competition on armaments export markets. Britain's interest in participation in joint European armaments projects has grown accordingly.

Against this background, it becomes obvious why Anglo-German armaments co-operation is characterised by joint participation in tri- and multilateral projects with European allied partners. There is no major project carried through bilaterally by Britain and the Federal Republic. Their co-operation, which started in the late 1960s, has developed most favourably. Table 16.2 gives a comprehensive survey.

Opportunities further to intensify bilateral relations in the armaments sector are under discussion at various levels of Anglo-German co-operation. Few people know that the extent of this co-operation is in no way inferior to that of French-German co-operation – a lack of awareness that may be due to the fact that co-operation has become such a smoothly functioning routine. Consultations take place – in some cases several times a year – on the following levels:

— Anglo-German summits between the Ministers of Defence
— meetings of the Armaments Directors of both countries
— Anglo-German Vice Chiefs' Talks
— Anglo-German Army Equipment Commission (AGAEC)
— Anglo-German security policy consultations
— Anglo-German meetings at General Staff level

Within the framework of these consultations, the opportunities for Anglo-German co-operation, for instance on Future Armoured Combat Systems (FACS), are currently being examined. This is a "family" of weapon systems comprising Self-Propelled Anti-Tank Vehicles (SPAT), Mechanized Infantry Combat Vehicles (MICV), Long-Range TRIGAT/Anti-Helicopter Vehicles, Recce Vehicles and the Main Battle Tank 2000. For the Federal Republic, these items – excluding the Main Battle Tank 2000 – constitute a development and procurement project worth DM12bn. The financial volume alone should make co-operation look worthwhile. Yet differences in national planning seem to be causing problems. The British side, at any rate, seems mainly interested in co-operation on the Battle Tank 2000. Another project discussed in Anglo-German talks is the Anti-Radar Drone (KDAR), which at present is at the definition stage. Total expenditure will amount to DM1.2bn. Agreement on bilateral development and production seems at least possible.

Taken all in all, it becomes apparent that Anglo-German co-operation on joint armaments projects, although it started only 20 years ago, has already reached a noticeable volume, as can be seen from Table 16.2. This is certainly also due to the fact that the first joint large-scale project, the MRCA Tornado, has proved a great success, contrary to the predictions of its critics who doubted its feasibility. This weapon system has given proof of its efficiency in flight and bombing accuracy tests also in the US. Its broad international acceptance is reflected in export orders from both NATO and non-NATO countries – orders partly obtained despite severe US competition.

Major problems in co-operation have only occurred in the field of armoured vehicles. The failure of the Main Battle Tank 70 project was due to differing military priorities (UK: protection, FRG: fire-power and mobility) and to a lack of political will, on both sides, to implement it jointly. Another reason may have been that in the 1970s, the financial conditions on both sides were still fairly favourable for developing and producing a battle tank in a national go-it-alone effort. Unlike today, national prestige, which has always played a particularly important role in decisions on major weapon systems, at the time carried more weight than budgetary constraints. The causes that were responsible for the failure of the trilateral development (UK, FRG and Italy) of the Self-Propelled Howitzer 155-1 (SP-70) were of a different nature. This development project, which was started in 1973, was discontinued in

1986. A major reason, apart from technical problems, was probably the inadequate organisation of the project management; there was no main contractor responsible for the overall management. All three nations will, therefore, produce their own howitzers nationally until the late 1990s. It should be noted, however, that they have agreed to develop the next generation of howitzers – the Howitzer 2000 – in trilateral co-operation again. Lessons have been learned from negative experiences in the past, so that sufficient knowledge is now available for successful future co-operation, especially with regard to the need for tight central management.

For understandable reasons, Britain had long pursued a policy of keeping its national defence industry as independent as possible. It has now substantially abandoned this policy and committed itself to the idea of division of labour as reflected in project co-operation within the framework of European partnership in the armaments sector. From the German point of view, this should greatly encourage the further expansion of Anglo-German armaments co-operation, as well as provide fresh impetus to this co-operation and enable joint projects even in areas traditionally reserved for national activities, as in the case of armoured combat systems.

An important point in the overall picture of Anglo-German defence relations is the extent to which industrial co-operation results. Table 16.3 only roughly depicts the situation. The relations and interdependencies between the two countries make an appreciable contribution towards strengthening the foundations of their partnership in the armaments sector and enhancing interest, on both sides, in further joint projects. Mutual knowledge of each other's technological potential, reliability and readiness, as well as ability, to engage in integrated project activities also generates industry-to-industry co-operation with a dynamic drive of its own. It thereby helps to broaden the range of joint possibilities and mutual interests in future weapon developments within the Alliance. From the German viewpoint, it should be noted that the privatisation of the Royal Ordnance Factories (ROF) is likely to have a beneficial impact on future Anglo-German armaments co-operation. It will help to remove structural differences *vis-à-vis* German private defence industrial companies, which have been an obstacle to co-operation. Both industries will in future have to operate on the same principles of profitability, and this will greatly enhance mutual understanding and at the same time lead to a more cost-effective co-operation.

The subject of "armaments exports" was for a long time a problem in Anglo-German defence relations. These exports are of considerable political and economic weight in Britain. Planned armament developments have, therefore, always been assessed and decided upon partly in terms of their export chances. In the Federal Republic, the situation is quite different: on the basis of the Military Weapons Control Act

Table 16.3   British defence industrial links with German companies:

Alvis	Euromissile: HOT compact turret
British Aerospace	MBB: Tornado, Experimental Aircraft Programme, EFA, Future International Military transport Aircraft FIMA
Dynamics Group	MBB: AMRAAM, Sea Skva (KWS Sea King), ALARM Warhead, ISS: NATO Frigate 90; BGT: Sidewinder AIM 9L, ASRAAM, AMRAAM: Blohm + Voss: Meko
British Shipbuilders	ISS: NATO Frigate 90
Dowty	Diehl: Copperhead Liebherr: Primary flight guidance system EAP Rheinmetall: Field Howitzer 155-1 Panavia: Tornado fuel system
E.O.-Systems	Siemens: Electro-optical products
Ferranti	Panavia: Tornado navigational system MBB: Helmet visor, Seaspray Mk, 3 and datalink for Sea King KWS
Gomba Stonefield	KHD: Engines
Graviner	DEUGRA: Fire fighting equipment for armoured vehicles
Hunting Engineering	EPG: MLRS Diehl: MLRS-3-Consortium
Laser Engineering	Porsche: Hydro shock absorbers for battle tanks
Lucas	Panavia: Cockpit covers for Tornado EPG: MLRS BGT: Sidewinder components Pierburg: Fuel controlling device RB, 199
Marconi	Panavia: Tornado avionics AEG Telefunken: TORNADO avionics BGT: Tornado Command Stability Augmentation System AEG: MLRS-3-Consortium Siemens: Triffid radio system under licence AEG: ACCS (joint consortium)
Martin-Baker	Panavia: Tornado ejection set Autoflug: Ejection seat servicing, tank seat for the PAH-2
MEL	Dornier: MAREC Radars for DO-128 and DO-228
Muirhead	Siemens: Ptarmigan facsimile under licence
Normalair	Panavia: Tornado air conditioning MBB: Transall air conditioning
Oceonics	Siemens: HEROS components
Plessey	Siemens: HERMES components

Racal	AEG: Decca chain
	Dornier: Avionics for DO-228
	ESG, SEL: part of the AMS consortium for
	ACCS
	Werftem: Radar and telecommunications
	equipment
Rolls Royce	Turbo Union/MTV: RB, 199 TYNE
Royal Ordnance Factories	EPG: MLRS
	Krauss: Maffei: 105 gun for the LEOPARD I
	Rheinmetall: FH-70 and 155-1
	Wegmann: Improved Lance
Smiths Industries	Teldix: HUD for Tornado
Trackpower Transmissions	EPG: MLRS
Thorn-EMI	Diehl: MLRS-3-Consortium
	Rheinmetall: fuses for artillery munitions
United Scientific Holdings	German subsidiary
Vickers	Rheinmetall: FH-70, 155-1
	IKL: Submarines
Westland	Westland Sitec – a German subsidiary

Source: *Wehrtechnik*, No. 9/1084, p. 27

(*Kriegswaffenkontrollgesetz* – KWKG) and the Foreign Trade Act (*Aussenwirtschaftsgesetz* – AWG), the Federal government has been pursuing a policy of restricting arms exports to Third World countries. Today's guidelines for this policy are drawn from the "Political Principles of the Federal Government for the Export of Military Weapons and Other Defence Equipment" adopted on April 28, 1982[2] by the social-democratic-liberal coalition of SPD and FDP. Under these guidelines, arms exports to non-NATO countries are only permitted subject to general exemptions that are stipulated for special political reasons or if, in individual cases, vital interests of the Federal Republic of Germany warrant an exceptional authorisation. "Vital interests" means foreign and security policy interests of the Federal Republic with due regard to the Alliance's interests. Problems such as used to arise from this restrictive export policy for Anglo-German co-operative projects have been removed by the Anglo-German export agreement of May 25, 1983[3], which corresponds to the 1972 French-German agreement on the export of jointly developed weapon systems.[4] It stipulates that all co-operation agreements are subject to a consultation procedure, which affords both partners – the German and the British governments – the possibility of objecting to export projects planned by the partner country. The partner is obliged to examine the objection, but cannot ultimately be prevented from carrying out the originally-planned arms export. In that case, the objecting partner must fulfill his obligations under the co-operation agreement within the framework of the export deal concerned. On this basis, Britain was able to realise its planned exports of 80 MRCA Tornados to Saudi Arabia and Oman.

Anglo-German armaments co-operation in Europe

Together with the French-German "axis", Anglo-German armaments relations form the basis of armaments co-operation in Europe. In the German partner's view, it will be essential further to expand this and to move to comprehensive and systematic armaments co-operation, if a strong and efficient European defence industry is to be secured on a long-term basis. The aim of the European NATO partners is to increase their self-sufficiency in armaments procurements. This is by no means to call into question transatlantic relations in the armaments sector. The US itself has repeatedly pointed out that a strong European pillar is an indispensable prerequisite for equal partnership in the Alliance, and has stressed that this necessarily includes a competitive defence industry. But the Europeans are unmistakably faced with growing problems in financing new weapons projects. Large-scale projects, as a rule, can now only be carried out co-operatively in Europe. Co-operation is seriously inhibited, however, by national interests. France, for instance, backed out of the EFA project in favour of its national RAFALE development. Even among the remaining partners (UK, FRG, Italy, Spain) problems continued to arise, prompting the Germans, for cost reasons, to consider the purchase of a suitable fighter aircraft in the US. Given the significance of the EFA project for military aircraft construction in Europe, the Federal Government is not very likely, though, to decide in favour of a purchase in the US. Yet such considerations are clear evidence of the problems experienced by the European defence industry *vis-à-vis* US suppliers. The British assessment of the situation is probably no different. Here, mention must be made, for instance, of the purchase of shares of Westland Helicopter Company by US companies (UTL and General Electric) and the resulting US influence on the further development of British helicopter technology. Reference must also be made once again to the previously mentioned Trident II project. It seems most unlikely that it will be possible to raise the enormous amount of £14bn. required for this project without adverse effects on the nature and scope of conventional armaments programmes. These few examples may serve as an indication that the European defence industries are faced with a challenge that can only be met by "closing ranks". Otherwise Europe risks losing its ability to develop its own weapon systems and becoming increasingly dependent on procurements from the United States.

This is also the underlying assumption of the Wise-Men-Study[5] published by the Independent European Programme Group (IEPG). This analyses the state of armaments co-operation in Europe, sets out the need for comprehensive and systematic Europe-wide armaments co-operation and submits proposals for the gradual creation of a European internal market in armaments. On the German side, government and industry attach great importance to the discussion of the statements and proposals contained in this study.

US-European armaments projects

Britain, the Federal Republic of Germany and France, in particular, are called upon to stand shoulder to shoulder within the framework of those projects already agreed upon, or to be agreed upon, with the United States on the basis of the Nunn Amendment. The US has scheduled a total of $2.9bn. for these projects in the period up to 1992. These funds will be made available to American armed forces exclusively for joint projects with the European NATO partners. Thus, if they want to draw on these funds, the US forces must engage in co-operation with the Europeans. However, funds from the "Nunn budget" may only be used for financing orders placed with US industry. Thus, to the extent that the Europeans wish to take part in a Nunn project, they must provide their own financial means.

Table 16.4 depicts the seven projects agreed upon by the Committee of National Armament Directors (CNAD) in 1986 and co-financed by the US under the Nunn Amendment. Of these, Britain and the Federal Republic have signed six and five projects respectively. The implementation of these projects is to be entrusted to International Project Management Offices (IPMO). Principles of Co-operation have meanwhile been adopted for the organization and operation of these offices. They provide for all projects to be handled jointly on the basis of a clearly-defined management structure. The leading positions in each IPMO are to be occupied by nationals of the participating countries in accordance with their financial contributions to the project concerned. The project leader is nominated by the host nation. The project leader chooses one deputy from each of the participating nations. All information compiled by an IPMO will be made available to each participant free of charge. The principles and objectives to be observed in co-operation on a "Nunn project" are to be laid down in a general project Memorandum of Understanding (MoU).

In recent years, the Europeans, including Britain and the Federal Republic, have called for efforts, at all political and administrative levels, to expand transatlantic armaments co-operation. By adopting the Nunn Amendment, the US has responded with what might be called a "crushing" offer to Europeans. This offer in fact amounts to $2.9bn for joint projects in the period up to 1992 if the Europeans are prepared to make a fair and adequate financial contribution. To date the European allies have not even been able to develop anything

Table 16.4   European–US cooperative projects ("Nunn projects")

Project	Participants	STI/MoU*)
ADA Programming Support Environments (APSE)	US, UK, GE, BE, CA, DA, FR, IT, NL, NO, SP, NACISA/SHAPE	MoU
Autonomous 155mm Precision Guided Munition (PGM)	US, UK, GE, CA, FR, IT, NL, SP, TU	STI
Modular Stand-Off Weapons (MSOW)	US, UK, GE, CA, FR, IT, SP	STI
Multi-Functional Information Distribution System (MIDS)	US, UK, GE, CA, FR, IT, NO, SP	MoU
NATO Identification System (NIS)	US, UK, GE, BE, CA, DA, FR, IT, NL, SP, TU	MoU
Stand-Off Airborne Radar Demonstrator	US, UK, FR	MoU
Battlefield Information Collection and Exploitation System (BICES)	US, IT	STI

*) STI = Statement of Intent
   MoU = Memorandum of Understanding

approaching a strategy to meet this challenging offer from the US. A consensus was achieved merely on the "Principles of Co-operation" proposed by Germany. A more comprehensive co-ordinated response is unlikely to emerge in the near future, as both Britain and France are obviously seeking to expand armaments co-operation with the US on a more bilateral basis.

Obstacles to greater co-operation

The Federal Republic has ample experience in armaments co-operation not only with Great Britain, but also with the other European NATO allies, as well as with the US and Canada. This is illustrated by two figures: Today, 60% of all German development and procurement projects are implemented in co-operation with other allies. These projects account for 70% (about DM8.5bn.) of the German defence budget means appropriated for development and procurement. This armaments co-operation has not, of course, come about from one day to the next. It is also fair to say that the Federal Republic, because of its front-line position in Central Europe and the presence of Allied troups along-side the Bundeswehr, finds itself in a special situation, which makes armaments co-operation seem particularly useful and desirable, be it only for Alliance policy reasons. Britain is in a comparable situation with regard to its security requirements in the Northern Flank sea areas and the Atlantic, which – among other reasons – justify its special interest in armaments co-operation with the US. To mention yet another special case: as stated earlier, the German-French partnership in the armaments sector must be seen against the background of the 1963 Franco-German Friendship Treaty, a political act prompted by mutual national interest in reconciliation. Generally, however, it is precisely national interests that run counter to armaments co-operation, and this dispite the knowledge that co-operation is both advantageous and necessary

— militarily (use of standardised/inter-operable weapon systems and equipment),
— economically (sharing of R&D costs among partners; cost advantages through greater production runs; common logistics and training),
— technologically (greater efficiency through a pooling of knowledge and experience),
— last but not least, for Alliance policy reasons (strengthened cohesion among the allies).

The following national interests, in particular, tend to obstruct armaments co-operation:

— National prestige, which for a long time played a decisive role, especially in decisions on the development and procurement of major weapons systems. This is best illustrated by the fact that Britain, the Federal Republic and France are still individually pursuing the development of battle tanks. It is the high costs of new weapons systems that have finally led to a change in attitude. Examples are the MRCA Tornado, the NATO Frigate 90 and the EFA project. Due to its expensive liquid-fuel, laser or electromagnetic gun technology, the Main Battle Tank 2000 is also likely to become so costly that it will no longer be possible for any one NATO partner to finance it alone for purely political reasons.
— The interest of those responsible for defence policy in maintaining a national defence industry will always remain an important aspect in decisions on co-operative projects with other countries. While the financing problems linked with new weapons systems restrict the scope for decisions, all partners in a co-operative project will normally try to obtain as large a share as possible of the interesting technology packages for their national industries. Only those who have the necessary national defence industrial base to develop proposals for new weapons

systems, and who can prove their feasibility, can really influence weapon technology developments within the Alliance.

— Another obstruction to armaments co-operation is, of course, that each country has a substantial economic interest in maintaining existing defence industrial capacities. On the face of it, the main concern is to avoid endangering jobs. Much more important, however, is the economic policy interest in preserving competitive positions in industrial high technology, which receives in many areas essential stimuli from defence technology. Another important aspect, from an economic viewpoint, is the fact that procurements of defence material from national sources are about 40% less expensive than those from abroad, because a portion of the purchase prices paid to national firms is recovered, *eg* in the form of tax revenues. Finally, the government's interest in improving its trade balance and foreign exchange position in individual cases should not be underestimated.

The cited examples of national egotism only show some of the problems confronting European armaments co-operation. Yet another important aspect is the difference in the structures and operating conditions of national defence industries, as well as the problem of insufficient "early-stage co-operation":

— In fact these structures are in some countries characterized by private companies (FRG), in others by arsenals and government-owned companies (US, France, UK). This causes differences in competitive conditions, as well as in business risks with regard to the utilisation and maintenance of capacities. These differences in turn obstruct private initiatives for industry-to-industry co-operation among the countries named above. In Anglo-German relations, the problems facing industrial co-operation will now be removed by the privatisation of the Royal Ordnance Factories.

— Co-operation in defence research and technology ("early-stage co-operation") is still in its infancy. Yet it is a precondition for broadly-based and systematic European co-operation in the armaments sector. Otherwise European armaments co-operation will continue to be no more than the incidental product of converging interests of several European NATO partners in individual projects. The IEPG states have addressed this problem and identified 31 technical areas (TAs) for European research and technology co-operation. The five areas that are of particular interest for the Federal Republic are presented in Table 16.5. Britain is also interested in all of these areas and has assumed the role of pilot nation in three of them.

Table 16.5   Research and technological cooperation among IEPG member states

Technical Areas (TA) which are of priority interest from the German perspective

TA No.	Designation	Participating	Lead nation
1	Microelectron components – gallium arsenide	FRG/UK/F	UK
9	Conventional warhead design	FRG/UK/F I/NO/E	UK
14	Compound materials for ballistic protection	FRG/UK/F/I, NL	NL
15	Computational methods in aerodynamics	FRG/UK/F/GR I/NL	UK
21	High strength light weight materials	FRG/UK/B/F/I NL/Sp.	I

Lessons for future co-operation in Europe

A characteristic feature of Anglo-German armaments co-operation is its integration into tri- or multilateral European development and production projects. This situation seems likely to persist in the future. Co-operation with other European partners means additional difficulties, due to the need to agree on joint projects and their implementation. Ultimately, however, this co-operation is in the partners' mutual interest because it strengthens the European pillar of the transatlantic Alliance. From experience gained in the last two decades, it appears that the following principles must be observed if European co-operation, based on Anglo-German partnership, is to be continued successfully:

(a) *Emphasis on complex weapon systems*: these are particularly suitable for European joint projects, because the costs of their development and production would overtax national defence budgets, thereby endangering other necessary armaments procurements. Moreover, it is precisely in these projects that the economic benefits of co-operation become apparent. The higher the development costs as a proportion of total project costs, the greater the benefits. Admittedly, the financial requirements of a tri- or multilateral development project are considerably higher than those of a national one, due to the complicated process of co-operation. However, the sharing of the total costs greatly relieves the financial burden on the individual partners.

(b) *Ex-ante agreement on common specifications*: political agreement is an absolute necessity for the implementation of co-operative

projects. Yet, despite the political will to co-operate, a project may
fail because of divergencies between military requirements and the
resultant technical specifications. Thus, in the case of the EFA project, there was originally political agreement on quintilateral
development and   production. However, France subsequently
backed out of the project because of differences in military and
technical concepts.

(c) *Fair balance of interests between participants*: As a rule, co-operation on an armaments project is attractive only if the partners can
expect technological and economic benefits commensurate with
their financial contributions. Against this background, past experience suggests the following approach:

— The planning and development work should be carried out by
the partners on a *pro-rata* basis, according to their financial contributions. This will guarantee them a fair share in large-scale
production.

— The joint project should be broken up vertically (by components) for large-scale production. This helps to avoid costly
parallel investments. Each country's share of large-scale
production should correspond to its financial contribution.

— The integration of systems (assembly) should be carried out at
national level, *ie* in parallel. As the assembly requires only little
investment, the parallel integration of systems at national level
will not significantly affect the total costs of a project. On the
other hand, all partners share in the know-how derived from the
manufacture of the final product.

— Parallel assembly requires the right of use to be granted on a
reciprocal basis. In this context, the question must be settled as
to the treatment of self-financed developments, contributed to a
project by a participating company, and the protection rights
involved.

— The equality of know-how contributed – even to sub-sections of
a project – must be guaranteed. This will require a continual
exchange of technology, both at the development stage and during production.

— For exports to third countries, an agreement must be concluded
with due regard to the individual partners' interests. As far as
Anglo-German armaments co-operation is concerned, this
requirement has been fulfilled by the agreement of 25 May 1983,
which applies to all co-operative projects.

(d) *Selection of efficient procedures for project implementation*:
The failure of the trilateral development of the Self-Propelled
Howitzer shows that organisational structures can be decisive
for the success or failure of a project. The project management
should, therefore, be organised so as to create industrially efficient operations. Possible alternatives are:

— project-related co-operation groups with the tasks of a multi-national main contractor (*eg*: MLRS 3 team);
— national main contractors with an international steering body (*eg*: Panavia, Eurofighter);
— joint subsidiaries (*eg*: BBG Bodensee-Gerätewerk, British Aerospace GmbH);
— cross-border co-operative joint ventures.

Experience so far indicates that the second approach is usually the simplest and most practical one.

Summary and perspectives

Anglo-German co-operation in the development and production of defence equipment can look back on more than 20 years of experience. In historical terms, this is a very short period. Thus, taking everything together, the level of success so far achieved is quite encouraging, despite some failures (Self-Propelled Howitzer) and certain hopes as yet unfulfilled (common Main Battle Tank).

Balancing interests with the US within the Alliance requires the maintenance of a competitive European defence industry. As early as the 1960s, it became apparent that this would necessarily involve a pooling of governmental and industrial resources within the framework of European co-operation. In view of the jump in costs from one generation of weapons to the next, the need to plan and develop new weapons systems in cost-saving co-operation with other European NATO partners has become increasingly urgent. This trend will inevitably continue. The objective of staying superior to the Warsaw Pact in the field of weapons technology requires "science fiction solutions" (*eg* laser weapons, electromagnetic gun, etc.) that will only be realised through expensive technology. This means that the scope for national go-it-alone activities is shrinking in the case of all complex weapon systems.

Two developments of topical interest in transatlantic armaments co-operation are of particular importance for the future of the armaments sector in Europe. The Europeans will not be able really to influence the organization and implementation of joint armaments projects with the US on the basis of the Nunn Amendment, unless they join forces instead of acting as individualists. If the various countries simply pursue their own national interests, this will cause disunity among Europeans in armaments co-operation. Another major issue is the American SDI research programme. Europe obviously has not even begun to realise the dimensions of this challenge. The unprecedented volume of research funds mobilised by the US for this programme also serves to a large extent the further development of conventional weapon technology with the related Command, Control and Communication Systems. Even countries like Britain and the Federal Republic of Germany, which have demonstrated their interest by concluding a

Memorandum of Understanding with the US, have been awarded very few contracts, contrary to America's political promise to let its allies have a fair share of the SDI research programme. Of the 1986-7 SDI budget, which totals $2.75bn, contracts worth no more than $68 m. (2.5%) have been awarded to the European allies. Britain and the Federal Republic of Germany may congratulate themselves on having attracted the major part of these contracts. Even so, from an objective point of view, the failure to recognise the need for adequate European participation in the SDI research programme seems likely, in the long run, to give US defence technology a dominant position within the Alliance.

Notes

1. IEPG study "Towards a Stronger Europe", p. 1.
2. cf. Bulletin of the Federal Government, no. 38 of May 5, 1982, p. 309.
3. unpublished.
4. unpublished.
5. "Towards a Stronger Europe" – A Report by an independent Study Team established by Defence Ministers of Nations of the IEPG to make proposals to improve the competitiveness of Europe's defence equipment industry (IEPG Secretary, UK Delegation to NATO, OTAN/NADO 1110 Brussels, Belgium).

Chapter 17
Collaboration in Arms Production: A British View

KEITH HARTLEY*

Collaboration is a form of international transaction whereby the member governments create a protected market for one or more items of defence equipment. This international transaction is reflected in an inter-governmental agreement (contract) determining the rules for exit and for allocating work on the joint project between members of the club and their national producers. The result is a government-created, protected and regulated international cartel. On this view, collaboration represents the formation of an international club, with countries joining voluntarily and remaining members so long as they expect membership to be worthwhile.

Partner states will have different views about the value of club membership, the differences reflecting their policy objectives and the constraints within which they have to operate. A nation might join an international club for defence or for economic or political benefits which it believes cannot be attained at reasonable cost by other means (*eg* independence). Club membership will also be determined by the membership fee (*ie* what has to be sacrificed) and by such constraining factors as the size of a nation's defence budget and the existence of a domestic defence industrial base. These constraining factors form the economic environment which determines the opportunities for, and success of, international collaboration. After outlining the economic background, including the UK defence industrial base, consideration

* This study was undertaken as part of the author's NATO Research Fellowship 1986–7. Thanks are due to Dr Welter, NATO, and Nick Hooper, Research Fellow, ISER, University of York. The usual disclaimers apply.

will be given to the criteria for assessing international collaboration, the results of joint projects and the factors which are likely to determine success or failure.

The economic environment

In defence equipment, NATO countries are faced with two problems. First, rising weapons costs and limited defence budgets. Unit production costs of successive generations of defence equipment (aircraft, missiles, tanks, warships) have been increasing at an average rate of 5–10% a year in real terms.[1] Second, there is substantial duplication of costly R&D and relatively short production runs, especially in Europe. For example, within NATO, there are 18 firms in seven countries working on ground-to-air weapons.[2] However, such duplication represents a major constraint on policy changes since it reflects the existence of national defence industries which will oppose changes from which they are likely to lose. Efforts to achieve the economies of standardisation will require a reallocation of resources both within, and between, NATO members.[3] European nations believe that they will be amongst the major losers from such policy changes. They fear that the USA will acquire a monopoly of high technology defence equipment and the associated technical "spin-off", with the Europeans restricted to "metal bashing"[4]. Admittedly, this extreme view fails to recognise that the Europeans have some competitive advantages (*eg* missiles, VTOL aircraft). Nonetheless, it identifies national defence industries as major interest groups which will oppose policies on international arms co-operation and standardisation from which they are likely to lose. Increasingly, though, nations are experiencing structural disarmament.[5] It is claimed that no one country has a large enough domestic market to develop and produce weapons at a politically affordable cost. Rapidly increasing weapons costs mean that fewer units can be bought and the decline in numbers has resulted in structural disarmament. Within Europe, international collaboration and the eventual creation of a European defence industrial base are seen as the solution to this problem[6].

The defence industrial base

At the national level, there are few clear government statements of the meaning of a defence industrial base (DIB). In the UK, references have been made to the need for a "strong and broadly-based" national defence industry consisting of those industrial assets which provide "key elements of military power and national security"[7]. However, apart from a vague reference to the need to maintain a capability in air, helicopter and sea platforms, no clear operational definition has yet been provided of the "essential key" national assets required for the DIB[8]. Similarly, proposals for a European DIB seem attractive until they are subject to critical scrutiny. Answers are required to a set of questions such as:

i.   What is the meaning of a European DIB and why is it required?
ii.   What is the minimum size and composition of such a DIB? Should it include a capability in all defence equipment, namely, air, space, land, sea and nuclear systems?
iii. Should the capability be restricted to R&D or include production?
iv.   Will the European DIB support competitive firms or will it be dominated by monopolies? Will non-European firms be allowed to compete?
v.   Will parts of the European DIB be privately-owned and parts publicly-owned?
vi.   What is the optimal size of firm required to exploit all the worthwhile scale economies in each sector of the DIB?
vii. What are the costs of maintaining a European DIB and are European nations willing to pay the price?
viii. How is the European DIB to be created; who will make the choices, including decisions on procurement; and how, if at all, will the losers be compensated?

As a starting point in answering these questions, much more information is required on European defence industries, their competitiveness, their experiences with collaborative projects and the efficiency implications of different European procurement policies.[9] After all, the defence industries of Europe are the major source of the expensive and increasingly costly weapons which are leading to structural disarmament: hence the need to question the efficiency and competitiveness of these industries. In other words, sensible public choices about European defence industries and collaboration require a reliable data base, together with an understanding of the operation of weapons markets and the causes of any inefficiency.

Within Europe, the UK has one of the largest defence industries. Table 17.1 summarises the main features of UK expenditure on equipment. Typically, 80% of the equipment budget is awarded to UK industry, 15% is spent on collaborative projects and 5% on imports[10]. It shows that equipment and associated costs account for almost 50% of defence expenditure. The UK also supports a substantial defence R&D base, absorbing 13%–15% of military spending during the 1980s, most of which is awarded to private industry and public corporations[11]. Within the equipment budget, the development and production of air systems accounts for almost 40% of spending, with sea systems accounting for some 30% and land equipment about 20% (see Table 17.2). Interestingly, in terms of efficiency, the ratio of R&D to

Table 17.1   UK Expenditure on Equipment

Programme	Expenditure (£m)	
	1980–81	1986–87
1. Total defence expenditure (current prices)	10,785	18,479
2. Total defence expenditure		
(constant 1984–5 prices)	15,100	16,962
3. Procurement of equipment (current prices)	5,324	9,048
Of which:		
(i) Research and development:		
Sea systems	283	476
Land systems	182	303
Air systems	499	690
General support	663	868
Total	1,627	2,337
(ii) Intramural R&D, net	412	656
(iii) Extramural R&D, net	1,215	1,681
(iv) Production and repair of equipment:		
Sea systems	1,229	2,110
Land systems	722	1,409
Air systems	1,560	2,673
General support	186	519
Total	3,697	6,711

Note: Procurement expenditure includes associated costs of R&D establishments and Procurement Executive staff: see Cmnd 9763-II, 1986,
Table 3.1.

Source: Cmnd 9763-II (1986).

production spending on equipment has improved from 1:2.3 in 1980–1
to 1:2.9 in 1986–7.[12]

Some of the main features of the size, industrial composition and
competitiveness of the UK DIB are presented in Table 17.2. A thorough
economic evaluation requires a study of the structure, conduct and performance of these industries. This approach shows that industry performance depends on its structure with a distinction being made
between the two extremes of perfect competition and monopoly.
Obviously, some of the high technology sectors such as aerospace, tor-
pedoes and nuclear-powered submarines are domestic monopolies
(British Aerospace, Rolls Royce, Westland, GEC-Marconi, Vickers).
Table 17.2 shows the major defence industries and leading companies
in terms of annual sales and dependence on MoD contracts. Pre-
dictably, the list is dominated by aerospace, electronics, ordnance and
shipbuilding most of which are now privately-owned companies.

Table 17.2   The UK Defence Industrial Base, 1985

1. Industrial analysis of defence expenditure in UK (£m)	8,014
including:	
Aerospace	2,461
Electronics	1,638
Petroleum products	737
Ordnance and small arms	675
Shipbuilding and repairing	557
Other mechanical and marine engineering	407
Motor vehicles and parts	274
2. Percentage of UK industry sales to MoD (%)	
Ordnance industry	60
Aerospace industry	50
Shipbuilding industry	40
Electronics industry	20
3. Percentage share of MoD contracts by value which were priced by:	
Competition	39%
Otherwise by reference to market forces	25%
Incentive pricing under Government profit formula	27%
Actual costs plus a percentage fee	9%
4. International trade	
Exports of defence equipment (£m)	2,135
Imports of defence equipment (£m)	253
5. Employment due to (direct and indirect, 000s):	
MoD equipment expenditure	395
Exports of defence equipment	120
Total	515

6. Major UK defence contractors receiving over £100m per annum

British Aerospace	Racal Electronics
British Petroleum	Rolls Royce
British Shipbuilders	Royal Ordnance
Esso UK	Shell Transport & Trading
Ferranti	Thorn-EMI
GEC	Westland

Notes: (i) Data are for 1984–85, except for exports and imports which are for 1984 and contracts which are for 1985–6.

(ii) Industrial analysis is based on commodity groups and includes land, buildings, food, fuel and services. Equipment expenditure shown in Table 1 does not include works, buildings, land, stores and services.

Sources: Cmnd 9763 (1986); HCP 399 (1986).

An indication of the average level of competition in the UK DIB in 1985-6 is shown by the fact that 64% of MoD contracts were priced by competition and some reference to market forces and 36% were non-competitive; in 1980-1, the corresponding percentages were 36% and 64%, respectively, so that there has been a substantial increase in competitive procurement.[13] International trade is a further indicator of competitiveness and it can be seen that there is a substantial surplus on this account. By adding exports to home sales, it is possible to estimate the total output of the UK defence equipment industry which was some £10.3 billion in 1984-5.[14] On this basis, exports of equipment accounted for some 20% of total output.

The DIB in Britain and Germany provides the "inputs" and acts as a constraint on the development of international arms co-operation programmes. Each national industry differs in size, composition, technical skills, ownership and has different comparative advantages. National defence industries will also have a view about international collaboration and the range of eligible and acceptable partner nations and companies. Some indication of a nation's views about joint projects can be deduced from its record of involvement in collaborative ventures.

Britain, Germany and collaboration

Britain and Germany have been involved in collaborative projects embracing a variety of both equipment and partner nations. Some of the current collaborative projects involving either the UK or West Germany or both nations are shown in Table 16.2 in the preceding chapter, which suggests a number of generalizations:

i.   Collaboration involving both Britain and Germany always includes at least a third partner state. In contrast, for aerospace equipment, each country has reached collaborative agreements with only one nation, usually France. However, the UK has bilateral projects with Italy and with the USA.[15]

ii.   The list of projects indicates the scale and type of equipment which some governments are no longer willing to undertake as independent national ventures and where international co-operation and collaboration is believed to be worthwhile. The list is dominated by aerospace equipment, which are often costly projects in terms of both R&D and production outlays.

iii. For the sample (n = 32), the number of partner nations varied between two and eight with a median and average of three. Significantly, the collaborative projects *actually in service* have usually involved only two to three partner nations.

iv.   The states most extensively involved in the sample of collaborative projects are the UK (25), followed by West Germany (21), France (19) and Italy (10). The UK is collaborating in a complete range of air, land and sea systems whilst Germany has a substantial involvement in aircraft and missile programmes. These variations partly reflect the extent of each nation's domestic defence industrial base, its desire to maintain a high technology capability and its "willingness and ability to pay".

v.   The types of equipment *not* listed in Table 17.3 cannot be ignored. The obvious examples are in naval and land equipment, especially tanks and armoured vehicles. The absence of more collaborative ventures for such equipment can reflect the fact that cost pressures on such equipment are not yet sufficiently great to persuade nations to sacrifice their independence. For example, the ratio of development to unit production costs on warships is under one, compared with ratios of over 100 for combat aircraft and 1,000 for missiles: hence, there are greater cost incentives to collaborate on aerospace projects. Collaboration on warships involving seven equal partners each requiring three ships might result in cost savings approaching 10% compared with a national venture.[16]

Evaluation of collaborative projects

Major difficulties arise in evaluating the performance of collaborative projects such as Tornado which involved shared R&D and production work. These are:

i.   Different policy aims: partner nations in a collaborative venture are likely to have different policy objectives and to differ in their "willingness to pay" for the various benefits from a joint project. In some cases, it is not clear whether governments have been buying defence equipment to protect their citizens or to support and protect their defence industrial base!

ii.   The counter-factual: what would have happened in the absence of a collaborative venture? For instance, in the absence of Tornado, would the UK and Germany each have built an identical aircraft, purchasing the same quantity in the same time-scale?

iii.   There is only a limited population of joint projects.

iv.   International projects are heterogeneous, involving trainer and transport aircraft, various types of combat aircraft, helicopters, missiles and other land and naval equipment (Table 17.3).

v.   Different partner countries are involved.

vi.   Various forms of organisational arrangements have been used, including joint management committees, prime contractor

– sub-contractor relationships and new international companies.

In assessing international collaborative ventures, the criteria for success often focus on inputs rather than end-outputs. Reference might be made to the number of partner nations involved in collaboration, to the creation of a new international company or to the fact that a joint programme has been completed. But numbers of partners, new companies and completion are not necessarily evidence of economic success in terms of efficiency, marketability and profitability. Ideally, an economic evaluation requires an assessment of all the benefits and costs as seen by society. Surprisingly, in view of the frequent official references to the benefits of collaboration, especially its cost savings, there is an absence of publicly-available information especially from governments, on the magnitude of the benefits and savings. An official UK report concluded that "in reviewing the outcome of projects, it proved extremely difficult to establish the extent to which the potential benefits of collaboration – which in principle are very significant – were fully secured in practice".[17] It was also reported that MoD often cannot specify in a way that can be measured their original industrial, political and other objectives. Even so, MoD has stressed "the importance of wider political, economic and industrial considerations in collaborative projects which, though largely unquantifiable, might be as important as clear cost and military advantages".[18] There is, however, a cost-benefit study of the Anglo-French Concorde which in some ways resembled a military programme (a major technical leap; government funding; cost-plus contracts). After allowing for all costs and benefits, the study concluded that Concorde had resulted in a net loss to the UK of some £1.7–£2.3 billion; that the programme was an error and ought not to have been undertaken.[19] Although data are unavailable for a comprehensive cost benefit analysis of collaborative arms projects (*ie* the problem of measuring and valuing output), it is possible to identify the major qualitative benefits and cost and to assemble some limited evidence. Various indicators are available which can be used to assess to performance of a collaborative project, some of which represent "inputs" into a more complete benefit-cost study. The range of possible performance measures embrace *planned* and *realised* economic, technical and political criteria. They include such indicators as profitability, cost-savings, development times, total output, export competitiveness, performance against the original contract specification (*eg* cost escalation), wider economic benefits (*eg* jobs, technology), political integration and military standardisation.

The benefits of collaboration

European collaboration is reputed to result in major economic, industrial, technological, political and military benefits, which take the following form:

i. *Cost savings for R&D and production, including the production of spares.* Partners on a joint venture can share R&D outlays and, by pooling their national orders to achieve a longer production run, they can obtain economies of scale and learning. In the ideal case, two equal partners on an aerospace project would share R&D costs (50% each) and a doubling of output would reduce unit production costs by about 10%.[20] Collaboration has advantages where a project involves considerable technical advance, substantial risks, high R&D costs and where the participating countries can combine to create a large "home" market.[21] For instance, on the Tornado project, three nations shared the R&D costs and combined their national requirements to give a combined initial order of some 800 units (385 for UK, 324 for West Germany and 100 for Italy): this was substantially greater than the requirements of any one nation and was much closer to US scales of output.

ii. *The creation of a European defence industry able to compete with the USA.* Collaboration enables Europe to undertake advanced aerospace projects which would be too costly on a national basis. In this way, it can continue competing in high technology aerospace products (including spin-off for its economies), while retaining a European defence industrial base and preventing a US monopoly. These benefits reflect a European desire to avoid American technological domination (*eg* the desire to prevent Europe becoming a nation of "metal bashers") and also being "unduly" dependent on the USA (*eg* US equipment is cheap but you pay for the spares). Without collaboration each European nation has too small a home market to compete with the United States. For example, UK national orders for military helicopters are in the region of 40–200 units of each type, while the European military market probably represents 100 helicopters per year of all types. In contrast, US military orders for the Sikorsky Blackhawk are expected to exceed 1,750 units and might well exceed 2,500 units produced at a rate of 150 helicopters per year.[22]

iii. *Wider economic benefits.* These take the form of domestic jobs and balance of payments benefits from supporting a European defence industrial base. Sometimes this argument is developed further to suggest that many of the jobs (*eg* aerospace) will be high value-added involving high technology which is much less likely to be copied by newly-industrialising countries.[23]

iv.   *Political benefits*. Some of these have already been mentioned, such as a desire for independence from the USA. Others include the belief that collaboration demonstrates the Alliance's cohesion and credibility;[24] and that it contributes to the creation of a united Europe through reducing national barriers and prejudice.[25] More interesting is the claim that cancellation of an international programme is more difficult.[26] Others have suggested that collaborative projects are immune from cancellation[27]. An alternative view might be that this is a cost rather than a benefit!

v.   *Military benefits* due to the greater standardisation and interoperability of equipment within NATO.[28]

vi.   *Other benefits* have been suggested. For example, the greater funding available in the R&D stage compared with a national project may enable the equipment to enter service before it is nearly obsolescent.[29] Collaborative arrangements might also generate technical rigour and lead to a pooling of knowledge and a competitive stimulus from the partners.[30]

Evidence for the benefits of collaboration

Cost savings

Only limited information is available on what is often claimed by governments to be a major benefit from collaboration. The following examples are of relevance to Anglo-German collaboration:

(a)   It has been estimated that in the ideal case and compared with a national venture, collaboration on Tornado reduced unit costs to the UK (R&D and production) by a maximum of 30% on the strike version and 10% on the air defence version. For all three nations, the total savings on Tornado might in the ideal case be some £1,900m (1976 prices[31])

(b)   The savings to the UK from its participation in the 4-nation European Fighter Aircraft have been estimated at £1,000m. (1985 prices[32])

(c)   UK involvement in a joint European battlefield helicopter project might lead to savings in development costs equivalent to six Sea King helicopters or some £60m (1984–85 prices: [33])

(d)   An official report gave cost savings as a major reason for the UK's collaboration on the FH70 howitzer, Trigat, Tornado and ASRAAM. However, no quantitative estimates were provided. Instead, there were references to the "economic and financial benefits of sharing the costs and risks of R&D and reducing unit costs through longer production runs"[34].

(e) A 1979 study calculated that if Britain, Germany and the USA had standardised on the West German tank there could have been savings of some $2 billion on production costs and further savings on R&D[55].

(f) More generally, it has been estimated that standardisation in defence equipment through the exploitation of scale and learning economies, together with the gains from competition, international specialisation and free trade could result in unit cost savings of 20%–30%[36].

Industrial, technological and political benefits

A major element in the UK's policy towards collaboration has been the desire to develop an effective European alternative to what it was feared would otherwise become US domination of the arms market. Thus UK collaboration, initially with France and subsequently with Germany and Italy, "formed part of a general strategy of maintaining the European air defence industry and later came to be seen as having political attractions in the context of an approach by the UK to join the European Economic Community".[37] The UK's aim was to maintain an advanced European aerospace industry for its civil as well as defence potential, thereby "developing a more economic and more widely-based European alternative to the US challenge".[38] Interestingly, Anglo-German collaboration on Tornado has created a new international company (Panavia) based on the design and technical expertise of two firms which in 1940–5 were responsible for two world-famous and opposing fighter aircraft (Spitfire and Me-109). This might be another indicator of industrial and political integration.

Employment benefits

Little published evidence is available on the jobs benefits from collaboration. On Tornado there are some 70,000 employees, with about 36,000 jobs in the UK, most of which are in British Aerospace and Rolls Royce. However, these are gross figures which do not indicate how many jobs would have been created either from alternative aerospace projects or from other economic activity elsewhere in the economy.

Military benefits

Collaboration has contributed to increased standardisation. Tornado is the classic example with one basic aircraft replacing six different types throughout three nations. An official UK report on ten joint projects referred to standardisation as a major reason for collaboration on three programmes (Trigat, EH 101 helicopter and ASRAAM).[39]

The costs of collaboration

Collaboration might not result in all the benefits suggested by the model of the ideal case. Indeed, some of the alleged benefits might have been exaggerated. Critics claim that inefficiency in collaboration results from work-sharing, duplication, administration and the need to compromise.[40]

Work-sharing

At the outset, collaboration requires the partners to agree upon some acceptable measure of work. Cost is often used to measure the work undertaken but problems arise where productivity, labour costs and accounting conventions differ between partner countries. Work will then be allocated on political, equity and bargaining criteria and not on the basis of efficiency and comparative advantage. Each partner will demand its fair share of each sector of high technology work (eg airframe, engines, avionics). During the 1985–6 debate on the future of the UK Westland helicopter company, it was suggested that the European helicopter industry was characterised by over-production, over-manning and a lack of profitability. It was never made clear precisely how European collaboration would rationalise the helicopter industry and make it more competitive[41]. Critics of the proposals for European collaboration in helicopters feared the creation of an inefficient cartel supplying a protected European market, with all the costs of the Common Agricultural Policy!

Duplication

On aerospace projects, each partner will require a flight-testing centre and its own final assembly line.

Administrative costs

Collaboration is believed to involve substantial administrative costs with claims of excessive government bureaucracy, complex arrangements for monitoring and controlling the programme, duplicate organisations, frequent committee meetings, paper-work and delays in decision-making, especially where key decisions require the unanimous agreement of the partners. Delays on the FH70 project arose because of difficulties in co-ordinating the administrative procedures in Britain,

Germany and Italy[42]. Suggestions have been made for improving the management arrangements on collaborative programmes aiming at prime contractorship rather than management by committee[43].

Compromises

There are likely to be compromises in operational requirements as the armed forces, scientists and industrialists of different nations try to reach an acceptable agreement. Problems arise in harmonising requirements and schedules for deliveries. It is not unknown for each partner to insist upon modifications for its own national order, so raising R&D costs and reducing the economies from a long production run of one type. Resolution of these difficulties is complicated by differences in language, measurement, bureaucratic and management procedures, traditions and national pride. A new international company will lack the long experience and "tight" management required to develop and produce competitive equipment. As a result, joint ventures might take longer to develop and involve higher costs than a national programme. Even without exits, the costs of collaborative ventures can also be increased by the unilateral actions of one or more partners (eg national budgetary problems can lead to a slower delivery programme).

As a result of these inefficiencies, collaboration is likely to increase the total cost of a project compared with a national programme[44]. For aircraft, various estimates have been given of the premium for European collaboration:

(a)   On R&D an extra 30%–33%.[45] The R&D arrangements on the Tornado engine were estimated to cost an extra 25%.[46] Others believe that these estimates are "too high" and that if there are any extra R&D costs from collaboration, they are under 20%.[47]

(b)   The square root rule whereby the collaboration premium on R&D is equal to the square root of the number of partners: hence two partners increases costs by about 40%[48]. Total development time on joint ventures is approximated by the cube root of the number of partners: hence development time on a 3-nation project might take some 45% longer[49].

(c)   On joint production work, the inefficiency premium ranges from an extra 1%–2% at the lower bound to an extra 10% at the upper bound for a given output.[50] An industry view suggests a 5% premium on collaborative production due to "geographical distances, language and other peculiar features associated with collaboration".[51]

(d)   A study of the original F16 European Co-production Programme estimated that compared with a direct buy from the USA, the European Governments seem to have accepted a 34% cost penalty.[52]

Even with inefficiencies, collaboration results in cost savings for each partner compared with an identical national project. For two equal partners on a joint European aircraft project, a collaboration premium of 30% on R&D and 5% on production, means that each nation will save at least 35% on its R&D costs and 5% on unit production costs (assuming a 90% unit cost curve for production.[53] Alternatively, it has been estimated that for a modern combat aircraft, with collaboration inefficiencies of 33% on R&D and 5% on production, a doubling of the market from 200 to 400 units due to collaboration results in savings of about 20% on unit costs.[54] Such comparisons are usually between collaborative and national programmes. Further cost savings of up to 25% might be available if a nation were willing to purchase its defence equipment from the cheapest supplier in the world market.[55]

Competition with the USA

Has collaboration created a European defence industry capable of competing with the USA? Any evaluation of Anglo-German collaboration is complicated by the small population of in-service projects involving the two nations. Nonetheless, data are available on the size of firms, development time, output and exports for aerospace projects.

Size of firms

For Tornado, the creation of Panavia (airframe) and Turbo-Union (engines) resulted in international organisations whose total activities approached the size of the US giants. As shown in Table 17.3, the combined activities of the partner companies of Panavia resulted in it being the largest employer in the world aerospace industry and placed fifth in terms of sales. Turbo-Union, however, remains substantially smaller than General Electric and Pratt & Whitney. Table 17.3 shows the substantial differences in firm size between American and individual European companies, and between British and German firms, especially in engines. Equally striking are the productivity differences between American and European firms and the differences amongst the partner companies involved in Tornado.[56]

Development time

Joint projects are reputed to take longer to develop than a similar national venture. The extra development time might be estimated by the cube root of the number of participating nations[57]. Others have reported bilateral projects taking 40% longer, and trilateral programmes some 70% longer.[58] As shown in Table 17.4, Tornado seems to have required considerably longer to develop than similar American

Table 17.3 Size of Aerospace Firms, 1985

Company	Sales (ECU millions)	Employment	Productivity (Sales per employee: ECUs)
1. *Panavia*			
British Aerospace	4,535	75,823	59,810
MBB	2,693	36,915	72,915
Aeritalia	1,430	12,321	116,062
Total	8,658	125,059	69,231
2. *Turbo-Union*			
Rolls Royce	2,742	41,700	65,755
MTU	536	6,613	81,052
Fiat	308	3,604	85,461
Total	3,586	51,917	69,072
3. *US Companies*			
Boeing	18,237	98,700	184,772
McDonnell Douglas	13,916	83,310	167,039
Lockheed	12,752	70,200*	181,652
General Dynamics	10,919	85,100*	128,308
General Electric	7,811	37,818	206,542
Rockwell	7,100	45,700	155,361
Pratt & Whitney	7,019	47,842	146,712
Northrop	6,763	46,900	144,200

*Figures for 1982
Source: EEC (1986)

Table 17.4 Performance Indicators

	Total Output	Development Time
1. Tornado	929	12 years
2. *U.S. aircraft*		
F-14	950 +	3 yrs, 9 mths
F-15	1,479	5 yrs, 11 mths
F-111	586	7 years
3. *National averages*		
European combat aircraft	"	9 yrs, 6 mths
US combat aircraft	"	6 years

Note: National averages based on a sample of 8 and 10 combat aircraft for Europe and the USA respectively.

Source: Hartley (1986).

aircraft (F-14, F-15, F-111) and 2.5 years more than the average time required for a typical European combat aircraft.[59] Similarly, for army equipment, development problems have caused major delays with the 3-nation SP70 howitzer programme.[60]

Output and exports

It is argued that successful collaboration results in an output approaching US scales of production and leads to greater export sales. Typically, US orders for its armed forces are in the region of 1,000–2,800 units for a combat aircraft produced at rates of 12.5 to 15 units per month. In contrast, Britain and Germany might each require 200–300 units of a combat aircraft. By combining their domestic orders, the 3-nation Tornado achieved a home market of some 850 units produced at a rate of 9 + per month, which is approaching US scales of production. Export sales have not been impressive, accounting for under 10% of output. However, Tornado is a highly specialised aircraft and it could be claimed that its closest substitute is the American F-14. By the end of 1985, the Tornado and F-14 had similar records of both total output and exports. Whilst the export records of joint ventures are useful performance indicators, it has to be remembered that national projects are also sold overseas (*eg* Harrier, Hawk, Mirage). Ideally, a comparative economic evaluation requires life cycle data on the unit costs and prices of collaborative, national and imported defence equipment.

Reasons for success or failure

Any evaluation of the reasons for the success or failure of collaborative projects encounters two problems. First, criteria have to be specified for assessing success or failure. Here, there is an absence of clear statements of the policy objectives of each partner nation at the start of a collaborative venture. Usually, independent commentators offer judgements after the event and with the benefit of hindsight! Second, various factors determine success or failure, and collaboration forms only one variable in a complex model. All other relevant influences such as the type of contract, the number of rival firms and the complexity of the programme have to be held constant.

Nonetheless, some generalisations can be formulated, although it is not yet possible to quantify their relative importance to success or failure. If choices reflect preferences, it can be deduced that the fact that a collaborative project has started and been completed without cancellation indicates that the partners believed that the venture was worthwhile. Of course, the problem is to determine each partner's view of what constitutes "worthwhile". Here, it is possible that each government's publicly-stated objectives in collaboration might not be its real aims. However, the trend towards more international collaboration suggests that this is becoming a preferred solution. An obvious example is the 4-nation Eurofighter which can be regarded as a follow-on from the trilateral Tornado project and organisation. Successful collaboration or failure is the result of economic, political, military, industrial and organisational factors:

i. *Economic factors* are relevant and take three forms: first, the rising development and production costs of defence equipment means that increasingly nations are finding that independence is "too costly". This is especially the case for projects involving a major technical advance, high risks and costly R&D. These difficulties are exacerbated in Europe, where nations have only a small domestic market so limiting their opportunities for achieving the economies of large scale production. Second, limited defence budgets and rising equipment costs means increased pressure to seek lower-cost methods of acquiring equipment. Where nations are unwilling to import defence equipment, they are likely to be attracted by the perceived benefits of some form of international collaboration. Third, international collaboration seems to offer wider economic benefits reflected in possible jobs, advanced technology and balance of payments benefits.[61]

ii. *Political factors* are reflected in a nation's desire for independence, and in its ability and willingness to pay for independence and security of supply (including national pride). As a result, a nation might seek to maintain "key" parts of its defence industrial base. Nations also differ in their willingness to associate with certain other countries[62]. And in negotiations about collaboration, a nation will use threats, bluff and bargaining skills to obtain the most favourable deal.

iii. *Military factors*. Collaboration requires nations to agree on a joint operational requirement and on the time-scale for the programme. Difficulties arise where each nation's armed forces have different tasks and genuine differences in defence strategy and tactics. Complications also arise where nations differ in the timing of their new equipment programmes. Inevitably, collaboration involves a willingness of the partners to compromise in both operational requirements and timing. Once again, a satisfactory international agreement is likely if each partner feels that the benefits of collaboration will outweigh its costs. The spectrum of benefits and costs will be wide-ranging and their valuations will differ between nations. With collaboration, there are extensive opportunities for bargaining and trading between objectives. For example, a nation willing to make sacrifices on its military and timing requirements might be compensated with a beneficial work-sharing package or be given the lead on some high technology work.

iv. *Industrial factors* reflected in the size and technical competence of a nation's defence industrial base. Each nation's defence industry will have a view about international collaboration and the range of "eligible and acceptable" partner nations and companies. Some of these views might reflect previous experience with collaboration. A nation's defence industry will be especially concerned about:

(a) The possible cancellation of a national project in favour of a collaborative venture
(b) Work-sharing arrangements. A nation with a high technology defence industry will seek its "fair share" of advanced technology work on the collaborative project.
(c) Possible losses of national technology and the likelihood that current partners will become future rivals.
(d) The delays involved in reaching international agreements and in the arrangements for monitoring joint projects.
(e) The likely costs and marketability of the resulting joint project.
(f) Possible restrictions on overseas sales if several governments are involved[63].

v. *Organisation and management factors*. Government departments, the armed forces, the defence industries and scientists-technologists in each partner state are likely to have different bureaucratic structures, different administrative approaches, different methods of procurement, contracting and reimbursement and different management philosophies. In other words, international collaboration initially involves "doing business with strangers"; such problems are likely to diminish with experience.[64]

Conclusions

Some collaborative efforts have failed in that the partner nations have withdrawn or cancelled, or failed to reach an agreement to proceed to the next stage of the development process. Examples of failures include the Anglo-French Variable Geometry aircraft (1967), the UK choice of Nimrod rather than the NATO AWACS (1977), the UK debate over the future of the Westland Helicopter Company and its participation in European helicopter projects (1986) and the long-running saga of possible collaboration on tanks. One study concluded that joint tank projects have foundered because of a political preference for national domestic interests, because of distinctively different tank philosophies, because of industrial and technology considerations and because of domestic electoral factors.[65] In other words, collaborative ventures will be strongly opposed where established and powerful domestic interest groups such as bureaucracies, the armed forces and industry believe that they are likely to lose from collaboration. This suggests that collaborative ventures which are supported by national defence industries are likely to benefit producers rather than a nation's citizens and taxpayers.

Notes

1. B. Field, "Economics and Defence Resources: The Prospect", *NATO Review*, October 1985, pp. 24–28.
2. J. Houwelingen, "The Independent European Programme Group: The Way Ahead", *NATO Review*, No.4, August 1984, pp. 17–21.
3. T.A. Callaghan, *US-European Economic Co-operation in Military and Civil Technology*, Georgetown University 1975.
4. K. Hartley, "Defence Procurement and Industial Policy", in J. Roper (ed.), *The Future of British Defence Policy* (London: Gower 1985).
5. See Callaghan, *op. cit.*
6. House of Commons Defence Committee, *The Defence Implications of the Future of Westland plc*, Report and Minutes of the Evidence, HCP 518, London, HMSO: 1986, p. xxxviii.
7. HCP 518, *op. cit.*, p. xxxvii.
8. House of Commons Defence Committee, *The Defence Implications of the Future of Westland plc*, House of Commons Defence Committee, Report and Minutes of Evidence, HCP 169, London: HMSO.
9. In November 1984, IEPG commissioned a study into methods of improving the competitiveness of the European armaments industry. Planned completion date for the study was late 1986. See *Statement on the Defence Estimates*, Cmnd 9673, London: HMSO 1986, I, p. 18.
10. Cmnd 9673-I, *op. cit.*, p. 42.
11. Council for Science and Society, *Military R&D*, London 1986.
12. Cmnd 9673-II, 1986, p. 16.
13. House of Commons Defence Committee, *Statement on the Defence Estimates 1986*, HCP 399, London: HMSO 1986, p. xiii; p. 143.
14. Home sales were estimated to be 95% of procurement expenditure for 1984–5 – *ie* 0.95 × £8,573m including associated costs. The estimates are for equipment only, and do not include expenditure on food, fuel, land and services. In 1984–85, these items account for a further £3.3 billion of MoD spending: hence total output of UK DIB might be some £13.6 billion for 1984–85.
15. C. Bluth, "British-Defence Co-operation: A Historical Survey" in this volume.
16. P. Pugh, *The Cost of Sea Power*, Chap. 13.
17. Ministry of Defence, *International Collaborative Projects for Defence Equipment*, National Audit Office, London: HMSO 1984, p. 1.
18. National Audit Office, *op. cit.*, p. 3.
19. P.D. Henderson, "Two British Errors: Their Probable Size and Some Lessons", *Oxford Economic Papers*, Vol. 29, July 1977, pp. 159–205.
20. K. Hartley, *NATO Arms Co-operation: A Study in Economics and Politics* (London: Allen & Unwin 1983, Chap. 8).
21. House of Commons Defence Committee, *Ministry of Defence Organisation and Procurement*, Vol. I, HCP 22-I, London: HMSO 1982, p. xliv; M. Edmonds (ed.), *International Arms Procurement* (Oxford: Pergamon 1981, Chap. 1).
22. See HCP 169, *op. cit.*, pp. 273, 394; K. Hartley, "Defence, Industry and Technology: Problems and Possibilities for European Collaboration", in G. Hall (ed.), *European Industrial Policy* (London: Croom Helm 1986).
23. K. Hartley, *NATO Arms Co-operation*, *op. cit.*, p. 83.
24. National Audit Office, *op. cit.*, p. 5.
25. B.O. Heath, "MRCA Tornado: Achievement By International Collaboration", *Journal of the Royal Aeronautical Society*, September 1979, pp. 329–343.
26. Edmonds, *op. cit.*, p. 12.
27. HCP 22-I, *op. cit.*, p. xliv; B. Udis, 'European Perspectives on International Collaborative Ventures in Aerospace', in Edmonds, *op. cit.*

28. T. Taylor, *Defence, Technology and International Integration* (London: Frances Pinter 1982, Chap. 3).
29. HCP 22-I *op. cit.*, p. xliv.
30. Hartley, *NATO Arms Co-operation*, *op. cit.*, pp. 148–151; HCP 22-I, *op. cit.*, p. xliv; Royal Aeronautical Society, *European Collaborative Projects*, Spring Convention, London, May 1981.
31. K. Hartley, 'Defence and Advanced Technology', in D. Dosser *et al.* (eds.), *The Collaboration of Nations* (Oxford: Martin Robertson 1982).
32. HCP 169, *op. cit.*, Q1541.
33. HCP 169, *op. cit.*, Q230.
34. National Audit Office, *op. cit.*, p. 2. pp. 10–11.
35. C. Groth, "The Economics of Weapons Co-Production", in Edmonds. *op. cit.*, p. 79.
36. Hartley, *NATO Arms Co-operation*, *op. cit.*, p. 67.
37. National Audit Office, *op. cit.*, p. 2.
38. National Audit Office, *op. cit.*, p. 6.
39. National Audit Office, *op. cit.*, pp. 10–11.
40. Hartley, *NATO Arms Co-operation*, *op. cit.*, Chap. 8; Hartley, "Defence, Industry and Technology", *op. cit.*
41. HCP 169, *op. cit.*, pp. 62, 67.
42. National Audit Office, *op. cit.*, p. 8.
43. HCP 22-I, *op. cit.*, p. xliv.
44. W.B. Walker, "The Multi-Role Combat Aircraft (MRCA): A Case Study in European Collaboration", *Research Policy*, Vol. 2, January 1974, pp. 280–305.
45. Sir George Edwards, *Partnership in Major Technological Projects*, Seventh Maurice Lubbock Memorial Lecture, (London: Oxford University Press 1970, p. 23;) Hartley, *NATO Arms Co-operation*, *op. cit.*, p. 161.
46. *Third Report from Committee of Public Accounts*, Minutes of Evidence, London: HMSO 1974, p. 151.
47. Hartley, *NATO Arms Co-operation*, *op. cit.*, p. 151; Pugh, *op. cit.*, p. 357.
48. Hartley, *NATO Arms Co-operation*, *op. cit.*, p. 153.
49. Hartley, *NATO Arms Co-operation*, *op. cit.*, p.153.
50. Hartley, *NATO Arms Co-operation*, *op. cit.*, p. 161.
51. Edwards, *op. cit.*, p. 23.
52. M. Rich, et al., *Multinational Coproduction of Military Aerospace Systems,* (Santa Monica: Rand 1981, p. 111).
53. Hartley, "Defence, Industry and Technology", *op. cit.*, pp. 253–254.
54. Edwards, op. cit., p. 24.
55. Hartley, *'Defence procurement',* *op. cit.*, p. 180.
56. The productivity figures are based on sales turnover rather than value-added. Differences can arise due to variations in a firm's R&D activity or due to its involvement in work under license or under sub-contract. See European Economic Community, *The European Aerospace Industry: Trading Position and Figures*, Brussels, October 1986, pp. 24–28.
57. Hartley, *NATO Arms Co-operation, op. cit.*, p. 153.
58. Taylor, *op. cit.*, p. 173.
59. Hartley, 'Defence, Industry and Technology', *op. cit.*, p. 254.
60. HCP 399, *op. cit.*, p. 153.
61. Sir Frank Cooper, *Pre-Conditions for the Emergence of a European Common Market in Armaments*, Brussels: Centre for European Policy Studies 1985; Edwards, *op. cit.*
62. Taylor, *op. cit.*, p. 96.
63. HCP 22-I, *op. cit.*, p. xliii.
64. M. Metcalf and M. Edmonds, "RSI and the Main Battle Tank 1970–80", in M. Edmonds (ed)., *op. cit.*; Edmonds, *op. cit.*, Chap. 1.
65. Metcalf and Edmonds, *op. cit.*, Chapter 9.

Chapter 18

What Future for the Partnership?

KARL KAISER and JOHN ROPER

The geopolitics of the two triangles

Any examination of the present or future relationship between the United Kingdom and the Federal Republic of Germany on defence or security matters has to be seen in the context of the Western Alliance which provides the basis for both countries' security. Within that Alliance Britain and Germany are two major European members, and their relations with the United States and France, the other two major members, are of critical importance for the security of the centre of Europe.

In many ways the politics of the Western Alliance and in particular the Anglo-German relationship can be seen in terms of two triangular relationships in which both countries are involved. The first of these, the transatlantic triangle has Washington at its apex and Bonn and London as the other two corners. The second European triangle links Bonn with its two European partners in Paris and London.

The security of Western Europe in the post-war period has relied on the American military guarantee. Relationships with the United States have therefore been central to British and German security policy. The multilateral institutions of the Alliance, political and military, have played some part in day-to-day management and the formulation of Alliance-wide policies but both British and German governments have felt that its meetings were often too large to be effective. They have therefore placed particular stress on their direct and privileged relations with Washington. Together with France their Foreign Ministers have maintained the tradition of meeting on the eve of every NATO ministerial meeting, nominally to discuss matters affecting Germany and Berlin but in practice to enable common positions to be established where possible in advance of the larger meeting.

British Prime Ministers in the post-war period have made much of their "special relationship" with Washington which was based on the wartime partnership. The relationship was not always reciprocated from Washington; nevertheless the continuing working co-operation in the field of intelligence and, after an interruption in the late 1940s in nuclear weapons technology have been extremely close. At some stages London felt that it could provide a bridge between the United States and her European allies. Such a role of messenger has not proved particularly successful in either direction, and certainly gave rise to Britain being seen by some on the continent as a Trojan horse for Washington. American nuclear weapons in Europe were first deployed in Britain and the UK has remained a key base for air- and sea-launched components of American nuclear forces. Britain's relative decline has created problems for the relationship, and the adjustment from junior partner to dependent ally has not been easy. However this has not reduced the importance of the transatlantic link in British defence thinking and policy. The implementation of the Labour Party's defence policies would substantially strain that link.

The Federal Republic has by reasons of geography and economic strength a central place in NATO. The United States has therefore given the highest priority to maintaining good relations with Bonn, and this has been reciprocated by successive German governments. Not only are the overwhelming majority of American land forces in Europe based in the Federal Republic but West Germany makes the largest European contribution to the forces on the Central Front. Germany has bound itself by treaty to being a non-nuclear weapon state, but nonetheless believes strongly in the need for a nuclear component in NATO's deterrent strategy. Questions of nuclear weapons policy have therefore a potential for tension within Germany and require the closest political relations between Bonn and Washington to prevent differences appearing.

Two sides of the transatlantic triangle, Washington-London and Washington-Bonn have therefore strong links. The third side, the link between London and Bonn, does not have the political strategic imperative which drives the other two but it has, for much of the last 20 years, been one of the strongest bilateral links for both partners. With France's partial withdrawal from NATO, Britain and Germany as the two main European countries in NATO's integrated command worked closely together from the 1960s in developing European positions on nuclear forces in Europe and on a variety of arms control issues. In addition Britain provides, after the United States, the largest number of forces deployed to the Federal Republic and British and German officers have worked very closely alongside each other within the NATO command structure. Consequently a close working relationship has developed, albeit one that has not been over demonstrative. Not surprisingly, therefore, this relationship has too often been taken for granted.

The second triangle which requires consideration is the European triangle based on Bonn and with Paris and London as the other two corners. The relationship between Bonn and Paris is one of the greatest political importance. The removal of historical fears and prejudices and the development of effective military collaboration for the defence of the Central Front after France had left the integrated military command has been an important task for French and German governments. Much has been achieved, and a framework has been established for doing more on a bilateral basis. This could provide part of the structure for a new approach to European defence co-operation.

Franco-British security relations have been less close. There has not been the same pressure on either side for co-operation, and the disagreements in the 1960s over British membership of the European Community, coupled on the British side with annoyance with France for its withdrawal from NATO's integrated command and French resentment at the privileged Anglo-American nuclear relationship, have kept the countries apart. More recently with Britain as a member of the Community and in the belief that Western Europe's two nuclear powers do have certain shared interests the prospects that the third side of the European triangle will have a reality have been strengthened.

Neither of the two triangles is balanced, some of the bilateral relations are stronger than others, but the sets of relationships they represent do provide two important parts of the political framework in which Anglo-German defence co-operation must be considered.

The evolution of the Alliance's military strategy

The bilateral Anglo-German defence relationship has always to be seen against the wider NATO Alliance. Britain and Germany, as two principal European partners in the Alliance, have played an active part in the development of its strategic doctrine. More often than not this has amounted to a European reaction to American initiatives on strategic thinking, developments in weapons technology or in some cases arms control proposals.

There have been two aspects of strategic doctrine which have been of continuing and particular importance: one is the role of nuclear weapons and the second, the most effective posture for the defence of Germany against a Warsaw Treaty attack. Earlier chapters of this volume, and in particular the introductory survey, have discussed the history of both these issues in some detail.

The questions that arise in the late 1980s are how far the traditional

NATO doctrine of flexible response is likely to be eroded on the one hand by changes in United States strategic thinking and increased reliance on strategic defences and on the other by changes in NATO's nuclear force postures resulting from US-Soviet arms control agreements. At the same time, in both Britain and Germany opposition parties have challenged the traditional consensus positions on the role of nuclear weapons in European defence.

The last decade has seen the recurrence of a debate on the basis of NATO's nuclear doctrine, the morality of nuclear deterrence has been challenged by churchmen on both side of the Atlantic, "no first use" of nuclear weapons has been advocated by leading figures in the United States, and an increased role for strategic defence has been advocated by President Reagan. Both Britain and Germany have been reluctant to endorse changes in NATO's doctrine or force posture until it can be unmistakably shown that these will clearly strengthen their country's security.

There is an understandable fear that some aspects of Mr Gorbachev's plans for a denuclearised Europe would increase the risks of conventional war in Europe. Reducing the importance of nuclear weapons has led to increasing concerns about the conventional balance in Europe. Whatever the merits of the arguments over the exact figures, the geographical asymmetry presented by the United States on the other side of the Atlantic and the Soviet Union only 350 miles (560 km) from the intra-German border means that many West Europeans feel the need for a continued nuclear component in NATO's deterrent forces.

The uncertainties in the present situation have led to an increased appreciation in West Germany of the contribution to Western security provided by British and French nuclear forces. We consider below arrangements for formalising this European nuclear relationship.

The second area of strategic doctrine in which there has been controversy in the mid-1980s has been the defence of the Central Front. Here the controversy has been both over official proposals, such as SACEUR's Follow-on-Forces Attack and United States Air-Land Battle doctrine, and unofficial proposals attacking "forward defence" and supporting ideas of "defensive defence". In spite of a good deal of debate on these issues, particularly in the Federal Republic, it seems that changes in NATO's force posture are extremely slow to be made and are more likely to be the result of financial and demographic resource constraints than debate about doctrine.

Evolution of the political environment of East-West relations

If one reviews Western economic and political strategy *vis-à-vis* the socialist countries one is struck by the remarkable similarity of British and German positions on the central issues, notably those that have at times been the subject of disagreement between the United States and its European allies.

In the field of economic relations both countries, while subscribing to the notion of prohibiting and even tightening the transfer of military technology, have resisted American attempts to further restrict the transfer of technology to socialist countries in the civilian field. The gas pipeline issue brought these disagreements to a head. Today both Britain and the Federal Republic adhere to the notion that a certain transfer of modern technology is a necessary part of economic interaction between industrialised countries in East and West and that a prohibition should be strictly confined to military technology.

With regard to credits, the two countries pursued different policies in the past, but for some time both Bonn and London have agreed that credits granted to socialist countries should remain unsubsidised (with the possible exception of some future government-backed loans to smaller socialist countries within a policy of differentiation).

The similarity of British and German views on the general philosophy of East-West economic relations is probably most important. Although the Federal Republic conducts some 6% of its trade with COMECON countries and Britain less than 2%, London and Bonn like other West European governments shared the goal of the Nixon administration that economic relations could create a web of interaction and a vested interest in peaceful intercourse within the Soviet Union. Indeed, there is widespread support in both Britain and the Federal Republic that economic relations remain a particularly important and expandable area of East-West interaction outside the military relationship. This is all the more true since other areas like culture, human relations or political intercourse tend to run into difficulties associated with ideological competition. While neither side adheres to the naïve notion that trade guarantees peace, both wish the East-West relationship not to be confined exclusively to competition in the field of security.

But it is in this area that significant differences in philosophy did arise between American and European governments during the Reagan administration. Neither Bonn nor London (nor any other West European government) shared the view supported by parts of the administration that *any* trade with the Soviet Union represented in the last analysis "trading with the enemy" (except, as Washington always put it, the sale of grain). Nor was there support on the European side for the notion that it was possible or desirable to bring the Soviet Union to her knees by economic boycott.

In the field of political relations with the East, Britain and the Federal Republic share a relatively broad conception that stresses the political, economic and cultural factors along with arms control and military security and therefore somewhat differs from the American approach which puts greater stress on the military elements of the competitive relationship, inevitably seen in the context of the competition between the two superpowers. For similar reasons Britain and the Federal Republic, like other West European governments, while being aware of the global nature of the East-West conflict, do not always share the American perception of certain conflicts in the Third World which Washington puts into an East-West context whereas Europeans tend more to stress their local origins.

For these reasons both the British and the German governments attach particular importance to the CSCE process, an appreciation that is not always shared by Washington which has a greater tendency to focus its attention and energies on the Soviet Union, whereas Britain and the Federal Republic like other West European governments are historically and culturally closer to the smaller East European countries. Consequently they are often more familiar, engage in more intensive contacts and have a particular understanding for their dilemmas and therefore regard the CSCE process not only as a way to engage the Soviet Union and the other socialist countries on a broad range of issues in East-West relations but to provide the smaller socialist countries with a forum where they can play a legitimate role of their own.

Finally, the requirements of reconciling the demands of managing the American-Soviet relationship with the necessity of consultation within the Alliance has created a problem that is as old as NATO. Repeatedly, eg during the Brezhnev-Nixon agreements of the early 1970s or the summit at Reykjavik in October 1986, both the British and the German governments considered themselves insufficiently consulted on issues central to their own interests. In such moments both countries are reminded of the necessity for a stronger European co-ordination of policies in order to create better conditions for inserting their interests into the superpower dialogue.

The definition of British and German interests in reacting to, and attempting to exert influence on, East-West relations will have to pay particular attention to the evolutionary trends of American and Soviet policies toward Europe. American differences in perspective and policy vis-à-vis Eastern Europe, as described in the preceding pages, are likely to remain a problem within the Western Alliance. But given the strong common interests in the field of security that tie the members of NATO together and considering the experience of handling differences for the last decades, it is likely that the disagreements on strategy vis-à-vis the East will, in the last analysis, remain manageable. Could the same be said for certain other trends within the United States?

The reservations that can be observed within the United States with regard to American nuclear commitments to Europe present the first and foremost problem. For a number of years now there has been a growing tendency for the United States to structure nuclear deterrence in such a manner as to avoid as far as possible the extension of nuclear conflict to US territory. The strategy of flexible response itself, as well as developments within this strategy and American proposals for its revision (as, for example, the proposal of an agreement about no first use of nuclear weapons), is an expression of this tendency. In the 1980s, however, the endeavour to limit nuclear conflicts has combined with a fundamental nuclear malaise. It affects conservatives and liberals alike, and includes President Reagan himself, who, in launching his Strategic Defense Initiative, evoked the immorality of nuclear deterrence and thereby strengthened existing anti-nuclear trends within the United States. The implementation of the INF "double-zero option" finds support in the United States on the basis of similar motivations. The removal of nuclear options that allow strikes on Soviet territory from Western Europe reduces deterrence to reliance on those nuclear weapons that would mainly be deployed on German soil (resulting in a self-deterrence of the West German government against their use) and to the American strategic arsenal (where the United States is self-deterred against its use).

In view of these developments, it is in the obvious interest of both Britain and the Federal Republic to use their influence to reconcile a desirable process of nuclear arms control and disarmament with the necessity of maintaining a minimum nuclear deterrence that does not undermine the credibility of America's nuclear commitment to Western Europe. Furthermore, the new developments in the area of nuclear disarmament should lead Great Britain and the Federal Republic to engage, together with France, in closer co-operation and a "Europeanisation" of the British and French nuclear forces. Such a process should not remove national control from the two governments, but it would redefine the function of these forces. This would have to be supported by the formation of a European Nuclear Planning Group which would regularly discuss all the issues connected with their tasks. Moreover, Bonn and London should conclude from the current developments in arms control that the European structures with NATO need to be strengthened in order to avoid a possible isolation of the Federal Republic and a consequent weakening of West European solidarity.

A second problem is the growing trend among American political élites to consider a reduction of the American military presence in Europe.

The third problem lies in the latent and occasionally acute temptation for Washington to engage in American-Soviet bilateralism that tends to bypass the European Allies and therefore creates problems for Bonn and London. Although experience shows that there is no formula for guaranteed success, there seems to be a great deal of wisdom in the prevailing point of view in Bonn and London that a functioning and cooperative bilateral relationship provides a better opportunity to introduce one's point of view into the Washington policy-making process than an approach that does not shun confrontation. In any case both Britain and the Federal Republic are well advised not to respond to

American-Soviet bilateralism by attempting their own respective excessive bilateralisms with Washington but by an effort to commit Washington to a process of multilateral consultation within the Alliance.

Finally, part of the effort to maintain a functioning security relationship between the United States and Europe will always consist of protecting the core of common interests in the field of security against the erosive impact of other issues on which the United States and Europe disagree, notably the problem of protectionism and of monetary destabilisation.

Let us turn to Soviet policy toward Western Europe. Here British and German policies have to be considered within the context of a distinct revival of Soviet interests in Western Europe. Gorbachev's major problem consists in preserving and strengthening the domestic economic and technological base through fundamental reform, otherwise the Soviet Union will face increasing difficulties in playing a world role. To pursue this policy he not only needs peace with the United States but also good relations with Western Europe.

Although the United States will remain the main addressee of Soviet policy when it comes to questions of peace, Soviet policy will no doubt continue to be interested in exploiting divergencies between the United States and Europe to put pressure on Washington to pursue policies more acceptable to the Soviet Union. For these reasons a number of Soviet initiatives in the field of arms control and disarmament are addressed to the European publics and politicians in order to influence American policy.

In the economic field "Europe first" is likely to be the prevailing trend in Moscow. Given the thorny history of boycotts and of restrictions on technology transfer between Moscow and Washington, Europe appears to be a more interesting partner for Gorbachev's new course of opening his economy to more co-operation with the West. As in the past, Soviet policy is likely to continue to try subtly to induce Western Europe to opt for support of cautious evolution rather than destabilising change in East-West relations, thus inadvertently preserving a Soviet sphere of influence, though under conditions of internal change.

In the face of these Soviet policies towards Western Europe, Britain and the Federal Republic have several interests in common. Their first priority should be, while recognising differences in approach and interest, to maintain the American-European relationship in a time of East-West change and to strengthen it where common interests exist. Second, both countries should use the Soviet interest in improving relations with Western Europe by encouraging Soviet policies that take into account West European interests in the field of arms control and political evolution in Central Europe. In many cases such a policy presupposes acting together within the Alliance and with the United States.

It is in the obvious interests of both Bonn and London to insist on essential requirements for arms control, notably effective verification and adequate balance in the nuclear and conventional field.

In the field of economic relations both countries should have an interest in responding positively to Soviet attempts to open relations with the West, including joint ventures and the transfer of modern technology, without however creating new forms of dependence and by observing the obvious limits of military technology in a policy of transfer of technology. Both countries should also abstain from subsidising credits although they may make occasional exceptions for smaller socialist countries.

Both governments are interested in pursuing a differentiated approach toward East European countries that supports the enhancement of human rights or the increase in foreign policy autonomy wherever possible. Both countries must be interested in change that leads to a substantial evolution within a socialist world without inducing collapse and repressive intervention.

Resource constraints on British and German defence

In considering their defence programmes for the remainder the century both Britain and Germany face considerable difficulties in attempting to maintain their present force structure.

These problems arise because in neither country under governments of any imaginable complexion is there at present a perception of the military threat which would lead to an increase in the share of public expenditure to be devoted to defence or in the share of the population of military age which could be enrolled in the armed forces beyond the measures already agreed.

Significant constraints are therefore imposed on the effectiveness of defence policies in the two countries. The first constraint is financial: the commitment to maintain expenditure at a level adjusted to take account of the general rate of inflation is unlikely to cope with the disproportionately rising cost of increasingly sophisticated defence equipment. The second constraint is imposed by the falling birth rate of the 1960s which is having its impact on the numbers available now for service in the armed forces.

In the United Kingdom the period from 1978–9 to 1985–6 were seven fat years for defence expenditure with the NATO target of 3% annual increase in defence expenditure being broadly achieved. Within this increase there was a particularly substantial increase in expenditure on defence equipment which rose at twice the rate of expenditure as a whole and reached some 50% of the total defence budget. The general restrictions on public expenditure of the Conservative Government in Britain have also affected defence spending and for the remainder of the decade there will be a slow fall in the level of expenditure – about 1.5% per year in real terms – within which it is likely that the effect on the equipment budget will be disproportionately large. The fact that these "seven lean years" coincide with the expenses of replacing Britain's strategic nuclear forces adds to the controversy surrounding this decision.

It is sometimes thought that the fact that the United Kingdom armed forces are an all volunteer force means that the demographic factors are less severe than is the case with most other Western European armed forces who rely to a much greater extent on the conscription. This is not entirely true. In the 1970s Britain needed to recruit one in 12 of those entering the 16–19 age group in order to maintain the level of her armed forces. By the end of this decade it will require to recruit one in eight of the same group. While the adverse economic situation of the first half of the 1980s probably helped recruiting, this is not necessarily a per- • manent factor. It is likely that to retain the increasingly highly-skilled personnel required in the armed forces of the future will mean that pay will have to rise at a higher rate than in the economy as a whole. This will be a further financial pressure on a limited defence budget.

Within the Federal Republic defence expenditure had a relatively substantial growth (in real terms) between 1971 and 1974 (around 4% average), dropped down to slightly negative rates in the mid-1970s and picked up slightly in the late 1970s and early 1980s. During the mid-1980s, however, a pattern of maintenance seems to have been the rule; *ie* the defence sector roughly keeps its share in the national budget with the likelihood of small increases in the order of magnitude of frac- tions of a percent during the remainder of the 1980s. Given a budget policy that stresses fiscal stability and given the strength of the demands from other areas, notably social policy, defence has to content itself with more-or-less the same share of national resources as in the mid-1980s.

Given the negative demographic trends in the Federal Republic the present peacetime strength of the armed forces of 495,000 would drop to 300,000 at the end of the 1990s if no compensating measures are undertaken. The prolongation of compulsory service from 15 to 18 months – no easy decision in peacetime – the voluntary prolongation of service, a new system of stand-by readiness, an increase of reservist training are all intended to maintain the fighting strength of the armed services but will consume significant resources at a time when modern armament disproportionately absorbs rising funds. As a result the Federal Republic faces a particularly difficult task of reconciling the needs for modernisation and measures which compensate for the demo- graphic decline with political resistance to an increase of the defence budget.

Co-operation in arms procurement

As in other areas of the defence relationship, such co-operation on joint arms production as has taken place between Britain and Germany has been given relatively little publicity. A recent estimate suggests that up to August 1986 the Federal Republic had purchased some £2.3 billion (DM4.3 milliard) of military equipment from the United Kingdom. The two countries had been involved in some of the largest joint defence projects in recent years. Although in most cases other countries were involved, Germany and Britain were most frequently the two largest partners (for example with the Tornado aircraft) and the current plans for the new European fighter aircraft indicate the extent to which the requirements of the two air forces are jointly procured.

The obstacles to greater collaboration have been both the general ones which affect all multinational defence procurement and some reasons that are particular to this pair of countries. The former include differences in national staff requirements (including, in Britain's case, the requirement to operate much equipment in tropical as well as Central Front environments), differences in timing of requirements for particular pieces of equipment, and resistance to equipment not developed and produced in the home country.

These general problems are intensified by asymmetries between the defence industries of the two countries. Britain has attempted to maintain a capacity for the largest degree of self-sufficiency in arms procurement while the Federal Republic, having seen its arms industry dismantled at the end of the war, has rebuilt its capacities frequently in co-operation with foreign partners. In the case of the aircraft industry and subsequently anti-aircraft and anti-tank missiles it was France who offered to assist in the redevelopment of German capabilities, Britain believing in the 1960s that she could continue on her own, while France saw sooner the need for such co-operation. A particular example of this was the attitude towards the delicate question of the export to third countries of jointly-produced weapons systems. The Federal Republic has a very restrictive policy on arms exports outside NATO, while its partners felt that to restrict the market for weapons jointly produced to NATO members would be uneconomic. France reached an agreement with the Federal Republic on the procedures to be followed in such cases as early as 1971, but a parallel agreement between Britain and the Federal Republic was only reached in 1983. It has since been used to cover the export of Tornado aircraft produced co-operatively to Saudi Arabia.

Successful bilateral agreements on arms production require effective co-operative links at political, military, civil service and industrial levels. In practice, within the two administrations the system of contacts and co-operation is similar in the British-German case to that which occurs in the more widely publicised Franco-German case. The two national armaments directors meet once or twice a year and always prepare a report for the annual ministerial summit where the Federal Chancellor meets the British Prime Minister together with a number of their ministers. These meetings of national armament directors carefully review the whole pattern of arms co-operation both at a bilateral and a multilateral level. There are, in addition, two standing British-German arms commissions, one for the army and one for the navy. Their annual meetings, together with the regular inclusion of procurement issues at the annual discussions between the General Staffs, ensure that there is a regular formal mechanism for co-operation.

This co-operation between administrations is gradually being underpinned by a growing network of industrial links between British and German industry. The best known and most successful of these has been the Panavia consortium for the production of Tornado. There are inevitably conflicting temptations for companies between "teaming" as a junior partner with an American firm and thereby gaining access to American technology and sometimes American markets, and co-operating with European partners. This was seen at the end of 1985 in the case of Westland's helicopter projects. The same dilemma may arise over the various proposals for extending air defence to provide some protection against theatre ballistic missiles.

In the field of arms production, as is in other areas of defence co-operation, British-German projects do not get the same publicity as Franco-German projects. This is in part because they do not have to fulfil the additional political function of symbolising French commitment to the defence of Western Europe. British-German co-operation is a natural part of their partnership within NATO's integrated structure and has not therefore been seen to require the same public demonstration.

Security concerns outside the NATO area

European security interests can be at stake outside NATO for several reasons. First, when the free supply of essential raw materials is threatened. This question no longer provides the nightmare for Western policy-makers that it posed during the 1970s in the wake of the first oil crisis as a result of diversification of energy supplies, energy saving measures and institutional innovation. Nevertheless, the threat still has to be taken seriously. Second, certain regional conflicts could escalate into conflicts that involve NATO partners, in particular the US, some with the further potential of spilling over into the East-West conflict in Europe. For the time being the Middle East seems to be the area where such contingencies are still thinkable, although under present circumstances the probability is low.

As observed earlier in the context of American-European differences on East-West relations, there is sometimes a difference in perspective between the United States and Western Europe on regional crises. Britain and the Federal Republic, like many other West European governments, do not always share the American perspective. The United States tends to view such crises in the context of the East-West conflict, whereas the European perspective is inclined to stress the local and regional origins of the crises.

If one reviews British and German interests in dealing with crises out-side the NATO area, the first priority should be given to a recognition of the simple fact that there are, indeed, cases where European security interests can be at stake outside the NATO area and that it is not in Europe's interest to abdicate their safeguarding to the United States alone. Consequently both Bonn and London should support an active European role in addressing European interests outside the NATO area and in creating the prerequisites for a European capacity to safeguard its interests.

The notion of European interests, a European role and an identity in world politics can best be served within the context of the European Community, using co-ordinated diplomacy within European Political Co-operation, by making use of the Community's economic resources, by mediation and by supporting countries of strategic importance.

Whenever the safeguarding of European interests outside the NATO area requires military means the difference between Britain and the Federal Republic should be clearly noted. Britain still has numerous bases outside Continental Europe (Hongkong, Cyprus, Belize, the Falklands) and is a nuclear power. Its navy is still structured in such a way that it can act outside Europe. However, as a result of history, the Constitution, post-war tradition and strong domestic constraints, the Federal Republic of Germany is unwilling and unable to play a military role outside the NATO area. Nevertheless, it is in the obvious interest of both Britain and the Federal Republic that Britain maintains its naval capability which can safeguard European interests in exceptional crisis situations. Indeed, it could be in the interest of both countries and of Europe to release Royal Navy capacities in the Atlantic for outside pur-poses by strengthening German naval presence there. Moreover, the time has come to entertain the notion that German armed forces should take part in peacekeeping operations or give logistic support to such undertakings.

New institutional approaches

Anglo-German co-operation in the field of security has functioned con-sistently and been without major problems ever since the stationing cost issue was left behind. Both countries have a similar outlook with regard to political and economic strategies of East-West relations, both take part in the integrated structure of NATO, both make an indispensable contribution to NATO's strategy of flexible response, and both Bonn and London regard the British participation in forward defence through the BAOR as indispensable. Within Germany there has been effective co-operation between the armed forces.

Co-operation between Britain and the Federal Republic also takes place within the existing institutions of NATO, WEU, and the various sub-bodies. Nevertheless there is a growing need for strengthening European institutional approaches basically for three reasons.

First, the growing disparity between the rising cost of manpower and modern armament on the one hand and the budgetary limitations on the other hand force both countries to pool their resources in the field of arms production more effectively. The long and thorny history of attempts at co-production has shown that it is easier to agree on projects which represent genuine co-production within Europe than across the Atlantic. Moreover, both countries agree that for major weapons it is essential to maintain a European industrial base. Britain and the Federal Republic should therefore do all they can to standardise and co-produce their weapons with Europe. Such an attempt will be promoted by placing it within European institutions such as the IEPG, the WEU and by creating a link with the common industrial policy of the European Community.

Second, in order to create a better opportunity to formulate and bring to bear within the Alliance their European interests on central questions of East-West relations, such as arms control or economic and political relations, Britain and Germany should actively promote and support the strengthening of a European sub-structure of NATO. Such an approach should give priority to WEU which has the advantage of comprising countries with a similar outlook in foreign and security policy. In addition, the European Political Co-operation of the European Community should be used to broaden this process, notably on economic and political questions of security. In the long run, however, both countries should seriously examine whether the existing institutions can fulfil the requirements of a stronger European role within the Alliance. If necessary a transformation of WEU in the direction of certain features of the former European Defence Community could be worth considering.

Third, a stronger European pillar within the Alliance must be seen as a fallback and insurance policy in case domestic tendencies in the United States lead to a weakening of the American presence in Europe. As mentioned earlier, both Britain and the Federal Republic should do their best to prevent such a move unless it occurs within a negotiated process of East-West reductions. If such a reduction occurs, both countries should be prepared to respond through strengthened European institutions.

What conclusions should Britain and the Federal Republic draw with regard to an implementation of new institutional approaches?

First, both give high priority to maintaining the transatlantic relationship realising that it must be adjusted to changes on both sides of the Atlantic. Consequently Britain and Germany will have to make a particular effort to make sure that a strengthening of European approaches does not undermine the relationship with the United States.

Second, Bonn and London should focus on the strengthening of WEU for defence policy, arms control and disarmament issues. In addition the question of nuclear co-operation will have to be faced in a double context: in order to make the best use of scarce resources a growing co-operation between Britain and France appears desirable in the nuclear field, but from the point of view of Europe it appears desirable to give both nuclear forces a European role. Such a European role would be strengthened by creating a European Nuclear Planning Group which, without changing the national prerogatives of decision, would regularly review the central problems of the roles and the potential uses of both forces. At the same time Britain and Germany should continue to consider wider questions of Alliance nuclear policy within NATO's Nuclear Planning Group.

Third, both countries can improve not only their contribution to European and transatlantic institutions but also their bilateral co-operation. Progress is desirable and called for in this area. In the case of British-German relations there is not the need for an elaborate structure comparable to that created by the Elysée Treaty between France and Germany which has to carry the burden of functions which are taken care of by NATO in the British-German case. The existing consultations at summit, ministerial and official level already cover the areas of defence policy, arms co-production and East-West relations. These should be strengthened.

Since British-German defence co-operation has functioned well and is based on a similarity of outlook, it has been taken for granted in both countries and the rest of Europe. British commitment of a major part of its land and air forces to the defence of Central Europe in the past 40 years has been an indicator of its acceptance of the indivisibility of European defence. That commitment and co-operation within NATO has led to a close if underestimated bilateral security partnership between Britain and the Federal Republic. If an effective European pillar for NATO is to be developed, it will need to build upon this strong existing relationship as a central component in the network of bilateral links and multilateral institutions which together provide the sinews of European defence co-operation.

Appendices

Table A.1 British Defence Expenditures

(a) Levels of defence expenditure, 1960–87

	1960	1965	1970	1975	1980	1985	1986	1987*
Defence budget £ billion	1.5959	2.1205	2.380	4.548	10.78	18.059	18.479	18.782
According to NATO definition	1.655	2.091	2.444	5.1654	11.24	18.4052	18.9	19.3
Defence budget as % of GDP	6.26	6.06	5.24	5.299	6.22	5.177	5.2	5.1
According to NATO criteria	6.49	5.93	5.38	6.018	6.41	5.276	5.1	4.8
Expenditure per head of population (in £)	30.598	39.26	42.67	80.55	192.84	321.72	326.0	334.0
According to NATO criteria	31.73	38.71	43.82	91.48	198.99	327.89	335.0	342.0

(b) Real growth in defence expenditures, 1972–87

	1972	1973	1974	1975	1976	1977	1978	1979	1980	1981	1982	1983	1984	1985	1986*	1987*
Defence Budget	+4	+6.9	−6.3	+0.1	+4.3	+1.3	+8	−2.6	+0.9	+8.2	+5.1	+8.3	−1.1	+3.4	−1.0	−1.0
NATO criteria	+7.3	−1.3	+3.3	−3.1	+0.1	+0.1	−1	+4.4	+8.1	−5.7	+5	−10	+1	+3.6	—	—

* Estimates

Table A.2 German Defence Expenditures

(a) Levels of defence expenditure, 1960–87

	1960	1965	1970	1975	1980	1985	1986	1987*
Defence budget DM billion	7.450	17.758	19.414	31.247	39.364	48.872	50.188	50.852
According to NATO definition	12.115	19.915	22.573	37.589	48.518	58.649	60.131	61.551
including Berlin	12.889	22.176	25.790	45.506	61.096	73.861	75.768	77.632
Defence budget as % of GDP	2.4	3.9	2.9	3.0	2.7	2.7	2.6	2.5
According to NATO criteria	4.0	4.3	3.3	3.6	3.2	3.2	3.1	3.0
including Berlin	4.2	4.8	3.8	4.4	4.1	4.0	3.9	3.8
Expenditure per head of population (in DM)	143.95	315.42	329.05	499.15	642	801	822	833
According to NATO criteria	234.09	353.73	382.59	600.46	791.29	980	985	1009
including Berlin	245.79	394.86	440.56	733.9	1013.84	1227	1241	1272

(b) Real growth in defence expenditures, 1972–87

	1972	1973	1974	1975	1976	1977	1978	1979	1980	1981	1982	1983	1984	1985	1986	1987*
Defence Budget	+ 7.7	+ 3.5	+ 4.2	− 1.3	± 0	− 0.1	+ 1.2	+ 0.9	+ 1.1	+ 3.8	− 0.6	− 2.1	+ 0.3	− 0.1	+ 0.4	− 0.9
NATO criteria	+ 7.1	+ 4.4	+ 4.3	+ 0.5	− 0.1	− 0.5	+ 2.7	+ 1.5	+ 1.9	+ 3.5	− 0.5	+ 0.9	− 0.4	+ 0.2	− 0.5	+ 0.1
including Berlin	+ 8.5	+ 4.4	+ 4.5	− 0.1	+ 1.7	+ 0.2	+ 2.3	+ 3.1	+ 2.4	+ 3.3	− 0.7	+ 0.5	+ 0.2	+ 0.3	− 0.5	+ 0.2

* Estimates

Index